MAGIC AND MODERNITY

Magic and Modernity

Interfaces of Revelation and Concealment

Edited by BIRGIT MEYER *and* PETER PELS

STANFORD UNIVERSITY PRESS

STANFORD, CALIFORNIA

2003

Stanford University Press
Stanford, California

Publication of this book was made possible in part by a
grant from the Netherlands Organisation for Scientific
Research (NWO).

Printed in the United States of America
on acid-free, archival-quality paper

Library of Congress Cataloging-in-Publication Data
Magic and modernity : interfaces of revelation and
concealment / edited by Birgit Meyer and Peter Pels.
    p.   cm.
Includes bibliographical references and index.
    ISBN 0-8047-4463-7 — ISBN 0-8047-4464-5
    1. Magic. 2. Divination. 3. Witchcraft. 4. Spiritualism.
I. Meyer, Birgit.   II. Pels, Peter.
    GN475.3 .M34 2003
    306.4—dc21   2002014751

Original Printing 2003

Last figure below indicates year of this printing:
12   11   10   09   08   07   06   05   04   03

Typeset by Classic Typography in 10/14 Janson

CONTENTS

ACKNOWLEDGMENTS

This book is the result of the conference Magic and Modernity that we organized in June 1997 at the University of Amsterdam. Apart from a small subsidy from the Royal Dutch Academy of Sciences (KNAW), the conference was
largely funded by the Research Centre Religion and Society, Department of
Sociology and Anthropology, University of Amsterdam. We thank our colleagues at Religion and Society at the time—Gerd Baumann, Peter van
Rooden, Patricia Spyer, and Peter van der Veer—for their characteristically
generous intellectual and material support of our initiative. With two exceptions (Pels's introduction and his contribution to this book), all chapters
in this volume are based on the presentations given during the conference
by the authors. However, the conference would not have been such a success, nor would the book have been composed in the same way, without the
contributions—as paper presenters or as discussants—of Misty Bastian, Wim
van Binsbergen, Filip de Boeck, Penelope Gouk, Edwina Hagen, Wouter
Hanegraaff, Ute Luig, Tanya Luhrmann, Gananath Obeyesekere, Stephan
Palmié, Peter van Rooden, Lyn Schumaker, Patricia Spyer, and Peter van der
Veer. The production of a formally coherent manuscript would not have been
possible without the support of Ingrid van de Broek and Nienke Muurling.
We thank Brad Weiss, Vincent Crapanzano, and an anonymous reader for
Stanford University Press for their enthusiastic and perceptive comments on
the manuscript. At the Press, Nathan MacBrien expedited the review
process, even when faced with a manuscript that was far too long yet (according to both readers and editors) could not be reduced to a smaller size—
we thank Nathan for being so efficient and flexible. That problem was
solved with a subsidy from the Internationalization Fund of the Netherlands

Organisation for Scientific Research (NWO), for which we are very grateful. From the time of the manuscript's acceptance by the Press, Helen Tartar and Norris Pope took over from Nathan to expertly guide it into print. Last, we thank the University of Minnesota Press for the permission to reprint Michael Taussig's "Viscerality, Faith, and Skepticism: Another Theory of Magic" from Nicholas B. Dirks, ed., *In Near Ruins: Cultural Theory at the End of the Century* (Minneapolis and London, 1998) in modified form.

MAGIC AND MODERNITY

Magic and Modernity

PETER PELS

The reactions to Princess Diana's fatal car crash on August 31, 1997, persuaded many commentators that the British monarchy had lost its public appeal in competition with Diana's stardom. The contrast between country-
wide, even global, mass mourning and the cool response to the tragedy by the
Queen and the Prince of Wales led one writer to reflect on Walter Bagehot's
mid-nineteenth-century thoughts on the secrecy and the shrouding of royal
privacy that served to maintain the magic of monarchy: "[Bagehot] could not
have predicted the effect of bursting flashbulbs and the dazzle of halogen
upon magic. This week we saw a troubled and bewildered family fumbling
to do the right thing in response to a barely-understood clamour. We did
not see a family which in some mystic sense stood for us, or which interpeted
[sic] the nation to itself. We saw no reflection of ourselves at all" (*Guardian*
[August 9, 1997]:6). Similarly, Ian Buruma commented that Diana's success
as a "global media celebrity" eventually destroyed the "mystique" of monarchy. If the latter was based on secrecy and the shrouding of royal privacy, it

was obliterated by Diana's stardom, which like its movie and rock star equivalents "explodes the border between public and private" and flaunts the star's lifestyle, loves, opinions, and feelings before the consumers of global media gossip (Buruma 1997:7). A different style of publicity seemed to destroy the secretive magic of monarchy, replacing it with the relentless exposure of global stardom.

It was not, however, the first time that the publication of the British royal family's privacy threatened the magic of monarchy. In December 1936, the efforts of the British press to maintain a conspiracy of silence about King Edward's affair with Mrs. Simpson were overruled by American newspaper articles, and the king was presented with the choice between remaining the king and marrying a divorcée. As in 1997, this crisis also "exploded" the privacy of the monarch in the face of the public and produced similar doubts about the possibility and necessity of maintaining the magic of monarchy, in which the king was seen to stand for his subjects (K. Martin 1937). But from 1937 on, the "domestic monarchy" first inaugurated by Queen Victoria managed to reconstitute itself through Edward's successor, "family man" George VI, and his successor, Diana's mother-in-law (Buruma 1997; K. Martin 1937:100); and in 1999, as well, the magic of the British monarchy seems capable of personalizing itself once again in Prince Charles or his son William.[1]

In emphasizing the evaporation of monarchical magic in the glare of flashbulbs and desire for the transparency of the hitherto opaque royal center of the nation, such comments express a core feature of liberal political culture. This culture seeks to expose monarchy as a terminal institutionalization of what Leonard Woolf called "the flag-waving, incantation, medicineman frame of mind" (quoted in K. Martin 1937:103), or, more modest, as the "glimmering recognition that we are, after all, citizens rather than subjects," people who need no royal title but can do with Diana's "natural nobility" and "classless compassion and humanity" (*Guardian*, August 9, 1997:6). But republican fantasies of progress toward more public, rational, and democratic expressions of citizenship usually ignore that the magic of monarchy was itself a product of a distinctly *modern* type of publicity. After all, the way in which the modern king or queen came to "stand for" the people in a mystic sense, in such a way that Queen Victoria or King George or Queen Elizabeth would become "reflections of" British selves, only appeared by the late nineteenth century, that is, *after* the critical forces of British republicanism—very much alive at mid century—were defeated by the twin forces of monarchism and imperialism in the 1870s (K. Martin 1937:44–45; Cannadine 1983). The secrecy and shrouding of royal privacy—"the complete absence of serious discussion of Monarchy" that marks a taboo (K. Martin 1937:9)—went together with a modern discourse of representation, of "standing for" the people; a discursive form that reinvented royalty as a symbol of national power with which citizens could identify themselves, despite the fact that the constitutional monarchy had, at the time, lost whatever concrete political power it once possessed.[2] This form provided, as Max Weber said, a *Veralltäglichung* of royal charisma that constituted both the legitimacy of the monarchy and of the British nation.

One might even suggest that the "dazzle of halogen" of Diana's stardom signifies a shift to a different enchantment, one that is closer to the magic of film, or the New Age sacralization of self (see Birgit Meyer, in this volume; and Heelas n.d.). Whatever the case may be, the modern magic of monarchy perfectly illustrates the main themes of this book: First, it shows that *magic*— the term will be discussed shortly—can be modernized to such an extent that it works as a counterpoint to liberal understandings of modernity's transparency and rational progress. Second, it brings out that modernity not only constitutes magic as its counterpoint but also produces its own forms of magic. Third, it highlights that for an adequate understanding of the relationship between magic and modernity, we have to attend to the ways in which its forms of publicity and secrecy complement or supplement each other, that is, to the ways in which the persuasiveness of the symbols we live by thrives on a combination of faith and skepticism, revelation and concealment (see Michael Taussig, this volume). We hope that such reflections will reinvigorate scholarly thinking about magic—a subject that has lain dormant for too long—by resituating it in a series of novel theoretical and ethnographic reflections.

We have been encouraged to confront magic and modernity by the observation of a lacuna: whereas the demise of the evolutionist view that magic is quintessentially "other" was marked by scholars who, since Sigmund Freud ([1919] 1938), Ruth Benedict (1934), and Bronislaw Malinowski ([1935] 1965), acknowledged the existence of magic *in* modernity, this acknowledgment was rarely accompanied by theoretical statements that reflected on the ways in which magic *belongs to* modernity. As I will discuss in more detail below, magic designated a conceptual field—shared with such notions as *shamanism, fetishism, witchcraft, the occult, totem, mana,* and *taboo*—that was predominantly made to define an antithesis of modernity: a production of illusion and delusion that was thought to recede and disappear as rationalization and secularization spread throughout society. However, this image of magic as the other or the past of modernity was always balanced by less dominant arguments about magic's universality, either as hidden wisdom (as in Europeans' musings on Hermeticism; see Yates 1972), as poetic imagination (as in Denis Diderot's and Johann Gottfried Herder's thinking about shamanism—see below), as a wishful "omnipotence of thought" (Freud [1919] 1938:120), as reasoning by analogy (Benedict 1934:39), or as the "institutionalization of human optimism" (Malinowski [1935] 1965:239).

Rarely, however, has magic been theorized as being explicitly *of* modernity, that is, not merely tolerated (as a universal human trait) among modern institutions but culturally *at home* in the institutions and practices we associate with the Occidental world. Anthropologists such as Ruth Benedict and Bronislaw Malinowski could argue that, for instance, political oratory, advertising, and property were specifically modern forms of magic (Benedict 1934:41; Malinowski [1935] 1965:236), but such remarks were typically left without elaboration. In social science theory in general, much insight can be gathered about modern magic from the "grand theories" of Karl Marx, Emile Durkheim, and Max Weber—to name just those I shall discuss further—but rarely under the name *magic* as such. Thus, although I will deal with a number of seminal departures from this modernist fixation in this introduction, many students of modern magic still find it difficult to discuss magic outside the anthropological "witchcraft" paradigm (e.g., Luhrmann [1989] 1994). Conversely, they study present-day occultism without much reference to a tradition of anthropological scholarship on and analysis of magic (e.g., Heelas 1996). The chapters in this book are aimed at overcoming such gaps.

The paucity of theoretical statements and ethnographic analyses of magic in the past twenty-five years may be overcome by bringing two aspects of the relationship between magic and modernity to the forefront of analysis: The first is the specific nature of *the supplementarity of magic and modernity,* that is, the way in which many modern discourses position magic as their antithesis, reinventing it in the process. Thus, if modern discourse reconstructs magic in terms that distinguish it from the modern, this at the same time creates the correspondences and nostalgias by which magic can come to haunt modernity. Much of this, of course, refers back to a broader cultural background in which Enlightenment and utilitarian rationalizations were increasingly confronted by the sentimentalist, poetic, or voluntaristic tendencies they excluded, tendencies that were harnessed by romantic thinkers and that became fundamental to modern occultism as well as to anthropological theories of magic (C. Campbell 1987:3; Hanegraaff 1998; Heelas 1996:67; see the following section); but it also concerns the transformations that occur when culturally contingent traditions of yoga, shamanism, or witchcraft are reinvented to suit the universalist eclecticism of the New Age (Baker 1995; Johnson 1995; Simpson 1994; Van der Veer 2001:55–82). Second, one needs to ask what are the specific forms of *the magic of modernity itself*—those enchantments that are produced by practices culturally specific to modern states, economies, and societies—practices labeled as representation, commodification, and discipline. Both aspects are present in my opening reflections on the magic of the constitutional monarchy, where practices of nationalist representation were seen to produce a taboo on publicizing a royal domestic interior that could as well be interpreted as an antithesis of what modernity should consist of.

These two aspects of magic and modernity need to be set within an outline of the discursive field to which a concept such as magic belongs and an account of why, given that many social scientists shy away from the concept, we favor it for something more than its mere alliteration with modernity. This is why I devote the first section of this introduction to a historical sketch of the family of concepts used by anthropologists to designate humanity's dealings with the occult since the Enlightenment. Anthropology, more than any other scholarly discourse on magic, was responsible for the interpretation of magic as an antithesis of modernity and for the production of the peculiar ambiguity and entanglement of magic and modernity that is the focus of this book. A second step in the argument of this introduction is obviously a reflection on the use of the term *modernity* in light of current critiques of modernization theory and debates over whether one can at all use this concept in the singular. A second section will, therefore, discuss how, for central theorists of modernity such as Durkheim, Marx, and Weber, modernity was haunted by practices that a later, post–World War II theory of modernization was meant to define out of existence. This will set the stage for the three concluding sections, in which I will use the perspectives outlined in the different contributions to this volume to show, first, how one can think about the (re)invention of magic in modernity; second, about the enchantments that are specific to modernity; and, last, not only why our focus on the interplay between publicity and secrecy, revelation and concealment, indicates promising directions for future research but also why such research may be urgently needed for our understanding of contemporary society.

Anthropology and the Occult: Ambiguities of Revelation and Concealment

For most of its history, anthropology was a science of the "West" about the "rest," and it is now widely agreed that much of the discourse produced by anthropologists was Occidentalist and produced an image of Westerners for themselves (Carrier 1995). In this fashion, much of what anthropologists said about magic was a way of negatively distinguishing "savage" or "primitive" logic from a modern, Western one. But anthropology was entangled with magic in more complex and intimate ways. Anthropological discourse about magic was, from the time of some of the first ethnographic contacts with "others" onward, characterized by a central paradox: that by exposing the backwardness or delusions of shamanism, fetishism, magic, and witchcraft, anthropology and folklore studies also revealed their existence. Evidently, the temporal distancing of magic by classifying it as premodern could only take place in the anthropologists' own time and language. Anthropologists' own practices of translation explained the otherness of magic by referring to social and cultural traits in their own, modern society. In this way, anthropologists contributed much to the reinvention of the discourses in which Europeans dealt with the occult. By revealing exotic dealings with the occult at the same time that they exposed the illusions behind these dealings, anthropologists unmasked their deceptiveness or delusion at the same time that they offered them as possible alternative practices.[3] Anthropologists helped modern subjects to domesticate exotic magical discourses and practices but taught them at the same time to deploy such discourses and practices along the fault lines of European social contradictions.[4]

SHAMANISM AND FETISHISM

By the early eighteenth century, descriptions of Siberian, Northern European, and North American healers and magicians were available to European intellectuals, and by 1800 they came to be classified under the Germanized term *Schaman*. These reports emphasized two aspects that, taken together, would characterize the paradoxical presentation of magic in nineteenth-century Europe: the idea that the shamans' work was based on deception, and its counterpoint, that even if deceptive the work of the shaman was based on natural truth.

Joseph François Lafitau, for instance, the missionary hailed as the forerunner of comparative ethnology (Pagden 1986), called North American shamans *jongleurs*, or "jugglers," a notion that clearly connotes the magician's public revelation of skilled concealment (see Michael Taussig, this volume). In his *Mœurs des sauvages ameriquains* ([1724] 1983), he alternated this term with indigenous North American terms and European concepts such as "priest(ess)," *mage*, diviner, *hierophante*, druid, and *médécin*, showing the broad range of associations of *jongleur*. Lafitau himself, however, was anxious to counter the idea of deception that Protestant Europe ascribed to popular healers and Catholic priests. He argued that his jongleurs had "knowledge of things divine and human, knew the efficacy of plants, stones, metals, all the occult virtues and all the secrets of nature" (quoted in Flaherty 1992:61). Anticipating Romantic thinkers such as Herder, Lafitau argued that jongleurs have an innate divine quality, a state of ecstasy that allows them to apprehend the divine, intuit a patient's imagination, and manipulate it in such a way as to achieve a cure (Flaherty 1992:63). Europeans would still be cured by jongleurs if European medical doctors had not overcomplicated medicine and turned what should have been accessible to all into an "impenetrable enigma" (Flaherty 1992:66)—a critique of the professionalization of medicine echoed later by Victorian occultists (cf. Flaherty 1992:108; Pels 2000; this volume) as well as by twentieth-century alternative therapists and popular representations of medical doctors (see Jojada Verrips, this volume).

These ambiguities found their way in Enlightenment European discourse through the Romantic interest in shamans displayed by, among others, Diderot and Herder. The possible consequences of such an interest were discerned by Diderot's correspondent, Empress Catherine the Great of Russia, who was wholly committed to the Enlightenment project, infused it with Protestant fervor, and ridiculed and persecuted the Siberian shamans in her

Eastern colonies. Catherine wrote to Diderot deploring the excessive amount of articles in the *Encyclopédie* on shamans, theosophists, and other obscurantist forces, showing she was aware that publications about shamans, even when ridiculing the latter, could also promote interest in their existence. Diderot himself based the aesthetics of fanciful, irrational, enthusiast, and frivolous nephew Lui (in *Le neveu de Rameau*) on his knowledge of Siberian shamanic performances (Flaherty 1992:127). Lui defends deception: "Nothing is more useful to the nations than lies, nothing more harmful than the truth" (quoted in Flaherty 1992:128). Lui sacrifices the truth, rationality, coolness, and common sense of his interlocutor, Moi, to the achievement of sublimity, and this shows that Diderot merged enlightened European understanding of the shaman with the novel category of "genius," identifying the performing artist as the shaman of higher civilization (Flaherty 1992:131). Similarly, Herder fused the Western genius and the Renaissance Magus with the exotic shaman, emphasizing the power of music and placing song at the origin and foundation of language, as a form of privileged access to reality (thus anticipating another hardy perennial of Occidental discourse on magic: the speculations on alternative sensory regimes that allow for a more profound knowledge of the world [see Pels, this volume]). For Herder, Orpheus was the epitome of the "noble shaman," standing for everything humane, just, helpful, and magnanimous (Flaherty 1992:139). Like Diderot, Herder defended deception, especially in arguing that James MacPherson's *Ossian* (the Scottish national epic that had been denounced as a fraud) was true to the spirit of the people and that "forgery was therefore neither a relevant concept nor a possibility" (Flaherty 1992:140). This anticipated Sir James Frazer's and Bronislaw Malinowski's idea that magic, even if deceptive, could be progressive and functional.

Comparable ambiguities characterize the other major category under which Enlightenment intellectuals discussed exotic magic: fetishism. Introduced into European thought by the ethnography of the Dutch merchant Willem Bosman in 1704, and popularized by the anticlerical Charles de Brosses in his *Du culte des dieux fétiches* of 1760, fetishism suggested a novel category of religion, dominant in Africa: a materialism incommensurable with Christian theology, conceived "as the worship of haphazardly chosen material objects believed to be endowed with purpose, intention, and a direct power over the material life of both human beings and the natural world"

(Pietz 1988:106). This idea of a primordial religion was promoted by Diderot, Christoph Meiners, and others and made it possible to think about intellectual progress in a way that "did not ultimately derive from the sorts of beliefs treated by theology but rather from prescientific conceptions of the powers of material objects to produce desired outcomes" (Pietz 1999:59). Auguste Comte radicalized the idea, leading to the ambiguous conclusion that a post-theological age of science and social engineering should revive people's capacity for "pure," pretheistic fetishism so that sociology could itself become a new religion, "an enlightened fetishism that fused humankind's religious sensibility with scientific reasoning" (Pietz 1999:59). I shall have more to say about fetishism below—suffice it to note here that, despite the efforts of anthropologists such as James Cowles Prichard and Edward Tylor to subsume it again under a spiritualist theory, the materialist notion of fetishism became prominent in Marxist theory, deploying an understanding of exotic magic along European fault lines of intellectual debates. This shows that, like shamanism, fetishism was a colonial exotic that Europeans exposed as illusionary and backward while simultaneously revealing its existence in order to conduct political and religious controversies and to upset the monopoly of certain hegemonic categories in the classification of intellectual progress.

MAGIC

The academic analysis of magic emerged in the second half of the nineteenth century, and it has commonly been characterized by statements that it must be regarded as a "monstrous farrago" (Tylor 1873:1:133), a "spurious science" hiding behind "bastard art" (Frazer 1911:53). However, few scholars have reflected on the paradox that such evolutionist confidence (if any; see below) arose in a period that can also be regarded as romantically "reenchanting" the world (Gay 1995:37ff.). Indeed, the high imperialism of the late nineteenth century, which tried to come to terms with, among other things, the Paris Commune, the Indian Mutiny of 1857, the foundation of the First International in 1864, and the Jamaican slaves' revolt of 1866 was also a period of high bourgeois anxiety. In addition, Tylor and Frazer were faced with a multiplicity of modern reenchantments. Folklore studies had long been the refuge for Puritans fascinated with the rites and spells that their own religion abjured, and scores of fat volumes demonstrate early versions of the Tylorean and Frazerian paradox of publicizing in extenso the survivals that one actually wants to see abolished (Dorson 1968). Folklore combined with literature to produce, from the 1764 publication of Horace Walpole's *The Castle of Otranto* on, a "gothic" novel that worked as a counterpoint to the dominant realist tradition, one that prepared the ground for the "mysteries" of Mary Shelley (*Frankenstein*, 1817), John Polidori (*The Vampyre*, 1819), Edgar Allan Poe, Charles Dickens, and Edward Bulwer-Lytton—all announcing modernist literature's persistent displacement of reason by magic, the occult, and the irrational. While all these writers drew on folklore studies (Bleiler 1966:xxxix), Shelley, Poe, Dickens, and Bulwer-Lytton also added scientific metaphors, especially of ether, magnetism, galvanism, electricity, and telegraphy, to the creation of modern mysteries (Bulwer-Lytton [1871, 1859] 1928; F. Kaplan 1974, 1975; see also Pels, this volume and Verrips, this volume). They thereby modernized magic by associating it with the imponderabilities of science, just as Frazer thought that magic was "bastard science" and postulated a "secrect sympathy" such as the notion of "ether" to explain the magician's identification of cause and effect and whole and part (Frazer 1911:54).

If, unlike Frazer, Tylor was tempted to compare magic to religion rather than magic to science, he shared Frazer's anxieties that magic might not be securely relegated to a primitive past. Although he predominantly tried to describe magic as a primitive survival, he sometimes also resorted to an alternative conception that emphasized that magic harbors a universal mythopoetic or "analogic consciousness," the loss of which one can nostalgically regret (Hanegraaff 1998:259).[5] Thus, Tylor's nostalgia shows an ambiguity in his explanations that supplements Frazer's seeming admiration of the progressive, "scientific" qualities of magical thinking. Moreover, Tylor's anxiety that magic or witchcraft might revive in his own time becomes apparent from his dealings with an important precursor of modern occultism, the Spiritualist movement (Pels, this volume), just as Frazer shared with his contemporaries the fear that civilization was only a "thin crust" easily rent by the savage forces of human nature (Frazer 1911:235–36). However, there are indications that Frazer was more sensitive than Tylor to the intellectual climate in which the Orientalist anthropology of Friedrich Max Müller was fused with the new literary mysteries of Bulwer-Lytton in modern occultism.[6]

Those who adopted the term *occultism* as a nom de plume in the 1880s presupposed a secret knowledge that surpassed the public certainties of both established science and religion and that was accessible by personal training and private experience.[7] In a comparable way, Frazer put much more emphasis than did Tylor on the affinity of magic with science, as well as the preoccupation of magic with secrecy. In postulating a "secret sympathy" like ether Frazer anticipated fellow anthropologists who also claimed that secrecy and privacy were the hallmarks of magic (Mauss and Hubert [1902] 1972:24). This went together with a renewed emphasis on the deceptive nature of magic, Frazer arguing that the magician's deceptive powers made him the first agent of intellectual progress, and Marcel Mauss that the key to the social authority of magic lay in "the moment of the conjuring trick" (Frazer 1911:215–16; Mauss [1902] 1972:123; see below). The discursive affinities between Frazer's work and contemporary occultists at least partly explains how this apparently self-confident rationalist came to be the—direct or indirect—inspiration for a number of modern occultist movements.[8]

The new emphases on science and secrecy in anthropological theorizing about magic were accompanied by a third important modernization of magic: its psychologization. Many founding fathers of psychology (Jean-Martin Charcot, Pierre Janet, Wilhelm Wundt, William James, James Braid, and Freud) were experimenting with or convinced of the reality of telepathy, clairvoyance, and like phenomena (Hacking 1988, 1995). Associationist psychology was central to Tylor and Frazer's conceptions of animism and magic, whereas Durkheim's and Mauss's point of departure for their thinking about magic and religion was the agenda set by the novel discipline of crowd psychology (Crapanzano 1995; Nye 1995). Likewise, occultists made a "discovery of the unconscious" (Ellenberger 1970) parallel to that of psychology, incorporating a topological conception of the person, one that argued that one needs to remove layers of convention to discover a "true" or "Higher" self (Blavatsky 1889:178; Heelas 1996) or to release the primary force of the will (Blavatsky 1877:57; Crowley, quoted in Willis 1985; cf. Hanegraaff 1996:433). The emphasis on psychology would also condition thinking about magic in the interwar years and help to shift it toward the thesis that magic is a human universal, as in Freud's argument about the desire toward the "omnipotence of thought" ([1919] 1938), Benedict's argument that magic consisted of wish fulfillment realized through the universal capacity of reasoning by analogy (1934:39), and Malinowski's idea that magic was an elaboration of the infant experience that a certain utterance could bring about the gratification of specific wants ([1935] 1965:233). The argument implied the identification of specifically modern manifestations of magic: neuroses for Freud; a superstition about education or property for Benedict; the persuasive formulas of advertising, political oratory, and even law for Malinowski. As argued earlier, however, these critiques of an evolutionist model did not explicate the "patterns of culture" of *modern* magic, and they stuck to the argument that either magic was a voluntary concealment of a threatening reality (Freud) or a form of coordinating actions for which other controls were lacking (Malinowski).

WITCHCRAFT

The emergence of *witchcraft* as an object of anthropological analysis gives rise to an intriguing question: why did this term emerge and come to dominate anthropological writings at the expense of the term *magic*? Although British anthropology usually dismissed Malinowski's theories in favor of his pioneering ethnographic work (Nadel 1957:190), the theories' pragmatist and processual sophistication has recently invited reappraisals (Comaroff and Roberts 1981:11; Thornton and Skalnik 1993:40–41).[9] Malinowski's mature theory of magic—one that identifies the human capacity for the magical use of language as a universal trait pragmatically acquired in infancy (Malinowski [1935] 1965)—can be read as inspired by James (Leach 1957) and prefigured Ludwig Wittgenstein's critique of Frazer (Tambiah 1990; Thornton and Skalnik 1993:40). Given this pedigree, one wonders why Malinowski's theory wasn't put to more use in the 1930s. Despite the fact that Edward Evans-Pritchard himself initiated a comparative discussion of Malinowskian theory (1929), by the time he published *Witchcraft, Oracles and Magic Among the Azande* (1937), the linguistic pragmatism of the magical act that characterized Malinowski's mature work had been superseded by Evans-Pritchard's emphasis on witchcraft as a system of specifically "other" beliefs. This paradigm would generate much discussion about the specificity of African morality and political equilibrium and the universal nature of rationality but implicitly assumed that comparable magicalities and irrationalities were, in the West, a thing of the past.

The emergence of the witchcraft paradigm was partly due, I submit, to the specific context in which Evans-Pritchard was confronted with it. Two years before the publication of *Witchcraft, Oracles and Magic*, in an introduction to a special issue of *Africa* (the audience of which consisted of anthropologists, missionaries, and colonial administrators), Evans-Pritchard described witchcraft as "an imaginary *offence*" (1935:418; my emphasis). The legal term displays the origin of his problematic in the legal practice of colonial rule: the difficulties experienced in implementing Witchcraft ordinances that declared that witchcraft accusations—as features of the indigenous cultural order potentially useful for the maintenance of indirect rule—were classified as imaginary and illegal (Fields 1982). The movement in anthropology that replaced the emphasis on pragmatic magic as a universal human trait with the intellectualist agenda of studying witchcraft as a local system of beliefs (a system that would disappear with the institutions supporting it; cf. Evans-Pritchard 1935:421) was at least in part fed by the problem of controlling and modernizing colonial societies. This problematic of witchcraft and social order was especially prominent after 1945, when British anthropology became far more intertwined with the colonial establishment than before (Richards 1977). Of course, Evans-Pritchard's account in *Witchcraft, Oracles and Magic* also included the specifically academic question of why people held on to apparently irrational beliefs, but that does not explain why Evans-Pritchard's approach superseded Malinowski's equally universalistic answer to that question. The postwar witchcraft paradigm dominated anthropological writings on human dealings with the occult, and Evans-Pritchard's interest in issues of universal rationality would not reemerge until 1970 (Douglas 1970:xiv).

Yet, even at its zenith, the witchcraft paradigm showed ambiguities. If, on the one hand, witchcraft was predominantly studied in terms of an African language of micropolitical equilibrium or as a form of institutionalizing local morality in reverse form (Marwick 1952; Mitchell 1956), it could, on the other hand, be seen as its opposite: as an expression of a modern social crisis when "witch finders" responded to the shattering of indigenous institutions by colonial rule (Richards 1935:458; Willis 1968). An even more disturbing version of Zande witchcraft resulted from an unintended effect of Evans-Pritchard's epistemological interests: the use made of *Witchcraft, Oracles and Magic* in both the attack on and the defense of Peter Winch's relativist conception of social science, resulting in a debate about the nature of rationality—often dominated by somewhat frantic attempts to exorcise the threat to modern certainties provided by a radical translation of Azande "witchcraft" (Wilson 1970; Hollis and Lukes 1982). Even during a period of hegemonic "modernization," the crossover of African magical practices into Western discourse by means of their translation as witchcraft produced problems of how to contain it to the "Dark Continent" (for a more extended discussion, see Pels 1998b).

CRITIQUE AND THE EMBARRASSMENT OF MAGIC

Thus, it may not come as a surprise that from the mid-1960s, the relevance of the witchcraft paradigm—in which the vanishing trick of magic had been completed by its replacement by the term *sorcery* (Evans-Pritchard 1970; Middleton and Winter 1963)—rapidly decreased. Apart from the internal contradictions of the paradigm, and the way it was made to destabilize modern understanding of rationality, anthropologists now also argued that *witchcraft* was a bad translation of African practices (Crick 1973, 1979). The generally pejorative connotations of magic and witchcraft seemed to have been an embarrassment to anthropologists working in the atmosphere of the critical theories of the late 1960s and early 1970s. For a period of about fifteen years, studies of witchcraft and magic became scarce. The studies that appeared showed a strong reflexive turn, in the sense of critically investigating the language through which occult practices were usually translated (Crick 1973, 1979; Favret-Saada [1977] 1980). Judging from the pages of journals such as *Man* and the *American Ethnologist*, the terms *magic* and *witchcraft* lost much of their appeal and were often joined or superseded by the terms *shamanism, spirit possession*, and so on. In this context, it is significant that one of the few recent overviews—and a most thoughtful one at that—of the anthropology of magic and religion in relation to science and rationality concludes with a critical view of rationality, rather than of magic and religion (Tambiah 1990).

For some, the most radical form of critique was one that pretended to reverse centuries of Western disrespect by arguing for the real or potential truth of magical, witchcraft, or shamanic practices, critiques that could be taken up in the countercultural, New Age celebrations of alternative perceptions of the world (Boshier 1974; Castaneda 1968; see also Johnson 1995). This revival of the romantic celebration of separate, alternative or visionary realities continues to this day in what can be called a postmodern form (Stoller 1989; Stoller and Olkes 1987; Gibbal [1988] 1994; cf. Willis 1985).

Olivier de Sardan (1992) has rightly pointed out that these studies often fall back on a rarefied, Eurocentric perception of the occult that owes its existence to the elite occultism that emerged in the late nineteenth century and that ignores other, Christian, or everyday European practices of magic. Employing a typically Occidental genre of the visionary quest (Crapanzano 1973:473), "sorcerer's apprentices" among anthropologists often maintain that one has to make a choice between joining occult practices and writing about them (Castaneda 1968:7, 198; Stoller and Olkes 1987:229), suggesting an unbridgeable gap between occult practice and ethnographic description that seems to be a venerable trope in Occidental discourse (Pels 1998b). One does not need to make a proclamation on the truth or falsity of such descriptions and experiences to note that, first, they tend to ignore that to those not initiated in their mysteries, magic and witchcraft are often a dangerous and violent presence (Geschiere and Ciekawy 1998:3), and second, that the ethnographic study of such phenomena still threatens to unsettle modes of translation and perception dominated by Western models (Pels 1998b; Van Dijk and Pels 1996).

Next to these "postmodern" initiatives, there have been other recent revivals of the anthropological study of magic and witchcraft. The study of modern occultism seems to have burgeoned, especially in a large number of doctoral theses currently being prepared in Britain (Heelas 1996:8). Those studies that have appeared to date, however, either fall back on questions derived from the witchcraft paradigm, which take as assumed the irrationality of such beliefs and movements (Luhrmann [1989] 1994), or, while regularly suggesting that the New Age is saturated by magical assumptions, do not employ the heritage of anthropological thinking about magic and witchcraft at all (Heelas 1996).[10]

From the late 1980s, those studies have been joined by studies that address the relationship between magic and modernity more explicitly and that make the study of magic and witchcraft an embarrassment to discourses on modernization in a very different way than the anthropological sorcerer's apprentices employed. These studies stress that newly enchanted perceptions of the world play a crucial role in trajectories of modernization and have coproduced the "New World" (Taussig 1980, 1987). Along with Michael Taussig, Africanist anthropologists in particular have stressed that our understanding of the modern has to theorize such alternative trajectories, especially because they include the permanence or revival of witchcraft in politics and economy (Fisiy and Geschiere 1990, 1991; Geschiere 1988; Rowlands and Warnier 1988). The essays in Jean and John Comaroff's collection (1993) and the book by Peter Geschiere (1997), in particular, have pioneered the ways the study of the creative (re)invention of ritual activity and witchcraft discourses allow one to "plumb the magicalities of modernity" and the "occult economies" of late capitalism (Comaroff and Comaroff 1993:xxx, 1999). As the contributions to this volume testify, it is on these initiatives that this book builds,[11] especially by showing that it is not just in the "Third World," but in global culture in general, that the problem of the containment of human dealings with the occult turns out to be inherent to modern societies (cf. Comaroff and Comaroff 1999; Geschiere and Ciekawy 1998).

So where does this leave the concept of magic? In this section, I have mostly emphasized that it is one of several concepts denoting a similar discursive field, in which different Occidentalist definitions of deluded or illusory beliefs were accompanied by doubts about the extent to which they were deluded, illusory, backward, or irrational. *Magic* seems to be the largest common denominator of this field, although this by no means implies that a definition of the word can substitute for all the relevant distinctions within this field designated by its affiliated concepts—between individual optimistic action, collective explanations of misfortune, the workings of the subconscious, the interplay of suggestion and deception, and so forth. It is perhaps even more important to recognize that the conceptual slippage from magic to other notions (the occult or even the irrational) is itself constitutive of modern discourses on magic, whether they involve the demarcations of philosophy, the fantasies of popular culture, or the playfulness of modernist literature.[12] The attempt to define magic runs into the same kinds of problems that Talal Asad identified in relation to the definition of *religion*: the attempt to produce a definition not only has to confront the problem that its constituent elements are the product of a specific history but that any general definition of magic—or witchcraft, or fetishism, or shamanism—is itself the product of a history of Christian discipline and Occidental science (Asad 1993:29; see also Pietz 1988). Following Asad, I maintain that it is more important to study the practices and power relationships in which those things that we tend to call magic (or label with related terms) are caught up—to a large extent because the effort to translate non-English notions with terms such as *magic* and *witchcraft* can only be kept transparent by recognizing the power inequalities of languages and the way in which the powerful language of English and its attendant cultural repertoire may transform the meanings that others employ (cf. Asad 1993:171ff.). But this already implies that one needs to examine practices—such as anthropological translation—that we tend to classify as modern. This will be the subject of the following section.

Haunted Modernities: Durkheim, Marx, Weber

> The pomposity of scientific control is carried ad absurdum, where there is nothing to control. The same rationalistic and empirical apparatus that has bumped off the spirits is being employed to impose them on those who no longer trust their own reason.
>
> —THEODOR ADORNO, *"Thesen gegen den Okkultismus,"* 1951

The trajectories of anthropological thinking about the occult traced in the previous section exemplify the kind of seesaw movement of denial and recognition that I also tried to pinpoint in the work of the individual theorists discussed. The invention of fetishism was closely related to Enlightenment materialism and its critiques of the enchantment and obfuscation produced by established religious metaphysics. Shamanism was used, by the likes of Diderot and Herder, as a Romantic counterpoint to Enlightenment rationality and common sense. The ambiguities about the place of magic in human intellectual evolution of Tylor and Frazer must be understood in the context of a similar reaction to rationalism, this time attacking mid-century positivism; whereas, inversely, the witchcraft paradigm that emerged in the context of 1930s and 1950s functionalist and modernization discourses swung the pendulum back to an emphasis on rationalization and disenchantment. Lastly, the embarrassment about the ethnocentric categories of magic and witchcraft in the 1970s, and the recent attempts to study the occult in terms of critiques of and alternatives to "modernization," emerge from a critical anthropology that desires a counterpoint to the all too unilinear and rationalistic notions of development and globalization. Because the interpretation of magic and ritual as obfuscating and conservative has Enlightenment roots, this seesaw movement of thinking about human dealings with the occult exemplifies the dialectic of the Enlightenment, which, in its attempt to achieve an abstract and transparent apparatus that will guarantee human freedom from both human and natural misfortune and disaster, sees this apparatus time and again turned precisely against these ends (Horkheimer and Adorno [1944] 1987:27).

Such doubts about the effectiveness of modernization were often silenced by the optimism of a post–World War II fantasy of social scientific engineering—a fantasy that did not lose its force until the early 1970s and that is, although enfeebled in the academic sense, still a potent ideological force. The fantasy obscured that such optimism was by no means universal when industrial society was still in the making. Its doubts are neatly captured in the experiences of that quintessential capitalist, Ebenezer Scrooge, and his attempts to dismiss as "Humbug!" any attack on his abstract, calculating conception of "business." In Charles Dickens's 1843 "A Christmas Carol," Scrooge is convinced of the impossibility and inhumanity of this vision of modernity by a series of visits by spirits, announced by the dreadful spectacle of his deceased partner, Jacob Marley, who tells him to heed their advice if he wants to escape the fate of wandering the earth after death, clanging a commercial chain (of "cash-boxes . . . , ledgers, deeds, and heavy purses wrought in steel" [Dickens [1843] 1971:57]).[13] Scrooge is first haunted by a spirit who presents him with his memories of a past of family ties, loves lost, and exotic fantasies ("Why, it's Ali Baba!" [Dickens 1971:72]), memories that Scrooge's dedication to impersonal commerce has silenced. Subsequently, the Ghost of Christmas Present shows him how the abundance of Christmas commodities should be enjoyed in gifts to family, to his underprivileged employee, and to the destitute (while threatening Scrooge by the children of "Want" and "Ignorance"). Lastly, the silent Ghost of Christmas Yet to Come shows Scrooge that, if he persists in his impersonal calculations of business, he will pass away into oblivion, forgotten by all except for the material value of the assets he has left behind.

This section discusses three similar ways by which to understand how modernity is haunted by ghosts of its own making: the construction of memories of a lost past, of the (proper or improper) ways to circulate commodities, and of the human oblivion that threatens when one indulges in an impersonal discipline of calculation. In a sense, ghosts of this ilk also haunt the understandings of modernity of three of its most profound theoreticians: Emile Durkheim, Karl Marx, and Max Weber. I do not claim to give an expert analysis or do more than suggest alternative readings of their and some of their followers' work, mostly helped by scholars who studied their work in more depth. But I hope these sketches will help to show that one needs to reread classical theorizations of modernity in a way that brings out how helpful they are in thinking about modernity beyond "modernization"—a modernization about which these thinkers were hardly as confident as those writing in their wake in the 1950s and 1960s. Even if Durkheim, Marx, and Weber retained hopes that modernity could purify itself of its own shadows, they wouldn't have been as "classic" if they had not also attempted to theorize these shadows themselves.

DURKHEIM, MAUSS, AND THE
MAGIC OF REPRESENTATION

Emile Durkheim's vision of modernization is commonly captured in the formula that with the increasing division of labor and differentiation of functions in society, social order shifts from a "mechanic" solidarity—a value consensus shared by all members of society—to an "organic" solidarity that develops out of a division of social roles and frees individuals from a number of external controls except for their increasing dependence on each other. An equally common view is that, in a later, more idealist phase, Durkheim started to doubt this vision of interdependent and organic solidarity and stressed that it still needed the cohesion of a *conscience collective* in order to work (Coser 1971:131–32). The main work in which this was spelled out was supposed to be his last, *Les formes élémentaires de la vie réligieuse* (published 1912), in which aboriginal Australians' religious solidarity—mechanical, if anything—was used to demonstrate the desired moral cohesion of all societies. Voilà the Ghost of Christmas Past, presenting a nostalgic memory of humanity's primitive childhood as the salvation of modern social cohesion.

Recent commentators argue that this distinction between an earlier, positivist Durkheim and a later, idealist one was produced by modernization theory—by Talcott Parsons in particular—but can no longer be upheld (Taussig 1993a:227; B. Turner 1992:xxix). Earlier essays, produced simultaneously with or shortly after his most positivist works, *The Division of Labor in Society* ([1893] 1984) and *The Rules of Sociological Method* ([1895] 1982), already show Durkheim's interest in the "hyperspirituality" that should make social life cohere and his interest in the State—with a capital *S*—as the organ of social, that is, moral thought (Durkheim [1906] 1974:34; 1992:51).

It is interesting to contrast this vision of the moral cohesion provided by a State with the essay on magic of Durkheim's pupils, Mauss and Henri Hubert (published 1902). Mauss and Hubert saw their theory of magic as contributing to the study of collective representations, and, in particular, of a notion of "vague power," mana, that acquired its cognitive status as the cause of certain effects "only at the moment of the conjuring trick" (of extracting an evil substance from the patient's body) when the individual subjective states of patient and conjurer joined in a momentary collective synthesis (Mauss [1902] 1972:123–26). In other words, the collective signifier or representation of magic emerges in the absence of a stable signified, as a "pure symbol" having "zero symbolic value" (Lévi-Strauss, quoted by Pocock 1972:4), in a "non-referential moment . . . where there is only timeless but effective tautology" (Crapanzano 1995:104) and where, as Michael Taussig puts it (in this volume), revelation and concealment, trick and technique, and faith and skepticism work in tandem. Mauss and Hubert therefore posited magical representations at the limit of representation, where neither the magical formula, nor the magical properties of things, nor the spiritual presence invoked are sufficient to justify the beliefs of (deceiving) magician and (deceived) patient and where the "residue" of efficacy, "this idea of a vague power," is the "total representation" of the magical rite (Mauss and Hubert [1902] 1972:98, 105).

It is at such moments of referentiality's absence, where the signifiers of magic escape stable signifieds, that Durkheim sought, unlike Mauss, a kind of referential stability in society (Crapanzano 1995:110) by "a somewhat mystical act of faith" (Malinowski [1935] 1965:235). In *The Elementary Forms*, Durkheim finds a referent for mana in the effervescent energy of the ritual crowd, that "electricity" that is materialized in the "only concrete object" on which it can fix itself: the totem (Durkheim, quoted in Crapanzano 1995:106, 109).[14] Totemic power functions for Durkheim as mana does for Mauss: it gives empowered and empowering reality to objects—symbols—that have, in and of themselves, neither reality nor power (Crapanzano 1995:112). Similarly, Michael Taussig notes that it is from the way that, according to Durkheim, sacred objects embody as well as erase the embodiment of society that they derived their sacred power and that it is this "peeling off of the signifier from its signified" that gives the representation not just the power of the represented but power over it as well (1993a:230, 235). In Taussig's essay on state fetishism, his rereading of Durkheim's reification and deification of society is directly coupled with the cultural construction of the modern state (Taussig 1993a). Indeed, Durkheim himself identified his argument that society is a moral being qualitatively different from (the aggregation of) the individuals it comprises as similar to Immanuel Kant's defense of the existence of God (Durkheim [1906] 1974:51), and Durkheim's argument about society runs completely parallel to his theory of the modern state.

In this theory, most succinctly put in Durkheim's posthumously published *Professional Ethics and Civic Morals* (1992), one can see the positivist, reifying moments of Durkheim's thinking most clearly coupled with his idealist, deifying intents, creating a magical tautology of how society is collectively represented by the State that has recently been identified as typically modern. He starts with defining the State as "a group of officials *sui generis*, within which representations and acts of volition involving the collectivity are worked out." The State does not embody collective consciousness, for that goes beyond the State (just as Mauss's notion of mana defines a residue beyond magical ritual). The State is a "special organ" in which certain representations that hold good for the collectivity are worked out, representations that are distinguished from other collective representations by their higher degree of consciousness and reflection. The State is "the very organ of social thought"; its principal function is to think (1992:49–51), and its fundamental duty is to "persevere in calling the individual to a moral way of life" (1992:69). This conceptual slippage from a "group of officials *sui generis*" to the moral brain of society—a slippage from concrete and particular signifiers of the state to the presupposition of the State's existence as signified—is impossible without a legitimizing tautology.

Taussig identifies this shift not merely as a retreat of an old sociologist, frightened by his own vision of modernity, from a positivist sociology to an unempirical idealism—as Parsons is supposed to have it—but as Durkheim's permanent and positive desire to theorize the symbol that is the State with a capital *S* (Taussig 1993a:229). I suggest that it is much the same kind of conceptual slippage that has recently come under attention as the "magic of the state" (Coronil 1997; Taussig 1997), which has earlier been theorized in terms of the state's illusory qualities (Abrams [1977] 1988), and that we also find in the example with which I started this introduction: the magic of the constitutional monarchy, presenting itself to the nation as an empty symbol capable of "standing for" a wide variety of imaginations of its citizens. This magic of representation, which suggests that *State, Society,* and *Nation* are material and authoritative presences in everyday life, is actually the effect of a host of different, dispersed, and detailed practices of symbolic repetition (Mitchell 1991a; Trouillot 2001)—among them, of the "state familiars" (registers, flags, etc.) that Martha Kaplan discusses (in this volume) and the repetitions of the imagery of monarchy that we find in national coinage and in the kind of public ritual that I discussed at the start of this introduction. Such a magic of political representation and its theological effects have also been identified as being central to strategies of establishing the modern colonial state (Mitchell 1991b).

THE FETISHISM OF COMMODITIES

> As soon as [the table] performs as a commodity, it changes itself into a thing both sensuous and super-sensuous. It no longer has its feet on the ground, but turns right round on its head, setting itself over and against all other commodities, developing whims in its wooden head that are much more miraculous than if it were to start dancing by itself.
>
> —KARL MARX, *Das Kapital,* 1867

Karl Marx's vision of progress was based on the idea that the history of humankind was a story of the increasing control of man over nature as well as the increasing alienation of man. If progress could be measured by the increase of the objectification of and control over nature, this led simultaneously to the alienation of man from the object he produces, from the process of production, from himself, and from his fellow human beings. In the present, bourgeois mode of production, the class struggle between capitalists and workers would create increasing contradictions that should lead to a modernizing revolution creating a classless society from which all alienation would have disappeared (Coser 1971:43–57). This identification of alienation as a social evil shows that Marx was one of the foremost theorists of the dark side of modernity. Instead of discussing alienation in general, I would like to focus on only one of its main features: the fetishism of commodities. On the one hand, Marx seems to have identified commodity fetishism as providing a more objective view of civil society than the monotheism of the

Protestant bourgeoisie. His main purpose, on the other hand, seems to have been to unmask it as a form of false consciousness. Beyond that, one might even suggest that the temptations of property were a threat to the ability of the proletariat to recognize its exploitation and realize progress toward a classless society. Thus, commodity fetishism appears, like the Ghost of Christmas Present, as a glimmering recognition of the necessity to properly redress material "Want" and "Ignorance," as well as a reckless surrender to consumerist desire.[15]

Perhaps the best way to enter this argument is by acknowledging that in contrast to sexual fetishism—in its Freudian form as well as in the semiotic reworking of the latter by Jacques Lacan and others—commodity fetishism is not a theory about a psychologized universal human nature but a materialist, and therefore historically contingent, critique (Pietz 1993). Unlike the former, it is therefore specifically directed at an analysis of the specificity of *modern* magic. As Marx famously argued, the mystery of the commodity form is founded on the way the commodity represents the social—and concealed—character of the labor that produced it as the concrete character of the product itself. Thereby, it also represents the social relationship between producers as a relationship of objects that exist independently of them ([1867] 1974:86). The commodity form is, therefore, "phantasmagoric"; it is an *Alltagsreligion*, a popular epistemology of social relationships that was worked out in more intellectual detail by the "secular theology" of political economy (Pietz 1993:145 n. 66). But as William Pietz argues, commodity fetishism (like political economy) is not only false but also functional.[16] It represents an epistemological advance, the fulfillment of a critique of the religious and secular universalism of Christianity and Hegelian "statism" in particular. Fetishism and political economy are closer to the true world than monotheism and statism, and they unmask the universalist spirit of the latter in favor of a contingent and materialist worldview inherent in the former (ibid.:142). But even if the knowledge of fetishized capital and an awareness of the existing ways of commodity distribution signify a more materialistic way of understanding the world—one that provides a more direct insight into the existing relations of inequality—they still remain phantasmagoric, a set of illusions to be superseded by the even more superior forms of perception of historical materialism and communism. For Marx, the direction of progress seems clear. Yet, there is a certain ambiguity about the relationship between subjective and objective perceptions of social progress. This ambiguity is underscored by the fact that elsewhere, Marx regarded Protestant Christianity and its image of abstract humanity, rather than fetishism, as the "proper form of religion" of a society of commodity producers ([1867] 1974:93).

The ambiguity may be better understood by recognizing that commodification is neither restricted to capitalist societies nor to the exchange of goods. Marx's tendency to discuss commodity exchange mostly in relation to capitalism may obscure that it characterizes many other societies (Appadurai 1986:9). Instead, the specificity of capitalist society may be better approached by recognizing that it marks an unprecedented social expansion of the commodity *form*, most notably through the commodification of human labor— and this was, of course, also the basis of Marx's famous discussion of commodity fetishism in the first part of *Capital*. This points to a way to approach the tremendous reach and variety of mystifications that characterized modernity's reliance on the commodity form as well as the extent to which such magic is inherent in its self-understanding. As Michael Taussig argued, we may well expose the quantity of disguised exploitation in terms of surplus labor time accruing to the employer (which requires at least a minimal mastery of the language of quantitative statistical calculation), but "the quality of that exploitation cannot be measured" (Taussig 1980:27). Indeed, if the labor represented by the commodity is social, and therefore "supersensuous" and invisible, the fact that its relations of power are hidden leads to all kinds of novel forms of revelation of what it keeps secret, revelations in terms of the work of the devil (Taussig 1980), of white vampires (Pels 1992; White 1993), or of other evils that commodities have acquired when passing through global markets (Meyer 1998a) that we can only understand by ethnographic description.[17] In fact, the closely affiliated historical provenances of Occidental definitions of *fetish* and *fact* show that such relations between the object's false appearance and its functional revelations were constitutive of Occidental culture (Pels 1998a). The most exquisite example of the inevitability of this ambiguity of commodity fetishism is that of Marx's own overcoat, the garment of respectability that he needed to wear to be able to enter the British Library for his studies but which he also had to pawn in order to be able to buy food for his family and the paper on which to write *Capital*: the overcoat, doubly fetishized—as respectability and as capital—was an indispensable means of producing the critique that would unmask the fetishism of commodities (Stallybrass 1998).[18]

The Ghost of Christmas Present haunted Ebenezer Scrooge with the image that the plenitude of commodity consumption could not be justifiably enjoyed without proper redistribution; what haunted Marx was that the classless redistribution of commodities in a utopian future would be preempted by the triumph of private property—by the "nightmare" that the bourgeoisie, rather than the proletariat, would turn out to be the turning point in history (Gouldner 1980:382). In that case, Marx's identification of commodity fetishism as the paradigm of modern ideology, based as it was on a conception of private property—on the salvation expected from the possession of things, worked out in such cultural detail by Walter Benjamin—gains importance the more one criticizes Marx's focus on the production rather than consumption side of modern capitalism.[19] In this respect it is interesting to note that Colin Campbell, in his revision of Weber's *Protestant Ethic*—according to Campbell, an ethic of capitalist production—makes the argument that a study of the specifically *consumerist* ethic of the bourgeois personality identifies it as a double one. This double personality wants, on the one hand, to critically expose—especially in the Bohemian phase of youth—its own alienation produced by the commodified relationships of capitalism and bureaucracy, only to resolve that problem in middle age by the comforts of pervasive commodity consumption (1987:223ff.) This suggests a rather more bleak vision of the place of the critique of commodification in society than that contained in Marx's progressionist view.

The challenge to a socialist utopia by commodity magic was spelled out by Benjamin's image of Paris at the time of Charles Baudelaire, where the revolutionary "miracles" of the anonymous professional conspirator (for Marx, the "alchemists of revolution"), of the enchanted perception of the city by the flaneur, and of the impersonal satisfactions provided by the prostitute are all linked together in the image of the commodity, and the "incognito" toward concrete, historical relationships that it maintains (Benjamin [1955] 1979). He linked the *Zauber* (magic) of cinema stardom and totalitarian dictator in an even more ambiguous prediction of twentieth-century political culture (1977:154).[20] Perhaps one can find yet another form of this commodified "incognito" in the continuous reproduction of the images of constitutional monarchy, already referred to above, especially in the serial repetition of the portrait of the king or queen on national forms of currency—the commodity par excellence—which, ubiquitously, inescapably, and close to anonymously make the monarch "stand for" the nation.

STRAINING AGAINST AN IRON CAGE: WEBER'S CHARISMA

The ghost that haunted Max Weber was the empty shell of the Calvinist entrepreneur, a *Berufsmensch* (professional person) who disenchanted himself by shedding all magical means of achieving the certainty of salvation and who became totally attuned to the duty of rational calculation or, as Weber quoted John Wesley, the exhortation "to become rich" (Weber 1947:197). As the duty to work and rational self-discipline came to outlive the spirit of Calvinism itself, the desire to master all things by calculation turned into the "driving gear" of the modern economic order, one that today determines the style of life of all those who are born into it with an "overwhelming force" and that will, perhaps, determine it "until the last hundredweight of fossil fuel is burnt" (ibid.). For the Puritans, the concern for worldly goods should have lain like a light cloak on one's shoulders, but

> fate decreed that the cloak should turn into an iron shell (*stahlhartes Gehäuse*). Since asceticism sought to enter and reform the world, material goods have gained an increasing and finally an inexorable power over the lives of people as never before in history. Today the spirit of religious asceticism—whether finally, who knows?—has evaporated from this shell. In any case, since it rests on mechanical foundations, victorious capitalism no longer needs its support. The rosy humor of its laughing heiress, the Enlightenment, seems also to be irretrievably fading, and the idea of duty in one's professional calling prowls about in our lives like the ghost of dead religious beliefs. (Weber 1947:203)[21]

As the Ghost of Christmas Yet to Come showed Scrooge, his exclusive preoccupation with the worldly goods of business and the rational calculation of their profit would result in personal oblivion after death. Indeed, Weber echoed Leo Tolstoy in arguing that progressive disenchantment made death—and by implication, "civilized life as such"—meaningless (Weber 1948:140).

It is amazing, in retrospect, how modernization theorists could distill a deterministic optimism out of Weber's tragedy, his Nietzschean genealogy of disaster (Lichtblau 1993:192; Peukert 1989). They were helped, in any case, by some tricks of translation that made Weber more deterministic and less historicizing than he was. Talcott Parsons's translation of the *Wahlver-wandtschaften* ("elective affinities") between Puritanism and capitalism as "correlations" inserted Weber's theorizing, against its explicit intent, into a universe of deterministic laws, ignoring, at the same time, the alchemical etymology of the term that reached Weber through Goethe (Lichtblau 1993:193).[22] Similarly, Parsons's translation of *stahlharte Gehäuse* with *iron cage* seems to shift emphasis to a determinism of social systems, at odds with the original, more individualistic idea of a personal "cloak" turning into an "iron shell."[23] In contrast, Weber's methodological individualism shows in his emphasis on the person being "born into" *Berufspflicht* (professional duty), a person also faced with the necessity of making choices in the "poly-theism" of values that characterizes modernity (Weber 1948:148; Schluchter 1988:362–63). Modernization theory obscured the historical Weber—his-torical in both senses, of Weber as a historian and as a historical creature of his own time.

Of course, the recognition of Weber's historicizing temperament does not deny that he did, indeed, promote an Occidentalist image of progressive dis-enchantment and reified Western rationality; nor does it imply that his his-tory was all correct. As Colin Campbell has argued, Weber made "his" Protestant ethic into "the" Protestant ethic, despite the fact that he recog-nized that there existed, for instance, a Lutheran mystique of sentiment next to the Calvinist turn to ascetic action (C. Campbell 1987; Weber 1947:108).[24] As a result, Weber may have exaggerated the identification of modernity in terms of the iron shell of *Berufspflicht* and downplayed the contradictions within modernity that he was confronted with in his own life. As is well known, the iron shell was to Weber also an existential problem, and it was a personal crisis, forcing him to leave his profession and partly caused by his fa-ther's Calvinism, that led to the writing of *The Protestant Ethic*. While publicly defending, with his wife Marianne, the Protestant ethos of monogamous sex-ual fidelity and the rejection of all sensual culture that went with it (Lichtblau 1993:185–86), he kept private his experiences, in later life, of (extramarital) sexual passion, while perhaps sublimating some of them in an increasing in-terest in the opposition between an ethical, ascetic, and progressive rational-ity, on the one hand, and a far more ambiguous awareness of the existence of a Dionysian, more feminine, and charismatic desire for intoxication on the other (Mitzman 1970:301–2). Thus, Weber personally experienced the contradictions between the different sides of the bourgeois personality identified by Colin Campbell, and this sheds a different light on Weber's statement that science can only give clarity by showing the possibilities of *choice* and his exhortation that each modern person has to find and obey "the demon which holds the fibers of his very life" (Weber 1948:151, 156).

At the very least, this shows that for Weber, *Entzauberung* (disenchantment) did not imply *Entgötterung* (the loss of belief in gods) (Schluchter 1988:347 n. 21). In the polytheism of values of modern society, "many old gods rise from their graves" and "resume their eternal struggle" in disenchanted and impersonal form (Weber 1948:149). Before one interprets this statement—as modernization theorists did—as a way in which Weber disengaged an essentially contested world of values from the world of scientific fact and rational method, one should take into account the fact that *Wissenschaft als Beruf* (science as vocation) clearly identifies the scientific disenchanted attitude *itself* as one of the "demons" that one may seek out and obey. In other words, the values of "value-free" science and rationality are themselves part of the field of battle of disenchanted moralities. This is underscored by Weber's view that whoever lacks a real vocation for science—whoever lacks the experience of the "strange intoxication" and "passion" of "the idea that the fate of his soul depends on whether or not he makes the correct conjecture at this passage of this manuscript"—should stay out of it (Weber 1948:135). But to include the outcome of the historical process of intellectualization—in the form of its "most important part": science (ibid.:138)—in a battlefield of intoxication and moral passion would seem to crack the iron shell—or, given Weber's well-known respect for science, at least fill it with a spirit and ethos different from the Protestant God and ethic that deserted it. How *stahlhart* is this shell, anyway?

Answers to this question may be sought in two directions. One follows from holding on to the "strong" idea of the iron cage, arguing that we are imprisoned in a technological world of our own making. Such an interpretation accuses Weber of "misguided optimism," both about breaking from the iron shell and about disenchantment, because he underrated the extent to which the omnipresent and omnipotent technology from which humans seek authorization and satisfaction has "re-enchanted" society (Germain 1994). There is much to be said for such a view: the reenchantments produced by modern technologies of communication, domination, and self-discipline—for example, by the routinization of royal charisma through the serial production of its imagery through coinage and mass media—ought in any case to be important topics for research. For the understanding of Max Weber's personal views, however, the second direction—of further penetrating the cracks in the iron shell—seems more appropriate. The voluntarism of Weber's position in *Wissenschaft als Beruf* was radicalized by his idea that a scientific genius could both reflect the values of an epoch and decisively influence them.[25] This capacity was based on the contingent appeal of his ideas and values to society at large—in short, on a charismatic authority emerging from the battleground of values played out in scientific discourse (Peukert 1989:25–26). Indeed, by discussing a scientific vocation in terms of intoxication and passion, Weber had already brought the Dionysian characteristics of charisma into the sphere of dispassionate analysis and fact. *Charisma* turns out to be a residual form of authority that is necessary both to the maintenance of enchanted traditions (Weber 1947:250) and to the production of prophets of disenchantment (Weber 1947:94 n. 3, 269); that is out-of-the-ordinary yet can be routinized in quite a number of ways (Weber 1956:140, 142); and that therefore defies classification in relation to the process of disenchantment and rationalization (Mitzman 1970:302). Charisma seems the way to think of an escape from the iron shell, the charm with which to lay the "ghost of former beliefs that is *Berufspflicht*." Thus, Weber's vision of a process of disenchantment in which the magic of tradition is being replaced by the rationality of law is haunted by two magicalities: the reification of so-called rational institutions and the impossibility of dismissing the social role of charisma.[26]

SO WHAT TO DO WITH "MODERNITY"?

The previous paragraphs show how little sense it makes to talk of a singular modernity or of a unilinear process of modernization. Haunted by their own diagnoses of the process of modern development, even the classical theorists of "modernity" acknowledged how much it was riven by contradiction, regression, and paradox. A singular modernity was never an empirical, historical fact except as a Eurocentric ideology of a universal teleology of the evolution of social systems, such as provided by modernization theory (Comaroff and Comaroff 1993:xi–xii). We have, indeed, "never been modern" (Latour 1993). Any attempt, therefore, to reduce the real diversity of human action by the indiscriminate application of such a label needs to be criticized empirically. However, talk of modernity is itself an empirical fact, and it is not mere talk: throughout the world, one can identify "modern" discourses that produce real effects—such as some of the processes divined by Durkheim, Marx, and Weber. Whether one argues that modernity is a singular, Enlightenment project, characterized by the nation-state and realized globally in different histories (Van der Veer 1998) or that one needs to affirm the existence of modernities in the plural by generalizing about different religious, cultural, or economic trajectories of globalization (Featherstone and Lash 1995; Hefner 1998), it seems obvious that for an empirically adequate analysis, we need to account for *both* the ideological *and* the practical effects of modernity—that is, make them operational in such a way that one can also talk about what modernity is not.

Ideologically speaking, one needs, at the very least, to take *modernity* to refer to the global (but not hegemonic) spread of a *consciousness of radical temporal rupture* (Habermas 1987; cf. Miller 1994:58ff.). Whether magic is made to define "tradition," or whether it finds a place in the practices of the New Age movement, it is, in both cases, crucial for the definition of something specifically "new." This proposition still leaves open whether such consciousness of temporal rupture is ideological and obscures social processes that have far more continuity than presumed, or whether it is discursive, that is, has come to modify social practices in such a way that social reality has (partly) turned into its image. Both dimensions are present in the practices of inventing or reinventing magic in modernity: even if magic is denounced as "bad" tradition and backward, it is often, in the process, reconstructed in novel ways that may come to influence social practices at a later stage. The best example of this has been discussed above: Frazer's novel emphasis on the secrecy and psychology of magic, which was taken over by some of the modern occult movements that *The Golden Bough* inspired. This haunting of modernity by the magic it represses is the focus of the first set of contributions to this volume.

On the other hand, one cannot deny that, practically speaking, there are certain modern forms of action that achieved tremendous historical modifications of human behavior. Here, one can apply the Foucauldian insight that rather than looking for the discontinuities in modern history in the field of the history of ideas, one should focus on *the practical transformation of technologies of conduct* (Rose 1996:300). I have argued above that such technologies of conduct may generate their own magicalities: for Durkheim and Mauss, by the effervescence of the crowd and the imagined communities of the *conscience collective*; for Marx, by the constitution of modern subjects through commodity production and consumption; and for Weber, by the steel shells of rational discipline, economy, science, and bureaucracy as well as by the romantic liberation promised by "charisma." The second part of this volume deals with these issues.

There is, however, a third aspect of the relation between magic and modernity that provides a backdrop to all the contributions to this volume and grounds them in a particular (trajectory of) history: the fact that most theories of magic (or modernity) discussed above seem to stress that *the modern study of magic is largely a study of human subjectivity*. Whether they mark questions of how human beings make intellectual associations, of what they can and cannot perceive, of how they constitute their desire for the future, of what makes the practices they engage in persuasive, or of whether and how they can be called rational or deluded, no present-day speculation about magic can escape the modern discursive boundary between the ideal, modern subject that makes true perceptions and practices a rational discipline and a magical subject that is set up in contrast as backward, immature, or dysfunctional. All contributions to this book assume that both the modern rationalist and the magically backward subject constituted by such theories are modernist myths that need to be scrutinized by empirical research. They also indicate that both modern and magical subjects are constituted in ideological as well as practical ways. Nikolas Rose has argued that one cannot assume the existence of a modern, individual subject without an ethnographically and historically sophisticated study of how it constitutes its interiority or "self" by practices of "infolding" exterior forms of authority, specific to time and place (Rose 1996:300). This goes for the study of the magical subject as well, and explains this book's—and especially the final chapter's—focus on magic's dialectics of publicity and secrecy, and revelation and concealment—on the moments and ways in which external authority conjures up magical beliefs and subject positions.

The Impossible Return of the Repressed: (Re)inventing Magic in Modernity

Following Bruno Latour (1993:11; see Margaret Wiener, this volume) we might say that the radical distinction between magic and modernity is a form of modernist purification that is constantly being betrayed by the translations and mediations needed to relate the two. Thus, magic is reinvented in modernity, an "invention of tradition" that does not create continuity with the past as much as it distances itself from it (cf. Hobsbawm and Ranger 1983; Fabian 1983). The invented opposition of an unchanging magical past and a dynamic, disenchanted modernity ignored metropolitan transformations of magic into occultism, based on the practices of phrenomesmerism and Spiritualism (Pels 2000, this volume), just as much as it forgot about colonial developments in which the understanding of Indian "superstition," against which James Mill and Thomas Babington Macaulay directed their initiatives for reform, relied upon a modern transformation of Brahmanic tradition into a European vision of foundational and supposedly unchanging texts (Pels 1999b:86, 94). In other words, the magic repressed by modernity may return, but in an encounter that transforms both.

In his chapter, Gyan Prakash offers a particularly insightful account of the positioning of a reinvented magic in the development of modernity in colonial and postcolonial India. The thinkers of the Arya Samaj reform movement had to recast indigenous culture in the image of Western reason at the same time that they had to make modern authority emerge on the basis of India's ineluctable difference from the West. They did this by trying to divest indigenous culture of its magicalities, not in a battle between science and religion but by disengaging the latter from "superstition." The resulting attempt to "scientize" and disenchant the Vedas created a doubly haunted modernity. On the one hand, it created a hybrid of modern science and Vedic Hinduism that subverted the former's illusory purity and that became a compelling image for the construction of the modern Hindu nation and its subjects—modern subjects now placed over and against a reachable God, who was to be reduced to their personal knowledge and experience. On the other, this national subject was itself not secure, for it was born in a failure to appropriate the magicalities that were incommensurable with it, and this incommensurability required a constant policing of the boundaries of Vedic

Hinduism by interpretations of the "superstitious" Puranas—a failure to suppress magical difference that haunts the image of an Indian "people." Alcinda Honwana, in her contribution to this volume, gives another example of an attempt to define the nation—in her case, Mozambique—over and against a past of magical practices classified as (needing to be) superseded. The Marxist modernization policy of Frelimo came to be haunted by the practices of the healers (*tinyanga*) that it tried to define out of existence (in a way comparable to the treatment of balian under Dutch colonial rule; see Margaret Wiener, in this volume), especially when the transnational guerilla against Frelimo was instrumentally "localized" in these healers by the opposition movement, Renamo. Her account of the way in which, after Frelimo was once more victorious in the polls, the spirits of dead Renamo soldiers come to haunt the living presents an interesting comparison with the role of spirit possession in "modern" Europe (Peter Pels, in this volume).

If Prakash and Honwana concentrate on the impossibility of securely relegating magic to a past from which modernity tried to purify itself, the next two chapters criticize the historical fictions on which such purification is based, by juxtaposing them with alternative histories that live on in the magical practices negated. Rosalind Shaw discusses, on the one hand, how the Sierra Leone rebel war is being "jujuized" by global media, especially in producing a newly hybridized image of modern weaponry combined with magical practices, in such a way that this image, spread, in a world of U.S. dominance, by networks of diplomatic correspondence, becomes an alibi for the international isolation of African countries. On the other, Shaw argues (elaborating on earlier work, Shaw 1997) that this can only happen on the basis of a specific kind of historical amnesia about a trajectory of modernity in West Africa that emerged already in the fifteenth century, initiated by the violent commerce of the slave trade—a trajectory that produced the forms of magical protection against war and robbery that have been transformed to novel uses in the rebel war. Although he does not go back as far, Laurent Dubois deals with a similar background, in showing the historical purifications that characterize both the archives and published representations of the Haitian revolution of 1791, purifications that reinvented Haiti from being a colonial failure into a justification of a civilizing mission. Although Haiti's revolution (which combined "fetish" and modern freedoms) was constitutive for the construction of a modern French nation, a historiographical trance silenced its importance in French history. This silence stands over and against the "reliving" of the emergence of a Haitian modernity in Vodou ritual practiced in present-day Paris. Such a critique of the magic of hegemonic historical representations indicates how constitutive magical practice was as a route to the development of modern nationalities (see also Derby 1994; on magic as a progressive force, see Martha Kaplan, this volume).

In the last two chapters in this set, Margaret Wiener and Peter Geschiere take the critique of the attempt to purify modernity from its magicalities a step further. Starting from the apparent contradiction between colonial modernization and indigenous magical practice, in which Dutch colonizers perceived the *balian* as offering no service and therefore lacking proper and honest employment (much like Alcinda Honwana's *tinyanga*), Wiener argues that, on the contrary, "colonialism *required* native magic, as its foil and ground." Employing Latour's vocabulary, she argues that the purificatory moves of colonial discourse generated new and uncanny hybridities: forms of indigenous knowledge (trance, rumor) that the colonial order could not accommodate (comparable to Gyan Prakash's Hindu national subject when faced with the Puranas); colonial iconoclasm that, in destroying indigenous images, attributed power to them as well; and unofficial discourses that enchanted Europeans by making them vulnerable to the "hidden forces" of indigenous culture.

In a way that, because more contemporary, is yet more disturbing, Peter Geschiere takes his seminal work on the modernity of African witchcraft a step further by focusing on a comparison of hidden dimensions of African and American politics, inviting us to think about parallels between U.S. political propaganda and the recent resurgence of "witchcraft" in Cameroon. Despite the fact that he points out parallels rather than identities between witch doctors and spin doctors, the vehement reactions of some of his colleagues to the comparison show how deeply rooted the oppositions of magic and modernity still are. Criticizing the tendency to portray Western politics as transparent by producing an imagery of African politics as "witchcraft-ridden," his comparison shows "the inadequacy of current terminology and the oppositions it implies between magic and science, transparency and occultism." By provoking such an encounter between seemingly opposed entities, Geschiere—like the authors of the preceding chapters—has pushed the discussion forward from seeing magic as modernity's counterpoint, antithesis, or malcontent, toward the recognition of the magic of modernity itself.

The Magic of Modernity: Representations, Commodifications, Disciplines

In my discussion of the haunted modernities of Durkheim, Marx, and Weber, I already tried to indicate some of the enchantments produced by modernity itself, especially in its forms of representing the nation-state to its citizens and of constituting subjectivity through commodification and rational discipline. Even if the emphasis of Chapters 2 through 7 of this book lies in modern magic as an antithesis rather than a product of modernity, they already show that modernity generated its own enchantments: the citizens' trances, the pollster's spins, the slave's protections, to name a few. The next four chapters elaborate on this and emphasize the way modern technologies of conduct—both ritual and rational, symbolic and substantial—determined the content and form of modern magic. However, because the content of *magic* was mostly defined in relation to a past superseded by modernity, *magic* is a term rarely applied to such modern enchantments.[27] The modern use of the family of concepts is often provocative, as in Theosophy's adoption of occultism as a nom de plume, Aleister Crowley's psychologistic reinvention of "magick," or Gerald Gardner's invention of "witchcraft," or wicca, in the form of a secret fertility cult—words meant to shock a predominantly Christian and scientific Occidentalist consciousness. Beyond that, the use of such concepts borders on, or disappears into, metaphor—even though these are metaphors we (want to) live by, as when creative marketeers portray themselves as modern magicians or management gurus are described as witch doctors (Micklethwait and Wooldridge 1996; cf. Peter Geschiere, this volume), when film theory likes to speak of the magic of film (see Birgit Meyer, this volume), or when one compares junkie scares or rumors about satanic child-abuse to witchcraft (Beets and Stengs 1992; La Fontaine 1992). The discussion of such modern magicalities often turns to other, related but more diffuse notions—the "spirits" or "monsters," for example, of Charles Dickens's "Christmas Carol" or Shelley's *Frankenstein* (cf. Pels, this volume; Verrips, this volume).

In this context, Martha Kaplan uses a neologism—*state familiars*—to highlight a specific aspect of the magic of the modern state (already referred to above in several ways). She focuses less on the magic of representation of the nation-state as such than on its material signifiers: books of registration, flags, gun salutes, and the like. Starting from an idea already discussed above, that the effort to separate the magical from the real will produce its own uncanny reminders, she outlines a number of ways in which the printed word, in particular, was a key aspect of the magic of the colonial state. Moreover, she thereby breaks with the idea that magic is only obfuscating and conservative, emphasizing, again, that to its practitioners, modern magic can be enlightening, creative, and progressive (cf. Comaroff and Comaroff 1993; cf. also Dubois in this volume). In her contribution, Birgit Meyer discusses how magic figures in a rather different enlightenment than that envisaged in the West. Popular cinema in Ghana brings about a break with the modernizing intentions of colonial cinema, in the sense that magic is not exposed as a tradition to be superseded but revealed as constituting modernity's present: popular film allows Ghanaians to reveal that magic and witchcraft cause improper inequalities in consumption patterns at the same time that the public "development" that colonial cinema wanted to achieve makes room for a moral focus on a feminine and domestic—typically modern—ideal of the nuclear family.

If Kaplan focuses on state representations, and Meyer on commodification and consumption, the last two chapters in this part of the book deal with the new magicalities of rational discipline. Jojada Verrips concentrates on the possible magical content of the medical discipline, and Peter Pels focuses on the magicalities that emerge from two different forms of intellectual and social discipline—while both define the world of health and healing as outstandingly susceptible to the development of modern magic. Verrips argues that popular discourse, gleaned, for example, from cinema and from mystery and horror novels, provides a running critique of medical science. This stance is partly fed by a popular suspicion that modern medicine can create unnatural beings (such as the Frankenstein monster). Moreover, medical doctors themselves not only contribute to popularizing medical discourse by bringing medical metaphors (such as germ theory) into everyday life but also anthropomorphize their own work as a struggle against evil entities in the body. When this is extrapolated to the social realm, the medical doctor turns into an inhuman monster himself—as we now know, H.G. Wells's Dr. Moreau was, so to speak, incarnated in Josef Mengele. Pels zooms in on a debate between Edward Tylor and Alfred Wallace about the immediate predecessor of modern occultism—Spiritualism—to which Wallace was converted. By interpreting the debate as one about the proper construction of British public culture, he shows that the objects of investigation of Tylor and Wallace—mind and spirits, respectively—pose, in their explanations, as causes of sociality but are actually effects of specific political anatomies, a panoptic and expert discipline in the case of Tylor and an experimental and domestic one for Wallace. The eventual victory of the Tylorean approach has obscured that both disciplines were crucial for the constitution of modern subjectivity but that Wallace's subordinate form survived in the realm of domesticized occultism, providing a paradigm for twentieth-century New Age practices.

Conclusion: Revelation and Concealment

The last chapter in this book is Michael Taussig's, and it is distinguished from the other contributions in the sense that it does not restrict itself to discussing magic *versus* modernity or the magic *of* modernity—although it addresses both—but suggests a novel and playful approach to magic in general. Taussig argues that if magic has commonly been seen as a tradition of belief that stands opposed to modern skepticism, a rereading of two classics of the anthropology of magic (the account of his career as a shaman of Franz Boas's most important Kwakiutl assistant, George Hunt, and Evans-Pritchard's *Witchcraft, Oracles and Magic*) shows that faith and skepticism actually work together to produce the persuasiveness of magic. This movement "in" and "out" of "belief" finds a parallel in the visceral quality of magical tricks and their (simulation of a) movement in and out of bodies. Quoting Goldman, Taussig argues that the power of magic emerges from "secret matters that are always hidden and can be experienced, therefore, only in simulated form"—a mimesis that necessarily wavers between technique and trick, cure and deception, revelation and concealment, faith and skepticism, seriousness and play. He goes further to suggest that the texts authored by Boas (with Hunt) and Evans-Pritchard—although they want to expose fraudulence rather than reveal magical prowess—are themselves "shamanic," or at least that the anthropologist is so obsessed by exposing the tricks of the witch doctors that he forgets where his technique of "observation" itself turns into a trick. Taussig hereby points to a field of ambiguity of faith and skepticism that not only helps constitute the efficacy of magic but can also subversively invade practices of disenchantment them-selves (as Margaret Wiener's discussion of colonial iconoclasm, or Peter Pels's discussion of Edward Tylor's research into Spiritualism bring out as well).

It is at this moment where the variable skills of revelation and concealment coincide that the subject is constituted, whether as patient, skeptic, magician, or fraud—the moment at which, as argued above, the infolding of exterior, culturally available repertoires of authority occurs. As such, Taussig's chapter may help to explain why modern theories of magic have always been such ambiguous attempts to construct subjectivity: they usually declared one side of the magical coin—the skeptical one—to be characteristic of modern sub-jectivity in general, although a mere toss of that coin could make repressed "faith" return. It is precisely Taussig's transformation of the purifying *distinction* between faith and skepticism into an embarrassing *mediation*—a mediation constitutive of the persuasiveness of magical "tricks" and "techniques"—that makes his contribution so important for a book about magic and modernity. The theoretical insights one can draw from it can be made to explain the mag-icality of modernity's attempt to oppose magic, to provide directions for re-search into the magic of modernity itself, and to make us play with the extent to which we have indeed never been modern. The chapters in this book show the need for such a task: the more they uncover the discursive tricks and prac-tical techniques by which modern identities—the Hindu nation, African Marx-ism, the "Juju" soldier, History without Vodou, colonial disenchantment, ra-tional politics—conceal the vulnerability and violence of modern forms of power, the more urgent a critical interrogation of the magicality of such forms of power—cinematic enlightenment, spinning statistics, ethereal ex-periments, the monstrosities of medicine—becomes. Thus, modernity's "burst-ing flashbulbs" may come to be recognized to constitute, as much as they expose, magical technique.

ONE

Between Science and Superstition

Religion and the Modern Subject of the Nation in Colonial India

GYAN PRAKASH

In 1988, California Institute of Technology received a letter from a Bengali village in India, written by a Mr. Biswas. It was a letter with a strange request and an unusual enclosure. It read:

> I am an Indian writing to you with a good hope in our Indian culture.
> Recently (on 27.6.1988) my wife has given a [*sic*] birth of our first child (female), our hope that she (child) will be genious [*sic*] and will go abroad for higher study in future. In our culture, we consider the "Umbilical Chord" of new born child very auspicious and generally we keep this underneeth [*sic*] the ground in places of tradition such as University, College, Temple, Church etc., with a hope that she/he will become famous according to the place where the "chord" is kept.
> I believe that at present your Institute is one of the greatest Institutes in the world. So with a great hope, I am sending that auspicious "umbilical Chord" of my child to you with the request to put in anywhere underneeth [*sic*] of the University campus. My wife wishes that our daughter will go to

U.S.A. in future for higher study. Once again, I request you to consider our sentiment.[1]

The "chord from Mr. Biswas" is not only a moving expression of parental love and ambition but also an extraordinary cultural artifact that registers a powerful faith in the authority of Western science. So powerful is this authority that not even the enunciation of "our culture" can escape its force. Thus, the loving parents send the umbilical cord of their child thousands of miles away from their native Bengal to California, asking for the performance of a Hindu rite at the California Institute of Technology, a renowned institution of modern science and technology.

If the letter expresses a touching faith in science, it is the umbilical cord that doubles as a sign of science's power. Science's cultural force surfaces when it is dislodged from its "proper" location in the laboratory and relocated "improperly" in the umbilical cord. So, even as a traditional Hindu rite is subordinated to the authority of modern science, an institution of modern science and technology is defined as one of the "places of tradition." The structure at work here is not dialectical but disseminatory, for the process of signification does not oppose one to the other; rather, science's authority comes alive at the site of its alienation in the dead tissues of the umbilical cord.[2]

The signification of science's authority through dissemination suggests that science cannot completely subordinate and appropriate the difference that enunciates its power. In serving as the material that rearticulates the self, the constitutive other haunts the self's identity and authority. Such an approach offers refreshing perspectives on science's position as a sign of modernity. First, it locates the articulation of science's cultural authority in the dissemination and negotiation of incommensurable knowledge and power, not in a unilateral assertion of despotic power. This approach promises to provide an understanding of how modern science's power is universalized. Second, by identifying otherness as a category produced by the failed attempt to appropriate difference, it positions science's others as demons internal to its life at the same time as that which remains outside its grasp, and haunts its dominance.

We can observe such an articulation of science's authority in nineteenth-century British India. Then, the reform-minded intellectuals faced the conflicting pressures of two opposite demands. On the one hand, the emergence of Western science as a sign of modernity demanded that the indigenous culture cast off its difference and be recast in the image of Western reason. On the other hand, the association of science with colonial power required that reason speak in the language of the indigenous culture, that India's ineluctable difference serve as the medium for the emergence of its authority of reason. It was at the site of this dilemma that there arose a powerful project to rid the indigenous culture of its "superstitions" and "myths." Not surprisingly, the principal object of this reformist project was religion. Or perhaps it is more accurate to say that the effect of reform was to identify and constitute religion by stripping it of what appeared unscientific and irrational. In this sense, science was not locked in a battle with religion but concerned with specifying its domain, disengaging it from what appeared as superstition. Science worked its magic by rescripting religion, by identifying it in reformed and hierarchized texts, by divesting it of "improper" accretions, by devising new standards of its order and intelligibility. Underlying the reformation of religion and the vigilant defense of its boundaries was the composition of a new stance toward God. No longer was God unreachable, an unknowable difference beyond the self; instead, it was now reducible to the knowledge and experience of the subject. This was a crucial transformation, for it placed the self, armed with the power of reason, in an all-powerful position. For this self the world was nothing but an extension of its being, and God was well within its horizon of knowledge. Denying that self's existence was bound up with an otherness beyond its comprehension; such an assertion of the subject's autonomy positioned religion to offer the material for the articulation of the notion of a community, a nation.

On the borderlines of science and magic, then, there appears a story of religion's secularization, its subjection to the logic of reason, that permitted its staging as the basis of a modern identity. Tracing the modern emergence of religion, this chapter asks if the process of bringing "a people" into existence could escape the pressure of knowledge and tradition named and stereotyped as magic and superstition. I argue that if science's authority was produced in the simultaneous configuration and division of the indigenous culture as religion and magic, then it is in this double movement that we must analyze science's legitimation of the idea of a people. It is in this sense that I argue that science's authorization took shape in the failed attempt to produce otherness in the image of the self. It was this failure to appropriate difference—reflected in the designation and stereotyping of the recalcitrant otherness as superstition—that produced reformed Hinduism and led to the identification of the Hindus as a community. It is from the vantage point of the subaltern, from the perspective of that which the discourse sought to expunge, that I wish to present the history of science's authority. I should stress, however, that my aim is not to retrieve the "real" history of the subaltern. Because I view superstition as the product of a failed attempt to absorb difference as an extension of the self's experience and knowledge, I identify it as a disfigured, displaced image of science, not a subaltern figure to be retrieved. It is precisely in this disfiguration that there arises another history of science's authority, another view of Hinduism's functioning as the stage for identifying a people.

Hindu Revivalism and Science

In 1895 a bitter dispute broke out in a north Indian town. In the acrimonious debate, the Arya Samaj, a Hindu reform and revivalist group, was pitted against a group of orthodox Hindu intellectuals. Established in 1875, the Arya Samaj had quickly emerged as a powerful voice for "purifying" Hinduism, embroiling it in numerous controversies. What sparked the 1895 dispute was its questioning of the rationality and legitimacy of *shrāddha*, the ritual of ancestor worship. The Arya Samaj denounced this and other Hindu rituals as manifestations of superstitious beliefs invented by priestcraft and contrary to the scientific wisdom contained in the Vedas, which it considered as the authentic source of Hinduism. The orthodox Hindu intellectuals took exception to the Arya Samaj's relentless attack on shrāddha as unscientific and illegitimate and agreed to a debate. The disputation was held in May 1895, and it was charged to answer the question of whether or not the ancestral ritual should propitiate only the living or both the living and the dead. The proponent of the orthodox case wrote an essay in Sanskrit defending the ritual against the Arya Samaj, which was represented by two scholars who jointly wrote an essay on the subject (*Śāstrārtha* 1896, 1–16).

The two sides disagreed on the impartiality of the Indian Orientalist judges, and forwarded the essays to Max Müller at Oxford for arbitration. Müller replied in September 1896, stating that ancestor worship arose "simply from a very natural human feeling to give up something that is dear to us, to those who were dear to us" (ibid.:19). No one asked if the departed came back to eat the offerings made, and the ceremony was held when remaining members of the family gathered at a meal. As the living also partook of the meal offered, the shrāddha encompassed both the departed and the living. Soon, however, superstition took over and people began to believe that the departed returned in bodily shapes to partake of the offerings. Müller then quoted from the Vedas to establish that the ceremony honored both the dead and the living. The Arya Samajists, stung by Müller's verdict, responded by hiring drummers, who paced up and down the town, drumming the charge that the letter was forged.

At the center of the dispute over shrāddha was its authorization as a rational and scientific ritual. Such a framing of the authority of Hinduism illustrated the extraordinary burst of conviction in the antiquity and authenticity of Hindu science that British India witnessed during the late nineteenth century. This conviction was shared by Hindu intellectuals ranging from religious reformers to practicing scientists who spoke repeatedly and obsessively of a forgotten but true religion of the ancient Hindus and contrasted it with the "irrationality" and "corruption" of contemporary Hinduism. Attributing the contemporary state of Hinduism to the loss of ancient Hindu science, the intelligentsia seized on such issues as the existence of the caste system, the condition of women, and the grip of priesthood and rituals to demonstrate that irrationality and unreason had so overpowered the Hindus as to render them powerless before the West.

The criticism of indigenous traditions was not new; contrary to British beliefs, Hindu practices included a lively tradition of critical thought. What was new, however, was the invocation of science's authority in the critique. The beginnings of this authority can be traced back to the early-nineteenth-century "civilizing mission," which identified reason with the West. A sense of "awakening" to reason and "renaissance" took hold among the emergent Western-educated elite, which saw itself uniquely placed to reform and revive traditions (Kopf 1969). Its project of reform expanded and took on a new shape after the 1830s, when colonial policies began to change under the combined influence of utilitarianism, evangelicalism, and the successful attack against Orientalist learning. As new technologies of governance—geological and land surveys, census operations, mining, telegraphs, railways, medical and sanitary establishments—emerged, they became modes of articulating science's authority. Science came to signify not just scientific research in laboratories but also new forms of rule and authority; it became a metaphor for rationality, modernity, and power (Prakash 1999). Thus, even as Indians took up scientific education and research, the reach of science's authority extended far beyond the laboratory to function as a grammar of social and cultural transformation. Formed in this milieu, the Hindu educated elite projected science as the true heritage of its religion and culture and represented itself as the agent for the "recovery" of the nation lost to myth and superstition. There appeared powerful movements to reconfigure the "flawed" body of contemporary Hinduism in the immaculate shape of ancient Hindu science, and Hindu intellectuals reached back for the ancient knowledge of the Hindus to recover the space of the modern nation.

Underlying the representation of Hinduism with the sign of science was a far-reaching transformation under way in colonial India that involved the meaning of the very term *Hindu*. This term is derived from the Sanskrit *Sindhu*, the name of the Indus River in present-day Pakistan, and was used originally by Persians to refer to the inhabitants of the Indian subcontinent. The Muslim chroniclers in the thirteenth and fourteenth centuries invoked this term to identify the non-Islamic peoples of India and to describe their beliefs and practices. The earliest use of the term to describe the Hindus as a community occurred in the fifteenth century. In the nineteenth century, the two senses of the term—as inhabitants of the subcontinent and as a community—became combined to constitute the Hindus as "a people," that is, as a nation. Crucial in forging this combination was the specification of Hinduism as a religion. This occurred largely, though not exclusively, in response to attacks on indigenous beliefs and customs mounted by missionaries and colonial officials. Defending the Hindus against the charge that their religious thought and social arrangements were irrational and backward, the intelligentsia claimed that Hinduism was a body of rational and internally consistent beliefs and practices. To substantiate this claim, they located Hinduism in authoritative textual sources and campaigned against customs and rituals that appeared to conflict with the rational principles enshrined in texts. By the 1850s, such efforts to constitute Hinduism as a religion qua religion, and equal to Christianity, had acquired a prominent place in the discourse of the elite Hindu intelligentsia.

In the colonial context, the constitution of Hinduism as a religion had profound political implications. For to assert that Hinduism was a religion was to claim a universality equal to that of Christianity. Implicit in this claim was also the assertion that the Hindus were entitled to the identity and authority of a people insofar as they possessed the cultural universal of religion. This proclamation positioned Hinduism as an emblem of identity, as the national religion of (Hindu) Indians. It was this desire for modern identity and authority that animated late-nineteenth-century Hindu revivalism, that is, movements to reconfigure Hindu society and religion according to what the intelligentsia saw as authentic traditions.

No leader exemplified Hindu revivalism better than Swami Dayanand Sarasvati. Born to a Brahman family in Gujarat in 1824, he studied religious texts and Sanskrit, fled home in order to escape marriage, and became a preacher in 1860. It was then that he decided that Hinduism had to be rescued from its contemporary "degenerate" state and restored to the ancient greatness and purity of the Vedas. He was not unique in the turn to the Vedas; Hindu reformers across the subcontinent turned during the nineteenth century to the Vedas and the Upanishads in their search for the textual basis of rational Hinduism (Jones 1989). In fact, the pursuit of rational religion was not confined to India. As Peter van der Veer shows, the British also configured Christianity as a rational religion in defining themselves nationally and in pressing their colonial claims (Van der Veer 2001). Science's authorization of reason as the supreme form of knowledge molded the constitution of religion, nation, and empire in the nineteenth century. Thus, it is no surprise that Dayanand also sought to establish the authenticity and antiquity of Hinduism as a body of rational knowledge.

A charismatic and audacious preacher and reformer, Dayanand disseminated his program of reviving the Vedic Hinduism of the ancient Aryas (Aryans) across northern India during the late nineteenth century. To spread his message, he established the Arya Samaj in 1875, which quickly made its mark among educated Hindus, particularly in the Punjab (Jones 1976:13–29, 36–66). Asserting the superiority of Vedic Hinduism over all religions, the Arya Samaj's mission was to restore a pristine and classical Vedic religion cleansed of such "corrupt" accretions as priesthood, the caste system, idol worship, child marriage, and prohibitions on widow remarriage and female education. This vision of a pure, scientific Hinduism of the Vedas was based on the authority and originality that Dayanand claimed for the Vedas as science. The turn to science sprang from the desire to represent Hinduism as a monotheistic religion. This desire grew in response to Christian attacks on Hinduism as idolatrous and polytheistic. As Hindu intellectuals responded to these charges by reinterpreting Hinduism as a monotheistic religion, they invoked the authority of science. Insisting on the fundamental indivisibility of science and religion, these intellectuals cited positivist ideas of Herbert Spencer and Thomas Henry Huxley to assert their belief in the oneness of all phenomena and in the existence of one supreme power. Just as science had one truth, so did Hinduism as an "essential religion" (Prakash 1999:75–81).

Dayanand was a leading figure in the milieu defined by the effort to recast Hinduism as a religion endowed with scientific thought. Thus, when the leaders of Theosophy, Helena Petrovna Blavatsky and Henry Steel Olcott, became interested in Indian religions, they turned to Dayanand and the Arya Samaj. Theosophy's origin lay in movements of religious dissent within Christianity. In the late nineteenth century, however, it developed as a spiritualist philosophy for the modern world. Offering a heady mix of clairvoyance, mesmerism, and hypnotism, Blavatsky claimed that her doctrine surpassed the understanding offered by modern science, and that it penetrated beyond the material realm to reveal underlying principles and consciousness (Blavatsky 1893–97; Campbell 1980). Convinced that the origins of occult science lay in Hindu and Buddhist ideas, Blavatsky and Olcott arrived in India from the United States in 1878. Dayanand welcomed Theosophy's turn to Hinduism. On their part, Blavatsky and Olcott were so impressed with Dayanand's ideas that they renamed their New York–based organization the Theosophical Society of the Arya Samaj of India, and placed Dayanand at its head (Van der Veer 2001:55). This collaboration, however, proved short lived. Dayanand found Theosophy's immersion in the occult at odds with his own commitment to an austere, uncompromising rationality. The Hinduism that the Theosophists championed, he thought, was full of hocus-pocus, nothing resembling the true scientific spirit of the Vedas. Thus, he denounced the Theosophists in 1882. They, in turn, returned the favor (Van der Veer 2001:55–56).

Theosophy's advocacy of the virtues of Hindu spiritualism, however immersed in the occult, strengthened the cultural opposition to British rule and laid the basis for an enduring association with Indian nationalism. Dayanand also contributed to the nationalist opposition, but the scope of his project was greater. Not confined to posing a cultural challenge to colonial rule, his project's goal was to reconstitute Hinduism itself so that it could function as a body of knowledge and practices for acting upon the modern world. Philosophical arguments about the scientific basis of the Vedas were neither nativist boasts nor matters of arcane discourse. For him, the constitution of Hindus as modern subjects was at stake. It is for this reason that he set about bitterly attacking everyday rituals and beliefs of the Hindus, giving speeches and sermons asserting the superiority of Vedic Hinduism over all religions; staging debates in which he charged orthodox Hindu pundits, Christian missionaries, and Muslim theologians with ignorance and superstition; and claiming that modern science confirmed the Vedic understanding of the universe.

Dayanand thrived on creating controversy and provoking opposition, and his rhetorical strategy in the verbal combats he staged was to refute and ridicule his opponents with relentless appeals to reason and science. In one such verbal duel staged in 1877, the combatants included Dayanand, a Hindu representative, four missionaries, and two Muslim theologians, and its avowed purpose was to ascertain true religion by addressing several questions formulated by Dayanand (Prasad 1889:29–33, 36–41, 70–78). Addressing one of these, which asked with what God made the world, at what time, and for what purpose, the Christian representative, Rev. Scott, was dismissive. He replied that he found the question useless but went on to state his views: God created the world out of nothing because there was nothing but God alone in the beginning; He created the world by fiat; and though the time of creation is not known, creation has a beginning. Rev. Scott was followed by Mohammed Kasim, who declared that God created the world out of his own body. The question of time, he thought, was a futile one (Prasad 1889:168–71). Then came Dayanand's turn. He was sharp and combative, and his appeal to the authority of science was revealing:

> God has made the world out of Nature or atoms, which are thus the material cause of the universe. The Vedas and the profane sciences prove the matter or the aggregate of atoms to be the primary and eternal substance of the phenominal [*sic*] world. The Deity and nature are both unbeginning and endless. Not one atom of the underlying substance of visible things can be increased, decreased, or annihilated. . . . Now, what is the doctrine of the nihilists, who

maintain that the world has come out into existence from nothing. They point out fiat or sound as the cause of the world. This theory, being opposed to science, is incorrect. .∴. No science can prove that the effect follows the cause. It violates the law of causation, the foundation of science, and subverts the law of association, the basis of reasoning. (Prasad 1889:171)[3]

Significantly, the acknowledgment of a self-exceeding infinity did not force Dayanand to admit that God was unavailable to the subject's consciousness, that it was an area of radical exteriority, a transcendence that both constituted and extended beyond the self. On the contrary, he claimed that the "Vedas and the profane sciences" were privy to the constitution of God and nature as "unbeginning and endless." Endowed with this knowledge, the Hindu self was self-sufficient, confident that its consciousness encompassed the nature of God itself.

Having bestowed the Vedas with the knowledge of God and asserted their superiority over other texts and traditions because they alone were consistent with science, Dayanand went on to also assert their antiquity. Claiming that "formerly knowledge travelled from India to Egypt, thence to Greece, thence to Europe, and so forth," he declared that no other religion could possess "the genuine history of this country"; only the Aryas, the most ancient people and the possessors of the "the most ancient records of knowledge," could answer questions about creation and offer their country's "genuine history" (Prasad 1889:171).

Such a claim on behalf of the Vedas and for the Aryas' right to represent their nation's history could not be confined to philosophical matters but had to extend to the daily practice of Vedic religion if the modern Hindus were to be refashioned in the image of their scientific forebears. This meant that the Vedic rituals—of which *homa*, or the sacrificial fire, was the most important— had to be represented as scientific in inspiration and purpose. This was important because Dayanand's reinterpretation of the Vedas was formed in opposition to popular Hindu rituals of worship and devotion. Anticipating that the Vedic sacrificial fire and the recitation of hymns might be subjected to the same critique that he had directed at popular Hinduism, Dayanand offered explanations that invoked the authority of science. In *Satyārth Prakāsh*, the canonical text of the Arya Samaj (Sarasvati [1882] 1963:55–56), Dayanand first recommends homa, the sacrificial fire, and then poses questions that he answers:

(Question)   What is the use of *homa*?

(Answer)   Everyone knows that foul air and water breed disease, diseases cause unhappiness in human beings, whereas fragrant air and water promote health and the destruction of disease provides happiness.

(Question)   It is useful to apply the sandalwood paste on someone's person and to offer clarified butter in a meal. The knowledgeable do not destroy and waste them in fire.

(Answer)   If you knew the laws of matter, which state that a substance is indestructible, you would never say such a thing. Look, when *homa* is conducted, men living in places far away from its site breathe the fragrant air just as surely as they take in the foul air. This is because fire breaks matter into fine particles which mix with and are carried by air to great distances, and negate pollution.[4]

To suggest that the Vedic homa purified the atmosphere by fragmenting matter into fine, light particles was to throw science—the sign of the modern nation—into the ordeal of the Vedic fire. Science emerged from this sacrificial fire with an ancient Hindu rationality, staging the practice of Vedic rituals as the performance of the modern Indian nation. Such a performance of the nation appealed to educated Hindus, who flocked to the Arya Samaj and found the subjectivity of modern India signified in its Vedic rituals.

Such modern restaging of the Vedas occurred, above all, in the Arya Samaj's successful program of education and social reform. The Arya Samaj integrated science in the Sanskritic education it offered at the Dayanand Anglo-Vedic College, and it established research institutes that sent speakers on tours to deliver lectures on science and technology (Jones 1976:72, 162–64). The emphasis on science did not suffer when the organization split into moderate and militant factions in the 1890s. On the contrary, the militant Gurukul wing stressed the "Vedic" rather than the "Anglo" part of education to "nationalize" the curriculum,[5] and the Vedas themselves were interpreted as science.

The militant Arya Samajists emphasized Vedic education with the strident claim that the Vedas constituted the sole source of science. This was the guiding vision in the writings of Pandit Guru Datta Vidyarthi, a professor at Lahore Government College, who led the militant faction until his death in 1890 and inspired the program of Vedic education imparted in the Gurukul school. Vidyarthi outlined his position in his collection of essays, *Wisdom of the Rishis*, by first refuting the argument that the Vedas were myths that embodied natural truths in an imaginative language (Vidyarthi n.d.:5–25). Unlike myths, which are concrete, the Vedas, he argued, were abstract and philosophical; they gave birth to philosophy, and mythology evolved afterward. Having thus established the Vedas as philosophy, he questioned the authority of the European Orientalists whose interpretation of the Vedic hymns as the mythology of a primitive people he dismissed as prejudiced and the product of mistranslation of Sanskrit (ibid.:26–91). The European Orientalists, Vidyarthi charged, did not know the law of Vedic Sanskrit grammar properly; they treated Vedic terms as nouns when they were actually *yaugika*, that is, terms that conveyed a derivative meaning consisting of a reference to the root together with modifications effected by the affixes. As an example of such a mistranslation, Vidyarthi cited a translation from Max Müller, the German Orientalist: "May Mitra, Varuna, Aryaman, Ayu, Indra, the Lord of Ribhus, and the Maruts not rebuke us, because we shall proclaim at the sacrifice the virtues of the swift horse sprung from god" (cited in ibid.:60).

Vidyarthi offered the following translation instead: "We will describe the power-generating virtues of energetic horses endowed with brilliant properties, or the virtues of the vigorous force of heat which learned or scientific men can evoke to work for purposes of appliances (not sacrifices). Let not philanthropists, noble men, judges, learned men, rulers, wise men and practical mechanics ever disregard these properties" (ibid.:59–60).

Vidyarthi's translation differs greatly from Müller's, and its purpose was to demonstrate that Vedic religion did not enjoin the worship of deities. The Sanskrit term *devatā*, he argued, did not mean a deity but signified a process; Agni and Marut were not nouns but terms that referred to processes and properties. Through such subtle reinterpretation and relocation of terms, Vidyarthi realigned the relationship between the Vedas and science. He placed the philosophy of the Vedas in a scientific register and organized his essay on the Vedic term *vayu* as a treatise on atmosphere, on the "gaseous envelope" composed of molecules of air charged with energy. "Is not, then, a *light, mobile, tremor-communicating, effluvia-carrying medium* a better and a more exact appellation for this masterly creation of the Architect of Nature than the ugly, unmeaning, inexact, and half-articulate word *air*," he asked (ibid.:92–93).

As Vidyarthi housed the concepts of mobility and medium in the Vedic term vayu, he shifted both science and religion out of their "proper" domains and mixed them "improperly" to change their meanings. The Vedic vayu, when placed in relationship to changing temperatures and currents, revealed itself not in accordance with the opposition between science and religion but as a concept formed in their precipitous mix. It is thus that the Sanskrit word *rig* came to signify nature and its properties, and Vidyarthi construed the Rig Veda to mean the knowledge of the "physical, chemical, and active properties of all *material* substances as well as the psychological properties of all *mental* substances" (ibid.:98). Whether this is the real meaning of the Sanskrit term is irrelevant; what is pertinent is that the Vedas were infused with the authority of Western science, whose position, in turn, they invaded and dislocated. We can observe this double operation performed in Vidyarthi's assertion that "long before Cavendish performed his experiment on the composition of water . . . the true philosophy of the composition of water was recorded in the Vedas and perhaps understood by many philosophers of the east" (ibid.:102). Here, if the reference to Cavendish acknowledged the power of Western science indirectly, it also placed the Vedas as the authentic anteriority of modern science. Such a collision and collusion of different authorities and different times permitted Vidyarthi to relocate the Vedas as neither science nor religion in their usual sense but as a body of timeless truths that embodied and exceeded the authority of modern science: "The measure of Vedic truth is not its power to grow and spread, but its inherent power to remain the same ever to-day and to-morrow" (ibid.:105).

The timelessness of the Vedas, produced in the flux of "to-day and to-morrow" and negotiated from the hybridization of modern knowledge and ancient heritage, became a compelling image for the construction of the modern Indian (Hindu) nation. It established the Hindu as an all-knowing subject, one that claimed authority over all that was meaningful, an ability to determine that Agni and Marut were not deities but processes. The impulse at work in Dayanand's representation of the Vedic sacrificial fire, and in Vidyarthi's interpretation of the Sanskrit word *rig* as a term signifying nature and its properties, was the denial of transcendence. Not even God escaped the Hindu's knowledge: God was an object of knowledge revealed to the Vedic Hindu. Nothing exceeded the ideas and experience of the Hindu subject, nothing existed outside the subject's experience and competence. Insofar as science and reason enabled this denial of transcendence, this repudiation of the inappropriable alterity, it authorized the representation of the modern (Vedic) Hindu as an all-knowing, self-contained subject. This was the real significance of the Arya Samaj; it made the Hindu subject so utterly sovereign that not even the unseizable alterity of God—*illeity*, as Emmanuel Levinas calls it (1981)—could escape its grasp. Hinduism emerged from this reconstitution as a religion for modern national subjects, as a means for bringing India within the reach of the Hindu.

Vedic Hinduism and Its Other

The relocation of Vedic Hinduism as the stage for representing Hindus as "a people," however, was crucially dependent upon drawing lines between religion and superstition; it entailed an anxious policing of the boundaries of Hinduism so as to expel from the domain of religion all that which was considered alien. The identification of Hinduism's "improper" accretions of myth and magic served as the means for representing what was "properly" religious. Such a strategy of appropriating otherness in the interest of projecting an all-knowing Hindu self meant outlining a history of Hinduism in which beliefs and practices attributed to the epic literature of the Puranas (composed between 500 B.C.E. and 500 C.E.) could only appear as perversions of the authentic historical trajectory.

All the sciences and arts and religions, Dayanand asserted, originated in Vedic India (Dayanand 1882:272). But then came the Great War of India, the Great War of the *Mahabharata*, when learned men and philosophers were slain on the battlefield. Knowledge declined; the religion of the Vedas disappeared or was perverted by the Brahmins, who had become ignorant; fraud, superstition, and irreligion flourished; and numerous religious sects were born. An Indian priesthood took root, convinced the Kshatriya warriors and kings that their word was the pronouncement of god himself, and flourished in the lap of luxury. It invented idol worship, temples, and the idea of incarnations to ensnare the masses and prevent them from accepting Jainism. Thus arose Puranic Hinduism, a system of false beliefs and idolatry (ibid.:272–300). How could such false beliefs overpower the true knowledge of the Vedas? According to Dayanand, Puranic Hinduism was victorious because people, "naturally prone to indulgences of imagination and ignorance," were unable to live the difficult life imposed by the science of the Vedas. As people succumbed to the bewitching charms of poetry, "science gave way to the spell of mythology, which soon spread over the world with the speed of electricity" (Prasad 1889:235). Ridiculing the Puranic mythology, Dayanand wrote: "For instance, Baly, a monkey king of Mysore, wrestled with Ravan, the ten-headed giant king of Ceylon, and, having got the monster under the armpit, forgot to take him out for six months. They don't tell us if he was given regular rations all the while" (Prasad 1889:239).

Such stories told by the Puranas were more likely to appeal to people's "degenerate sense" than the dry, abstract truths of the Vedas, and they produced idolatry and fanciful notions of incarnation. As a result, wrote Guru Datta Vidyarthi, the militant Arya Samaj leader:

> The broad and universal distinction of all training into professional and liberal has been altogether lost sight of in the Puranic mythology, and like everything else has been contracted into a narrow, superstitious sphere of shallow thought. The Vedas, instead of being regarded as universal textbooks of liberal and professional sciences, are now regarded as simply codes of religious thought. Religion, instead of being grasped as the guiding principle of all active propensities of human nature, is regarded as an equivalent of certain creeds and dogmas. (Vidyarthi n.d.:99)

In the cold light of reason and science of the Vedas, Puranic Hinduism, whose myths, legends, and deities formed the stuff of the daily popular religion, appeared childish. Puranic Hinduism had managed to even pervert the meaning of Vedic philosophy; "instead of being regarded as universal textbooks" of science, the Vedas became a religion—a body of "certain creeds and dogmas."

This sense of the decay and loss of the science of the Vedas animated the Arya Samaj's powerful reformist critique of Puranic Hinduism and plunged it into numerous controversies. These critiques and controversies were not inconsequential debates on arcane theological matters but vital contests concerned with creating a new national subject in the regenerated Arya. Aimed at renewing the Aryan personality by refashioning daily life, this project drew inspiration from Dayanand's *Satyārth Prakāsh*, much of which was devoted to outlining rules of daily living. Dayanand's bitter denunciation of astrology as superstition, for example, was animated by the concern to diminish the influence of priesthood on the daily life of the Hindus. He argued that once people gained the true knowledge of the physical world contained in the Vedas, they would cease to depend on the priests and astrologers who hoodwinked the ignorant by attributing diseases and misfortunes to planetary influences (Dayanand 1882:23–24). Later, the bilingual journal of the militant Arya Samajists devoted to women's issues hammered home the same message: astrology fed on ignorance and was contrary to the authentic texts of Hinduism (Pānchāl Panditā [1900] 1901:10–11). The reform of daily life was also a principal concern in Guru Datta Vidyarthi's text, *Wisdom of the Rishis*, which devoted a chapter to the organization of the household and marriage, subtitled "A Scientific Exposition of Mantras Nos. 1, 2, and 3 of the 50th Sukta, of the first Mandal of the Rig Veda bearing on the subject of the household" (Vidyarthi n.d.:103).

The Arya Samaj carried Dayanand's legacy forward by conducting pamphlet wars on Hindu rituals and beliefs. At issue in these wars was the appropriation of difference. Having endowed the Hindu subject a consciousness that encompassed the transcendence of God, the Arya Samaj was not about to concede that the interior of the Hindu self was riven with contending definitions. The constitution of the Hindu as an undivided and self-contained subject demanded the containment of the contagion of difference. It is thus that the Arya Samaj sought to establish the authority of the Vedic reason by representing and vigorously attacking the Puranas as myth and poetry. Such a strategy did not shy away from difference but courted it in order to contain it. This can be observed in a Hindi pamphlet that the Arya Samaj published in 1893 to refute the ancestral ritual of shrāddha attributed to the Puranas (*Mritak Shrāddha Khandan* 1893:3). Consisting of a fictional disputation between an Arya and a Pauranik (a Puranic believer), the text rigs the discussion in favor of the Arya Samaj, demanding that the efficacy of the shrāddha ritual be proved and demonstrated with evidence. The Arya commands that the Pauranik explain how his ancestors return from the world of the dead to consume food offered in the ritual, and it then disputes the explanation offered.

> *Arya:*   Okay, let us assume that they shed their gross bodies to re-enter this world, as they did earlier to depart from it upon their death. I assume that just as we cremate a lifeless body, so do they in the world, or else the blood would cause the body to rot. If this is the case, then it seems you have committed a

> murder by performing a *shrāddha*, because now they are neither in the other world nor here. Where will they go now?
>
> *Pauranik:*   No, my view is that they live in fine, spiritual bodies. They do not need gross bodies. Therefore, they can travel as they please.
>
> *Arya:*   This is impossible because, if they did not leave this world of their own will, how can they now travel as they please? Besides, you believe in rebirth. If they left their bodies here, who will be reborn? (*Mritak Shrāddha Khandan* 1893:3–4)

Admitting his error, the Pauranik amends his argument, stating that ancestors do not reenter this world to accept the offerings made in the ritual; rather, the food offered to the Brahmin in the shrāddha ceremony is carried across to the ancestors. The Arya then moves to clinch the argument:

> *Arya:*   This is very doubtful. If the fluid from the food consumed by the Brahmin is sent across, then it will not turn into blood, and the Brahmin will die. If it transforms into blood and reaches your ancestors, then they are guilty of drinking the blood of the Brahmins, committing their murder. Besides, the Brahmins should become weak from the lack of blood, but we observe instead that the Brahmins fed during the *shrāddha* become strong and healthy from the fifteen days of feasting. So, your argument does not make sense. Nor can you say that your ancestors consume the food offered them by inhaling the Brahmin's breath, because they could not possibly survive breathing the foul air, that is, "carbonic acid gas," that we exhale. (*Mritak Shrāddha Khandan* 1893:3–4)

The dialogue is set up to establish the writ of science and reason, but the Arya's strident refutation of the Pauranik's beliefs is strained. An uncertainty surrounds the authority of the Arya Samaj's knowledge, as it loses itself in a reverie of explanations for the means of communication between this and the other worlds. Even as the Arya institutes the authority of science, he is forced to dislocate it in the Pauranik's explanations. He must ask, How do the ancestors travel? Do they shed their gross bodies? How can they be reborn? Does food turn into blood before its consumption by the ancestors? Such questions are rigged with the intent to establish the power of the Arya Samaj, but to fulfill this intent the Arya had to first allow the Pauranik to cut into the discourse, permitting his ancestors to gnaw at its authoritative core. Only then, after the Arya has explored and exhausted every one of the Pauranik's explanations, contorting his discourse to follow the mythic meandering of the bloodthirsty and Brahmin-murdering ancestors, can the Arya display the sign of his authority. Distortion and vulgarization of the opponents' explanations—"it seems you have committed a murder by performing a *shrāddha*"—become necessary in order to authenticate the Vedas. This strategy turned the Puranas into the enemy of the Hindu nation and accused them of having caused its loss through myths and fantasies.

A Hindi text from 1895, written as an allegory, orchestrates such an accusation against the Puranas (*Swarg Men Subject Committee* 1895). It describes the deliberations of a special committee—a "subject committee"—instituted in heaven to register complaints and investigate charges against the Puranas. A correspondent describes the preparations for the meeting. Upon receiving notice of the meeting of the committee, the deities came from all over—from Calcutta to London and Bhopal to Nainital, crossing rivers from the Ganges to the Thames and mountains from Meru to the Himalayas. Riding on swans, bulls, buffaloes, and trains, the deities of everything, including tables and chairs, and numbering 900 million ("the population of the deities had increased greatly in the most recent census"), arrived at the meeting to air complaints (*Swarg Men Subject Committee* 1895:12–15). Every deity lodged a complaint that the Puranas' fanciful tales had incurred it untold harm and disrespect. Lord Brahma proposed that Vyasa, the sage who is said to have composed the Puranas, should be expelled for writing defamatory accounts of the gods. Lord Krishna joined in, stating that he had been greatly embarrassed by the Puranas: he had never stolen butter and carried on amorous relationships with milkmaids. Lord Vishnu endorsed the proposal for Vyasa's expulsion, charging that he had been smeared by the accusation that he had left his consort to make love to a demon's wife. Lord Shiva complained that Puranic stories had turned his lock of hair into a waterspout; people expected to see the Ganges flow out of his hair. After everyone had aired their grievances and asked unanimously for Vyasa's expulsion, the president of the committee agreed that the Puranic myths had made a mockery of the deities and reduced them to curiosities displayed in the museum. Vyasa, he agreed, must explain his conduct. But Vyasa pleaded innocence. "I never composed even a single Purana. If I had, why would I have given a slanderous account of my own birth?" In reality, he argued, the atheists (the Charavak philosophers) were responsible for composing the Puranas. "I trained my disciples only in the Vedas and composed the Vedantic texts to determine truths, in addition to writing a short historical account of the Mahabharata consisting of 24 thousand verses" (*Swarg Men Subject Committee* 1895:19).

It is striking that the discourse uses the language of law to contain the force of Puranic beliefs. The encounter between the Vedas and the Puranas does not take the form of a dialogue but of a judicial proceeding that confers the Vedic discourse with the force of law rather than the hegemony gained from consent. Such a discourse of power distorts the representation of heaven itself, reducing a lofty celestial body into a mundane earthly body engaged in interrogation and punishment. The pressure exerted on the dominant discourse shows up in the very form of ridicule and mockery that it uses to subordinate the authority of the Puranas. Thus, the text dislodges the Puranic myths and legends from the field of cultural beliefs and practices and places them in the incongruous arena of censuses, committees, newspaper correspondents, and railroads in order to contain their force. The discourse impoverishes rich myths and reduces them to ridiculous facts. Thus, the text has Shiva complaining that the Puranic image of him as the source of the river Ganges reduces him to waterspout. But mockery can be read as a sign of the menace the Vedic discourse recognizes in otherness.

As the text mocks the Puranas relentlessly, it also repeats the Puranic myths compulsively to demonstrate the authority of Vedic knowledge. In order that a new national subject may be recovered, every deity and each story tell the tale of the loss of Vedic reason to fanciful myths. The revived Hindu nation, however, bears the mark of its loss of vitality to the Puranic myths. So, as Vyasa declares his allegiance to the Vedas, the strategy of mocking and stereotyping difference returns to shadow the Vedic authority: Vyasa acknowledges the power of the Vedas, but his speech mimics the language and tone that the text mocks. This mimicry contains and regulates the menace of otherness and assimilates the stereotyped Puranic myths as the medium for the rearticulation of the Vedic nation. Such a revival of India relied on a compelling appeal to the Vedic past, but it also inhabited the recalcitrant difference of the Puranas in the representation of the nation. Placed intimately beside the Vedic nation, the bewitching spell of the Puranas exerted a constant pressure, rendering the nation's narration unending and uncertain.

Conclusion: Modern Religion and Modern Nation

The Arya Samaj was only the most prominent instrument of a widespread effort in the late nineteenth century to resignify Hinduism with the authority of science. This effort included the wide circulation of the concept of Hindu science, which was originated by Orientalists and championed by Indian religious reformers and practicing scientists. It is not difficult to understand the desire to seize something that was associated with colonial power and make it one's own. But precisely because the cultural translation of science was identified with alien power, it was violent; it necessitated the absorption of otherness, its reconstitution in the image of self. The nineteenth-century religious reform movements were crucial instruments and expressions of this process. For it was religious reform that produced a modern, autonomous subject for whom even God did not mean a realization of the self's limitation. The Arya Samaj, for example, projected the Hindu as a modern self for whom religion did not mean an awareness of his/her transcendence by other knowledge. Quite the contrary, the Arya stood as a figure that spoke the language of science to bring the world within his reach as an object of his knowledge and experience. Intervening in both subtle, philosophical matters and everyday life, the Arya Samaj sought to produce the Hindus as a nation, community, "a people" that embodied science, God, the infinite. It is in this light that we should see the revival of the Vedantic philosophy in the late nineteenth century. Frequently combined with the philosophies of August Comte and Spencer, this philosophy expounded nondualistic conceptions of the world, placing it at the command of the Hindu self. It is thus that Hinduism emerged as a modern religion that, equipped with the authority of science, claimed to provide the basis for identity. In this sense, the identity-fulfilling function of Hinduism was related to its transformation by science, to its resignification as a religion of the undivided, colonized subject. Not surprisingly, Hindu symbols pervaded the language of secular nationalism, and the abiding belief in the achievements of Hindu science nurtured the struggle for a modern secular state.

The reinscription of Hinduism, however, was born in failure, a failure to appropriate what Levinas calls the absolute Other, the other that is incommensurable with the self, and hence outside its understanding and resistant to suppression. I read the creation of categories such as magic and superstition, and the campaign against the Puranas, as expressions of this inability to extinguish the self-exceeding exteriority. I am not suggesting that the Puranas constituted this radical exteriority but that the distortion and displacement of the discourse necessitated by the effort to stigmatize them as myths and fantasies—asking how ancestors travel to receive the food offered in the shrāddha ceremony, the indictment of Vyasa by the "subject committee"—register the failure to suppress otherness; that the stereotyping and naming of beliefs as superstition and myth operated as modes in which the self was compelled to speak as it failed to order difference into the same. We can identify the recalcitrance of otherness not in the Puranas that the discourse mocks but in the contortions forced upon the discourse as it struggles to bring the epic literature within its domain of understanding and critique. It is there, where the discourse produces magic and superstition and separates them from the Vedic religion, that the failure to suppress difference gives rise to the menace of otherness that haunts the image of "a people."

TWO

Undying Past

Spirit Possession and the Memory of War in Southern Mozambique

ALCINDA HONWANA

In May 1996 *Media Fax*, a daily Mozambican newspaper distributed by fax, reported the sudden death of soldiers belonging to the battalion of the government army in the District of Govuro. The soldiers were all Maconde and were reported to have participated in the killing of Laquene Nguluve, the "traditional" chief of Vuca, a small locality in the District of Govuro.[1] The killing happened in 1986 during the war between the Frelimo government and the Renamo rebels, because Nguluve was accused of supporting Renamo. Ten years later, in 1996, the Maconde battalion stationed in Govuro started to be afflicted by the retaliation of Nguluve's spirit: in two months, six of its members died in strange circumstances, and the commander who ordered the killing of Nguluve underwent a serious mental breakdown. Members of the battalion and their relatives turned to local diviners for help. Divination revealed that the spirit of the dead chief wanted revenge and asked for the life of a Maconde child to be taken with the very same gun that had been used to kill him. The Maconde apologized and pleaded with the spirit to accept as a settlement three goats, a bottle of brandy, and a virgin Maconde girl, who would be offered to take care of the hut of the spirit. Apparently the spirit of Nguluve rejected that offer, and people fear that he will continue to afflict and kill the soldiers of the battalion until his demands are met. The matter has become a public concern, and local authorities in the Govuro District (the government, the Association of Traditional Healers, and the Association of War Veterans) have been involved in trying to mediate the conflict.

This incident characterizes the situation in the rural areas in postwar Mozambique, where the living are haunted by the spirits of the dead and where spirit possession is not a matter of the past but is at the very heart of modernity. In this chapter I examine the role spirit possession and exorcism play in the politics of national culture in Mozambique. Despite having no formal space in the modernization discourse of the state, spirit possession plays an instrumental role in processes of healing, cleansing, and social reconciliation in the aftermath of the war in Mozambique. I will discuss spirit possession in the context of state politics of culture in the postindependence period, especially during the war between the Frelimo government and the Renamo rebels. My analysis of spirit possession in present-day society is developed against the backdrop of historical sources with regard to the phenomenon in the nineteenth century and their memorization in present times. Showing the ways in which spirit possession has been constantly renewed, I will pinpoint its transformative and dynamic character. My main argument is that in contrast to modernist claims, in Mozambique spirit possession cannot be relegated to an obscure dimension in human experience or a distant past but has to be acknowledged as a constitutive part of everyday life. Spirit possession is a public, visible, contemporary reality that allows individuals and groups to reconstitute their identities by treating ill health and promoting social well-being. Although spirit possession constitutes a stabilizing factor in social relations, it is by no means a static regulator of human endeavor and identity. On the contrary, it is precisely its capacity of making possible individual and collective changes of identity that explains much of its forceful dynamics and successful adaptation to modernity.

Frelimo, Renamo, and Politics of Spirit Possession

This section discusses Frelimo's and Renamo's attitude toward "traditional" beliefs in spirit possession during the postindependence period, that is, since 1975. The war between Frelimo and Renamo started in 1977 and lasted for about fifteen years.[2] During that period, both political groups eventually accommodated beliefs in and practices with regard to spirit possession in order to reconstitute their own sense of being and purpose. For Renamo, who desperately searched for a political ideology, resorting to spirit possession was a way to gain some legitimacy and popular support from the outset. In the case of the originally Marxist-oriented Frelimo, spirit possession was initially regarded as mere superstition, which was to be replaced by a secular materialist philosophy. This attitude only changed in the late 1980s, when Frelimo eventually adopted a more moderate line, reformed its political system, opened the economy to free market forces, and created some space for religion. The war came to an end with a peace accord, which resulted from international mediation and peace talks, signed in 1992. Frelimo won the 1994 democratic elections and formed a new government. In order to understand the dynamics of the war and both movements' interactions with spirit possession, one needs to examine some of its antecedents.

During the sixties, the creation of Frelimo and its struggle against colonialism sparked a process of social and political change in the country that was accelerated by independence from Portugal in 1975. Frelimo's Marxist orientation favored a materialistic view of social reality in opposition to what it labeled as superstitious and obscurantist beliefs and practices of traditional society. Frelimo's vision of real, as opposed to formal, independence was to be realized through a national project, which made a decisive break from colonialism, capitalism, and "traditionalism." Frelimo's Marxist ideology offered a consistent discourse of opposing colonial and capitalist exploitation and favoring a nation-building project beyond ethnic divisions and in which "traditional" religion and lineage relations had no role to play.

In a speech in September 1970 Samora Machel, Frelimo's second president, expressed the party's position toward "traditional" society.[3]

> Although the colonialists dealt a powerful blow to traditional society, traditional education is still the dominant form of education in Mozambique.

Owing to their superficial knowledge of nature, members of traditional society conceive of it as a series of forces of supernatural origin . . . that superstition takes the place of science in education. . . . Taking advantage of the superstition . . . certain social groups are able to maintain their retrograde rule over society. In this context education aims at passing on tradition, which is raised to the level of dogma. (Machel 1981:34)

This summarizes Frelimo's attitude toward traditional society during the armed struggle against colonialism. This position did not change in the years after independence. Under Frelimo's rule, many "traditional" institutions that dealt with so-called superstitious beliefs were abolished and had no formally recognized political and social functions in society. Traditional chiefs (many of them believed to have collaborated with the colonizers) were replaced by popularly elected officials who composed the Grupos Dinamizadores, that is, elected councils with the task to "dynamize" workplace and neighborhood, and later by the Party Committees, both with the mission of fighting traditional values and implementing the new secular policies. The *tinyanga* (healers, diviners, and spirit mediums) were not allowed to operate freely. In order to effectively break the power and influence of traditional political and spiritual leaders, Frelimo also took action against those ceremonial practices that ideologically legitimated the authority of the traditional leaders. Rain and fertility rituals, and other rituals to venerate the ancestral spirits such as *ku pahla* or *timhamba* were prohibited (Young 1978; Roesch 1992). People were encouraged to deal with their health problems by attending modern institutions of health care such as the hospital and dispensaries, at least when these were available. In line with socialist policies, health care and education became free for every citizen, and there was a massive effort to create medical and educational centers even in the most remote areas of the country. New policies of rural development were implemented with the aim of bringing about rapid social and economic development.[4]

Chirindja, traditional chief of Munguine, was very frustrated when after independence Frelimo decided to outlaw local religious traditions. In his words:

With the end of the power of the chiefs of this land came the end of the performance of our *ku pahla* ceremonies, which are addressed to the ancestral spirits of this land. . . . As a result people ceased to enjoy ancestral protection, and things went wrong. Drought came and we starved because there was no rain: we did not perform the rain rituals. Later the war also came to our land because we were not protected by our ancestors: we did not honor them. The whole life in the community became disrupted, as there was no longer respect for the elders, no respect for the ancestors, no respect for our traditions.[5]

Chirindja's statement brings to the fore two fundamental aspects of the relationship between Frelimo and traditional practices: First, the fact that "traditional" leaders no longer had formal power over the communities made them resentful of Frelimo. Second, Frelimo's rejection of traditional religion and its moral values, and its failure to provide an effective alternative, was regarded as the source of the moral crisis to which Chirindja refers.

Recourse to tinyanga was seriously discouraged. Some people mentioned cases of tinyanga being arrested in situations such as the death of a patient, because they were not recognized as capable of providing proper health care. Also in the course of Operação Produção in 1983, an operation aimed at sending the so-called unskilled urban unemployed (who were described as "parasites") to the rural areas to work the land (for a critique, see Clarence-Smith 1989; Geffray 1990), some traditional practitioners were considered unemployed and sent to remote rural areas. Their profession as diviners, healers, and spirit mediums was not recognized by the state. Despite all this, people continued to make use of these religious and health care institutions. Even many Frelimo militants, especially grassroots militants, continued to have recourse to the tinyanga. Yet instead of engaging in these activities in daylight, they would do so during the night and in secret and would often deny it to avoid being considered "obscurantists," "superstitious," and hence attached to the old values. Denial and secrecy about recourse to diviners and healers were more frequent among urbanized middle class and the party militants.

Naturally, Frelimo's opposition toward traditional religion created some tensions between the government and the rural population, who were strongly attached to traditional beliefs and practices. Many peasants felt disempowered by the government's antagonism to the rural cultural heritage and traditional authorities and by its policies of forced "villagization" (Geffray 1990). There clearly was a struggle going on between the new and the older, long-standing sets of values. On the one hand, spirit mediums and chiefs in particular wanted to maintain these long-standing values and "traditions" in order to preserve their power and authority. On the other hand, a new generation and a new political order sought to change the previous state of affairs and create a new worldview, based on a scientific interpretation of the world that would promote "progress," "development," "modernization," and a new pattern of power relations. These tensions were exacerbated during the 1980s, as the hardship and pressures created by the escalation of the war with Renamo rendered Frelimo's rural development project unsustainable. Schools and hospitals were destroyed by the rebels, "communal villages" (which provided community services) were attacked, and agricultural fields burned. Life in such a devastating social and political environment became so unbearable that many people turned to their ancestors for help and protection. In this situation, the limits of Frelimo's program of modernization and secularization as well as the incapacity of its ideology to respond to people's actual problems became obvious. With its economy devastated and development projects paralyzed, the country became increasingly dependent on foreign aid. As a result, the government decided to undertake far-reaching economic reforms, abandoning its former Marxist policies in favor of political and economic liberalization. In 1990 a new Constitution was adopted, enshrining the principles of multiparty democracy. Furthermore, with its resources dissipated by years of war, the government was incapable of imposing a military solution to the conflict.

In the same vein, and as a result of these pressures, the government reconsidered its position toward the role and space that traditional culture and religion would occupy in its modernization ideology. It realized that to be effective, its political project had to be harmonized with the beliefs and practices of the majority of the population. The government became more tolerant of traditional values, especially those connected to beliefs in impersonal forces and beings.[6] Of course, the pressures caused by the escalating war with Renamo had a direct impact on accelerating these changes.

The Mozambique National Resistance (Renamo) was created in 1977 by the Rhodesian Central Intelligence Organisation (CIO). The Rhodesian government created and sponsored the rebel movement in retaliation for the Frelimo government's full implementation of the UN-mandated sanctions and, more important, its support of ZANLA's (Zimbabwe National Liberation Army) armed struggle for the independence of Zimbabwe. Immediately after Mozambique's independence, a number of Portuguese settlers and former members of the colonial army left Mozambique for Rhodesia, as a result of their opposition to Frelimo's policies. This provided the Rhodesian security services with a recruiting pool for founding members of Renamo. At its inception Renamo (initially known as MNR) was totally dependent on Rhodesia and served a twofold purpose: first, to assist the Rhodesian forces in operations against ZANLA inside Mozambique, mainly through intelligence gathering, and, second, to implement the agenda of those resentful Portuguese settlers who wanted to unseat the "communist" government of Frelimo. Therefore, Renamo initially possessed few local roots. In the beginning, Renamo's mentors kept the military wing separate from the political wing, which was almost completely controlled by white Portuguese-speaking Mozambicans. With the independence of Zimbabwe in 1980 following the Lancaster House agreements, Renamo lost its Rhodesian support and was taken over by South African Security Forces, and some groups in Western countries. While the external support allowed Renamo to make significant military progress, its political and ideological project remained very weak (Hall 1991; J. Honwana 1995, 2000).

To deal with this tension, Renamo tried to harness popular support inside Mozambique by adopting a traditionalist approach, which filled the void created by Frelimo's denial of traditional chiefs and of traditional cultural religious beliefs and practices. Such a move provided Renamo with a local base among sections of the peasant population. This turning to traditional beliefs and practices seems to have compensated for Renamo's initial lack of political and ideological substance.[7] Renamo quickly capitalized on Frelimo's disregard for traditional religion and the consequent flowering of peasant resentment. It presented itself as a movement against the disrespect for Mozambican traditions. Renamo leaders are reported to have said that "Frelimo has angered the ancestors in Mozambique, they did not honor them" (Vines 1991b:31–32).

Alex Vines (1991a) refers to the Matsangaissa myth that was widespread among the population of Gorongosa,[8] in the central region. According to the myth, Matsangaissa was given magic powers by a respected spirit medium (*mhondoro*) in Zimbabwe (see Lan 1985). These powers protected Matsangaissa and his troops from the effects of bullets as long as they respected the local population. However, as some Renamo soldiers broke this code of conduct by abusing local young women, the magical powers were broken. Not knowing this, and believing himself to be still protected by these powers,

Matsangaissa and his men stormed a government position and were slaughtered by machine-gun fire. Matsangaissa died in that attack. The myth has several variations, but its essence remains the same. It brings into focus the role of supernatural powers in Renamo's war, and the way in which the organization utilized a powerful set of traditional religious symbols in order to attract the local population. It also helped promote the idea that Renamo's success was due to its close relationship with the spirits, which in turn legitimized its activities.

Renamo created a space for traditional leaders and spiritual authorities until then marginalized by the government. In many Renamo-occupied zones in the country, traditional chiefs were given a role in the leadership structure, and many diviners, healers, and other religious leaders became central to Renamo's efforts to legitimize its religious ideology and traditional standing. However, in the southern region the relationship between Renamo and the local population was more complex. This complexity derives from the nineteenth-century wars over the establishment of the Gaza State in the region, in which the Tsonga people of the southern region clashed with the Ndau people of the central region (Renamo's stronghold). Despite the difficulties in creating a strong support base in the south, Renamo recognized the symbolic and ideological value of the spirit mediums and other religious practitioners, such as the Zionists, and incorporated many of them into the movement by force. Yet there are also cases of tinyanga who volunteered to join Renamo. Traditional religious practitioners as well as prophets from Zionist Churches (see below) were often abducted to work in Renamo military camps. Major decisions, in particular those of military strategic nature, were usually taken after consultation with the spirits. The spirit mediums were used to protect Renamo camps by making them "invisible" to Frelimo soldiers through their magical powers. They assisted the soldiers by telling them how to wage the war, where the enemy was, and where to fight in order not to upset the spirits, thereby avoiding the sacred places. They guided them in their long journeys in the forest and performed rituals to make the combatants strong and reinforce their morale. Many Renamo fighters were credited with supernatural powers, including being bulletproof. These powers were supplied by spirit mediums whose fame also served as a way of attracting recruits to Renamo's ranks. David Lan's (1985) work on Zimbabwe also shows how spirit mediums had a powerful influence on the young guerrilla soldiers.

In the district of Manhiça, for example, there is the legend of a strong female spirit medium known as Mwamandjosi, who was one of the most famous spiritual leaders of Renamo in southern Mozambique. Some informants pointed out that she had been captured in one of Renamo's attacks on Manhiça and was forced to work for them. Mwamandjosi was reported to be very good at discovering where the enemy was hiding and at protecting soldiers and civilians in Renamo camps. In Manhiça many informants acknowledged the powers of Mwamandjosi by saying that she made the bullets of the government soldiers miss their target and that she made their guns fail in the middle of battle.

Sitoe, a spirit medium from Mandhlakazi who lives in Manhiça, was also abducted by Renamo and forced to work for them. Here is his story:

> In 1992 a group of *matsanga*[9] raided the village, at around six o'clock in the evening. I was just chatting with some friends when the whole thing started. They took me immediately because they thought that I was a militia and they wanted my gun. I told them that I had no gun, but they did not care and started to beat me. Then somebody said that I was a *nyamusoro* [a specific kind of diviner-healer of the type of *nyanga* (singular of *tinyanga*), see A. Honwana 1996], and they stopped beating me. They took me and my wife to their military camp . . . to work for them.[10]

In the Renamo military camp Sitoe had to perform divination in order to reveal the position of Frelimo soldiers, when they would attack, and the like. He said that Renamo military chiefs also asked him to divine when money was stolen in the camp. As he was successful in discovering the thief, they gave him special treatment: instead of having to sleep outside, he got a tent and a woman (at their arrival in the camp, Sitoe and his wife were separated by the soldiers, and he has never seen or heard of her since).

Spirit mediumship and ancestor worship were prominent in Renamo's approach. The political propaganda refrain of the Renamo military commanders was that theirs was a "war of spirits"—a crusade, in which Frelimo was painted as a traitorous organization that was forcing people to abandon their ancestors and accept foreign ("communist") ideas. Renamo presented itself, in contrast, as having created an alliance with the ancestral spirits to return Mozambique to its traditions and ancestral ways. However, such a use of traditional religious powers to fight the war is not solely confined to Renamo. There are accounts establishing that government troops and militia, Frelimo's official antitraditionalist ideology notwithstanding, also made use of spirit mediums in order to protect themselves from harm and bring success to military operations (Vines 1991a; Roesch 1992). But whereas the Frelimo soldiers were circumspect in doing so and had to be secretive about it, Renamo forces treated traditional religion as an integral part of its struggle and as the core of the movement's mobilization ideology.

In the district of Mapulanguene (Gaza Province) a captain of a government battalion managed to save his men and defeat Renamo with the help of a female spirit medium of the area. The captain stated that before his alliance with the spirit medium he had lost several men, even before confronting Renamo on the battlefield. According to him, snakes sent by the spirits were killing about three to five men in each patrol. Following these incidents, the captain and his men asked the spirit medium to give him and his soldiers protection from snakes. She also helped them to build a strong combative morale and defeat the enemy. This shows that in practice spirit mediums supported combatants from both sides. Some took the side of the government forces and others the side of Renamo. Still others, like the *Naprama*, a spiritual army created by a spirit medium called Manuel Antonio in the northern provinces of Nampula and Zambezia (Wilson 1992), were against both armies and acted in defense of the civilian population (Wilson 1992; A. Honwana 1996).

As mentioned earlier, in the late 1980s and early 1990s Frelimo's attitude vis-à-vis traditional religion started to change. It appears that Frelimo was compelled into making these ideological changes in order to adjust its doctrine to the actions taken by its grassroots militants and soldiers, who were isolated from the ideological dogmas of the leadership through the brutal reality of the war. These fighters were the ones who (individually or collectively) reestablished or brought to the surface the links with traditional institutions such as the traditional chiefs and the spirit mediums (Lauriciano 1990; Wilson 1992). Thus Frelimo was, in a way, forced into these changes, for it had to regain support from the peasantry and the spiritual legitimacy of the ancestors in order to counteract Renamo's traditionalist strategy and be able to win the war (Wilson 1992). As gains and losses in the actual war in the countryside depended on the political allegiances of traditional spiritual authorities, Frelimo was forced to admit that its ideology was too far removed from local circumstances and formed an obstacle to victory. Clearly, in order to fight Renamo one had to go along with its attitude toward spirit possession and other traditional forces to a much larger extent than Marxian ideology would allow for.

In order to understand the conflict between Renamo and Frelimo, one has to get beyond the terms set by their ideological struggle, which is cast in an opposition of "tradition" versus "modernity." Their ideological discourses notwithstanding, neither of the two parties can simply be equated with one or the other position. Renamo's strategy should certainly not be mistaken as a mere return to tradition and as an expression of an antimodern stance. Such a view would take for granted the perspective of the modernization paradigm, which conceives of modernity as bringing about a break with long-standing traditions, and leaves no room for the possibility of inventing them. In the case of Renamo it is clear that both on the practical and ideological level, it actively made use of and recast *tradition* in order to represent itself as the true custodian of local identity. Frelimo's struggle with tradition, as we already saw, also pinpoints that tradition and modernity are entangled in myriad ways and that modern postcolonial politics cannot easily do without spirits.

Transformation of Spirit Possession

Apart from looking at the place of spirit possession in current political struggles, it is also important to examine it within a historical context so as to reveal the dynamic nature of the phenomenon and show how spirit possession is constantly changing and being renewed. In southern Mozambique, before the close contact between the Nguni and Ndau groups in the nineteenth century,[11] the Tsonga were only possessed by local spirits (*tinguluve* or *malhonga*),[12] the spirits of their direct ancestors. These spirits did not put the possessed in trance and did not "come out" and talk through a spirit medium. They only guided diviners and healers through dreams and visions. Spirit possession involving altered states of consciousness or "real" trance appears to be a relatively recent phenomenon in the region. It is only in the last quarter of the nineteenth century that the Tsonga peoples were exposed to "real" trance through their encounters with foreign Nguni and Ndau groups (Junod 1927; Earthy 1933; Binford 1971; Rennie 1973; Feliciano 1989). This interaction is a consequence of the Nguni migration from Zululand toward the north of Mozambique. In the course of this migratory movement the Nguni subjugated the Ndau (among other groups), forcing them to go down south as "slaves" in the Nguni Gaza state in Tsonga territory. In this process of interaction, all sides absorbed beliefs and practices of one another, and many local Tsonga became possessed by foreign *vanguni* and *vandau* spirits. The question of how and why this process of absorption or integration of spirits took place is an intriguing one. According to many informants, the Tsonga became possessed by Nguni spirits by intermarriage and through the *mpfhukwa* phenomenon. Possession by Ndau spirits, however, came basically through mpfhukwa, for very few Tsonga intermarried with the Ndau. So, what is mpfhukwa?

The Mpfhukwa Phenomenon

Mpfhukwa became a widespread phenomenon in southern Mozambique after the Nguni wars, which established Nguni rule in the southern Mozambican region. *Mpfhukwa* is a term that comes from the verb *ku pfhukwa*, which means "to wake up" and indicates "a person who wakes up from the dead," or "to resuscitate" (Helgesson 1971). *Mipfhukwa*, plural for "spirits," and also known as "spirits of the war" (*swikwembu swa matlhári*), were those of foreign soldiers (Nguni and Ndau) killed during the Nguni wars in the southern region. The spirits of soldiers and civilians killed during wars are believed to afflict the living (especially those who caused their death or mistreated them or their descendants in life). It may also be that they seek protection from the family of someone who helped them in life. People explain this return of the spirits of the dead by referring to the fact that the soldiers and civilians killed in war were not properly buried because their own families could not mourn them and perform the necessary rituals to place them in their proper positions in the world of the spirits. Thus, their souls were unsettled; they became spirits of bitterness. The mipfhukwa spirits can afflict a family until their will is respected. In order to be appeased, the mipfhukwa spirits generally ask for a hut (*ndumba*); a virgin girl to marry them; a cow or a female goat for reproduction; or just cattle, traditional beer, and sometimes money. In this way, local families are forced to accommodate nonkin spiritual forces from outside. Often, however, the afflicted consult powerful spirit mediums to exorcise these foreign spirits in order to prevent them from returning and disturbing the family. This can be viewed also as an attempt to emphasize local identity.

This notion of spirit possession is based on an embodiment of debt and moral fault, which is extended beyond the individual and his or her kin and concerns wider society. The following case illustrates how descendants are forced to pay for their ancestors' actions in the past. This case also shows how changes in an individual's personal history impact wider societal changes. In the present, histories of debt and moral fault are frequently memorized in people's accounts of this early period of interaction with the Nguni and the Ndau groups. Sengo from the town of Inhambane recalls what happened in his family: "During the *Nguni* wars Nhakele, my great-grandfather, was a soldier of Ngungunyane and he killed a Ndau named Mussarira. Years later, and after my great-grandfather's death, the spirit of Mussarira afflicted our family, killing people and causing illness and misfortune."[13] After consulting a diviner who caught the spirit and made him talk, the spirit of Mussarira asked for a girl to marry him, some cattle, and a hut for him to live in. Sengo's paternal grandfather offered his daughter Maria to become the spirit's wife and also complied with all the other demands.

As this case illustrates, people in the southern region believe that the Ndau spirits are very strong and powerful and that the mpfhukwa phenomenon is originally Ndau. There is a myth that mpfhukwa is a capacity that is acquired through the powers of a plant called *mvhuko*. The use of the powers of this plant is part of the Ndau "tradition," and many Ndau people drink the solution made from this plant just weeks after birth. The solution is believed to make the individual stronger, and once dead to be able to revive his or her spirit and seek revenge.

In sum, the nineteenth-century interactions between the Nguni, the Ndau, and the Tsonga transformed local Tsonga sacred representations and gave rise to personal embodiment and social incorporation of new categories of foreign, spiritual beings. Possession by these new spiritual entities induced practitioners into a deep trance, a practice that had not arisen before. Divination sessions no longer merely relied on the use of oracles or divinatory bones but also of trance. Concomitantly, in order to accommodate the new spirits, changes occurred with regard to the practitioners' regalia and paraphernalia (red pieces of fabric for the Nguni spirits and white for the Ndau; seashell necklaces for the Ndau and feather hats for the Nguni) and their personal habits (e.g., they could no longer eat fish, out of respect for the Nguni spirits). All this shows that spirit possession is a highly flexible phenomenon, which can easily be made to speak to changing historical contexts. The shift toward possession by foreign spirits not only has caused changes in actual practice but also forms a source for ongoing debates. The incorporation of new sacred representations has instigated conflict and contestation over what is genuine, or what should be absorbed or rejected, and what should constitute "true" possession. These debates not only keep on occurring among the practitioners themselves, for some of whom it is unacceptable to work under the influence of the Ndau spirits possessing them, but have also been extended to other arenas, for instance, Zionist Churches.

These churches have a distinct attitude toward spirit possession. Unlike the mainstream churches, they share the same kind of etiological thinking with those who come to them for help.[14] Seeking to bring about divine healing through the power of the Holy Spirit, these churches manage ill health and misfortune in similar ways to that of the tinyanga. In the same way as spirit possession constitutes the focus around which the activities of the latter gravitate, it also is one of the main features of the Zionist healing rituals. Zionist prophets are possessed by the spiritual agencies that inspire and help them in their healing task. However, in contrast to the tinyanga, the Zionists solely rely on local spirits, that is, the spirits of the ancestors (the tinguluve or malhonga) and seek to exorcise the foreign Nguni and Ndau spirits, whom they consider as downright evil.[15]

Clearly, with the emphasis on the evil nature of foreign spirits, the Zionists affirm and enhance people's skeptical attitude toward these spirits and their search for a "pure" identity uncorrupted by foreign powers and their spiritual counterparts. Ndau spirits especially were considered problematic forces from which one should better distance oneself. Associating these spirits with the widespread killing of the Tsonga, many informants believe that the Ndau never forgave the Tsonga their alliance with the Nguni invaders. The *Ndau mipfhukwa* are of ill repute in the southern region, and there is a general belief that they are very dangerous and of bad character (Rennie 1973). This links up with the tensions between the Ndau and the Tsonga of the southern region to which I already referred in the discussion of why Renamo had more problems in establishing a local base in the south. Due to Renamo's association with Ndau spirituality (Renamo's leaders were almost all Ndau, and Ndau language and religion were central to the movement's ideology), many Tsonga were loath to embrace Renamo, even though they might not have been content with the government's policies regarding traditional religion. Moreover, Renamo's brutality and terrifying methods of warfare might have created a lot of skepticism and made it unattractive.

Postwar Identities and Spirits of the Dead

In the postwar period a strong emphasis has been placed on "traditional" spiritual powers in order to bring about healing and envisage a new start. On the one hand, people believe that as the ancestral spirits are instrumental to protecting and helping them reorganize their lives, these spirits should be venerated. On the other hand, people feel vulnerable to the spirits of dead soldiers and civilians of the war who may haunt and afflict them. These are the mipfhukwa spirits discussed in the previous section. As we have already seen, the emergence of these spirits is considered particularly threatening after a war, when soldiers and civilians have not been buried appropriately. Many people believe that the mipfhukwa spirits of the war between Renamo and Frelimo will be as dangerous as the ones of the Nguni wars, because of the considerable involvement of Ndau, who formed the initial main support base of Renamo (this only changed in the last years of the war). Moreover, because there has been greater contact between the Tsonga, the Nguni, and the Ndau, the knowledge of mpfhukwa is no longer exclusively the Ndau's. For these reasons, many people fear that the mpfhukwa spirits will reemerge as forcefully as they did in the past. People assert that rituals to appease the spirits of the dead have to be performed in all those places where battles took place and people died. These rituals are considered as vital in order to calm down the spirits and place them in their proper position in the spiritual world. These rituals are usually performed by the traditional healers and spirit mediums as well as by Zionist prophets and other independent churches. In these rituals the spirits of the dead are acknowledged and appeased through a powerful set of symbolic procedures and performance.

Appeasing the Spirits of the Dead

The notion of social pollution is an important factor in the context of postwar healing in southern Mozambique. Pollution may arise from being in contact with death and bloodshed. Persons who have been in a war, who killed or saw people being killed, are believed to be polluted by death and other war atrocities. They are the vehicles through which mipfhukwa spirits might enter the community. These spirits constitute a threat not only to the individual who committed the offense but also to the whole group, because they can afflict family relatives and even passersby. After a war, when soldiers and refugees return home, they are believed to be potential contaminators of the social body. The spirits of the dead that haunt them may disrupt life in their families and villages. Thus, the cleansing process is seen as a fundamental condition for collective protection against pollution as well as the prerequisite for the social reintegration of war-affected people into society (A. Honwana 1998, 1999b; Reynolds 1996). In this postwar period, many families perform cleansing rituals to purify and protect themselves and their relatives from the atrocities of the war. This practice is more predominant in the countryside, where family solidarity, age hierarchies, and beliefs in spirits still wield considerable influence on people, especially in their struggles for better health. In urban and semiurban settings, where people are exposed to other ways of solving their afflictions, only some have recourse to the nexus of spirit possession described above, while others may combine a series of therapies or refrain from spiritual or therapeutic strategies altogether. Religious and political alliances also shape people's decisions in favor of a particular treatment. In the remainder of this section, I will analyze a number of cases and discuss how postwar identities are negotiated and constructed in this particular context.

Fabião from Manhiça shared a very interesting case with me. He told me that in April 1993 spirit mediums in Munguine were asked to perform rituals on the road that links Munguine with the town of Manhiça. The rituals were needed because as soon as it got dark, nobody could use this road to get to Manhiça. The mpfhukwa spirit of a Renamo commander killed nearby during the war was afflicting passersby. Local people reported that as they approached the place, they felt someone beating them, or heard voices of people sending them back, or became blind and could not see their way to Manhiça. The spirit mediums performed first a ritual called *ku femba*, which aimed at catching the spirit and making him speak. The spirit explained who he was and said that he wanted money and *capulanas* (local pieces of fabric that women wear) and to be accompanied to his homeland. Reputedly the local government in Manhiça got involved in the case and donated some money to offer the spirit. Members of the local population also contributed money to be given to the spirit and to buy the capulanas. A week later, the ritual took place. In the presence of all villagers the spirit was "caught" again by the spirit mediums present at the event, and the offerings were presented to him. Then the spirit mediums placed the spirit and all the offerings in the capulanas, tied them, and took them to be buried far away from the village, on the way to his homeland. Fabião stated that the mediums also put some medicine on the money and the pieces of fabric in order to prevent the return of the spirit. According to local people, since then no more incidents have occurred on that road. People believe that these rituals are necessary to bring back peace and restore the order impaired by the war.

Another example of mpfhukwa spirits afflicting the living is that of Laquene Nguluve presented in the introduction. The fact that several institutions sought to help solve the problem attracted some media attention. Interviewed by a journalist, the current traditional chief of Vuca, brother of the deceased, stated that "our spirits (the *Ndau*) are stronger than the *Maconde* spirits. . . . The spirit of my brother knows what he wants. I asked him to save the (*Maconde*) boy and accept their offerings but he refused, saying that he will finish that group who killed him unjustly."[16] This statement again confirms the view that Ndau spirits are very strong and powerful. However, recent reports on the case stated that the government managed to transfer the remaining members of the battalion to Mueda (hometown of the Maconde). After the performance of several rituals and continuous pleading by the relatives through the spirit mediums, the spirit of Laquene accepted saving the child and received as a settlement the suggested offerings. Cases that demanded the killing of an innocent child do not appear to be very common in the area. Threats like this might constitute a way of showing extreme anger and of forcing the offenders to plead with the spirit for forgiveness.

During this war young people were forcibly recruited to become soldiers, especially among the rebels. Many of them killed innocent civilians and committed the most terrible war atrocities (A. Honwana 1999a). Rituals performed for former child soldiers are also aimed at resolving the wrongdoing that happened during the war. Soldiers are believed to be potentially exposed to the anger and revenge from their victims' mipfhukwa spirits. Ritual performances serve to acknowledge such killings and to symbolically separate the soldiers who committed them from their deeds. For instance, a fourteen-year-old boy, who had been kidnapped by Renamo and forced to be a soldier, had to go through a cleansing ritual when, after the war, he was reunited with his family. On the day of his arrival, his relatives took him to the ndumba (the house of the spirits). There he was presented to the ancestral spirits of the family. The boy's grandfather addressed the spirits, informing them that his grandchild had returned and thanking them for their protection, through which his grandson had been able to survive. Then the family elders talked to the boy in order to find out how he felt and what had happened to him during the war. A few days later, the family invited a spirit medium to help them perform the cleansing rituals for the boy. The medium took him and his relatives and neighbors to the bush, where a small hut covered with dry grass had been built especially for this purpose. The boy, who wore the dirty clothes he had brought from the Renamo camp, entered the hut and undressed himself. Then the hut was set on fire, and the boy was helped out by an adult relative.

The hut, the clothes, and everything else that the boy brought from the camp had to be burned. This act symbolized the rupture with that polluted past. A chicken was sacrificed for the spirits of the dead and the blood sprinkled around the ritual place. The chicken was then cooked and offered to the spirits as a sacrificial meal. After that, the boy had to inhale the smoke of some herbal remedies and bathe himself with water treated with medicine. In this way his body was cleansed both internally and externally. Finally, the spirit medium made some incisions in the boy's body and filled them with a paste made from herbal remedies, a practice called *ku thlavela*. The purpose of this procedure was to give strength to the boy. During this public ritual relatives and neighbors assisted the medium by performing specific tasks or by merely singing, clapping, and being present.

When, after the war, refugees and displaced populations returned to their communities, the first ritual they underwent is the *mhamba* ritual. *Timhamba* (plural of *mhamba*) rituals are performed to venerate the spirits of the dead buried in the family land or symbolized by the tree of the ancestors (*gandzelo*). These rituals, also known as *ku pahla*, are aimed at restoring the liaison between individuals and their deceased ancestors and receiving their ancestors' blessing and protection to rebuild their lives. Timhamba rituals bring together members of the family, who all participate in an animal sacrifice, and are usually performed by spirit mediums, who address the spirits and decode the spiritual messages for the living. Zionists also perform both these rituals and those to cleanse former child soldiers. In this context of an increased quest for reconciliation and healing, there is considerable competition between the tinyanga and the Zionists, who both want to attract clients.

The problems described and the rituals performed testify to the complexities involved in the reconstruction of identities after a devastating war, when people have to start from scratch and rebuild their lives. In the postwar period, people have to deal with dramatic past events through which families were torn apart: sons who killed their fathers; child soldiers who were forced to raid their own villages; mothers with children who fought on different sides; cousins who killed cousins, and so forth. In these circumstances, rebuilding social life and reconstructing personal and collective identities become a pressing, yet incredibly difficult, project, and in order to achieve reconciliation and healing people turn to practices of spirit possession.

The performance of these rituals and the negotiations and arrangements that precede them go beyond the particular individual concerned and encompass the collective body. In some cases only family members, friends, and neighbors are involved, as for instance in the ritual for the former child soldier, which aimed at preventing any future afflictions from the spirits of the dead. In other instances such practices transcend the level of the family and immediate neighborhood and incorporate community organizations and government institutions, as in the case of the afflicted Maconde soldiers and in the ritual expelling the spirit of the soldier who haunted the people of

Munguine. The involvement of the larger group expresses the links between individuals and groups, as individuals are not perceived in isolation from their social and cultural environment. Their personal actions can contaminate the whole social body. Therefore, individual afflictions are, through ritual performance, transformed into a matter of concern to the whole group (be it a family, neighborhood, village, community, or district). Healing the person is to heal the collective—and for this reason even the Frelimo could not bypass, let alone abolish, local understandings and practices with regard to spirit possession.

Conclusion

The different positions taken by Renamo and Frelimo with regard to spirit possession clearly cannot be captured in the opposition of tradition versus modernity (Hobsbawm and Ranger 1983). This is a false dichotomy. As we saw, spirit possession—despite being identified as "traditional" by both parties—is a highly flexible, dynamic phenomenon that is part and parcel of modernity. By turning to traditional religious beliefs and practices to gain legitimacy and support, Renamo does not necessarily cease to be a modern organization, equipped with sophisticated weapons and fighting Marxist rule in Mozambique. Likewise, Frelimo's initial denial of the traditional spirits whom it sought to exorcise from its modernist discourse eventually had to be given up in favor of a harmonization of its political project with these practices of spirit possession. If in consonance with the Marxian perspective, spirit possession was initially denied "coevalness" (Fabian 1983) and recast as a matter of the past, it kept on haunting Frelimo and eventually enforced its acceptance.

Rather than being a matter of the past, in the context of postwar Mozambique for the people concerned, spirit possession appeared to offer practices suited to cope with the past. As we saw, spirit possession responds to the quest for reconciliation and healing as well as for the construction of new identities. The conditions in which people have to make sense of their lives and rebuild their social relationships are set within a modern context marked by the market economy and structural adjustment, democracy, and other globalized institutions and predicaments. In order to be effective, the responses of the tinyanga and the Zionists to people's afflictions have to be articulated in terms of these current dynamics. Rituals of spirit possession and exorcism address and appease the past in order to make sense of and transform the present. Apart from the importance of social healing—of literally laying the ghosts from the past to rest—these ritual practices illustrate the importance of continuity, of drawing strength from a reconstituted past to deal with the empty and painful present and help construct the future. For the time being, practices of spirit possession will certainly continue to play a constitutive role in politics of national culture and hence urge us to overcome the misleading conceptual boundary separating modernity and spirits.

THREE

Robert Kaplan and "Juju Journalism" in Sierra Leone's Rebel War

The Primitivizing of an African Conflict

ROSALIND SHAW

A rundown, crowded planet of skinhead Cossacks and *juju* warriors, influenced by the worst refuse of Western pop culture and ancient tribal hatreds, and battling over scraps of overused earth in guerilla conflicts that ripple across continents and intersect in no discernible pattern.

—ROBERT KAPLAN, "The Coming Anarchy," 1994

I will concede that Sierra Leone, from the perspective of the average American, is a deeply weird place. Once, in Freetown, Sierra Leone's capital, I met a member of the Kamajors, a traditional hunter society. He was wearing a red ronko, a "war vest," which, he said, made him impervious to bullets.

—JEFFREY GOLDBERG, "A Continent's Chaos," 2000

When Western media coverage of African wars such as that in Sierra Leone extends beyond discussion of African governments, political and military leaders, peace accords, and international organizations, "tribalism" and "juju" tend to be offered up as a recurring duo of inventions. Given that Sierra Leone's rebel war was not (for the main part) characterized by ethnic conflict but did include the use of ritual materials and practices to confer impenetrability or invisibility, these "magical" techniques of war and defense (often glossed as *juju*) were prominently highlighted in foreign media coverage. In the print media's longer features on the ten-year war in Sierra Leone (as well as on the recent civil war in neighboring Liberia), what I call juju journalism became part of an established genre. Here, the mingling of "modern" technologies such as AK 47s with "magical" techniques has been taken at best as a sign of "deep weirdness" and at worst as evidence that processes of counter-evolution are at work in the collapse of African states such as this one.

These primitivized representations of African disintegration form part of a set of understandings of Third World threat in the North Atlantic world—understandings that are also manifest, following the events of September 11, in the incarceration of, and secrecy surrounding, over six hundred detainees of Middle Eastern origin in the United States. Just as racially charged North Atlantic images of danger have been realized in very concrete outcomes, juju journalism's influence has not been limited to the sphere of representations alone: it has also had an impact on U.S. foreign policy toward Africa, as I explore below.

Most notable for its influence is Robert Kaplan's famous 1994 article, "The Coming Anarchy," in which he casts Sierra Leone and what he calls its "juju warriors" as the portents of a growing chaos that threatens to engulf us all.[1] While not all juju journalists covering Sierra Leone follow Kaplan in his prognosis of a return to a Hobbesian state of nature, they too have tended to seize upon ritual bulletproofing and invisibility as apparent signs of an ahistorical primitivism that is incommensurate with modernity. Before examining this form of journalism, then, I will turn to these techniques of ritual combat and defense, locating them in the history of this region.

Historicizing Closure and Darkness

The ritual techniques in question are called "Closure" and "Darkness" in many Sierra Leonean languages, including Temne (respectively, *kantha* and *an-sum*). Far from being the anachronistic signs of primitivism usually portrayed in the foreign media, these techniques proliferated with the integration of West Africa's upper Guinea coast into the globalizing system of the Atlantic slave trade. It was through the "Atlanticizing" of Sierra Leone during the slave trade centuries that accelerating warfare and raiding created a landscape of disappearance, commodified bodies, and death (Shaw 2002).

Two texts may help us begin to situate Darkness and Closure historically in the upper Guinea coast. The first, entitled *Geographical Account of the Province of Sierra Leone*, was written around 1615 by a Portuguese Jesuit missionary, Manuel Alvares, who spent almost twenty years in a mission in early seventeenth-century Sierra Leone. Alvares was writing a few decades after a conquest of local peoples (such as those who spoke Temne) by a migrant Mande-speaking people called the Mane. The Mane had become intermediaries in the European slave trade, and their wars and raids of conquest had come to be the principal means by which they obtained captives for sale as slaves (Rodney 1970:102–3).

According to Alvares, one local community strove to avoid discovery by the Mane through techniques of concealment: "The fearful respect these savages have for the conquering (Manes)," he wrote, "has made them so careful and cunning that, in order to conceal the path to their secret villages, they walk it backwards" ([1615] 1990:II:chapter 2:2). Alvares also described the resistance of neighboring Limba communities that, he claimed, used underground hiding places: "They are astute and clever, and inclined to be warlike," he wrote. "Hence their villages have underground places, in which they live with all the necessities of life when besieged. This is how they have preserved their independence (and avoided conquest by) the Mane" ([1615] 1990:II:chapter 2:3). From Alvares's account, we get a sense of how salient a concern was concealment in this landscape created by the conjunction of Mane conquest and European slave trading nearly four centuries ago.

This concern with concealment entailed more than the maintenance of secret physical spaces; it also entailed the spread of ritual techniques. By the time Alvares was writing, Temne-speaking groups had by and large become incorporated into a centralized Mane kingdom and by doing so had assimilated Mane techniques of political organization and warfare, included in which were Mane war medicines. Alvares writes, for instance:

> I shall conclude this chapter by describing the *nebrina* medicine. A village is approached by those bent on war. A fog then arises which prevents one man seeing another, and hence, God willing, the attackers have the victory. . . .
> The vessels in which they mix these potions are made of the horns of animals. . . . These are the infernal reliquaries of all the kinds of Manes, who arrived with these goods; and the native heathen when they received them paid for them with the money of idolatry. (1990:II:chapter 12:5)

These ritual materials that "the native heathen" obtained from the Mane were, of course, those that the Mane, "bent on war," had used against *them*. At a time when tropes and practices of concealment and protection were important for local peoples as forms of defense against the Mane, then, Temne-speaking groups were incorporating Mane techniques of warfare and ritual concealment—including the "fog . . . which prevents one man seeing an-other"—through submission to Mane rule. Using the very techniques that had been used against them, Temne-speaking communities learned to em-body the ritual powers of their own invaders.

The second historical text that I want to introduce here was recorded two hundred years later by a Church Missionary Society missionary named the Rev. C.F. Schlenker, who collected Temne narratives in the northwestern Temne town of Port Loko, formerly a major center of the slave trade. One of the narratives Schlenker collected tells of a powerful warrior and slave dealer named Korombo, who is described as having destroyed "the whole Temne country" (Schlenker 1861:3):

> Here at Port Loko he did not fight, he only traded with the Europeans. When he was ready to come here to Port Loko, at the towns, where he slept, he asked for boys; he took them and bought them, and went and sold them. When he met with a woman in childbed, he took out cloths and palmwine . . . , and gave (them) to the woman, and said: "When thy child is worth the amount, I shall sell it." He took out a gun, and gave it to the hus-band. They were not able to kill him; they chopped him, (but) the cutlass did not enter (his body); they shot at him with a gun, (but) the balls did not hit him; and he was able to fly. When he came to a town, he assembled the people, selected (a number of) them, and sold them. (Schlenker 1861:5)

So in his passage to Port Loko—a node of the Atlantic system in which he "traded with Europeans"—Korombo is depicted as not only fighting and raiding but also as transforming Temne social practices into commercial transactions that brought about social death. Relationships between guest and host, husband and wife, parent and child, the continuity of a community through its children, and practices of gift giving are all subverted, in this ac-count, from ways of creating and renewing social relationships into ways of accomplishing their destruction through the commodification of bodies, the disappearance of people, and the plunder of the household's and the com-munity's means of reproduction. Korombo's capacity for violent penetration enables him to reduce human bodies to commodities; moreover, this capacity, we should note, is linked to the impenetrability of his own body, and to its extra-human extension through powers of flight.

As well as generating an escalation of warfare and raiding, Sierra Leone's integration into the Atlantic system gave rise to many figures like Korombo: well-armed "big persons" (*an-fem a bana*) whose power derived from commercial wealth. Nor did the violence and terror end when the British Anti-Slave Trade Act was passed in 1807, or when, in 1808, the British took over a settlement of liberated Africans in Freetown, establishing the first British Crown Colony in West Africa.

As a substitute for the external slave trade, the British colonial government promoted what they called a "Legitimate Trade" in groundnuts and forest products such as timber, camwood, and palm oil. But ironically, this replacement for the Atlantic slave trade itself required slave labor for the production and transport of these goods, leading to the acceleration rather than the decline of slave raiding (Lenga-Kroma 1978:76–78; 153ff.). In addition, the rivers that had always been crucial routes of travel and transport in this region now became even more essential for conveying the goods of this colonial trade to the coast. Communities far from rivers now found their access to these commercial highways restricted by groups who controlled important tidewater trading centers: accordingly, new trade wars were now fought over access to these river entrepots (Ijagbemi 1968, 1973).

The chronic dangers of these trade wars and of the intensifying raids for slave labor that accompanied them were, moreover, magnified by another development: the professionalization of warfare. Nineteenth-century counterparts of Korombo—individual entrepreneurs who gained rapid wealth, power, and leadership through the Legitimate Trade—each maintained a permanent fighting force with which they enforced their own interests, often at the expense of established rulers, who, in turn, defended their authority by building up their own permanent bodies of warriors (Ijagbemi 1968:304). Often, moreover, these bands of specialized warriors broke away from their leaders' control, generating an escalation of indiscriminate attacks and plunder (Ijagbemi 1973:278).

What kind of landscape was created through the centuries of the Atlantic and Legitimate Trades? And how did people live in this landscape? In contrast to the power and freedom of Korombo's flight through the air, travel along roads and rivers was an extremely perilous enterprise for ordinary people at the height of the Atlantic trade in the eighteenth century, as the historian Walter Rodney describes: "'They never care to walk even a mile from home without firearms,' wrote John Atkins in 1721. This testimony clearly points to a state of insecurity bordering on anarchy. Another graphic illustration of this was to be seen in the dislocation of villages in Sierra Leone, and their re-siting in almost inaccessible hideouts, away from the main waterways and the slave-raiding chiefs" (Rodney 1970:259). And later, as another historian, E. Ade Ijagbemi, describes for the nineteenth century,

> To travel from Yonibana to Petfu, or from Ronietta to Bathbana—distances of about five miles each—in those days, one might find it necessary to sleep on the way; because one could not travel along straightforward roads, for fear of falling into the hands of warrior parties. . . . Sometimes it would be necessary to offer sacrifice before undertaking such journeys. If one was unlucky and fell into the hands of war parties on the way, one would be captured and sold into slavery. (1973:40)

With these circumstances in mind, it is apt that Korombo the warrior was depicted as able to fly. It was well-armed warriors such as Korombo who had the greatest capacity for a rapid, direct mobility that was far removed from the difficult, circuitous movement of ordinary people that Ijagbemi depicts.

Like the roads and rivers, the forest itself was an ominous space that could conceal raiding parties. During the nineteenth-century trade wars, Ijagbemi tells us, "Fear of sudden attack hung constantly over many towns and villages; for there was no knowing where the warriors might strike next. People moved together and built strongly fortified centers (Ro Banka, in Temne). Farmers and traders moved in groups, and carried arms and protective shebes (charms) with them" (1973:40). These fortified centers were stockaded towns, encircled by rings of defensive fences and ditches that protected their inhabitants from whoever (or whatever) might come out of the forest. Stockaded towns can be traced back at least to the sixteenth-century context of Mane conquest (Donelha [1625] 1977:103), but they became especially common during the nineteenth-century trade wars: people would leave them during the day to go to their farms and would then return to their enclosed interiors at night or when under attack (Fyfe 1962:565).

These techniques of fortified enclosure were combined with techniques of concealment. The stockaded towns that became common in the nineteenth century were built so as to be hidden from the outside (ibid.:565). When the nineteenth-century English traveler F. Harrison Rankin visited the town of Magbele, for instance, he found that it was defended not only by its solid encompassing wall but also, he writes, "in the narrow paths approaching it through the forest, winding in many curves, and allowing the advance of a single man only at a time. They [stockaded towns] are generally blocked by vegetation. . . . The town is completely hidden from sight at a distance of a few yards" (Rankin 1836:237–38). Today, many Temne towns still bear the name *ro-Mankane*, "the hiding place."

Outside the town's concealed and enclosed space, to travel unarmed, unaccompanied, and on the open road was almost unthinkable. The best that people could do was to conceal and enclose *themselves*: like a hidden fortress, the body was not only shielded by ritual Closure but also shrouded by medicines of Darkness that produced a zone of visual chaos strikingly similar to the "fog . . . which prevents one man seeing another" that Alvares described nearly five centuries ago. Thus both warriors on the lookout for potential captives and travelers wishing to avoid them wore Islamic amulets (*e-sebe*) and herbal medicines that they obtained from diviners, some of which ritually Closed their bodies from penetration, while others wrapped them in Darkness.

Of course, practices and substances that confer invisibility and impenetrability are unique neither to this part of Africa nor to the eras of the slave trade and slave raiding. But capacities for Closure and Darkness draw upon local and regional histories; they have acquired a particular regional and historical significance in Sierra Leone and its neighbors as first the Atlantic slave trade and then the colonial Legitimate Trade added new and terrifying dimensions to them. Integration into the Atlantic world, and then into Britain's colonial periphery, generated imperatives for concealment and impenetrability on an ever-increasing scale. These imperatives—inhabiting stockaded towns and hidden settlements, farming areas of bush that might conceal slave-raiding warriors, and traveling along hidden and difficult paths, avoiding rivers and direct roads upon which agents of physical and social death might be moving—shaped the landscape into a topography of disappearance and the body into a hidden fortress. Through their use of the very practices of Closure that slave raiders and warriors used as techniques of capture, ordinary people endowed themselves with "stockaded" bodies that could foil attempts to make them into commodified bodies. And through their use of techniques of Darkness, they gave themselves bodies that could inhabit this landscape of disappearance by controlling the capacity to disappear.

During the Protectorate era, Sierra Leone's second colonial period, established in 1896, circular stockaded towns were prohibited by the British colonial authorities. The British perceived the "war fences" that defended stockaded towns as a barbaric materialization of the "warlike" character of those who inhabited them and set about a transformation of the built environment. T. J. Alldridge, a colonial official based in the south, described the metamorphosis of the town of Pendembu from 1892 to 1908 in these terms: "In those days Pendembu consisted of three towns, each surrounded by dense war-fences. On my recent visit all was changed. The squalid huts with their barbaric war fences had given way to a town with a fine open quadrangle containing some of the best native homes in the country" (1910:175). Thus the fortified interiority of this stockaded town was turned into an open public space, reminiscent of town squares in Europe, and "squalid huts" were converted into "homes." This open spatial character was further modified by linear organization, as many towns and villages moved to the colonial roads and railway, stretching longitudinally in ribbon development formation.

In the late-twentieth-century landscape I knew before the spread of Sierra Leone's rebel war, the warfare of the nineteenth-century colonial period had been over for at least eighty years. Diviners, however, applied ritual defenses analogous to the bygone circular fortifications through techniques of ritual Closure that encircled bodies, houses, and farms with invisible defensive barriers offering a striking parallel to the stockaded town. These defenses were not (for the most part) raised against human enemies but against incursion from spirits and witches. Yet the protection they afforded was sometimes likened to that of ancestors or warriors fighting to defend their town against enemy attack. During my 1981 visit, for instance, I found that the wife of an eminent Poro cult association leader, Pa Yamba, had recently died after making a deathbed confession that she was a witch. A diviner had then ritually protected Pa Yamba from her witch shade by embedding seven tiny axes, each an inch long, in a block of wood by the front door of his house: "If her shade comes near," Pa Yamba told me, "the ancestors (*an-baki*) will seize the axes and fight her off." The ancestors' defense of ritual Closure, then, took the form of warfare in miniature, carried out with weapons appropriate to villagers protecting their endangered homes.

Another form of Closure—the ritual protection of the body against external penetration—has been of particular concern for many politicians, businessmen, and chiefs in the late twentieth and early twenty-first centuries. These "big persons" and their kin often go to diviners and herbalists to "bulletproof" their bodies against attack from their political and commercial rivals. Up until the outbreak of war in 1991 it was not so much assassination attempts with ordinary guns or knives that were anticipated; the most insidious attacks were carried out invisibly with weapons known as "witch guns" (*e-pinkar a seron* in Temne) that shoot tiny ritual missiles with deadly powers of penetration. To defend themselves, some big persons washed their bodies with medicine; some had steam baths over boiling infusions of herbs; some had an amulet (*an-sebe*) made; and some commissioned short versions of a gown known as *an-ronko*, formerly worn only by chiefs, warriors, and hunters. These gowns, as Opala (1982) argues, appear to have their origin in Mande "war shirts" and hunters' shirts (McNaughton 1982) that are treated with medicines and often stamped with potent Arabic writing to render warriors impervious to weapons. In both Limba-speaking and Temne-speaking parts of Sierra Leone these shirts are made by powerful diviners and blacksmiths, soaked in medicines, dyed reddish-brown with camwood, stamped with cryptic black symbols, and sewn with a pocket on the left-hand side containing dangerous medicines (Opala 1982). The politicians' and businessmen's version of this shirt is a short vest concealed under the clothes to render the wearer's body impenetrable to both conventional and invisible weapons.

These ritual defenses are not mere reflexes of the slave trade and Legitimate Trade. But, I suggest, experiences of the Legitimate Trade's violence were mediated by memories of the Atlantic trade, whereas twentieth-century upheavals and concerns seem themselves to have been configured by memories of the Legitimate Trade (Shaw 2002). Thus even in the absence of war, the Closure conferred by an invisible barrier in one instance and a war shirt in the other, as well as ritual simulacra of ax fights, shooting, and bulletproofing, have been salient in relation to late-twentieth-century experiences of the dangers lurking in both domestic witchcraft and in political and commercial rivalry.

In 1991 the rebel war began, following twenty-five years of "kleptocracy" by the All Peoples' Congress government, and the postcolonial state's withdrawal from border areas and valuable sites of diamond extraction, for which all sides in the conflict competed.[2] As towns and villages were raided and the roads once again became channels of death, ritual techniques for the protection of the body took on a new and horrific relevance. In 1992 I met Liberian refugees and internally displaced Sierra Leoneans who, in order to avoid the dangers of direct travel, had escaped from danger through the bush and had used Closure and Darkness techniques to conceal their passage. Not only displaced people but also combatants used ritual materials and techniques that either Closed the body against bullets or produced a Darkness that enabled them to see their enemies before they themselves were seen.

These techniques of mystical warfare, moreover, became incorporated into the fighting forces of the state itself. In the early 1990s, a reason commonly given by both soldiers and civilians for the army's failure to defeat the Revolutionary United Front (RUF) rebels was that the rebels' expertise in medicines and rituals of defense was superior to that of the Sierra Leone Army (Joseph Opala, personal communication, October 1997). The RUF used (and sometimes abducted) Muslim ritual specialists—*mori-men* in Sierra Leone Krio—to make amulets and other ritual materials that would produce Closure and Darkness. In response, the military government of Valentine Strasser created a special battalion called the Tamaboro with the help of ritual specialists in the northeast of the country.

Later, in 1995, Strasser's government brought in Executive Outcomes (EO), a corporation formerly based in South Africa that employed white ex-soldiers from the former apartheid regime as mercenaries. Executive Outcomes and its costly high-tech weapons were hired (at an estimated $1.8 million per month [Hirsch 2001:118]) to defend Sierra Leone's diamonds and other mineral resources—though not its citizens—against the rebels. It began to work with a very different fighting force: a civilian militia known as *kamajos* ("hunter" in Mende), which had been operating in the southern, Mende-speaking part of the country since 1993 (Muana 1997). This militia was a regionally based civilian group whose members are often depicted, and depict themselves, as "traditional hunters." It was, however, made up of farmers, traders, teachers, and university students. Although they were taught certain pieces of hunters' lore, medicines, and ritual practices—notably techniques of Closure and Darkness—these became legitimizing practices that substituted for a deeper knowledge (Ferme 2001:27). "The very visibility of [their] magic objects, clothes, and rituals," argues Ferme, "points to their superficiality, in a context where the combatants' youthfulness argues against their having deep interpretive powers" (ibid.).

In 1996, the kamajos became an arm of the state. During that year, Strasser was overthrown in a palace coup, democratic elections were held, and the new president, Ahmad Tejan-Kabbah, sent EO away after he signed the Abidjan peace agreement with the RUF. Tejan-Kabbah's government was not, however, able to control its army, which had been starved of funds for decades and was recently expanded through the recruitment of youth (including many under eighteen). Some soldiers raided the very communities they were supposed to protect and were accordingly dubbed *sobels* (soldier/rebels). Rather than investing in the army, the new minister of defense, Hinga Norman, gave government support, resources, and weapons to the kamajos, who formed a paramilitary unit later known as the Civil Defence Forces (CDF). Initially, as fighters mobilized to protect their own localities, and bearing the name of "hunters" with all its associations of "deep" knowledge and historical belonging, the kamajos became popular heroes. But as time went on, and as they became an extension of the state, they began to commit atrocities similar to those of the RUF rebels, although not on such a large scale.

Rather than anachronistic residues of a primal past, then, techniques of Darkness and Closure in the rebel war embodied both ritual memory and, for the kamajos, an authorizing discourse. If we regard these techniques as ritual memories, we might see them as methods for the construction of bodies that could (it was hoped) inhabit the world that the war created, tying together past and present experiences of a landscape transformed by the commodification of people (Shaw 2002). The memories these techniques incarnate, then, are those of Sierra Leone's modernity—a modernity born of the application of economic rationality, of a transregional circulation of commodities (first slaves, then products for the colonial trade, then diamonds). At the same time, Closure and Darkness authorized the kamajos' status as "traditional hunters" both by drawing upon Mende ideas of deep knowledge (Ferme 2001:27) and, as we will see below, by becoming emblems of the kinds of practices that have been deemed antithetical to modernity in European history.

Witchcraft Battalions and Deep Weirdness

For those who analyze African conflicts for the North American and European media, and for those who make foreign policy decisions, the blurring of European distinctions between magic and modernity is often disturbing. In the conjunction of ritual techniques and high-tech weapons in wars like Sierra Leone's, there seems to be a dissolution of boundaries that threatens to unravel the world that the Enlightenment built. Journalists covering both Sierra Leone's and Liberia's wars have thus regularly found shock value in juxtaposing icons of modernity with such signs of primitivism as "fetishes" and "juju."[3]

In one instance, a 1995 *New York Times Magazine* article entitled "A War Without Purpose in a Country Without Identity," the author—Jeffrey Goldberg—writes about a meeting he had with young members of one of the rebel factions, the Liberian Peace Council (LPC). This is how he describes his discussion with these teenage guerillas, who have named themselves Colonel Action, General War Boss III, General Rambo, General Murder, and Captain Mission Impossible:

> These young men are war criminals—"nasty killers," they call themselves—but there is something absurd, almost comical about them, besides their cartoon names. Throughout Liberia, guerilla "uniforms" usually consist of shorts and T-shirts collected long ago in American charity drives. General Murder's shirt celebrates a high-school wrestling team in Sioux City, Iowa; another L.P.C. fighter's shirt features a smiling girl and the tag line "Braces by Drs. Kessler and Morgenstern." The generals and I chat idly for a couple of hours. I ask them to describe their goals, almost as if I'm their school guidance counselor.
> "I want to kill Charles Taylor," Captain Mission Impossible says.
> But wouldn't you rather be in school, safe from the bullets?
> "Bullets don't kill us," he says, fingering a phallus-shaped fetish around his neck. He is 17 years old. (Goldberg 1995:38)

Our shock at the youth of these fighters, of their matter-of-fact attitudes toward killing, and their apparent indifference toward school and personal safety is presumed to be compounded by this supposedly "absurd, almost comical" image of teenagers who combine items of contemporary American popular culture with African "fetishes"—objects that, Goldberg also suggests, have an ominous resemblance to human sexual organs.

In coverage of Sierra Leone's war, the mere existence of the kamajos as fighters who combined conventional fighting techniques with such practices as ritual Darkness and Closure was considered startling enough in itself to merit attention. Mention of the kamajos became a recurring motif in the writings of foreign journalists based in Freetown, as in this *New York Times* report on the demobilization process following the Lome Peace Accord of 1999:

Sierra Leone: Fighters Disband

Traditional hunters who helped the West African peacekeeping force known as Ecomog to keep Sierra Leone's Government from being overthrown have begun returning to their villages. The Government ordered the hunters, who are known as kamajors and wear mirrors and crosses in the belief that they will ward off bullets, to disband after a peace agreement signed early this month with the Revolutionary United Front. (Norimitsu Onishi, *New York Times* [July 28, 1999]:A10)

When, a few years earlier, the kamajos cooperated with EO, some observers viewed this alliance in terms of an adulteration of apparently "premodern" communities with Western modernity:

The [Executive Outcomes] force came equipped with two MI17s and an MI24 Hind—Russian helicopter gunships similar to American Apaches—a radio intercept system, two Boeing 727s to transport troops and supplies, an Andover casualty-evacuation aircraft, and fuel-air explosives, bombs that suck out oxygen upon detonation, killing all life within a square-mile radius. . . . Once in country, they set about training an elite corps of Sierra Leonean soldiers, and they employed traditional Sierra Leonean hunters, known as Kammah Joes—a witchcraft battalion armed with old single-barrel muskets, special herbal potions, and supernatural war garments believed to repel bullets—as scouts in the unfamiliar jungle. (Rubin 1997:47)

This *Harper's Magazine* article is a critique of EO operations in Sierra Leone. Its author, Elizabeth Rubin, emphasizes Executive Outcomes' high-tech weaponry, exposes its mission of resource extraction and its thinly disguised neocolonial racism, and traces its links to multinational business interests—especially in the diamond trade. She underscores her criticism, however, by constructing a contrast between Executive Outcomes and its helicopter gunships, Boeing 727s, and fuel-air explosives on the one hand, and the "witchcraft battalions" of the kamajos with their "herbal potions" and "supernatural war garments" on the other—thereby drawing a trajectory of a soon-to-be-lost African innocence. Although her critique of EO is very telling, she effectively denies the kamajos—who are cast as "traditional Sierra Leonean hunters"—the capacity either to understand or to provide any meaningful critique of "modern" warfare or multinational corporations themselves.

Instead of being noble primitives cast by circumstances into encounters with a modernity they do not understand, the kamajos, remember, consist of men from a wide range of occupations. They have incorporated such concepts as "centuries-old tradition" into their self-identification and often define themselves through concepts such as magic and juju that connote a dichotomy between ancient and modern, darkness and light—and thereby seek to appropriate their power. They also feed these images back to journalists, as we see in this article from 1996:

> Bo, Sierra Leone—Traditional hunters in southern Sierra Leone have been joining forces to protect civilians from rebel attack, putting their faith in centuries-old "black juju" to ward off rebel bullets.
>
> The colorfully dressed Kamajor hunters, who say celibacy is vital if the magic is to work, are a familiar sight in the southern provincial capital Bo, wandering back from combat in the bush with shotguns on their shoulders and knives in their belts.
>
> About 200 Kamajors in Bo have set up an unofficial civil defence force to protect the town from rebels of the Revolutionary United Front (RUF), who took up arms in 1991.
>
> The chief hunter, Mohamed Samukai Billy, told Reuters the Kamajors special powers came from a ceremony mixing elements of Islam with traditional magic.

"We undergo a special ceremony which we call 'black juju' or 'magic,'
carried out by powerful Muslim Alphas or Morimen," he says. . . . "These
methods are very effective in making us immune against bullets—provided
we adhere strictly to the magic and do not break the laws accorded us."
(Sam Akintimoye, "Sierra Leone Hunters Use Ancient . . . Reuters News
Story," Posted on "Naijanet" e-mail Listserv [February 16, 1996])

Such accounts in the foreign media, as kamajo leaders such as the "chief
hunter" were no doubt aware, could extend the kamajos' legitimacy as "authentic" popular grassroots fighters, masters of locally rooted occult forces,
to a world audience.

Thus whereas foreign journalists have been drawn by the apparent in-
congruity of magic and modernity in the person and powers of the kamajo,
kamajos themselves have often highlighted their special powers in encounters with foreign journalists and other expatriates:

I will concede that Sierra Leone, from the perspective of the average American, is a deeply weird place. Once, in Freetown, Sierra Leone's capital, I met
a member of the Kamajors, a traditional hunter society. He was wearing a
red ronko, a "war vest," which, he said, made him impervious to bullets. He
was a little bit drunk, I think, and he proposed an experiment: I would wear
the vest, and he would then fire bullets from his AK-47 at my chest. I declined, which made him dangerously upset. He threatened to shoot me
without the benefit of his vest, for disrespecting his beliefs.

I think about this man whenever Americans tell me that Africa is one
great impenetrable, illogical mystery. I can't claim to understand his belief
system, but I understand what gets him up in the morning. The Kamajors
know that the terrorists of the Revolutionary United Front are the bad guys,
and they have lately been doing what they can to stop them. (Goldberg 2000)

Instead of promoting the kamajos' legitimacy, however, such challenges as
this can just as easily confirm Western images of an "African magic" that
transgresses its boundaries and overflows dangerously into the "modern"
world of cities and AK47s. Goldberg's account of his encounter forms part
of his critique of U.S. isolationism and its double standards toward African
wars: even people who believe in magical bulletproofing are committed to
"struggling against the chaos" (ibid.).[4] Yet at the same time his story con-

firms North Atlantic perceptions of Sierra Leone as a space of the "deeply weird" through its images of magical practices in the "wrong" places.

Juju journalism did not originate the perception that "Africa is one great impenetrable, illogical mystery." But if Goldberg heard this repeatedly expressed by Americans in discussions of Sierra Leone, it is more than likely to have been catalyzed by the writing of Robert Kaplan.

Robert Kaplan's New Age Primitivism

In Robert Kaplan's journalism and travelogue, the conjunction of modernity and magic is made into a particularly monstrous hybrid—and here, the threat represented by this conjunction is understood to be directed against a presumed "us" in the North Atlantic world. Aligning himself with the political "realism" of the U.S. foreign policy establishment, Kaplan represents himself as a purveyor of "brutal honesty" (1996:36), of gritty, no-nonsense analysis that "confront[s] the real world, slums and all" (1996:xiv). Setting himself against what he calls "dangerously optimistic accounts regarding democratic elections in Africa" (1996:13, n. 16), he uses his "unsentimental journey" (1996:11) from Africa to Asia as a basis for prophesy: "I wanted to map the future, perhaps the 'deep future,' by ignoring what was legally and officially there, and, instead, touching, feeling, and smelling what was really *there*" (1996:6).

His version of "the real world" in Sierra Leone is based on a visit to the cities of Freetown and Bo in 1993. There, according to the Sierra Leone chapter in his travelogue (1996), his opinions were formed through conversations with the following people: a U.S. diplomat, an ambassador from a Western embassy, a government minister, a medical doctor at the bar of the Hill Station club, two government officials at a dinner party, an American representative for Catholic Relief Services, and a Sierra Leonean youth who helped him find accommodation in Bo (1996:32–69). This youth is the exception; most of Kaplan's impressions seem to have been obtained either from elites and expatriates talking *about* ordinary Sierra Leoneans or from his own silent observations on the road. His quest to touch, feel, and smell "what was really *there*" is realized in a road trip to Bo punctuated by the usual indignities of roadblock harassment, mechanical failures, and flat tires.

In one such delay at a village, he has an epiphany of sorts: "the piles of garbage, the empty shelves in the single store, the buzzing flies, the vacant and surly stares of the numerous young men hanging out until our flat tire gave them something useful to do, the sheer nothingness of it all" (1996:62). As Richards points out, these apparently idle youth are, in fact, firewood sellers looking for work, but Kaplan "appears not to have engaged them much in conversation while they fixed his truck" (P. Richards 1999:17). Apparently uninterested in finding out about their lives, he looks no further than his own reading of their stares as threatening.

What Kaplan "learns" in this way does little more than to elaborate on the nineteenth-century social Darwinism that he brought with him. When he begins his journey at the border of the Ivory Coast and Liberia, for example, he encounters "authentic rain forest" (1996:26):

> Though I had seen no soldiers, let alone any atrocities or *juju* spirits, an indefinable wildness had set in. It occurred to me that, perhaps, the forest had made the war in Liberia. . . . The forest was partly to blame for the iniquities of humankind here—for President Doe disemboweling the previous president, Tolbert, and for Prince Johnson, in turn, cutting off Doe's ears; for Charles Taylor's teenage soldiers breaking into the bridal shops of Monrovia, dressing up like women-*cum-juju* spirits, and going on boozy rampages that ended in ritual killings. (1996:27)

This is just "traveler's intuition" (ibid.), he acknowledges, having no other basis for this startling piece of tree fetishism. Nevertheless, he goes on to develop this traveler's intuition into a sweeping theory of West African epistemology, underdevelopment, and war anyway. Forests, he claims, isolate those inside them from the rest of the world, hindering intellectual development and fostering emotional excitability by obscuring a clearer view, both physically and intellectually; those who inhabit them "tend to depend less on reason and more on superstition" (1996:28). Appropriately enough, this hypothesis is supported by a footnote referring us to Sir James George Frazer's chapter on "The Worship of Trees" from *The Golden Bough* ([1911] 1996:28, n. 40).

In Kaplan's brand of environmental determinism, in which he seeks "to see humanity in each locale as literally an outgrowth of the terrain and cli-

mate in which it was fated to live" (1996:7), the forest provides fertile
ground for the germination not only of vegetation but also of "irrational"
dispositions. What Kaplan calls (variously) superstition, animism, juju,
magic, juju spirits, and spirit culture appears, for him, to be a cultural outgrowth of the dark, dense tangle of roots, trunks, and foliage. Both forests
and juju, moreover, are presented as generative of strange and perverted acts
of violence. These connections between the forest, spirit culture, and brutal
violence appear materially self-evident to Kaplan as he stands by the Liber-
ian/Ivorian border, gazing at the imposing crush of trees and creepers, and
ruminating on stories from the Liberian civil war (1996:29).

But while, for Kaplan, the forest breeds "spirit culture," the destruction
of the forest breeds something worse: the "Coming Anarchy" itself. That the
forest in Sierra Leone is not, in fact, receding (P. Richards 1996, 1999; Fairhead and Leach 1998) is never confronted: environmental degradation and
overpopulation are as firmly rooted as menacing trees and juju spirits in Kaplan's West African imagination. Resource depletion, Kaplan argues, hastens
the urban drift of "animistic" populations that "drain" (a favorite verb) into
shantytowns, bringing superstition, tribalism, and communalism with them.
When magical, forest-born "spirit culture" occupies spaces of urban poverty,
"weakening" as it mingles with such products as "mass-produced weaponry,
and other artefacts of modern times" (1996:29), Kaplan suggests, the result
is "a new-age primitivism" (ibid.) manifest in the violence of "*juju* warriors,
influenced by the worst refuse of Western pop culture and ancient tribal hatreds" (1994:62). Thus he tells us:

> Many of the atrocities in the Liberian civil war have been tied to belief in
> *juju* spirits, and the BBC has reported, in its magazine *Focus on Africa*, that
> in the civil fighting in adjacent Sierra Leone, rebels were said to have "a
> young woman with them who would go to the front naked, always walking
> backwards and looking in a mirror to see where she was going. This made
> her invisible, so that she could cross to the army's positions and there bury
> charms . . . to improve the rebels' chances of success." (1994:46)

By placing this striking image of a naked, mirror-gazing woman whose backward steps create a spell of invisibility immediately after a suggested link between war atrocities and "belief in *juju* spirits," Kaplan resurrects nine-

teenth- and early-twentieth-century associations between representations of African "animism," "barbarism," and unclothed bodies in the European imagination.[5]

But in Kaplan's version of evolutionist thought, we are moving inexorably toward apocalypse instead of advancing toward progress. His "new-age primitivism" (1996:29), the transgressive hybridity of urbanism and animism, the modern and the magical, embodies the downward slide of civilization into primordial chaos. Thus Islam and Christianity, which Kaplan views as forces for progress, are weakened in West Africa by "syncretization." His friend, the Sierra Leonean minister, tells him: "Here in West Africa we have a lot of superficial Islam and superficial Christianity. . . . Western religion is undermined by animist beliefs not suitable to a moral society since they are based on irrational spirit power" (1996:33). This, Kaplan decides, is again the fault of the forest, "a green prison" in which Islam is "infiltrated" by spirit cults (1996:28). The resultant syncretization is a problem, Kaplan argues, because it interrupts the process of moral and intellectual development, diluting the relatively civilizing properties of Islam with a more regressive spiritual condition. Using exactly the same language as former French and British colonial officials in West Africa who regarded Islam as a source of moral and intellectual progress even as they feared its power for anticolonial mobilization (e.g., Crowder 1968:356–63), Kaplan writes: "Though Islam is spreading in West Africa, it is being hobbled by syncretization with animism: this makes new converts less apt to become anti-Western extremists, but it also makes for a weakened version of the faith, which is less effective as an antidote to crime" (1994:66).

The dissolution of boundaries between what, for Kaplan, are distinct spatiotemporal categories that correspond to different points along an evolutionary timeline—paganism and Islam, forest and city, nature and civilization, magical thought and modern technology—can only mean decay, breakdown, chaos (1996:63). For Kaplan the prophet, the map of the deep future is revealed: "A brief moment marked by the Industrial Revolution, which gave humankind a chance to defend itself somewhat from nature, may be closing" (1996:4). The title of part 1 of *The Ends of the Earth* says it all: "West Africa: *Back to the Dawn?*"

That Sierra Leone's and Liberia's wars *were*, in fact, characterized by appalling violence, that these two West African states *had* broken down were all the confirmation that Kaplan (and not only Kaplan) needed of the salience of his neoevolutionist map of the future as a sinking back into humankind's primordial past. "But Kaplan is right—Sierra Leone *is* in a state of anarchy," scholars I respected would sometimes tell me. What they meant by this was what Kaplan himself seems to mean by "being right." According to Paul Richards, who presented a critique of Kaplan's work at a 1999 event in London: "On Sierra Leone, Kaplan's line was if he was so wrong why was he so right? Apparently a *New York Times* editorial had called him to task for not predicting the democratic transition in Sierra Leone in 1996, but fighting since showed how right he had been all along" (1999:16). Yet how prescient did anyone have to be to predict that fighting would continue after the elections in 1996? The Sierra Leonean state still had no resources, the government was still unable to control its armed forces, and the RUF rebels were still out there. With sleight of hand, Kaplan tends to insert compelling realist *descriptions* of the violence itself (e.g., "video footage [showing] mutilated bodies and a man pulling a finger out of his wallet, claiming it made him 'disappear'" [1996:67]) to mesmerize his audience into swallowing an *explanatory* house of cards. His analysis, which anchors "drive-by" observations (P. Richards 1999:17) to a deterministic chain connecting thick forests, juju spirits, overpopulation, deforestation, urban migration, and reverse evolution, is "realist" only in an aesthetic sense.

Primitivism and Policy

In another chapter in this collection, Margaret Wiener argues that during the colonial era in Bali, the language of fetishism, magic, superstition, and its evolutionist paradigm created objects of official action and colonial control. What kinds of boundaries are inscribed and what kinds of official action—and inaction—have been facilitated by juju journalism? Kaplan's writing on European primitivism in the Balkans, *Balkan Ghosts* (1993), with its recurring images of dark churches, old monks, and ancient Balkan hatreds, had reportedly shaped President Clinton's decision against military intervention in Bosnia (Bringa forthcoming).

When "The Coming Anarchy" was published, so effectively did Kaplan's images of new age African primitivism tap into the Hobbesian imagination of the U.S. policy world that the article was faxed to every U.S. embassy in Africa (P. Richards 1996:xv).[6] According to an anthropologist who was based in Abidjan when the article first appeared, "The American ambassador made it required reading at the embassy, and back in Washington, it became canonical at the Africa section of the Foreign Service Institute" (Margaret Anderson, Nuafrica network [Listserv], posted August 17, 1998). Published four months after the U.S. withdrawal from Somalia and two months before the 1994 massacre in Rwanda, Kaplan's article, writes a former U.S. ambassador to Sierra Leone, "buttressed the growing trend in the Washington policy community of withdrawal from direct involvement in African crises" (Hirsch 2001:17). The significance of "The Coming Anarchy" in lending intellectual legitimacy to the 1990s trend of U.S. isolationism from Africa can be gauged from another Nuafrica Listserv participant's account of the article's distribution at a military meeting:

> When I came across the article, I dismissed it merely as an expanded version of the WAWA ("West Africa Wins Again") stories that used to pollute conversations with expatriates during my many years in Africa. I viewed it more seriously when the article was distributed to civilian visitors at a military conference I attended in June 1994. The sponsors evidently believed that the Kaplan article supported their anti-peace operation views. Why get involved in missions in cultures we can never hope to understand? As such, Kaplan's pessimism . . . both reflects and fosters growing US nativism and isolationism. (Walter S. Clarke, Nuafrica network [Listserv], posted September 1, 1998)

Thus instead of creating objects of colonial control, the neoevolutionist narratives of juju journalism were used to create objects of official *inaction*: "no-one can resolve this," the message seems to be, "it's juju-inspired violence."

Not all juju journalists, as we have seen, follow Kaplan in arguing that the conjunctions of magic and modernity in Sierra Leone's war signal the decline and fall of civilization: some view such conjunctions in terms of noble primitives or of a fairly harmless "deep weirdness." But regardless of their own interpretive spin, their writings are likely to be read—in the foreign policy world, at least—through the interpretive prism of "The Coming Anarchy." Even Kaplan himself no longer believes that "Africa is . . . a bellwether for politics for the rest of the world" (2000:xiii). After traveling through Cambodia, moreover, he developed doubts about his explanatory package, although he remained convinced that "culture . . . was still crucial to the question of why some states like Cambodia and Sierra Leone failed" (1996:412).

Yet the damage had been done. And it was not only Sierra Leone and Liberia whose wars were "primitivized." In answer to the question of whether NATO's "successful" 1999 intervention in Kosovo could be repeated to help end wars in Africa, for example, *New York Times* journalist Donald G. McNeil argued that "any mission for ground troops is . . . problematic," explaining: "The Congo cease-fire document expects the peacekeepers to disarm more than a dozen armed forces, including Unita, the Mayi-Mayi guerillas and the Hutu militias. Unita has been at war for 25 years. The Mayi-Mayi charge into battle naked, thinking they're bulletproof" (Donald G. McNeil, "Bombing Won in Kosovo: Africa Is a Tougher Case," *New York Times*, "Week in Review" [July 25, 1999]:16). How can naked African believers in magical bulletproofing, McNeil implies, be expected to be rational participants in a peacekeeping operation? Juju journalism provided a convenient rationale for an isolationist politics of knowledge in relation to African conflicts more generally in the 1990s. This is especially ironic in Sierra Leone, given that such techniques as Darkness and Closure did not develop in a supposedly "primal" African isolation but proliferated through integration into an expanding Atlantic world of human commodification and extraction. Recognizing the modernity of these forms of "magic" should also entail a recognition of North Atlantic entanglement—and accountability—in this region.

In the new century, the isolationism of the 1990s has undergone a reversal. The glaring disparity between international responses to Kosovo ($690 million, plus a further pledge of $2.1 billion [Hirsch 2001:95]) and Sierra Leone ($25 million [ibid.]) generated criticism of double standards that the United States, United Kingdom, and UN found embarrassing. At the time of writing, in 2001, demobilization and disarmament are well under way in Sierra Leone under the surveillance of several thousand UN peacekeeping troops, whose presence is generating an economic boom in Freetown. And tellingly, I have seen no more juju journalism for over a year.

FOUR

The Citizen's Trance

The Haitian Revolution and the Motor of History

LAURENT DUBOIS

Yes. I want to consult the record. Learn facts, the official documentary evidence, witness, proof. Simultaneously I must not neglect the many other ways the past speaks.

—JOHN EDGAR WIDEMAN, *Fatheralong,* 1994

In November 1791, the Marquis de Gallifet, the Parisian absentee owner of some of the most prosperous plantations in Saint Domingue, received bad news from across the Atlantic. "Your houses, Monsieur le Marquis, are nothing but ashes, your belongings have disappeared, your manager is no more. The insurrection has spread its devastation and carnage onto your properties" (Archives Nationales [AN], 107 AP 126, Millot to Gallifet, August 1791). A few weeks later, he received the details of his misfortune from one of his surviving employees, Pierre Mossut. "We were attacked by a horde of assassins, and could only offer meager resistance," wrote Mossut. "After the first volley, we took refuge in flight." If Mossut survived, it was only because a domestic slave appeared, miraculously, with a horse. A few days later, Mossut carried a telescope to the top of one of the hills outside Le Cap and examined the state of the Gallifet plantations. All of the buildings and all of the cane had been burned. The land where they once stood would become the site of one of the fortified camps of the insurgents (AN, 107 AP 128, Mossut to Gallifet, September 19, 1791; Fick 1990, 98–99).

Like many who followed him, Mossut blamed the insurrection on "the various writings published in your capital in favor of the Negroes," which had circulated in the colonies and were known to the slaves. Mossut's letter presented in embryo the interpretation of the insurrection that became standard among the planters and has haunted interpretations of the Haitian Revolution ever since. The overzealous Republican advocates of racial equality, he claimed, had undermined the social hierarchies that made possible the functioning of slavery; the well-regulated social order of Saint Domingue had been shattered through the inappropriate application of the doctrines of the revolution to a context that required its own particular laws. Yet Mossut also admitted that he was mystified as to what drove the slaves. "There is a motor that powers them and that keeps powering them and that we cannot come to know," he wrote. "All experienced *colons* know that this class of men have neither the energy nor the combination of ideas necessary for the execution of this project, whose realization they nevertheless are marching towards with perseverance." Mossut had questioned captured insurgents, hoping for some identification of who was behind the rebellion, but he learned nothing. "We have executed many slaves, among them ten from your plantation," he informed Gallifet, "but though they admit to being guilty and to having participated in the revolt, they have all observed an obstinate silence when questioned about who armed them and incited this odious trance" (AN, 107 AP 128, Mossut to Gallifet, September 19, 1791).

Mossut was making an oblique and perhaps unconscious reference to the mysterious ceremonies that had preoccupied administrators and plantation owners in Saint Domingue for decades. He may have suspected that the religious practices of the slaves had given an impetus to their revolt and had made possible their impressive interplantation organization. Yet he was also suggesting that only a trance induced by some malefic magician could account for the vitality of the slaves' insurrection. The "combination of ideas" necessary for their actions could not, according to Mossut, have emerged from the slaves themselves.

A few months later another captured slave insurgent likewise frustrated his interrogators' search for an explanation. But the objects they found after they executed him confronted them with a sign of the "combination of ideas" that lay behind the revolt. His captors found

> in one of his pockets pamphlets printed in France, filled with commonplaces about the Rights of Man and the Sacred Revolution; in his vest pocket was a large packet of tinder and phosphate and lime. On his chest he had a little sack full of hair, herbs, and bits of bone, which they call a fetish. And it was, no doubt, because of this amulet, that our man had the intrepidity which the philosophers call Stoicism. (Parham 1959; Fick 1990:11)

The objects carried by this slave suggest the complex ways in which insurgents brought together the languages of dignity and resistance of Republicanism with those articulated through African-based religion. It was a combination that surprised—and has continued to surprise—many observers.

The slave revolt of 1791, which shattered the plantation economy of Saint Domingue and ultimately brought about the abolition of slavery, confronted Europeans with what Michel-Rolph Trouillot has termed an "Unthinkable History." As he argues: "The events that shook up Saint Domingue from 1791 to 1804 constituted a sequence for which not even the extreme political left in France or in England had a conceptual frame of reference. They were 'unthinkable' facts in the framework of Western thought." In the face of the 1791 insurrection, contemporaries searched for the roots of revolution outside the slave insurgents themselves, in the propaganda of abolitionists, the conspiracies of royalists, or the imperial designs of Spain or England. Even those who advocated slave emancipation tended to argue that political rights could only gradually be granted to ex-slaves and were unprepared for the radical implications of the slave revolt of 1791 (Trouillot 1995:82).

Interpreters then—and since—have all too often overlooked the fact that the insurrection of slaves in Saint Domingue and elsewhere during this period was the military *and* ideological foundation for one of the crucial events in the history of democracy—the transformation of slaves into Republican citizens. In the early 1790s, slave insurgents often mobilized around false but prophetic rumors that claimed that metropolitan authorities had abolished slavery but that local authorities were resisting the decision. As groups of insurgents constituted themselves as a political force, this prophetic "news" was transformed into reality. Planters joined the anti-Republican camp and began turning to the English for support, and the idea emerged that in return for liberty slave insurgents could become the defenders of the Republic. In 1793, when hundreds of slaves rose up in Trois-Rivières, Guadeloupe, and killed twenty-three whites, they presented their actions to the officials of the island as an attack against the royalist conspiracies of their masters. "We have come to save you," they told the whites. "We want to fight for the republic, the law, the nation, order." Instead of punishing them, many whites called for the formation of a slave army to defend the island from English attack (Dubois 1998b). In Saint Domingue in 1793, the besieged Republican official Sonthonax offered freedom and citizenship to those slaves who would fight for France, a decision that turned the tide of conflict in the colony and which he ultimately broadened into a blanket emancipation. Deputies elected in the colony carried the news of the emancipation to the National Convention in 1794, declaring that the Republic had been saved by slave insurgents turned citizens. The convention ratified Sonthonax's decision, and it decreed the abolition of slavery "throughout the territory of the Republic," where "all men, without distinction of color, will enjoy the rights of French citizens" (Fick 1990:157–82; Gauthier 1995:203). Sonthonax later declared in Paris that "The Blacks are the true sans-culottes of the colonies, they are the people, and they are the only ones capable of defending the country" (AN, ADVII 20A, "Sonthonax . . . à la Convention Nationale," 2 Fructidor an II [August 19, 1794]).

During the 1780s, the royal government had explicitly identified African slaves as a danger to the national body, passing the Police des Noirs, a law that required those identified as "blacks" who lived in France to carry identity papers or be deported (Peabody 1996:106–36). Yet by 1794, Africans could be described as the only *true* citizens of the colonies. The revolutionaries of Saint Domingue had transformed the terms of national belonging and brought about one of the most radical gains of the "Age of Revolution"— the immediate and universal emancipation of all the slaves in the French Empire. By deploying an emerging Republican language of rights, in combination with demands for land and liberty rooted in the experience of slavery, the revolutionaries actualized the abstract universality of the Rights of Man and broadened the idea of citizenship. If the political culture of the French Revolution helped incite the slave revolutions of the 1790s, these in turn permanently altered the meaning of that political culture. Emancipation carried with it a fundamental reconfiguration of the relationship between metropole and colony, because Republican laws were to be applied equally to all peoples and territories of the French Empire. It therefore actualized a "universalization" of Republican law more radical than any advocated even by abolitionists at the time.

Under a Republican colonial regime, the French Antilles became the site of the first large-scale experiment in slave emancipation, which transformed the political landscape of the Caribbean and much of the Americas. As would be the case throughout the Americas, the process of emancipation was saturated with contradictions, as freedom was granted but immediately restricted through arguments about the incapacity of ex-slaves to be full citizens. These contradictions paved the way for the reversal of emancipation during the early 1800s, when Napoleon Bonaparte sent expeditions to the Caribbean to return the colonies to their pre-1789 situation. The French armies encountered much fierce resistance, and two years of war ultimately brought about the transformation of the colony of Saint Domingue into the independent nation of Haiti. The new Republic protected the principles France had rejected, as it institutionalized the abolition of slavery in its constitution (Fick 1990; James 1963).

Two nations were born together at the end of the eighteenth century: France and Haiti. They were both born through Republican revolutions that radically reshaped the social systems that had preceded them, and they were born symbiotically, linked materially and ideologically as they unfolded. Both revolutions profoundly changed the terms upon which citizenship and national belonging could be imagined, and both were linchpins in the production of the nations that followed them during the nineteenth and twentieth centuries. As Europe was fundamentally changed by the Republican revolution and by the Napoleonic campaigns that followed it, the societies of the Americas were deeply marked by the arrival of Haiti, whose actual and symbolic presence determined the course of the Latin American independence movements and the move toward slave emancipation throughout the Americas (see Blackburn 1988). Yet, throughout the last two centuries, whereas the French Revolution has become a symbol of the advent of modernity, the Haitian Revolution and Haiti itself have become symbols of political backwardness rooted in African superstition. Instead of being proof of the failure of the colonial venture, Haiti has been recast as its justification. The highly developed plantation economy and the radical political revolution that emerged from it have been primitivized, masked by the powerful image of a backward country practicing "Voodoo" in the absence of a guiding European influence. Through a trick of historical silencing, Haiti has been abolished from the West.[1]

The silencing of this past has been the condition of possibility for the production of broader historical narratives imbued with what Fernando Coronil calls the "Occidentalism" of "the West's self-fashioning as the self-made embodiment of modernity" (Coronil 1997:14). Such "Occidentalist" accounts, which represent the universal principles of democracy as products of European modernity, depend on the elision of the slave revolutions of the 1790s and the continuing exile of the nation they produced. For under an insistent silence, the heritage of transformation of slaves into citizens profoundly influenced the subsequent development of slavery and slave emancipation in the Americas, as well as the course of French colonialism there and in Africa. The fear of slave insurrection, made powerfully clear through the Haitian Revolution, impelled legislatures in the U.S. South to push for restrictions on the slave trade itself, not so much for humanitarian reasons as out of a fear that the continued importation of Africans would create the conditions for slave revolution (Frey 1991:226–42). In this and other ways, the history of the Haitian Revolution propelled the fulfillment of some of the broken promises of Republicanism through the gradual elimination of slavery throughout the Americas (Blackburn 1988). At the same time, the idea that Republican ideals could liberate suffering slaves in the Caribbean was transmuted into arguments about the need to abolish the slave trade within Africa itself—arguments that formed part of the foundation for French efforts to colonize West Africa. So the arguments for the elimination of slavery, propelled in the French Empire by slave insurgents who had demanded their freedom, became part of the arsenal of European "modernity" that was deployed as a justification for continued European colonization (Dorigny 1989; Largueche 1995).

Through all of this, as racial theories about the backwardness of Africans became an essential justification for the continued deferral of the rights the Europeans claimed they were bringing, the silenced colonial history of the Republic's ideas was productively erased in order to assure the progression of colonialism as the march of the Rights of Man emanating from Europe. The contradictions of this colonial project would of course explode—in ways that strikingly paralleled the events of the 1790s—during the post–World War II period, as the European empire was attacked and dismantled. But the forms created within the "imperial nation-state" of France (Wilder 1999) continue today to haunt the Caribbean, Africa, and France itself as the Republic confronts economic and political reconfigurations that resonate with those of the turn of the eighteenth century. In the midst of a crisis over the meaning of Republican rights and national identity in France, the forgotten spirits of the slave revolutions of the 1790s once again carry necessary lessons, and the forms taken by their evocation highlight the complexity of connecting the present to the past.

If, as Peter Pels suggests (this volume), the practice of magic is defined by the play of "skilled revelation and concealment," then it can be said that the Haitian Revolution has been subject to magical processes both through its concealment as a motor of history and through its skillful and selective revelation by various practitioners of the evocation of the past. Those who seek to unveil, expose, and call on the history of the Haitian Revolution operate at the crossroads of diverging, and perhaps incommensurable, strategies for communicating with the past. And in many ways, the questions first articulated in the midst of the 1791 insurrection remain unanswered: What incited the "odious trance" identified by Mossut? Is the name of the "motor" that he could not "come to know" hidden somewhere in the archives? Or is it embodied in the spirits from the past who, today, are still called from the past into the present through the rituals of Vodou?

History's Myth

> For some, this is fantasy; for others, history.
> —MICHELLE CLIFF, *Free Enterprise*, 1993

In 1988, Léon François Hoffman, a scholar of French Caribbean literature, presented a paper entitled "Un Mythe National: La cérémonie du Bois-Caïman" at a conference in Paris (Hoffman 1993). By tracing the ceremony's genealogy, Hoffman intended to deconstruct the "National Myth" through which the Bois-Caïman ceremony is represented as the root of Haitian independence. August 14, 1791, was a stormy night, according to the standard account. Hundreds of slaves slipped away from their plantation quarters in order to take part in a Vodou ceremony at Bois-Caïman, with the priest and insurgent slave Boukman officiating—accompanied (in certain versions) by a green-eyed *manbo* (priestess)—they danced, and many were possessed by Petro *lwa* (gods), notably the warrior Ogou. They vowed to rise up against their white masters and free themselves, sealing their pact by sacrificing a pig and drinking its blood. A few days later, the largest slave revolt in history began as thousands of slaves killed their masters, systematically destroyed the instruments of sugar production, and burned the cane fields of the Northern Province of Saint Domingue.

Hoffman argued that the first written description of this ceremony appeared over two decades after it took place, in the work of an ex-planter named Antoine Dalmas, who explicitly presented it as a barbaric event: "The religious ceremonies that the blacks practiced in slitting the pig's throat, the eagerness with which they drank its blood, the value they placed on possessing some of its hairs—a kind of talisman which, according to them, would make them invulnerable—serves to characterize the African." Dalmas concluded that "it was natural for such an ignorant and stupid class to take part in the superstitious rituals of an absurd and bloody religion before taking part in the most horrible of assassinations." As Hoffman noted, Dalmas had, like many French writers describing the victorious Haitian Revolution, a keen interest in making the slave insurgents seem as savage and superstitious as possible; his history of the revolution was followed by a tract arguing that the blacks could not govern themselves and that France had every right to reconquer Haiti and make it a slave colony again (Dalmas 1814:117–18, quoted in Hoffman 1993). The legend first described by a "racist planter," suggests Hoffman, was in turn developed by the "metropolitan abolitionist" Civique de Gastine, who added the detail that it was a dark and stormy night. All later sources, Hoffman claimed—from the work of Victor Schoelcher to that of Haitian historians and finally to textbooks of Haitian history—depend on these two deeply problematic sources. Hoffman concluded that the Bois-Caïman ceremony never happened, adding that it was important for "the liberty of People" to know the origins of their myths.

Hoffman's paper exaggerated the problem of sources surrounding the Bois-Caïman ceremony. Dalmas's work, for instance, though published in

1814, was actually written in 1793 and 1794, when the writer was in exile in Philadelphia. In the years before the revolution, the author had served as a surgeon on a sugar plantation in the Northern Province and had therefore had consistent contact with slaves, and he was in the region during the uprising. Although not a witness to the ceremony, and clearly hostile to the slave revolution, he could easily have heard echoes and some details about the event from slaves at the time. And the works of nineteenth-century Haitian writers Hurault Dumesle and Celigny Ardouin, which Hoffman wrote off as simply by-products of the writings of the French Civique de Gastine, drew at least in part from oral testimonies about the ceremony collected in Haiti in the early to mid nineteenth century, when survivors of the period were still alive.

As Hoffman noted, Dumesle clearly drew on Gastine's text in writing his poetic account of the Bois-Caïman ceremony. But he also added a crucial detail: a portion of the speech that the slave leader Boukman gave that night. The Haitian writer most likely did not simply make up this speech out of thin air. Dumesle's work was an account of a journey to the historical sites in the north of Haiti, and on this journey he seems to have heard something that inspired his account of the ceremony. There was, in other words, some historical memory of the ceremony present in the Northern Province in the early 1920s. Indeed, recent research in the area has unearthed the continuing oral transmission of information about the ceremony among Haitians, though it is difficult to know whether these traditions have their roots in local memories of the events or in the broader representations that have proliferated about them, especially in the twentieth century.[2]

During the discussion that followed Hoffman's presentation, the Haitian novelist Jean Metellus challenged Hoffman, saying that his paper was a perfect enaction of the usual foreign tendency to denigrate Haiti and had turned the conference into a *rigolade*—a farce—at the expense of Haiti. The story of Bois-Caïman, he added, was a foundational myth drawn from a historical event. The Haitian scholar Laennec Hurbon pointed out that Hoffman had not proven that the event never existed but rather that there was no proof that it had existed. Hurbon also noted the central epistemological problem at the root of Hoffman's intervention: that the social context that produced the revolt a priori excluded the voices of slave insurgents from the very documents that have been used to write its history. Trouillot has noted that the very constitution of the historical archives always creates a situation of documentary inequality, which facilitates the telling of certain stories and the silencing of others. "Silences are inherent in history because any single event enters history with some of its constituting parts missing," he writes. "Thus whatever becomes a fact does so with its own inborn absences, specific to its production." As Trouillot further argues: "The very mechanisms that make any historical recording possible also ensure that historical facts are not created equal. They reflect the differential control of the means of historical production at the very first engraving that transforms an event into fact" (Trouillot 1995:49).

The Haitian Revolution took shape in a society where slaves were systematically excluded from acting as agents in the creation of the documents that now form the historical archive of Saint Domingue. Slave gatherings of any kind were strictly policed, particularly because they not only provided a space in which slaves from different plantations could act in community but were also known to be the sites of religious rituals whose practice frightened and mystified whites.[3] The religious practices of the slaves developed in a context of surveillance, suspicion, and repression. As such, the documentary evidence they left behind was necessarily limited, refracted through the distorted fears of the whites who heard rumors or stories about what went on within them. Historical research that seeks to document the development of religious practices of the slaves of Saint Domingue thus confronts a complex task, and it confronts the epistemological issues raised by writing about what, on some level, is impossible to document. Trouillot suggests: "Silences of this kind show the limits of strategies that imply a more accurate reconstitution of the past, and therefore the production of a 'better' history, simply by an enlargement of the empirical base" (Trouillot 1995:49). The silence surrounding Bois-Caïman is a symptom of a broader constitution of the historical narrative of the French and Haitian Revolutions within a field of inequality constructed through and reflected by the inequalities in the constitution of historical narratives.

Hoffman's deconstruction of the "myth" of Bois-Caïman was marked by a desire to dispel the nationalist pretensions of the essentialist "negritude" of the dictatorship of François Duvalier, an amateur ethnologist who used a celebration of Haitian history and culture—notably the evocation of the Bois-Caïman ceremony—to strengthen his regime. Yet Hoffman's deconstruction also inscribed itself within a broader set of assumptions about the nature of historical narrative and historical facticity. It was not lost on those who responded to his paper that his deconstruction of the story of Bois-Caïman, although it was in some ways an act of resistance against a certain kind of historical mythologization, also fit all too comfortably with the broader erasure of Haiti from the history of modernity. For in effect the "myth" of Bois-Caïman must be seen as a complex reaction to the dynamics of historical silencing, a way of announcing the process through which the legally silenced, literally objectified slaves of Saint Domingue became citizens of Haiti.

The story of the ceremony confronts the larger denigration of Vodou religious practice by placing the root of Haitian independence in a religious ceremony, associating the creation of an independent black Republic with the "magic" of a religion that was and is commonly seen as a throwback to primitive African practice. To invoke Bois-Caïman in this way is to suggest a different vision of this religion, to perceive it as a motor in that most modern of events, a national political revolution, and therefore to gesture toward an account of the complex modernity represented by Vodou. The religion was only one element in the complex historical processes that drove the struggle against slavery and for Haitian independence, and so the myth of the Bois-Caïman ceremony produces a selective memory of that struggle (Mintz and Trouillot 1995:138). Those who created and passed on this myth modified the history of revolution in a particular way, choosing to highlight the importance of religion as opposed to the importance of other factors in the historical narrative, both confronting and deepening the stereotypes surrounding Haiti and Vodou. The struggle over the meaning of Bois-Caïman suggests some of the ways in which the production of national mythologies takes place in an archival and geopolitical field deeply inflected by the unequal distribution of power. It also illustrates the magical process through which Europe has come to hold its monopoly on the concept of "modernity," through which it continues to exercise its hold over the "development" of "elsewheres."

Historical myths condense historical narrative, providing a story through which to comprehend complex foundational events from the past. The contrast between the story of Bois-Caïman and that of one of the central figures of European mythology—the taking of the Bastille on July 14, 1789—highlights the imbrication between nationalist history, the creation of archives, and the production of ritual. The subsequent representation of the taking of the Bastille as a sign of the victory of popular sovereignty depended both on the rituals of the assailants themselves and on the inscription of the event in the "archive" of public memory by members of the National Assembly during 1789. In the week following the event, as its impact became clear, representatives contrasted the taking of the Bastille with other examples of "illegitimate" crowd violence and in so doing mythologized the event as a legitimate expression of the people's will. Archives were constituted—in one of the first reports of the event, a newspaper noted that "a quantity of books, of registers of imprisonment, of materials for history were found in the Bastille." Starting as early as July 15, the need for commemorative rituals was discussed (Sewell 1996:863). The ritualization of the taking of the Bastille continued during the early 1790s as part of an ambitious program of Republican ceremony. Robespierre instituted a series of highly stylized ritual celebrations which replaced saints' days with celebrations of the nation and the "Etre Suprême" (Supreme Being). Special prayers to such foundations of national strength were written and distributed in an attempt to transform the old order through a ritually based inculcation of the new values of nationalism (Ozouf 1988; Hunt 1984).

The changing rituals that surrounded the institutionalization of the Republic during the early 1790s were, as the historian Jules Michelet described them, part of a "new religion." For Michelet, the highest expression of this was the Festival of the Federation of July 14, 1790, when representatives from throughout France traveled to Paris, singing revolutionary songs just as religious pilgrims before them had sung hymns. They gathered to commemorate the fall of the Bastille and in so doing enacted the emerging vision of a supreme nation whose worship would sweep away all divisions between citizens. Throughout the country, wrote Michelet, old spaces of worship were transformed through the worship of a new god. "All the old emblems grew pale," as people swore at old altars, "before the Holy Sacrament," or in front of the "cold image of Liberty," worshipping justice and equality and creating "such a temple as had never existed before" (Michelet 1967:445, 451).

Writing in the second half of the nineteenth century, Michelet described how, at the end of the academic year, he communed with "the spirit of the Revolution," which "possesses a knowledge of which others are ignorant" and "contains the secret of bygone times." "In it alone France conscious became conscious of herself," he wrote. He noted that there was no monument to the revolution in Paris. The Champ de Mars, where the Festival of the Federation of 1790 had taken place, was an empty space, where "a forgetful generation" amused themselves with horse races. It was, however, haunted: "A mighty breath yet traverses it, such as you nowhere else perceive; a soul, a spirit omnipotent." For in its soil was "profoundly mingled the fruitful sweat" of the citizens who, "aroused by the cannons of the Bastille," had converged in 1790 "with the unanimity of one man, and decreed eternal peace." Michelet considered that it was the duty of the historian to commune with the spirit of the revolution, to communicate with the past that haunted Paris in order to bring France to its destiny as a Republic (Michelet 1967:3–4).

The continual condensation of memory surrounding the "spirit of the Revolution" has been built upon a silence, an erasure of certain aspects of this spirit—or of certain "foreign" spirits that threaten the established narrative. Michelet was only one among many historians of France who essentially ignored events in the Caribbean when he wrote about the birth of the French Republic. As Yves Benot has noted, Michelet described the Saint Domingue revolt in 1791 as "the worst war of savages that has ever been seen"—and then never mentioned it, or the abolition of slavery of 1794 it brought about, again (Benot 1989:205–16). The intertwined French and Haitian Revolutions were separated from one another and remembered in very different ways throughout the last centuries, in a context in which one power remained an imperial center, while the other was first isolated and then incorporated into the world economy on terms dictated from outside. Haiti's revolution was consistently delegitimized through the processes of history making and history writing by which France imagined its major colonial defeat and sought to limit the possibilities of independent Haiti. In this France would be joined by the United States, which reacted with fear to the birth of the black Republic.

In early-nineteenth-century France, the defeat of the Leclerc expedition and the desire of many exiled planters to see their own return to Saint Domingue gave rise to a massive production of writings on the causes and possible redress of Haitian independence. The argument of a majority of these writings was that the independence of Haiti was an illegitimate political event and that France should mobilize to take back its former colony.

The roots of the historiography of the Haitian Revolution lay in this literature about Saint Domingue, which set the stage for France's "recognition"
of Haiti's independence in an 1825 treaty that was a masterpiece of early
neocolonial policy. The Haitian government agreed to pay a huge indemnity
to the planters who had lost their property during the Haitian Revolution,
and so Haiti was made to "pay" for its revolution, tracing a prophetic and
precocious path in the reversal of history still called "Third World debt."
The history of Haiti was written in certain terms that justified and deepened
the country's political and economic isolation.

Although during the early nineteenth century there were some connections between independent Haiti and Britain, and especially British abolitionists, there was ultimately little support given to the new regime, even after the dismantling of slavery was initiated in the British colonies during the
1830s. In the midst of the crossroads between a process of emancipation
propelled in part by the development of liberal economic ideology (see Holt
1992) and the beginnings of the colonization in Africa, Haiti gained meaning as a testing ground both for the success of large-scale, immediate emancipation and for the capacities of individuals of the "African" race who, after
being exposed to slavery, were freed from the guiding influence of whites.

During the first half of the nineteenth century, a Haitian historiography
was launched by figures such as Thomas Madiou and Beaubrun Ardouin,
who faced (as Haitian writers continue to face) a situation of archival inequality in which many of the existing source materials on the Haitian Revolution are in French archives.[4] Although in some cases this work influenced
foreign writers on Haiti, it did not temper the popular representations of the
"State of Hayti," which increasingly turned to "Voodoo" as proof of the
primitiveness of Haiti.[5] In 1860, Gustave Allaux began a work on Haiti in
this way: "I am to talk of a country that has newspapers and sorcerers, a third
estate and fetishes, where worshippers of snakes have declared democratic
constitutions 'in the presence of the Supreme Being' and monarchs 'by the
grace of God' one after another for the past fifty years." Allaux told the story
of the Haitian Revolution as it emerged from the depths of "hills that hid er-
rant Africa," arguing that for "blacks transported from Africa, who had never
read the *Social Contract*," liberty was what had preceded slavery: "The right
to live as they had in Africa, to be killed by cow tails, white chickens and
black cats, to carry chiefs in feather headdresses who have the right over life
and death" (Allaux 1860:1:18–21).

Under a veneer of the forms of Western democracy, Allaux suggested, the heart of Haiti was nothing more than barbarous Africa. His text highlighted the impossibility for a European audience of imagining that the actions of African slaves during the Haitian Revolution had in fact been a crucial part of the development of the very language of universal rights with which Allaux disparaged Haiti. For it was the action of these slaves that had forced the Republican France of the French Revolution to overcome the glaring contradictions of its continued acceptance of slavery, so setting the foundation for the elimination of the slave trade and the abolition of slavery in the French Antilles in 1848, both events that allowed Allaux to stand on his moral high ground as an enlightened "Westerner."[6]

The specter of cannibalism and human sacrifice was invoked by a variety of authors writing about Haiti in the next decades (Hurbon 1988:93–98; Dayan 1995:10–13). This characterization helped justify the American occupation of Haiti from 1915 to 1934, which in turn created a new set of literature that associated "Voodoo" and Haiti with barbarism and despotism. The U.S. Marines campaigned against the *cacos*, who resisted the occupation, using descriptions of "'satanic' rites of 'Voodoo'" to justify the violence of the repression against them (Dayan 1988:305). U.S. doctors posted in Haiti associated "Voodoo" with sickness, asserting that "modern" knowledge would take the place of the backward religion.[7] The Gendarme d'Haïti, administrated by U.S. Marines, set up surveillance of those suspected of practicing Vodou and condemned those they caught to hard labor. Religious objects were burnt. One of those in charge of this process was Faustin Wirkus, a U.S. marine who authored a popular book that described the Haitians' "brute throwback to jungle ancestry." Another popular author who was also a U.S. marine, John Craig, concluded that "these people had never heard of democracy and couldn't have comprehended it had they heard. They had been ruled by despots, and despotism was the only government they could understand" (Dash 1997:27–28).

Yet those who fought the U.S. Marines remembered and referred to a national history that included the democratic possibilities of the Haitian Revolution. When, after the death of Charlemagne Péralte, a group of cacos gathered in 1919 to appoint Benoit Batraville their "Chief of the Revolution against the Americans on Haitian soil," they did so under a title that read "Liberty or Death; the Republic of Haiti" and followed the declaration of the soldiers with three pages of signatures. The cacos deployed the national slogans of their occupied country, slogans rooted in the Haitian Revolution, speaking of their struggle against the U.S. Marines as another revolution. One of them also deployed the memory of the past in another way. When they captured Benoit Batraville in 1920, the U.S. Marines also captured his papers, which wound their way to the National Archives in Washington, D.C. Among them is a sheet entitled "Oraison," which contains a prayer addressed to *Saint Jean* (Saint John the Baptist). It seems to refer to "father Toussaint" and to "Africa" in a plea that repeats the word "help." In addition to the writing, there are two crosses and one symbol in the shape of an *E*. Whom was the prayer addressed to? It could well have been a Catholic prayer, a text meant to be read for intercession from Saint Jean. In Vodou there is also a lwa named *Sen Jean Batiste*, who is often figured through the images and name of Saint John the Baptist. Is it too tempting to believe that the *oraison* was a call by Batraville or one of his comrades to a lwa who had helped Toussaint-Louverture fight against the French and who could help in the battle against the U.S. Marines? In the practice of Vodou, an oraison is often more than words written with the intention of being spoken or read. These words, once inscribed on a page, can be folded to enclose herbs and make a sacred object that can protect the person who wears it. The oraison stored in the National Archives was folded into six pieces; it got wet on the edges, and today it is falling apart. If it was a sacred object whose meaning resided not only in the words it carried but in its other elements and in its placement with a certain person, what is left of the oraison? Does the archive contain its "magic"? The archive has categorized it as a written text, unfolded it, and numbered it. I paid ten cents and made a copy of it, which I have carried with me and shown to people in the hopes that someone will be able to explain what it means. The original oraison lies unspoken, unfolded, and mute in the archives.[8]

The Republic's Magic

You have to know how to serve the spirits. Just like a country has a constitution, they have law. Civilized countries, serious countries have the law—you respect the constitution, you respect the law. This is the way I see the spirit.
—GEORGES RENÉ AND MARILYN HOULBERG, "My Double
Mystic Marriage to Two Goddesses of Love," 1995

Visiting Paris from Guadeloupe in 1997, a friend of mine joked: "What military dictatorship has come into power here?" In the metro stations and train stations, groups of soldiers armed with machine guns, accompanied by police, were stopping people—always selectively—and asking for papers. In "Europe without borders," the borders were multiplying. As the more solid border posts and checkpoints were abandoned, such new forms of policing—condensed in the roving CRS (State Security Police) buses that regularly set up roadblocks in Paris—were becoming more entrenched. The borders, once circumscribed, were now everywhere, and each outing could become an excursion into a border zone. Inside the national territory of France, a thousand shifting borders were present, invisible to many, inescapable for those who "looked" foreign. In a demonstration in Paris during the winter of 1997, a group carried a black, white, and gray version of the French flag, mourning a Republic that needed reminders of its democratic possibilities.

Jacques Derrida has suggested that in the crisis of the late twentieth century, "it would be necessary to learn spirits . . . to learn to live with ghosts, in the upkeep, the conversation, or the companionship, or the commerce without commerce of ghosts." Derrida turns to a dialogue with the spirit(s) of Marx, an outsider who, he suggests, "has not yet been received." "Marx remains an immigrant chez nous, a glorious, sacred, accursed but still a clandestine immigrant as he was all his life," writes Derrida. "One should not rush to make of the clandestine immigrant an illegal alien or, what always risks coming down to the same thing, to domesticate him . . . to assimilate him so as to stop frightening himself (making oneself fear) with him. He is not part of the family, but one should not send him back, him too, to the border." Through Marx, Derrida imagines the possibilities of a "New International," a new kind of international law whose content could exceed the limits of contemporary international institutions, which are weakened by the fact that "their norms, their charter, and the definition of their mission depend on a certain historical culture" and "cannot be dissociated from certain European philosophical concepts, and notably from a concept of State or national sovereignty whose genealogical closure is more and more evident." The "New International," suggests Derrida, would be "a link of affinity, suffering, and hope," one "without status, without title," that would be "a kind of counter-conjuration" (Derrida 1994:xviii–xix, 174, 85–86).

As I have already suggested, other forgotten spirits haunt the history of the political culture that is in crisis at the end of the twentieth century—spirits complicating the idea of international law that is only the product, as Derrida suggests, of "European philosophical constructs." In fact, the development of the idea of universal rights fundamentally depended on a transcultural process that took place in the plantation societies of the Caribbean at the end of the eighteenth century (Dubois 1998a). As Derrida examines the continuing ways a Marx proclaimed dead haunts the present, I therefore turn to another kind of productive haunting—the dialogue with the spirits of Vodou taking place today in the temples dotting the *banlieue* (suburbs) of Paris. These spirits, forged out of slavery and revolution in the Caribbean, carry the marks of the Republic's silenced history and—through the practice of one *oungan* (priest) named Erol Josué—possibilities for a different vision of the Republic's future.[9] In one of his songs, Josué describes his departure into exile: "I left Port-au-Prince, I arrived in Paris, with all my *divisions* behind me." The word *divisions* is the military term and refers to all the lwa (gods) and all the culture of Vodou that he brought with him. Josué mobilizes these divisions in calling for, and creating, a different vision of the possibilities of the Republic at the end of the twentieth century. He has intertwined his work as an oungan with his work as an activist in the *sans-papiers* movement, which in recent years has brought together undocumented immigrants from a variety of countries in a successful struggle for the granting of residency papers and the reform of immigration laws.

For Josué, Vodou and politics have always gone together. He grew up in Port-au-Prince in a family that practiced Vodou, with a temple attached to his house. After the fall of Duvalier, a wave of attacks against Vodou temples and oungans began as part of the larger campaign of *dechoukaj* (uprooting) taken up against all those who were associated with Duvalier; with the encouragement of Protestant missionaries, these attacks grew into a generalized campaign against Vodou. Josué was sixteen at the time, and he became involved in groups formed to defend the religion, meeting other activists and speaking out on the radio as part of a broad movement in defense of Vodou. It was this involvement that led him to his initiation as an oungan. Josué therefore has a complex relationship with the past of the Duvalier regime and to what has followed it in Haiti.

The dictatorial regime used the network of Vodou priests, as it used other networks of power in Haitian society such as the Catholic Church, to spread its influence and suppress its political opponents. Duvalier allowed rumors that he himself was an oungan to flourish in order to strengthen his political position, and in so doing he strengthened the position of the Vodou religion in Haitian society. The link between Duvalier and Vodou enabled Catholic and Protestant institutions (which themselves were also implicated with Duvalier) to encourage the violent anti-Vodou campaigns of the dechoukaj, and, in its wake, the stigmatization of the religion. The stigmatization operates in part through a fixation on practices of individually oriented "sorcery," which, though often shunned by many practitioners, gained increasing saliency in the tough years of suffering, surveillance, and suspicion created by the dictatorship. In present-day Haiti, the unallayed cycle of poverty and political violence continues to eat away at the rural foundations of Vodou and propel the proliferation of forms of individual "magic" interlinked with the practice of Vodou. At the same time, practicants of the religion who were first mobilized to resist the dechoukaj continue to argue that the fundamental tenets of Vodou as an ancestral, community religion must be part of the Haitian society of the future.[10]

A few years after being initiated as an oungan in Haiti, Josué left for Paris, where he worked as an artist and public spokesman for Vodou. Although he does not have a *houmfou* (temple) in Paris, he has a few initiates and conducts ceremonies in the houmfou built by one of them in a basement in Bobigny or else in his apartment in another banlieue. Organizing ceremonies is not always easy in Paris. Spaces of worship are difficult to construct and are usually placed in basements to avoid noise complaints from neighbors; carrying out animal sacrifices is sometimes difficult, and often money is sent to Haiti so a sacrifice can be conducted there or one is promised and then fulfilled on a journey to Haiti. Drummers who know the ceremonial rhythms are rare in Paris, and clapping or recordings often replace drums. For Josué, though, these adaptations are not important, as long as the practice of the religion and the service to the lwa continues. He keeps an altar in his closet, supplying the lwa Erzulie with French perfumes; he has found new paths through which to serve the lwa, in the form of a statue of a black virgin enthroned in a church in Switzerland, whose picture he keeps on his altar to Erzulie. Since he first saw the picture, he has discovered that other Vodou worshipers in Europe have also begun using the photograph as an intercessory for Erzulie. Through Ogou, Erzulie, Azaka, Aizan, and other lwa, Josué brings the history of Haiti to dialogue with the *sèvitè* (worshippers) of the lwa in Paris.

To Josué, the Bois-Caïman ceremony was a foundational moment both for the nation of Haiti and the practice of Vodou. He uses the story of the ceremony to describe the historical process through which the multiplicity of practices and languages among the slaves were brought together in the interest of solidarity against slavery. "Haitian Vodou, and the solidarity of Haitians, was born in August 1791, at the Bois-Caïman ceremony," he says.

> On that day, the slaves began to realize that they all were part of the same cause, that they had to fight together. It was both a religious and a political ceremony. From there, a language was born, Creole, and a religion was born, Vodou, and, eventually, a nation was born, Haiti. All the slaves had come from different tribes, and these different tribes all had their different practices; but starting with the Bois-Caïman ceremony they mixed their cultures to create a force we call Haitian Vodou, the assembly of the *lwa*. The slaves merged together to create Haiti.

Josué associates the three elements of religion, language, and political solidarity to narrate Haiti's past in a way that provides a history for his own practice as an oungan. I asked him of the controversy provoked by Hoffman's paper on the Bois-Caïman ceremony; he had followed the controversy and had hosted a radio program about the paper when he was still in Haiti.

> He can say what he thinks, what he wants to think. But it's too bad, I think, to tarnish the political and historical image of a country that has finally found its liberty, after so much struggle, so much misery, so much slavery. Now, 200 years later, a historian comes to shatter the image of Haiti. It's too bad. But you can't do anything about it because it's not written. If it's written it is they who write it down—the historians, always the historians. But the evidence is there because in the songs of Vodou, in the history of Haiti, the evidence is there. The evidence is there, it is alive and it is not we who have created all this. We inherited this power from the ancestors; there had to be a ceremony to bring together the slaves, to create a culture, a religion, to the work of religion and political consolidation. Of course there was re-

sistance before that, it prepared the ceremony, and afterward there were many other events. . . . But I refer particularly to the Bois-Caïman ceremony because, as an *oungan*, it has a great deal of importance for me, because it is there that the religion I have inherited was born. But also because I am Haitian and I believe in the Bois-Caïman ceremony, and every day of my life I live the Bois-Caïman ceremony, and in every one of my ceremonies I live the Bois-Caïman ceremony.

For Josué the ceremony becomes a way of speaking of the historical processes through which Vodou was formed, processes in which the political and the religious were deeply linked. The interconnections between the rituals of Vodou and the rituals of national belonging were evoked by Josué in his description of the *chiré Aizan*, which is a fundamental part of many ceremonies. He spoke of

Aizan, who is the *lwa* of virtue and is important in initiations, whose symbol is a palm tree, which is also in the Haitian flag. And in the Haitian flag there is a little bonnet on top of the palm, and we call this the bonnet of Aizan. You see, once again it's the history of *Haiti* that comes back. Aizan is a lwa of virtue, but also of liberty, and when in a ceremony all the people tear the palms of Aizan and distribute them, they are sharing liberty, tearing liberty and sharing it, giving liberty. . . . It's every day, it's open, it's an open book. Every day you see the flag, every day you see Aizan, every day there is a *chiré Aizan*, liberty is there.

The red and blue of the flag's colors also evoke the lwa Ogou and Erzulie, "the marriage of the woman and the man, who are the poles of Haitian culture." "The lwa are the mirror of society," says Josué. "The history of Haiti resides in them." Vodou songs "tell the story of the lwa, and they tell the story of society at the same time." Histories of slavery and of revolution are carried in songs sung to the lwa during ceremonies, some of which invoke revolutionary leaders such as Boukman, Toussaint-Louverture, and Jean-Jacques Dessalines. The history of the struggle for independence is made particularly present through the warrior lwa Ogou, who, in his many forms, embodies the complex and gendered ambivalence that military figures hold in the Haitian context, both as defenders and as enemies of the people, as ancestors of independence and contemporary destroyers of freedom (Brown 1989; Cosentino 1995).

The lwa of the Petwo nation, which, unlike the other nations of Vodou, whose names refer to African origins, was born in the Caribbean itself, are particularly marked by the memory of the violence of New World colonization and the violence that was used against it. In her 1953 work *Divine Horsemen*, Maya Deren wrote of the Petwo rites:

> It is the crack of the slave-whip sounding constantly, a never-to-be-forgotten ghost. . . . It is the raging revolt of the slaves against the Napoleonic forces. And it is the delirium of triumph. For it was the Petro cult, born in the hills, nurtured in secret, which gave both the moral force and the actual organization to the escaped slaves. . . . Even today the songs of revolt, of "Vive la liberté" occur in Petro ritual as a dominant theme. (62)[11]

History is present in Vodou rituals in multiple and complicated ways. If, for an observer such as Deren (or myself), the shock of the whip hitting the dirt floor during a Petwo ceremony powerfully brings the brutal past of slavery into the present, such a connection is not necessarily articulated by those who practice the religion. Josué told me that the whip may of course carry that connotation but that in his mind it is a part of the ritual, a way of opening the way for the lwa, of calling them to the ceremony. The whip is multivalent in its meanings, its resounding crack speaking both of oppression and resistance as it calls the spirits down.

The historical memory present in Vodou is perhaps most powerfully evoked through possession by the lwa. The act of possession—by an Ogou merged with the revolutionary hero Dessalines, by an ancestor spirit returning to the land—literalizes the powerful invocation of history as present. It is not only an evocation of past events but a literal making a present of this past, which always returns reshaped. For when the lwa possess a person, they come to dance, to chide, and to speak with the living. They may give advice, tell stories, criticize the ceremony, or interrogate someone about his or her behavior. They may demand a spiritual marriage with one of those present or may simply bless that person with a mist of rum. The major lwa have many manifestations: Ogou can be dangerous, but he can also be a calming and positive presence as he touches chins with the base of his sword or delivers someone a military salute, which is promptly returned. Erzulie, too, has many faces, as Erzulie Freda, a white coquettish figure who speaks French and demands perfume or as the black Erzulie Dantor, who is voiceless but speaks through her dancing and demands that worshipers approach by holding a knife to her chest. These lwa not only bring lessons from the past in what they say; they also embody through the form of their presence the history out of which they emerged. As Joan Dayan suggests, the lwa of Vodou tell a history of the intimate contradictions of slavery. She writes:

> If the colonizer exercised privilege by distorting or annihilating the African past, Vodou—the religion that kept alive the lives and deaths of the ancestors—re-imagined a unique relation to a brutal institution. Gods were born in the memories of those who served, and they not only took on the traits or dispositions of their servitors, but those attitudes and languages of the masters and the mistresses from long ago, tough revenants carried in the memories of the descendants of slaves. (Dayan 1994:10–11)

The lwa therefore carry stories that are often silenced in the official histories of the revolution, the stories of women who participated in the insurrection of 1791—embodied in the *manbo*, who, possessed by Erzulie, sacrificed the black pig at the Bois-Caïman ceremony—and their broader experience of oppression both within slavery and after emancipation. Through lwa such as Erzulie, a different history of the revolution emerges. As Dayan writes: "These rituals of memory could be seen as deposits of history. Shreds of bodies come back, remembered in ritual, and seeking vengeance" (Dayan 1995:35–36). Although the stories of revolution—notably the Bois-Caïman ceremony—have been appropriated by dictatorial regimes such as that of Duvalier, Vodou has also provided a space in which unfulfilled promises of the revolution can be invoked in a way that speaks out against the established order. The lwa also carry the hidden and unfulfilled possibilities of a revolution that asserted the equality of blacks and whites as it brought together multiple "nations" of African gods in a structure that allowed for their difference and continued transformation even as it united them in a struggle for liberty.

Born out of what must be understood as a deeply *modern* context—the factorylike plantation society of Saint Domingue, and the political revolution that emerged from it—Vodou provides a means of rereading the history of modernity not only through the memory carried in songs but also through possession, the poetry of dance, and the commentary made through the manipulation and placement of objects such as the Haitian flag, the palm, the machete, and the elements that form altars.[12] According to Josué, the lessons they bring from the past have a great deal to contribute to France's future. Today, he greets a growing number of French Antilleans as well as metropolitan French. "I hope in the future that more foreigners will come to our ceremonies. I am for this idea of having people from other nations, from other horizons, joining us in our practice." Many of these, driven by the stereotypes of the religion, first seek what they see as "black magic" to strike against enemies or ex-lovers, and Josué turns them away disappointed when he explains that the practice of Vodou is about transforming oneself, rather than attacking others. He takes on, however, the challenge of changing their vision of the religion, dispelling the myths they bring to it, and showing them what he sees as its true possibilities as a spiritual path. "They need to come to Vodou to truly understand our philosophy, and adapt themselves to our culture."

This is, for Josué, the starting point for a broader dialogue through which Vodou can contribute to the resolution of the conflicts and problems facing France at the end of the century. "We have a democratic culture, one that has no color," Josué told me. As he greets women and men from a variety of backgrounds and teaches them to serve and dialogue with the lwa, he crafts a practice of Vodou that seeks to effect a broader change in today's France. Openness, respect for women's autonomy, and tolerance and adaptation, he suggests, are fundamental tenets of Vodou, and it is therefore a religion that can greet those seekers who feel themselves abandoned in France itself. "The first lesson Vodou teaches is communal living. The *savoir-vivre* of Vodou is one that can be adapted to any people, and if the lesson is well learnt it can teach people to help each other not just materially but in the truer sense of the term." The teachings of Vodou and of the system of the *lakou* (family compound), in which each person helps the other, can help France confront the rising fascism and racism in the country as it shows people how to live in a community, because they instruct "how to accept one's neighbor, one's compatriot, a foreigner." "This is what we need," he told me, "to smash this fascism in France, to make people understand they are all united, on one planet, that we may be of different colors but blood has only one color."

Vodou crosses borders and boundaries, travels from the countryside of Haiti to the streets of Brooklyn and Paris, and carries with it the marks of the history it helped forge. It is a transnational and transcultural religion, one that provides another imagining of the Republic whose meaning is today in crisis. For in a sense Vodou is a Republic, a religion born out of enslavement and revolution against it, a religion that unites different nations of African and New World deities within a set of shifting but solid *règlements*. Within the variety of nations of lwa represented in the Vodou pantheon—who are brought together as they are worshipped in ceremonies, even as their particular separate histories are respected and reiterated by their classification— lies a history of enslavement and exile from Africa transformed into a new religion. It is a religion that both forged and was forged by one of the most important democratic revolutions of modernity, and it carries a necessary haunting to a forgetful Republic. Can it be heard?

History's Promise

In July of 1802, as the Leclerc expedition consolidated its strength in Saint Domingue, an ex-slave sent a letter to her ex-master to remind him of a promise he had made. "My name is Minny, daughter of Blanche," she wrote, "and my father, whom I never knew, was your esteemed manager M. Masson." Her full name was Marie-Rose Masson, and until 1793, she had been the property of the Marquis de Gallifet, who had agreed to free both her and her mother. She had paid for her freedom, but since the insurrection of 1791, Pierre Mossut, the employee who had written Gallifet with the bad news and who had taken over his affairs in Saint Domingue, had been "exercising an authority contrary to your justice" over her. The imminent reestablishment of slavery, she wrote to Gallifet, meant that "the arms among your property that still exist will, voluntarily or by force, have to return to their useful work." But Marie-Rose had a right to the freedom she had paid for, and she asked Gallifet to make good on his promise. She included an address in her letter, the address of a merchant in Le Cap, who would deliver Gallifet's response to her (AN, 107 AP 128, Marie Rose Masson to Gallifet, 8 Thermidor An 10 [July 27, 1802]).

In the end, Marie-Rose's freedom came not from the actions of her Parisian ex-owner but from those of her future co-citizens. After independence, Gallifet's plantations became the terrain for new struggles over land

and labor, as did those of his neighbor Millot, who had first written with the news of insurrection over a decade before. In the early decades of the nineteenth century, it was there that the Roi Christophe built his Sans Souci palace, with its multiple references to European architecture and defeated enemies (Trouillot 1995). Marie-Rose's letters give us a glimpse of a history that never happened. Yet on some level the reestablishment she feared *did* happen, as old forms of historical understanding overtook the new reality represented by Haiti's birth.

Over a century later, the Martinican Aimé Césaire railed against the continuing limitations imposed on the histories of slavery and resistance by institutionalized forms of narrative. In "The Verb 'Marroner,'" a poem dedicated to the Haitian poet René Depestre, he spoke from "a Seine night" where "as if in drunkenness I recall/the insane song of Boukman delivering your country with the forceps of the storm." New words, he suggested, were needed to speak this history; poems must not be "a mill for grinding sugar," and so he invited Depestre to "laugh[,] drink and escape like slaves" with him. "I too remember," he wrote, evoking the memories of the Haitian Revolution he carried with him, memories he insisted on even if they could never be verified as fact: "as a matter of fact *did* Dessalines prance about at Vertières?" Césaire argued that the restrictive forms through which these stories had to be told undermined the very possibilities of revolution; "the form taking its revenge/chokes the poems like the accursed fig tree." Commenting on the poem, James Clifford notes that "we still need a verb 'marroner,'" suggesting that the forms at our disposal continue to reinforce our forgetting and shroud necessary pasts. Césaire's lament still speaks from the banks of the Seine: "and the forms which linger/humming in our ears/are, eating the new which sprouts/eating the shoots" (Césaire 1983:371; Clifford 1988:181).

FIVE

Hidden Forces

Colonialism and the Politics of Magic in the Netherlands Indies

MARGARET J. WIENER

Looked at as a series of delusions, magic is distasteful to the modern mind, which, once satisfied of its practical futility, is apt to discard it as folly unworthy of further notice.

—EDWARD BURNETT TYLOR, "Magic," *The Encyclopedia Britannica*, 1883

For it must always be remembered that every single profession and claim put forward by the magician as such is false; not one of them can be maintained without deception, conscious or unconscious.

—SIR JAMES FRAZER, *The Golden Bough*, 1911

And he began to believe in a hatred that rose slowly around him out of the hostile soil, like a plague. He believed in a force hiding in the things of the Indies, in the nature of Java, in the climate of Labuwangi, in the conjuring tricks—as he continued to call it— that sometimes makes the Javanese cleverer than the European and gives him the power, a mysterious power, not to release himself from the yoke, but to cause illness, lingering illness, to pester and harass, to play the ghost most incredibly and hideously: a hidden force, a hidden power, hostile to our temperament, our blood, our bodies, our souls, our civilization, to all that seems to us the right thing to do and be and think.

—LOUIS COUPERUS, *The Hidden Force*, 1900

Magic is a tricky term, as slick and slippery as magicians themselves are said to be. In common parlance—and much anthropological theorizing—magic connotes both illusion and delusion, both the sleights of hands of profes- sional conjurers and false belief in supernatural powers. In accounts of magic, assertions about fallacy and fraud mingle with awe. In an important sense, magic is a comparative term, mired in relations of power. Like superstition (its occasional synonym), it is often used by those in some position of authority to speak of what is foreign, strange, troubling, dangerous, wrong, threatening, false. Perhaps one reason that so many anthropological studies of magic have been studies of witchcraft or sorcery is that more positive versions tend to accrue other characterizations: healing, folklore, psychology, transubstantiation.

It is the space magic occupies in the murky territory between fraud and fear in the imaginations of modern Europeans that I explore in this chapter. Although it is about magic in colonial Indonesia, I will have little to say about the practices of Indonesians. In any event, "magic" is a European category. Although there are a host of indigenous terms for the specialized knowledges (involving activities, images, words) that Europeans called magical, none of these map easily onto what Europeans meant or mean by magic. That Indonesians may now treat these terms as synonymous is due to the "work of translation" (see below) that formed such an important part of colonial rule—as well as current processes of globalization. Even recent use of a cognate, *magik*, does not indicate an identity of reference. Because the term *magik* does not suggest to Indonesian users violations of an order of nature radically different from an order of culture, it need not imply illusion and delusion (see, e.g., Koentjaraningrat 1985).

A number of colonial discourses about magic meet in fears about the "hidden forces" potentially mobilized by natives. The phrase comes from Louis Couperus's 1900 novel *The Hidden Force*.[1] In it, the family of a high-ranking colonial administrator in the Dutch East Indies—a figure Couperus repeatedly characterizes as hard working, practical, capable, manly, and eminently rational—is subjected to a series of supernatural assaults that ultimately result in his breakdown. Suturing together uncanny incidents with racial fantasies and sexual scandals, the phrase that Couperus repeats throughout the book and that is used as its title so resonated with Indies experiences and metropolitan fantasies about the mysterious East that it was instantly adopted as shorthand to refer to any sort of strange, occult, or sinister incident in the imaginative space of the Indies.

The expression *hidden force* (in Dutch, *stille kracht*) coalesced what until then had been a patchwork of disconnected tales and uneasy colonial anxieties. The most literal translation of Couperus's title would be "silent force."

As equivalents for the Dutch *stil*, dictionaries present "quiet or silent," "mute," and "hushed" but also "secret, concealed, hidden."[2] Couperus's English translator, in choosing to render *stil* as hidden, no doubt meant to evoke discussions of occult phenomena. In fact, since many of those who picked up Couperus's phrase in the Indies used it in just such discussions, it is indeed a good translation. In addition, *stil* conveys to speakers of Dutch overtones not evident from dictionary definitions, for example, of something approaching silently and out of sight. Critics frequently comment on Couperus's use of language to create the atmosphere of threat and foreboding that marks the book (Nieuwenhuys 1978:257–60).

Couperus's novel suggested both the limits of European common sense and the impossibility of ever fully knowing or dominating colonized peoples. In short, a sense of menacing hidden forces is precisely the point where, if I may borrow from another brilliant title, this one an essay by Indonesian historian Onghokham (1978), the "inscrutable" meets the "paranoid."

I begin my exploration by narrating the contents of a report written by precisely the kind of sober and conscientious civil servant who formed the dramatic focus of Couperus's novel. The report concerns the arrest of a Balinese *"wonderdokter"* (a charlatan or witch doctor) in 1921. Its author declared the event without political significance—a mark of his own success in containing that bugaboo of the Netherlands Indies regime: disorder. Regardless of its "insignificance," however, the incidents described and the report itself illustrate the most overt and palpable politics of magic in colonial Indonesia. Not only does the episode reported involve the actions of colonial administrators, obvious agents of state power, but they also engage in familiar kinds of modernizing discourses and practices, those of amelioration and social engineering. As we will see, however, the forms of power articulated through this affair go beyond explicitly governmental goals such as policing and reform.

The incidents described in this report provide an entrée into an official point of view on magic, expressed in the policies and practices of the Dutch colonial state.[3] Colonial states constituted one of many sites where hegemonic discourses about magic and modernity took shape. Their administrators shared with other European intellectuals—including missionaries and metropolitan anthropologists—the certainty that magic rested in some important way on false ideas.[4] Indeed, since twentieth-century civil servants in the Indies took degrees in Indology and ethnology, and commonly contributed to discussions of native practices in both learned and popular journals, it is hardly surprising to find congruencies between their understandings of magic and those of academics.[5] Their scholarly activities, along with the central role officials occupied in the social life of European communities in the Indies, lent a certain weight to their opinions. Thus the acts they performed as administrators implicated familiar elite positions on magic in attempts to transform and discipline subject peoples. Their reports reflect not only faith in the Enlightenment project but in their own right and ability to impose a particular understanding of reality and knowledge on those they governed.

European responses to magic in the Indies, however, were fractured. For one, the self-confident distinctions authorities attempted to draw between rational European and irrational native appear, upon closer examination, to involve considerable sleight of hand. Moreover, the cultural understandings and practices produced through patterns of everyday life in the Indies, revealed in part through narratives that attempted to discipline them, bear witness to the instability of colonial positions on magic and provide interesting subversions of the administrative voice. Indeed, as Couperus's novel shows, colonial officials could become objects, as well as producers, of discourses about magic.

In thinking about magic in the Netherlands East Indies, I am inspired by Bruno Latour's call for a "symmetrical anthropology," which would deploy the same kinds of arguments and explanations to speak about both science and magic, both Europeans and Indonesians (Latour 1987, 1988, 1993, 1997). More specifically, however, Latour's argument for why "we have never been modern" (1993) provides a stimulating framework for teasing out the logic of colonial discourses about magic and for revealing some of the problems with modern European beliefs about belief. In analyzing discourses about magic in colonial Indonesia, I borrow several of his concepts to explore the processes through which Europeans constructed modernity and magic in relation to one another in the intercultural encounters of late colonialism.

Disciplining the Sorcerer (If Not His Magic . . .)

In May 1921, Resident Henri T. Damsté, whose post entailed overseeing the governance of the islands of Bali and Lombok, received a frantic telegram from G.J. Kuys, a relatively inexperienced subordinate charged with administering Jembrana, a region in northwest Bali.[6] According to Kuys, a "fanatic" named Nang Mukanis was disrupting peace and order by representing himself as a healing balian and extorting divine veneration from the population.[7] Kuys recommended that Nang Mukanis be arrested and placed in seclusion, and, to accomplish this, he requested an armed brigade. Damsté sent two and headed to Jembrana himself.

On Damsté's arrival, Kuys filled him in. Kuys had first learned of Nang Mukanis from an anonymous letter. Its writer informed him that since Nang Mukanis had set himself up as a balian in a remote village a mere two weeks before, people from all over Jembrana had been streaming to his home with offerings.[8] Because he had heard nothing of any disturbances from the Balinese district head or other Balinese authorities where Nang Mukanis lived, Kuys initially paid little attention to this news, though he passed on the letter to the district head for comment. The latter's response, however, aroused his interest. Adamantly rejecting the letter writer's charge that he and other Balinese authorities in the district believed in Nang Mukanis's "miraculous power," the district head assured Kuys that there was no cause for concern. But he was clearly disturbed that Nang Mukanis had come to Kuys's attention. Kuys decided to look into the situation, and, dismissing the district head's protests that it was an uncomfortable and difficult journey, insisted on being taken to Nang Mukanis's compound.

There he found hundreds of Balinese, among them, to his disgust, the chief of police and the wife of not only the district head but of a member of the judicial council. Signs of ritual activity abounded: colored cloth draped all the pavilions, and incense burned everywhere before piles of offerings that Kuys calculated as worth hundreds of guilders; there was even a decorated sedan chair. Nang Mukanis himself, clad in the white clothing worn by Balinese who traffic with divinities and spirits, was just then making a circuit around the yard, singing an invocation to the gods, while followers held a parasol over his head to mark the presence of divinity. At Kuys's unexpected appearance, everything stopped. After staring at the interloper ("with eyes full of hate"), Nang Mukanis snapped the parasol shut and walked off. Sitting down, Kuys asked those assembled why Nang Mukanis had become so wildly popular but found their answers—which referred to successful cures—unhelpful. After a look around to confirm claims made by his anonymous informant, Kuys waited in vain for Nang Mukanis to return. He then consulted the Balinese officials, who professed that they could not understand why hundreds of people visited Nang Mukanis daily and claimed they had thought the matter too inconsequential to mention.

As Kuys later informed Damsté, the situation did not appear critical. Once people "noticed that offerings and homage are brought in vain," the mania would surely pass. In the meantime, he asked to be kept posted. An incident a few days later, however, changed his mind.

By chance in Nang Mukanis's district on a tour of inspection of new roads, Kuys encountered Nang Mukanis dancing with an upraised dagger at the head of a large procession. Kuys immediately dismounted and took several strides toward the balian, who turned in his direction, dagger raised, and (said Kuys) seemed to make defiant movements with his head. At this several girls fell to the ground shrieking, apparently possessed. As Nang Mukanis headed straight for him, the alarmed Kuys, who was unarmed, looked around for the district head, who rushed up and grabbed the raised fist containing the dagger. The district head, aided by the police chief, a constable, and some of Nang Mukanis's followers, led Nang Mukanis into a nearby compound and dispersed the crowd. Kuys noted with displeasure, however, that they had made no effort to disarm Nang Mukanis and seemed to entreat rather than order him.

Judging that things had gone too far, after concluding his inspection Kuys ordered Nang Mukanis's arrest. But that evening the district head and police chief reported that they had been unable to carry out his orders. When they had tried to take Nang Mukanis into custody, Damsté wrote,

> [he] invoked a demon, and immediately everyone [once again hundreds of people were crowded inside his compound] was as possessed! Many fell shrieking loudly on the ground, and others conducted themselves as if insane. And they themselves and the police agents—whose eyes already rolled and were bulging out of their heads!—had ducked out of the dangers threatening them by 'hastily withdrawing'! And they lacked the nerve to repeat the attempt!

It was then that Kuys had telegraphed Resident Damsté. Backed by armed brigades, however, Kuys felt he could return to his previous policy and wait for the affair to run its course. Damsté disagreed. Nang Mukanis must be arrested. To insure no further mishaps, he charged the police to round up Nang Mukanis before dawn, when he more likely would be home alone, and ordered that the local authorities not be informed in advance. After instructing the brigades to avoid bloodshed, Damsté added that should they not find Nang Mukanis, they were "to impound or destroy all of the concrete signs of his holiness." Although they apprehended Nang Mukanis without mishap, they executed this portion of his orders as well. Damsté reports:

> And what under those circumstances was not necessary, but all the same perhaps also not bad, the decorations in Nang Moekanis's dwelling, his white garments, and the elegant, now dismantled sedan-chair—that had been a gift of homage from the district head!—were chucked all in a heap in the yard and burned, without this [act] of the police being retaliated by gods or demons.

This act of iconoclasm was followed by another later that same day when the Resident assembled the Balinese authorities in the district capital for a dressing down. Berating them for failing to protect their people against "stupid tricks," he held up to ridicule their own credulity as well as their failure to inform Kuys about the commotion being caused by Nang Mukanis, a "mentally impaired commoner." (Because the Balinese officials were all members of priestly or aristocratic families, this reference to rank was meant to shame them further.)

From Resident Damsté's point of view, there was much cause for satisfaction with the outcome of events. After his harangue, the Balinese administrators appeared to be ashamed of themselves and, as he put it, appropriately "disenchanted." Nonetheless, he thought the whole affair spoke to the gullibility not only of ordinary Balinese but even of those with education and position. He noted with disgust that a member of the judicial council, scion of a priestly household who had had, moreover, the benefit of attending a Dutch school, had even removed the gold from his teeth on Nang Mukanis's orders and had had to go to Java to repair the damage.

Magic and Colonial Order

Damsté's report is a narrative of triumph: written in the "prose of counter-insurgency" (Guha 1988), it presents disorder successfully contained.[9] His apparently modest assertion in the conclusion of the report, that these were "not important events," underlines his own effective management of them. So does his observation that although the "seeds" were there for the crisis to escalate, and the Balinese "soil" receptive, no more "weeds" of this kind were likely to grow, at least not in Jembrana.

But if the whole matter were really so unimportant, why all the excess? True, no blood was shed—and here Damsté probably handled the affair better than some of his colleagues might have; elsewhere in the Indies, on no greater provocation, people had died. Nonetheless, a good deal of violence is evident in the report, ranging from Damsté's tone of voice (unremittingly sarcastic when it comes to Nang Mukanis and the Balinese officials) to his orders to seize and destroy Nang Mukanis's possessions, not to mention the arrest itself.

And what, after all, was the threat? Although a similar tone of ridicule and disdain informed other administrators' narratives about native healers (particularly those healers whose practice did not involve herbal remedies and therefore rested entirely on "magic"), they generally left such figures alone—as some of them lamented (Jasper 1932).

Perhaps another way to pose the question is to ask under what circumstances magic became the target of official action or what kinds of magic provoked a forceful response. For only some of the phenomena that Europeans regarded as magic became objects of surveillance. In contrast to colonial governments in Africa, for instance, Dutch authorities never passed laws punishing their subjects for accusing one another of witchcraft. Nor, despite arguments that the colonial state's indifference to sorcery encouraged criminality (Hitzka 1930; Lesquillier 1934), did they ever prohibit or even pay much attention to its practice. This sort of magic rarely engaged the fundamental concerns of the Netherlands Indies state.[10]

To see what did, it is instructive to look at the colonial penal code, newly instituted just three years before Nang Mukanis's arrest. Overriding the recourse to "customary law" that otherwise prevailed in matters concerning natives, the penal code targeted certain magical practices as disorderly. More precisely, state authorities isolated the circulation of certain objects or knowledges associated with supernatural power as potentially subversive. Specifically, it was against the law to teach any arts or *elmu* (knowledges) that might lead people to think that they could commit a crime without risk or to sell or otherwise make available amulets purported to have supernatural power.[11]

The anonymous author of an article published in the *Netherlands Indies Police Guide* in the same year as Nang Mukanis's arrest explained in some detail why amulets "deserve the utmost interest and vigilance on the side of the Police" (S. 1921:33). In general, he observed, the possession of amulets— and, he noted ominously, every native (at least on Java and Madura) had at least one—and "the blind faith of the population" often instigated criminal acts.[12] Spells and amulets that led people to think themselves invulnerable and supported by invisible powers were, however, especially problematic. Indeed, such amulets led inexorably to rebellion, for a conviction of their own immunity encouraged those who otherwise would avoid an armed confrontation to engage in seditious acts. Thus, "In case of *insurrection* against the Netherlands Authority, e.g., we can be assured *that the participants in the revolt without exception are provided with jimats* [amulets], while from the subsequent inquiry it continually appears *that education in the practice of elmus preceded the breaking out of the disturbances*" (S. 1921:33; emphasis in original).

This was no isolated opinion. Commentators on colonial policy frequently voiced such views, though some laid more stress on the dangerously charismatic figures who distributed amulets rather than on the objects themselves.[13] And authorities acted on such views. Two years before Nang Mukanis's arrest, an incident in Garut, West Java, resulted in the death of a haji and a number of his followers and family members and the wounding of several others. Newspapers suggested that the Javanese victims hadn't responded to warning shots because they believed their amulets prevented the bullets from striking them; during the investigation that followed, the police arrested parties suspected of supplying those amulets.[14]

But apart from the dangers of subversion, the article argues that the penal code had another equally critical purpose, namely, "to protect the credulous, ignorant population against *fraud* committed by . . . individuals whose only goal is to part the economically still far from financially sound population from its money" (S. 1921:33). This too is a common theme in official discussions of magic.

Peace and order were not the only goals of administration; equally significant was the paternalistic protection of an ignorant and poverty-stricken population. This was still the era of the Ethical Policy, adopted at the turn of the century, shortly after Damsté entered the colonial civil service. Its stated purpose was to pay back the people of the Indies for the wealth extracted from them by improving their welfare.[15] Particular emphasis was placed on education (at least of a minimal sort, and especially for the children of aristocrats) and material prosperity. It is hardly surprising in light of such concerns that some officials argued that the government should eradicate native superstitions on the grounds that they wasted both time and money that could be better spent in other ways (Habbema 1919)—or that the state would regard the prosecution of fraud as part of its mandate.

Although Damsté does not mention the penal code or explicitly address the issues of potential sedition and fraud, such considerations clearly informed Nang Mukanis's arrest. Most critical, of course, was his potential threat to peace and order. By calling Nang Mukanis a "fanatic" in his original telegram, Kuys had placed him in a familiar colonial category, likening him to other charismatic figures who had trafficked in mystical knowledge and (according to the government) either directly or indirectly instigated unrest or rebellion. Nang Mukanis's reactions to Kuys did not help.

In addition, both Kuys and Damsté mention the money that Nang Mukanis had collected. Though Kuys did not see any cash when he visited Nang Mukanis's compound (his anonymous correspondent estimated that Nang Mukanis had raked in somewhere on the order of 350 guilders in the short time he had been practicing), he took its presence for granted, given the abundance of offerings. This was a reasonable assumption, because when Balinese bring offerings on visits to healers, they include a special offering containing a donation, which the balian ordinarily keeps. Such donations, however, are entirely voluntary and usually quite small. (And the rest of the offering returns home with the client.) The two substantial chests filled with money the police found after Nang Mukanis's arrest probably testify more to his extraordinary popularity than to extortion. But then there was the sedan chair and since, in the eyes of the government, he was offering no service, *any* monetary gain would have been deemed out of order. Damsté even briefly wondered if Nang Mukanis might have been involved in a conspiracy with the family of the district head, many of whose kinsmen also were em-

ployed in the colonial civil service in Jembrana, among them the chief of police, a tax collector, and a member of the judiciary. But he regarded it as
more likely that they had been duped as well, taken in by Nang Mukanis's
fascinations.

So it is clear why Damsté berated the Balinese officials for failing to report
Nang Mukanis's growing popularity and for failing to protect people from
fraud. The remainder—his disgust at their credulity—is another matter.

As I argue below, this disgust involved more diffuse relations of power.
Damsté's assumption that what Nang Mukanis had to offer could not possibly be real made their regard for the healer problematic. It was one thing for
ordinary people to be superstitious and believe in wonderdokters; native officials, however, should have been closer to the European point of view, especially officials educated in Dutch-language schools.[16] As intermediaries
between the Balinese and the colonial state, these Balinese officials showed
themselves to be unreliably close to the wrong end of the spectrum. And
anyone who could have *this* kind of effect was dangerous indeed.

On the whole, the administration's views on magic are more complicated
and contradictory than its explicit policies and concerns might suggest. Some
hint of this appears in a number of incongruities marking Damsté's report.
Consider, for instance, the matter of efficacy. Nang Mukanis was threatening,
a danger to peace and order, precisely because he was, after all, effective, at
least in drawing crowds of Balinese. Thus he must have had some kind of real
power and real knowledge. Even if he were a fraud, deception involves skill to
carry off; indeed it is con artists' cleverness that makes them dangerous. Yet
after Nang Mukanis's arrest, Damsté dismissed him as a "mentally impaired
bungler." What had he bungled? And if he were indeed mentally impaired,
where would the threat lie? Why *not* wait for people's enthusiasm to pass?
Casting aspersion on his sanity seems to contradict the idea that he is a fraud.
But it makes perfect sense to have both attributions if magic simultaneously
evokes for Europeans both illusion and delusion.

Modernity and Disenchantment

Apart from concerns about disorder or fraud, a more pervasive colonial logic
informs Damsté's treatment of Nang Mukanis. The politics of magic is deeply

enmeshed in the contradictions of the colonial project, premised as it was on absolute difference yet justified by the possibility of identity through modernizing or civilizing processes, such as education. Colonialism *required* native magic, as its foil and ground. The "irrationality" of native superstitions and practices was necessary to demonstrate the rationality of modern European institutions, in particular science (disciplined observation and reason as the road to true knowledge vs. mere belief and custom) and government (rational bureaucracy as a mode of administration and justice vs. the exploitative and despotic regimes colonialism replaced).

Indeed, there are grounds to argue that "magic" was a ghostly product of the project of modernity itself. To see how, I turn to Latour, who asserts that what we call "modern" in fact refers to two sets of practices, which have complex relations with one another. The first, by means of translations or mediations, produces mixtures and hybrids. The second, by means of purifications, creates distinctions and differences. Latour goes on to note that "without the first set, the practices of purification would be fruitless or pointless. Without the second, the work of translation would be slowed down, limited, or even ruled out. The first set corresponds to what I have called networks; the second to what I shall call the modern critical stance" (1993:10–11). Latour adds that critique hides from itself the work of translation; indeed, it is because moderns overtly or explicitly disallow hybrids that they proliferate.

Latour primarily wants to highlight the mixtures between nature and culture created by the work of translation and the distinctions between human and nonhuman produced through purification. Although undermining this nature-culture divide is Latour's main intention (and this divide is highly relevant to the politics of magic, as will be seen shortly), the practices to which he refers are of general interest. Indeed, the ideas of hybridity and purification have stimulated much recent social theory, especially in the field of colonial studies.

Both to clarify Latour's use of these terms and to draw out the implications of his claims about their interrelation, it is helpful to see how hybridization and purification articulate within colonialism. The various activities understood under the rubric "colonialism"—from the settling of territories to the extraction of wealth, from the administration of subject peoples to the deliberate reform of their ways of life—all involved interactions between Europeans and those they ruled. Minimally, these required some degree of mediation, of cultural and linguistic translation, however problematic the communications that resulted. Indeed such processes never occurred without friction, without the production of new forms of culture and the transformation of meanings and practices. Nor was the colonial work of mediation solely discursive. It included other material relations, from the exchange of goods to sexual intercourse. The literature on colonialism makes increasingly obvious precisely how much hybridization occurred in colonial contact zones. Moreover, those involved in these processes were never solely human agents but included plants, animals, and microbes.

Yet at critical moments colonialism also entailed endless forms of purification, through which attempts were made to separate and distinguish subjects and phenomena. From living spaces and child-rearing techniques to scientific racism, from sanitation works to the codification of customary laws, colonial agents tried to classify, discipline, and cleanse in the territories they administered. Moreover, in doing so they obscured the prior and subsequent networks that traversed the divisions they made. As Ann Stoler and Frederick Cooper note, the continual generation of binaries and dichotomies—including the difference between European and non-European—so characteristic of colonial institutions in the late nineteenth and early twentieth centuries, was "out of sync with . . . quotidian experiences" (1997:9), with the myriad and diverse connections among people, objects, and practices.

By referring as he does to the *work* of mediation and purification, Latour forces attention to the fact that such processes are neither automatic nor mechanical. Each entails labor in and on the world, in specific and circumscribed circumstances. But this need not imply that such labor is always entirely intentional or that its outcome may be predicted.

Although Latour emphasizes that purifying and mediating practices occur simultaneously, his analysis seems to suggest that hybridization precedes purification. This certainly makes good historical sense. Without hybrids, there is nothing to purify. On the other hand, by constantly establishing new divisions the work of purification, including the Cartesian works of analysis and critique, multiplies the sites where further hybridization becomes possible.[17] Indeed, because moderns (according to Latour) refuse to accept or recognize hybridity, critique must be constantly brought to play.

To see the relevance of these matters to the politics of magic, one must follow Latour a bit further. Among the most significant products of modernity's work of purification, claims Latour, are two interconnected Great Divides (1993:97–103). The internal divide distinguishes nature from culture; the external divide differentiates European from non-European. What makes non-Europeans both scandalous and identifiable is their constant mixture of nature and culture, a common feature of those practices Europeans labeled magical. Europeans, on the other hand, uniquely insist on the distinction. What most radically sets the West apart from the rest is European science, which provides genuine knowledge, rather than mere representations, of nature.[18]

These interconnected divides form the fundamental elements of the colonial politics of magic. Claims that natives were deluded in their understanding of reality (and thus inherently inferior to modern Europeans) authorized colonial rule. Europeans' access to nature through science set them apart from other people, who merely had beliefs—that is, projections of culture. Assertions like this justified conquest and civilizing missions alike. Not only did the European intellectual edge make conquest possible through technologies created by science, but those very technologies often were presented as evidence of a superiority that by its mere display would make actual force unnecessary (Adas 1989). Such, at least, was claimed.

Such claims, however, are based on a problematic understanding of science as practice. Ascribing European supremacy to rationality or to the match between European knowledge and the working of the natural world (the well-known correspondence theory of truth) is a kind of philosopher's conjuring trick that obscures the way that facts are constructed through costly and difficult labor, involving inscription procedures, the generation of allies, and long networks of interconnections between people and things (Latour 1987, 1988).

Latour's analysis clarifies a number of moves common to discourses about magic. If the difference between magic and science in the broadest sense provides a rationale for distinguishing European and non-European, commentaries about or analyses of native magic relentlessly engage in further purificatory critique, by dividing nature from culture. Thus those who gave some credit to native knowledges insisted on the need to separate their truths from patent falsity, those elements that could be assimilated to natural science from those that were irretrievably cultural. This meant, for example, removing the pollutants of charms and spells (magic, false belief) and leaving the residue of purified natural material substance (true knowledge). Thus A.G. Vorderman, a famous colonial physician and researcher, divided Javanese *guna-guna* (the use of various means to make someone ill or mad) into superstitious acts involving spells and charms and "the administering of foreign supplements in the food or drink of the person to be manipulated." Only the latter was relevant to medical science; the former belonged to the sphere of the ethnologist (Vorderman 1893:81–82). Such forms of analysis purified local practices by splitting apart what they treat as inseparable—while simultaneously obscuring the insights they had to offer on what generates disease.

Both Damsté's report and his actions can be seen as instances of the modern colonial work of purification. He simultaneously presumes and reinscribes clear boundaries between Europeans and natives. Even his tone—disdainful, distant, derisive—contributes to this effect. At the same time, however, his purificatory practices generate uncanny uncertainties and hybridities.

In the remainder of this article, I point toward some of this hidden work of mediation produced by efforts to dominate and discipline, as well as toward hybridizing formations that incited critique and effects of difference. These investigations open up three fruitful perspectives on the colonial politics of magic. The first suggests that what appears "magical" may be a by-product of difficulties in incorporating occulted indigenous networks of knowledge and power. The second raises the question of whether in attempting to mediate with colonized populations in the name of peace and order, colonial practices inevitably exhibited precisely those "magical" qualities that experts ordinarily attributed to the colonized. The third widens the focus to situate colonial expertise and management within everyday life in the colonies. It is here that I address oft-told tales about magic in the Indies, in which (among other things) colonial officials themselves, such as the hero of *The Hidden Force*, appear susceptible to native magic.

The Magic of Occulted Networks

The notion of networks is tantalizingly suggestive for understanding the politics of magic operating in Damsté's report. Indeed, that report contains a surplus of information that has something of the slippery suggestiveness of magic itself. Throughout is the tracery of a number of overlapping networks of knowledge and power, some more apparent than others.

The first such network is the hierarchically structured chains of inscription and transmission of information that make up the "imperial archive."[19]

Damsté's report begins by referring to the cable he received from Kuys sent by way of East Java. This (Damsté writes) led him to telephone South Bali, where reinforcements were quartered, and then—because, he complains, the telephone between the residency capital in Singaraja and Jembrana's capital of Negara has not worked properly for two years—send *another* cable via East Java in response. Such references to communication and transportation technologies run through Damsté's report.[20] The same network is even invoked in the ritual acknowledgments with which the report begins and ends of a spectral reader, the governor-general, who constituted a key node in the knowledge-power relations of the imperial archive. Indeed, it is only because this incident was inscribed and then transmitted to Batavia, from which it was forwarded to the Ministry of Colonies in the Netherlands, whose records now reside in the General State Archives, that it can now be used to tell a tale of magic and modernity.

A second network evident in Damsté's report connects to these well-traveled roads by less defined paths. This is the network of rumors, of unattributed claims made within the space of colonial rule. Although less stable and predictable, and therefore more mysterious, this network may still be incorporated within the imperial archive, at least up to a point. Thus the cables sent via East Java spread word of "disturbances" in Jembrana through the grapevine, so commanders of troops in East Java anticipated that they might be called to Bali, and stories reached the governor-general's office in advance of Damsté's official report. Somewhat more problematic is the anonymous letter that started the flow of information. By including a copy in his report, Damsté accommodates it within the paperwork of rule. But here authoritative knowledge begins to show its limits.[21] Its unknown writer becomes a screen for administrative projections as Damsté imagines him as the ideal colonial subject: alert, omnipresent, critical, obedient, and even more suited for the civil service than those Balinese actually occupying such offices (or so writes Damsté). But surely the writer's motivations involved more than a desire to serve the colonial state. Although his letter shows him to be familiar with the concerns and claims of European rule, it also manifests less compatible critiques and interpretations. That Damsté so unproblematically presumes his cooperation rather than wondering what local disputes might have provoked the missive (was its writer a rival healer? someone envious of the success of the district head and his family? a traditional intellectual perturbed by the absence of authorities who might intervene to challenge Nang

Mukanis's claims about the divine sources of his power?) suggests that efforts to link this network to the first do not entirely succeed.[22]

More fragile and problematic still are pathways built on face-to-face communication. Although in theory more reliable (since based on direct observation), such knowledge is in fact more equivocal, for it posits an unproblematically interpretable native subject, whose acts and gestures are instantly transparent. Thus Kuys reads in Nang Mukanis's eyes hatred and defiance; Damsté notes the "strange gaze" of Nang Mukanis's brother, which he asserts once brought him "an aureole of holiness."

But it is where nothing is subsumable within existing networks that colonial knowledge breaks down and an inscrutable (and thereby potentially threatening) native reality appears. How is it that people fell down screaming in Nang Mukanis's presence? Strangely, Damsté makes no effort to deal with this question. Presumably, Nang Mukanis did have power of a kind, perhaps "the power of suggestion," since Kuys noted that people became possessed "under his influence." What did trouble the authorities was his popularity. How had word of his therapeutic talents spread throughout all of Jembrana, so that within two weeks of his becoming a balian (and without any telephones or telegraphs!) hundreds of Balinese flocked to his remote compound daily? When Kuys asked some of them how Nang Mukanis became famous, they answered by speaking of successful cures and noted that Nang Mukanis himself was healed after a long illness. But to Kuys, who took for granted that Nang Mukanis could not really heal, these responses made no sense; as he remarks, "no one imparted anything that could make understandable to me that sudden enthusiastic veneration." What answer *would* have satisfied him?

More to the point, Kuys may have thought he had asked a simple question and his interlocutors that they had provided straightforward answers. But there is nothing simple about a conversation whose participants share so little in the way of common experiences, assumptions, and past knowledge. Similarly, although Kuys himself witnessed something of Nang Mukanis's power, its sources necessarily eluded isolated observation. Power is constructed within a nexus of alliances, practices, dispositions, objects, and institutions. Viewed on its own—removed from the relevant networks—power is always vulnerable, just as Nang Mukanis was on the morning of his arrest.

Breaks in the construction of colonial knowledge rendered certain practices a threat. Not all of the ways in which Balinese mobilized could be incorporated into colonial networks of power/knowledge. Is it because some Balinese networks proved inaccessible, even (due to their unfamiliarity) undetectable, that certain indigenous practices appear so mysterious and dangerous, so much the opposite of European technologies?

Iconoclasm as a Pedagogy of Disenchantment

> Colonising refers not simply to the establishing of a European presence but also to the spread of a political order that inscribes in the social world a new conception of space, new forms of personhood, and a new means of manufacturing the experience of the real.
>
> —TIMOTHY MITCHELL, *Colonising Egypt*, 1991

As noted above, the modern work of purification conceals the myriad networks linking what is supposedly distinct. In arguing that colonial divides concerned with "magic" or the "supernatural" involved a good deal of mediation work and produced unpredictable hybridities, I begin with a question: is it possible to destabilize the separation between European and non-European by showing that *those* purified objects were constantly entangled?

Indeed, evidence of such mingling can be found in the acts of iconoclasm that accompanied Nang Mukanis's arrest: in both the destruction of the objects marking Nang Mukanis as someone involved with spirits and divinities and in Damsté's triumphant observation that this transpired without any supernatural intervention. Happily, such practices and pronouncements constitute an important element in the official politics of magic in colonial Indonesia. Moreover, they originate precisely in the conviction that a vast gulf separates Indonesian and European mentalities.

Damsté writes about these events as if what he calls the "signs" of Nang Mukanis's "holiness" should possess some inherent power, such that harming them would (if Balinese beliefs were correct) instantly bring upon the perpetrator the wrath of invisible powers. Thus the successful burning of these "signs" demonstrated the absence of Nang Mukanis's "holiness." The gesture satisfactorily brought about a purification that divided nature (material objects, inherently powerless) from culture (human—or rather native—projections and fantasies).[23]

Such acts of violence not only purified, however, but also constituted a spectacle of the real, a colonial lesson in disenchantment. Damsté presents the burning of Nang Mukanis's belongings as self-evidently demystifying. Like his harangue of the Balinese leaders, it serves as an educational occasion, befitting the improving aspirations of the Ethical Policy. Presumably word of the incident, witnessed by the district head and Nang Mukanis's family, would have spread along the same mysterious channels as those that made Nang Mukanis's reputation in the first place.

Colonial rule abounded in such pedagogic performances. The demonstration in Nang Mukanis's yard was not entirely original to Damsté. Some seventeen years earlier, J.E. Jasper, a contemporary of Damsté's who went on to achieve even greater renown than the latter within the colonial hierarchy, advocated strikingly similar measures in Javanese legal cases involving accusations of magic: "The police magistrate could not take better action in the interest of peace in the country . . . than to cause all the reported *tumbals, jimats*, sacred pieces of iron, sacred stones which they supposed would do evil, to be burned or destroyed in the presence of plaintiffs and defendants, to demonstrate that such hoo-ha is . . . of no value" (1904:132).

Indeed, virtually any action on the part of the colonial state, including acts of conquest or responses to potential or real insurrections, could be transformed into a lesson in metaphysics. So, for instance, a newspaper report of a massacre during the Dutch conquest of Bali's last independent realm describes various "magical" weapons the Balinese carried into battle and comments that Balinese "belief" in "magical force will be shaken in no small measure."[24] In accounts of such incidents violence even becomes a salutary intervention, palpably proving the false value of charms and fetishes or the long periods of fasting and prayer necessary for the mastery of various forms of esoteric knowledge. Thus numerous narratives smugly trumpet the fact that amulets ensuring invulnerability offered no protection against European bullets. Commonly, they continue by noting that after *this* such fantasies would be forgotten: *now* the natives would no longer be ignorant, would no longer harbor patently false beliefs.[25]

All the more troubling, then, that the lesson seemed so hard to learn. As the contributor to the *Police Guide* observed: "However often the effect of Netherlands bullets already brought disenchantment in a bloody way and proved the invalidity of such hocus pocus notions with facts, the unshakable belief in a more possible way to obtain invulnerability continually re-emerged again" (S. 1921:34). Consequently, such performances needed to be continually repeated. This could, of course, be taken as evidence of native irrationality, as "S" seems to imply. On the other hand, it raises questions about the "rationality" of their colonizers.

Certainly Damsté would have denied that the paraphernalia his agents burned had any power: what made them worth destroying was his assumption that *Balinese* believed this.[26] And it was their *belief* that he ultimately aimed to destroy. But how odd to think of fire as an agent for transforming people's points of view. How by burning certain objects could people be induced to think as he thought they should?

Damsté attempted to contain the problem of magic by isolating and destroying its apparent source, thus showing faith in it to be the opposite of good sense. But acting this way implies that native magic was indeed dangerous and threatening and thus affirms rather than undermines its power. In other words, it was highly unlikely that anyone would learn through such violence that what they believed to be powerful was not.

There is a strange materialist realism at work here: destroying the things makes the problem vanish too. Damsté's demonstration, like all pedagogic spectacles, is premised on a peculiar notion: once they see this, the truth will be evident. But to see the world the way European colonizers did clearly would require more than a single show. These political performances ultimately rest on a kind of sleight of hand. Stage magic works by cloaking the apparatus necessary to create appearances, not only the difficult skilled work but the networks of helpers manipulating lights and carrying objects. Damsté's efforts obscure the networks that produce his reality. Conversely, he has no sense of how Nang Mukanis managed to "invoke demons." Damsté writes as if "invoking demons" were a skill Nang Mukanis should command at all times and circumstances, instead of only being possible under special conditions.

But let me switch magical metaphors here. For if Damsté's account of what happened in Nang Mukanis's yard seems on the one hand a kind of conjuring act, on the other hand it seems suspiciously familiar to anthropologists of magic. Isn't believing that one will destroy someone's power by destroying what *represents* it (down to his clothing!) precisely what Frazer (1911) called "sympathetic magic," supposedly an expression of primitive thought? And the idea that one will disenchant through such displays reflects a kind of omnipotence of thought, since the need to repeat such demonstrations shows it to be untrue. But then since "magic" is an object produced through European concerns, it should not be surprising to find its traces in colonial practice.

Perhaps the best way to explain the repeated colonial remarks about how acts of violence would disenchant the natives is by recalling those theorists who emphasize the expressive and symbolic dimensions of magic. Dramas of proof were vital to the colonial project. To an important degree, colonial rule itself involved an elaborate sleight of hand. How else could a handful of Europeans—even with technologically efficient weapons—have controlled millions of natives if not through practices entailing illusion and delusion? But tricking themselves was as important as duping the natives. These dramas, in other words, might better be seen as directed toward Europeans than toward subject populations. They constituted spectacular occasions on which Europeans could convince themselves once again of their inherent superiority.

Apart from the issues raised by pedagogic iconoclasm in the Indies, in general efforts by colonial administrators to engage with native populations for whom "magic" was part of the fabric of everyday life invariably produced disconcerting hybridities. Indeed, colonial rulers, depending as they did upon enlisting the cooperation of native populations, could not maintain in practice the purity of their rejection of magic in theory. In attempting to act effectively in ways they thought would be meaningful to those they ruled, they tangled themselves in contradictions.

Take, for instance, the activities of a British district officer in Nigeria, who used the expertise in sleight of hand he developed as a boy to impress those he ruled with the powers he possessed and so ensure their compliance (Hives and Lumley 1930). Or consider the conundrums faced by other British district officers, who found that the Witchcraft Ordinances that prohibited Africans from making and dealing with accusations of witchcraft placed the regime in a dubious moral position, one not conducive to maintaining peace and order. As Karen Fields (1982) argues, by prosecuting those who attempted to rid communities of witches, administrators seemed to be protecting evildoers. Thus administrators came to find it necessary to think within the "logic" of witchcraft to maintain the authority of the colonial state.

Magic in Colonial Popular Culture

> If you can't share a ghost story, you're not a real Indo.
> —MARGUÉRITE SCHENKHUIZEN, *Memoirs of an Indo Woman*, 1993

Narratives such as Damsté's depend on clear demarcations between Europeans and natives, while being oriented to the ultimate eradication of those
differences by the successful work of education effected by enlightened administrators. Other narratives, generated in the course of daily life among
colonizing classes in the Indies rather than as official statements, demonstrate a more ambivalent involvement with native magic. In a wealth of rumors and stories from the late nineteenth century on, the supernatural aura
of the Indies played a leading role. These popular discussions of magic reveal that the border might be crossed in the wrong direction: rather than offering lessons in disenchanting natives, such narratives present "enchanted"
Europeans.[27] Although for some of those Europeans (such as for Louis
Couperus, whose famous—for some infamous—novel expressed his anti-
modernist sentiments) such enchantment mainly entailed fascination, for
others it went much deeper, generating a host of fears and fantasies.

I began this paper in Bali, but I can hardly remain there. For in Indies
lore about uncanny magic, it is Java that figures as the geographic center of
the colonial imagination, as it was home to most of the European population.[28] It was there, on the airy verandahs of old Indies houses and colonial
clubs, that Europeans shared tales about ghosts, sorcery, and inexplicable incidents or played at table turning and telling fortunes.

In the stories related in such spaces, native magic appeared not only potentially dangerous to public "peace and order" but to private safety and welfare. This was nowhere more true than in rumors about European victims of
guna-guna, the Javanese term that Europeans and Eurasians adopted to refer to native sorcery, usually involving seduction or revenge.[29] A more diffuse
threat to personal security informed other frequently shared tales, concerned with uncanny occurrences that undermined ontological certainties.
Couperus's novel portrays several such incidents, from a rain of stones (stories about these, in fact, inspired the novel) to the climactic famous scene
where the Resident's wife runs screaming and naked from her bath when wet
red splotches—betel juice? blood?—appear on her alabaster body. Following

the book's publication strange incidents tended to be attributed to unknown "hidden forces," sometimes, as in the novel, under the command of native experts in occult knowledges. In these various tales of magic, popular culture, instead of carefully separating the causal agents recognized by European science from those it deemed fantastic, drew upon *all* the vulnerabilities Europeans felt in the Indies, concentrating them in images of inexplicable hostility.

Such stories circulated among a very diverse population. The broad category "European" included *totoks* (people who came to the Indies from Europe as adults, and commonly expected to return there), *Indos* (Eurasians, people with connections somewhere in the female line to Indonesians), and Creoles, who, along with Indos, could also be referred to as "Indies people." Male and female, rich and poor, members of these communities had attitudes that overlapped in some ways and differed in others, including their responses to hidden forces.

Although such anecdotes no doubt had been imparted for generations among Europeans living in close proximity to or intimacy with Indonesians, they first appeared in print when they came to the attention of totoks, who arrived in the Indies in increasing numbers beginning in the 1870s. Some wrote because they found these tales curious, interesting, intriguing; others because they thought them absurd; still others in defense of their truth. In many such stories the victim of magic is a totok, often a skeptic, as in Couperus's novel.

Totok reactions to such tales no doubt were stimulated both by changing patterns of Indies life and by discussions of the occult in Europe, prompted by movements such as Spiritualism and Theosophy. For instance, although the "hidden force" narratives on which Couperus drew can be traced back to an incident that occurred in the home of an Assistant Resident in 1831, it took the spread of spiritualist performances in Europe, and the various controversies these provoked, to loosen the narrative floodgates.[30] As for guna-guna tales, these became increasingly relevant as more European women emigrated to the Indies, and the practice of marrying or cohabiting with native or Indo women became problematic.

Such tales both reflected and shaped European experiences of living in colonial Indonesia. Doctors, for example, reported visits by male patients who feared that various symptoms indicated that their deserted native mistresses had used magical spells and poisons against them (Kohlbrugge 1907:18–19).

Indeed, some European men claimed their ongoing involvement with native women was itself the consequence of sorcery (Van Hien 1934:48).

Anxieties about occult native powers could also affect the way that civil servants carried out their official duties. In an article appearing a few years after Couperus's novel, Jasper (1904) noted that some administrators feared the magical repercussions of infringing upon local customs.[31] This, he complained, made it difficult for them to distinguish between mere superstition and "customary law," respect for which was a cornerstone of administrative policy.[32] Jasper complained that such officials "imagine[d] so much of the hidden force that emanates from the Javanese . . . that [they] also ascribe[d] to him the great power to make [the] perfectly hale and hearty suddenly seriously ill, by the administering of mysterious, not existing, or having no effect, sometimes indeed entirely innocuous, things." All in all, he proclaimed that "the European population at the expense of everything is coming more and more under the influence of the morbid myth concerning magical power in the native" (1904:132). Like Damsté, Jasper entered the colonial civil service near the inception of the Ethical Policy, and its civilizing impulses clearly influenced his disgust at colleagues who let anxieties about supernatural retribution affect their work.

Uncanny rumors illustrate the murky uncertainties of colonial society. It is tempting to subject such narratives to the kind of analysis anthropologists made famous in the study of African witchcraft: namely, to see them as indicative of strained social relations. Certainly such anecdotes expose a subterranean colonial anxiety about native subordinates.[33] Indeed, popular lore revealed and exercised the fault lines of colonial society.

On the whole, tales of magic implicated those Indonesians most intimately involved in Dutch lives. Apart from mistresses, these included aristocrats incorporated into the state apparatus through the Native Civil Service; thus in Couperus's novel, the agent responsible for the hidden force manifestations that destroy the Resident's life is a Javanese regent, furious over the Resident's dismissal from office of a member of the regent's family. Servants—and every colonial household had a minimum of four—formed a particular locus of concern. For magicians to work their spells, they required material that had had extended contact with their victims' bodies (e.g., clothing, hair, nail clippings); in turn, those bodies had to be put in contact with specially constructed objects. Because a professional magician was unlikely to have such intimate access to Europeans, he or she had to work through intermediaries. And these, tales warned, were inevitably one's servants. Even those who dismissed the reality of native powers could attribute to servants numerous motives for playing frightening tricks or assisting others in doing so, ranging from money to a desire for revenge against employers who were excessively demanding or who refused advances on their pay.

Not all narratives about native magic inspired fear, however. Some found such tales merely entertaining. Others enjoyed the new metaphysical vistas they opened, asserting that living in the Indies made one realize that "there are more things in heaven and earth" than European science could imagine.[34] Fascination or conviction led some to want to know more about Javanese knowledges or the occult in general. Books on Javanese "secret doctrines," informed by various streams of European occultism, proved immensely popular. These were the specialty of H.A. van Hien, author of the multivolume *The Javanese Spirit World*, which went through six editions between 1894 and 1934. A compilation of local lore informed by the writings of Theosophists, Orientalists, and ethnologists, it included detailed descriptions of Javanese divination methods and accounts of places Javanese considered haunted and of the spirits likely to be responsible, as well as discussions of guna-guna and hidden force (Van Hien 1934). Catering to the market created by Couperus's novel, Van Hien also published a collection of Javanese incantations, under the title *Formulas for Hidden Force* (1924).

Others defended the existence of hidden forces on the basis of experience. As the editor of a Surabaya newspaper wrote in 1916:

There are still people in the Indies who think that Hidden Force does not exist. They ground that opinion in the main on the fact that what they cannot comprehend or get to the bottom of with their human senses also cannot be. How absurd that opinion is, and to how much shortsightedness it testifies, we have argued frequently in this paper. In the more than thirty years that we [have] reside[d] in these colonies, so many unsolvable puzzles have been placed before us which all go back to the existence of forces and influences not perceptible with our senses—forces of which the limits are utterly indeterminate, that crop up most unexpectedly and are not to be opposed with our means—that we can no longer deny the existence of the so-called hidden occult forces and phenomena, [even] if we also absolutely cannot explain their cause and effect. And no scientific, developed man may contemptuously shrug his shoulders at such an opinion; that leaves us cold. It is only because he has not yet become acquainted or wants to become acquainted with the above phenomena. Only when those phenomena press themselves upon him by chance with crushing persuasive force is he converted.[35]

Tales of such conversions, in which skeptical totoks came face to face with the irrefutably eerie, comprised a recurring theme of fiction, as well as of newspaper and magazine articles.[36] Typically, the convert is male; because women were presumed more suggestible, their conversion could not make as dramatic an impression.

Clearly, stories about magic and hidden forces provoked counternarratives. If these did not question the stories altogether, as merely anecdotal rumor, they commonly sought to strip away any mystery by explaining strange occurrences in "natural" terms, trying once again to shore up the divide between native and European, nature and culture. Some of the tools used to do so are familiar to anthropologists: the claim that belief in occult forces rested on the power of suggestion. Others are less so: Europeans who claimed to have been bewitched were diagnosed as suffering from temporary or chronic mental disturbances.[37] Not all explanations relied on psychology. Some ascribed to natives an astounding skill in legerdemain and equally astounding depths of deception, resentment, and propensity to form conspiracies. Hidden forces still! But ones that preserved the crucial ontological and ethnological distinctions.

At times commentators went further, declaring that Europeans who believed themselves bewitched, or who believed stories that Europeans could be bewitched, only proved the genuine danger of life in the tropics. Rejecting the progressivist optimism of those promoting civilizing missions, they interpreted totok conversion as a symptom of degeneration. Those who came to believe in hidden forces no longer counted as fully European. Protecting the association between rationality and European identity, they considered that such persons had "gone native" (*verinlandscht* [the assessment of a priest named M. Timmers in 1918]) or been "Indicized" (*verindischt*), a fate some warned was inevitable if Europeans spent too long in tropical colonies (Kohlbrugge 1907; Kerremans 1923; also see discussions in Gouda 1995, chapter 5).[38]

Take, for instance, the judgment of Jacob H.F. Kohlbrugge, a physician who spent several years in the Indies, wrote widely on the Javanese and their (native and colonial) rulers (to approximate the title of a book he published on his return to Holland, which collected several essays), and eventually occupied a chair in ethnology at Utrecht. According to him, Van Hien's claim that he had encountered a number of wretched Europeans who had been victims of guna-guna showed that Van Hien—who originally came to the Indies in the 1870s to serve in the army—had been Indicized. (Kohlbrugge even proposed the suggestive influence of native animism as the agent responsible! [1907:18].) Indeed, Kohlbrugge warned, in a tropical climate it was impossible to retain, or for that matter to acquire, the moral and intellectual dispositions associated with European civilization. Critical of some of the assumptions informing the Ethical Policy, he regarded attempts to "improve" Javanese as equally doomed to failure as attempts to maintain or reproduce in the next generation of colonizers a truly European identity. On the other hand, natives who moved to Holland would become more and more Dutch. For both native and European, belief in magic was a symptom of the pernicious effect of the tropical sun.[39]

Although some tried to purify a European identity by insisting that any concession to the truth of hidden forces indicated a problematic slippage in the direction of the native, in practice different positions did not map easily onto multiply positioned colonial lives. For instance, Creusesol (1916), scion of an old Indies family who managed a plantation and wrote books on the side, undoubtedly would have scoffed at Kohlbrugge's warnings. Himself skeptical about hidden forces, he maintained that reports of strange incidents proved the susceptibility of totoks to native chicanery. Unlike planters from Indies families who "understood" the natives, newcomers made easy marks. Colonial officials especially spent a relatively short time in the Indies, and their position kept them at some remove from native life. This explained, he claimed, why they were the stars of stories about hidden force phenomena.

Note that colonizers drawn in by Indies magic did not, in fact, "go native"—Kohlbrugge's neologism is more precise than that of Father Timmers. They were *Indicized*, that is, they developed new hybrid subjectivities that were monstrously anomalous from the point of view of the metropole—but also strange from the perspective of those they colonized. Indeed, constructions of magic and native knowledge in Indies popular culture and everyday life were as much European as indigenous.[40] For one, commonly they were articulated in relation to science or Christianity: thus Marguérite Schenkhuizen

(1993), an Indo, prefaces her account of becoming the victim of a sorcery attack by asserting her former skepticism and then declaring that her Christian faith had protected her from serious harm. In addition, discussions of magic increasingly ignored Javanese explanations (e.g., that spirits called *gendruwo* could cause hidden force manifestations) in favor of the comparative categories developed in controversial metropolitan sciences (the poltergeists of parapsychology or psychical research). Indeed, being in the Indies encouraged some to experiment with European forms of occultism such as Spiritualism and Theosophy.[41] Moreover, not only did converts insist on divisions where none existed locally (i.e., supernatural vs. natural causes), but their stories often sensationalized magic and nonhuman forces as sinister, in contrast to the protective or helpful role such forces and practices might play locally.

Nor did such cultural hybridity necessarily lead to renouncing European superiority. In a novel by Van Wermeskerken (1922), for example, when the skeptical totok main character begins to accept the reality of the spirits that his Indies wife and mother-in-law take for granted, he declares European Spiritualism superior to the spirit beliefs of his native servants on the grounds that at least Europeans can converse with, rather than merely invoke or propitiate, spirits. If popular culture broke down the divide between European and non-European in some areas, it reinscribed it in others.

Nonetheless, that Europeans living in the Indies could come to believe in magic undermines the opposition some tried to draw between magic and modernity, upsetting implicit chronologies and even geographies of magic. Nor did these conundrums only exist overseas. Metropolitan science also continually had to grapple with evidence that undermined efforts to portray magic as a feature of Europe's unenlightened past or at worst a rural relic. Tylor, faced with the fad for Spiritualism even among respectable Londoners, was forced to conclude that magic ("the philosophy of savages") could undergo a revival ([1871] 1958:155; Peter Pels, this volume). For Freud, magical thinking persisted within civilized modernity, and could reemerge under the right circumstances in all but the most rational of men. In such attempts to police threatened boundaries appear the debris of history, effects of relations of power that also shaped the internal constraints and pressures, the "structures of feeling" (Williams 1977), of later ethnographers. In the end, theories of magic have much to say about efforts to conjure modernity.

Concluding Remarks

This article has explored two kinds of politics of magic in colonial Indonesia: one at the level of explicit and implicit policy, another within the broader framework of debates over the reality or interpretation of popular rumor and anecdote. If native magic formed an object of concern for colonial administrators, it also constituted an object of fascination, fear, and disciplining knowledge within the wider colonizer community. The interweaving of purification and mingling characterized not only the practices and discourses of officials but permeated Indies popular culture and everyday life. Despite continual efforts to align magic with native backwardness, constant hybrids ensued that undermined distinctions between "us" and "them."

Having begun by using Damsté's report to explore the politics of magic in a modernizing colonial state, I want to end by returning to colonial administrators, this time as objects rather than originators of discourses about magic. In colonial societies, not every European modeled modernity equally. Ultimately, European superiority had a particular tone of voice, demeanor, and emotional style, that of the dispassionate, hardworking, self-assured bourgeois male who rose to the top of bureaucratic hierarchies. The main character in Couperus's *Hidden Force* exemplifies precisely the kind of colonizer subject who thought himself impervious to native (and feminine) occult nonsense: a resident in the colonial civil service, someone very much like Henri T. Damsté. Couperus suggests that such subjects labored to maintain the modern rationality that formed the foundation of claims to European superiority through specific practices and forms of self-work—and showed they were not after all impervious.[42] Outside of the networks (the imperial archive) that provided grounds for their self-confidence, such officials sometimes could prove vulnerable—as vulnerable as Nang Mukanis, found home alone on the morning of his arrest.

It is clear why Couperus's novel would have reverberated with readers in the Indies, for in it colonial power was attacked on all fronts. Not only would administrators find the mysterious incidents that dot the text "politically significant" (since they are instigated by a Javanese regent), but they constitute threats to the patriarchy that ordered colonial society (undermining the Resident's ability to sustain what Couperus calls his "masculine simplicity" or to exert authority in his own household) and challenge the boundary formations on which the construction of modernity depended.

The eventual popularity of books such as Couperus's and of less literary Indies "ghost stories" among reading publics back in Europe reverses the ideal flow of wisdom, indicating that the monster of magic could not be contained after all. Equally relevant here is the market for anthropology, which— whatever its attempts to distinguish itself from such popular culture—shared in the simultaneously pleasurable and spine-tingling aura of the exotic that was produced by the colonial project.

SIX

On Witch Doctors and Spin Doctors

The Role of "Experts" in African and American Politics

PETER GESCHIERE

One of the more unsettling aspects of developments in postcolonial Africa is the all-pervasive role of *witchcraft*, *sorcery*, and *occult forces* (or whatever term one prefers) in modern sectors of society, notably in politics.[1] Examples will hardly be necessary for anyone who follows the press. Let me just refer to a striking enumeration by Jean-François Bayart in his new book *L'illusion iden-titaire*—all the more striking because he shows that not only leaders such as Sékou Touré, Mathieu Kerekou, or Jean Bédel Bokassa were deeply involved with witchcraft, using all sorts of "experts" to affirm their power and attack opponents, but that also more generally respected figures such as Félix Houphouët-Boigny or Thabo Mbeki saw or see fit to maintain their own links with this discourse and its practices.[2] The Western press avidly capitalizes on sensational rumors and images; compare, for instance, the wide circulation in various newspapers, November 1996 (so still in Sese Seko Mobutu's days), of an indeed-striking photo of three Hutu soldiers of the Zairean army, completely naked apart from a huge Kalashnikov for each of them (and a pair of heavy boots for one of them). The association of nakedness with magic invulnerability is a recurrent theme in many African wars.

This prevalence of the occult seems to confirm, more than any other aspect, the image of Africa as a continuing "heart of darkness." As Peter Pels emphasizes in his introduction to this volume, magic is often characterized as "the antithesis of modernity": it is deemed to be either a kind of preliminary stage, preceding science and even religion; or it is seen as basically different from such more "civilized" modes of thought. The proliferation of witchcraft ideas and practices seems, therefore, to offer the ultimate proof of Africa's "Primitivism" or at least of its "Otherness." As will be clear from the title of this contribution, this chapter's tenor will be very different. My aim is to show that such simplistic oppositions, which are often implicit and therefore all the more basic in much Western thinking, distort our understanding of Western politics as much as of what is going on in Africa. Comparing "witch doctors" to "spin doctors," the publicity experts that can "spin" anything—the press, an item, an image—and who, therefore, are supposed to play a crucial role in "selling" politicians to the public—is not a gratuitous play of words.[3] On the contrary, this terminological convergence, which to some may seem just a fad, can offer a firm footing for exploring the rationale of the simplistic but tenacious oppositions that dominate much of current thinking on "the West versus the Rest."

In earlier publications (Geschiere 1996, 1997), I briefly referred to certain parallels between the role of witch doctors in African politics and the emergence of publicity experts as crucial actors in the politics of Western democracies (notably in America, but increasingly so in Western Europe as well). This evoked very mixed reactions, notably from political scientists. For instance, during a Social Science Research Council conference in Niamey, my 1996 paper had the honor of being discussed by a distinguished political scientist, Paul Brass, who was quite positive about most of its contents, but rejected with quite surprising vehemence (surprising to me at least) this parallel between African witch doctors and Western PR experts.[4] To others as well it clearly seemed to be equally shocking. The precise arguments varied, but it was clear that my comparison sinned against a whole series of conceptual oppositions: transparent versus occult, scientific versus magical, or even rational versus irrational.[5]

This text takes up this challenge. Is this comparison indeed enlightening or is it just fashionable nonsense? Taking up this challenge forced me to delve into the vast literature on American politics, for me a somewhat frightening terra incognita. Clinton's turbulent career—and especially his spectacular reelection in 1996 after having been generally considered as down and out only two years before—offered a convenient entry point. In this contribution, I focus especially on Dick Morris, called "The Man Inside Clinton's Head" by the press and compared to Rasputin or even "a mind altering medicine," and notably on his own larmoyant story (1996) of his rise and fall as the president's closest advisor; and furthermore on *Primary Colors* (1996), a novel that seemed to reveal so much about Clinton's campaign that the anonymous author was long thought to be one of Clinton's intimates. Moreover, I will make some references to books by other Clintonian sharks, notably those by James Carville (1995 [with Mary Matalin and Peter Knobler], 1996) and George Stephanopoulos (1999). Of course, this is only a very small selection of the rapidly growing literature on the role of such "spin doctors." Indeed, since I started working on this contribution (1996), there has been some sort of hype about their role, culminating in two Hollywood movies (not only *Primary Colors* after the book mentioned above but also *Wag the Dog*), a sequel novel to *Primary Colors*, and many other books. Moreover, this somewhat shady profession is apparently no longer special to American politics only. Tony Blair's irresistible electoral charm is generally associated with the genius of his own spin doctor, Peter Mandelson, who was even appointed as Minister in Blair's new cabinet. And François Mitterand's death released a whole stream of publications on his more or less hidden collaborators.[6] Apparently, spin doctors are on the rise, and they may be with us for the time to come. However, because the aim of this text is to tackle more general conceptual issues by starting with concrete examples, I prefer to stick to the concrete stories, mentioned above, about all the spinning that is supposed to have taken place around a towering figure—towering both in terms of power and in his capacity to generate rumors—such as Clinton.

The leading questions for this text are, therefore, whether the prevalence of "witchcraft" in African politics is, indeed, proof of the continent's "Otherness"? Or does a comparison between African witch doctors and American spin doctors rather highlight all sorts of correspondences? Could a view from Africa on Western politics even be enlightening, in the sense that it suggests an alternative reading of these American stories? My aim is certainly not to try and show that someone such as Morris is just another kind of witch doctor or that Western society is full of witchcraft. It certainly is, but the issue at stake is much broader: it is rather about the tenability of prevalent conceptual oppositions—magic (or witchcraft) versus science, occultism versus transparency, and so on—and their role in current analyses of politics. The question is rather how to surpass these terms and their inherent oppositions, which seem to evoke inevitably unilinear visions of "political development" as leading to ever greater transparency and an ever more rational organization of politics. Such oppositions are highly problematic, not only because they ultimately boil down to an all too simplistic contrast between "us" and "them" but also because they help maintain a flat and distorted view of politics in the West. The more the politics of "the other" are marked by witchcraft, magic, and irrationality, the more "our own" politics seem to be transparent, scientific, and rational.[7] Comparing witch doctors and spin doctors may help to highlight that at a deeper level, similar issues play a role in *both* African and American politics: for instance, a precarious and constantly changing balance of secrecy and publicity, revelation and concealment, which may be inherent to the exercise of power in general.

Below I will first try to outline certain general principles—notwithstanding huge regional and historical variation—in the role witch doctors play in contemporary African politics; a case study from my fieldwork in southeast Cameroon will serve as a starting point. In the second part of the chapter I will explore to what extent witchcraft logic allows for an alternative reading of Morris, *Primary Colors*, or of Carville.

"Witch-Doctors" in African Politics

A quite spectacular case during my second period of fieldwork in East Cameroon (1973) can serve—even though, by now, it dates back nearly thirty years ago—as a useful starting point for trying to highlight certain general principles in the role witch doctors play in modern African politics.

> In the early 1970s, an old dispute between Pierre Mimbang and André Bekobe, two eminent politicians in the *arrondissement* of Nguelemendouka (Cameroon, East Province) took an unexpected turn. Their conflict went

back to the 1950s, when they were competing fiercely for the position of *chef de canton*. In those days, Mimbang—after he had just become chief—had even physically attacked Bekobe in front of the French administrator. The latter had dismissed Mimbang on the spot and given his post to Bekobe. Since this incident, the hostility between the two had led constantly to new confrontations.

Mimbang, who had a better education than Bekobe, was more successful when political parties were established at the time of independence. He became mayor of the commune and filled many important posts in the *soussection* of the single political party (then the Union Nationale Camerounaise of President Ahmadou Ahidjo). Bekobe remained canton chief and only received more modest positions in the party hierarchy. Over the years, there were constant rumors about new confrontations between the two adversaries and constantly changing coalitions with other politicians of the *département*. However, under the obsessive authoritarianism that marked one-party rule in Cameroon, these intrigues always took place in secret. The villagers reiterated these rumors but could only conjecture about what really had happened. A sure sign that something was wrong was when the famous black Mercedes of Mr. Malouma, the member of parliament for the whole region, passed by people on its way to Nguelemendouka. At this, the more curious villagers would comment: "Ah, he's going to discipline them, now they'll have some heat!"

In 1973, a dramatic development transpired: Mimbang had a fatal car accident. On return from a visit with his *nganga* ("witch doctor"), his driver lost control over his Land Rover and the car sped off into the bush; Mimbang died on the spot. In itself, the accident was not that surprising: it had happened at a point on a muddy road that was notoriously difficult; moreover, it had just rained and the driver had a reputation for being "trop dynamique." But in the villages rumors immediately sprang up. People said that the road had been strongly "armored" (*bwima*; always translated as *blindé* in French); this was why the car had suddenly swerved off into the forest. These rumors were reinforced when people heard that certain sworn enemies of Mimbang had taken refuge with their own nganga. These refugees were none other than Bekobe and François Mimbang, another politician who had his own reasons for being in conflict with the victim, Pierre Mimbang.[8]

An informant who had links to the entourage of the deceased gave me his interpretations of the incident. He "knew" that André Bekobe and François Mimbang had prepared the death of Pierre Mimbang. To do so, they had obtained the collaboration of Pierre Menkambe, a renowned witch of the Bekobe family. Hadn't this Menkambe been seen creeping into Mimbang's courtyard during the night? In the dark, there had been a confrontation between Menkambe and the witches who guarded Mimbang's house. Apparently, Menkambe had been the stronger and he had decided, in keeping with the demands of Bekobe and François Mimbang, that at the start of the following month, Pierre Mimbang would no longer live. The next day, Pierre Mimbang felt ill. Warned by his entourage of the sinister plans of Menkambe, he went quickly to the village of his nganga to be cured. After a few days, he felt better and decided to return home to participate in an official meeting. His nganga warned him not to go, because his enemies had left formidable barriers on the road, but Mimbang left none the less. Ten kilometers from the nganga's village, the car swerved off the road and Mimbang died. This was only one of the interpretations that circulated in the village (probably the version put forth by those close to Pierre Mimbang). But other villagers as well affirmed that Bekobe, François Mimbang, and Menkambe had taken refuge with their nganga. This was generally seen as "proof" that they were involved: apparently, they feared the vengeance of Mimbang's kin. It was said that the first wife of Mimbang had already visited a very famous nganga. Bekobe and the others might indeed need the protection of their own experts!

Such entanglements certainly do not occur only at the lower levels of the political hierarchy. The crucial role of nganga (witch doctor) in the struggle between Mimbang and Bekobe in the case above strongly reminds, for instance, of the stories about how president Bongo of Gabon uses witchcraft experts in order to both eliminate his opponents and subject his confidants to his will (Cinnamon 1996; Péan 1983:35). And, as mentioned before, similar stories circulate about many other presidents and higher politicians (Bayart 1996; Geschiere 1997). Of course, the role of the occult in national politics becomes very different when Islam is involved, but it is certainly not less important, as is illustrated, for instance, by the spectacular career of the Malian marabout Cissé, who—through his much advertised pact with the devil—was supposed to have accumulated so much power that he was recruited successively by Presidents Sékou Touré (Guinea), Sese Seko Mobutu (Zaire), and Mathieu Kerekou (Benin; see Banegas 1998:495).

Stories like these may seem to be pure fantasy to many Western readers, programmed as we are to equate magic with superstition and irrationality. Yet, despite all sorts of variations and differences, such stories follow certain basic principles and in this sense partake in a rationality of their own. The performance of the *nganga*—a term current throughout the extensive Bantu area in central and southern Africa[9]—has certain characteristics that are common to most experts of the occult. What is precisely the role these nganga are supposed to play in politics?

First of all a nganga has to *see*. Nganga, who can be both women and men, are supposed to have "a second pair of eyes." Indeed, the acquisition of such a second pair of eyes is the very first stage of any initiation into the realm of witchcraft (see de Rosny 1981). These extra eyes enable the nganga to see the witches who are conspiring against his (or her) client.[10] However, this additional visionary power has its reverse: it enables the nganga to see the witches but it makes him at the same time visible—and thereby within reach—for all the witches of whatever origin.

Second, the nganga has to *armor* (as said, in francophone areas people often use the term *blinder*) his client. He has to empower him so as to make him both impervious to the attacks of his jealous opponents and invincible in his attacks on others. A crucial stage in this empowerment—and this is a third common characteristic—is the *confession*. The nganga has to *reconstitute* the client in order to take away his misfortune. This calls for a "deconstruction" of the client's personality through an often drawn-out "confession," in which all sorts of hidden secrets have to be brought out (a crucial question is often to what extent the client himself has "gone out"—that is, left his body in order to join the witches). Only after such a confession—which often requires a series of sessions and, of course, has its costs, not only spiritual but also material—is it possible to "armor" the client.

Another common aspect is that the nganga will require a *sacrifice* of his client. Nowadays, this sacrifice will consist mainly of money. In postcolonial Africa, the occult has become highly monetized. To my Maka informants, it was, for instance, self-evident why the same politician succeeded in accumulating all important political posts in the region (MP, mayor, president of the regional party committee, etc.) throughout the 1960s and the 1970s. The reason they gave was simple: he had accumulated far more money than any of his rivals on the regional scene and, therefore, he could buy the services of the best nganga. Indeed, it is clear that many nganga simply sell their services to the highest bidder. However, the stories about nganga refer also to a more personal kind of sacrifice. In the local discourse, there is a diffuse but general idea that an initiation into witchcraft in general is supposed to require the sacrifice of a close relative.[11] This theme turns up also in stories about the relation between a nganga—who is viewed as some sort of a "superwitch" (see below)—and his clients. It is especially this notion of sacrifice that gives this relation a somewhat amoral shade. It is also this aspect that risks making a nganga's support counterproductive: the latter may require such a heavy sacrifice that, in the end, he destroys the client.

It is important to note that the nganga in general have a *highly amoral aura*. In many respects, they are beyond the opposition between good and evil. Their very role is marked by a basic ambivalence.[12] They are supposed to be able to armor—or heal—only because they have developed their witchcraft to a spectacular degree. This is why people describe them as "witches who have beaten all records." Nganga themselves will always emphasize that their "professor," who taught them his secrets and thus helped them to develop the witchcraft in their belly, bound them with strong prohibitions against using their knowledge for killing rather than for healing. But in many regions, people are not so sure that the interdiction against killing will be observed. After all, nganga are witches and, therefore, there is always the risk that the basic instinct of witchcraft—that is, to betray and eat your own relatives—will break through. Indeed, in many areas, there is a diffuse but basic idea that nganga themselves could only be initiated after they have sacrificed a close relative. To put it more succinctly: a nganga can only heal because he has killed. This basic amorality—the nganga can only help because they have placed themselves beyond considerations of good and evil—seems to equip them particularly well to play their role in "the politics of the belly," which according to Bayart (1989) and other authors is characteristic of postcolonial Africa (but certainly not only for the politics of that continent).

The relationship between the nganga and his client are furthermore characterized by a somewhat paradoxical emphasis on *intimacy and distance*. A nganga is supposed to penetrate into the intimate sphere of his client. Only then can he really armor him. But he is, at the same time, an outsider. People often prefer to go to a nganga elsewhere—sometimes in villages several hundreds of kilometers away—or, conversely, nganga work at a considerable distance from their home country (in Cameroon, for instance, witch doctors from Nigeria are nowadays supposed to be particularly efficacious). Again, this is certainly not a new trait. As Elisabeth Copet-Rougier (1986) emphasizes for the Kako (East Cameroon), a nganga should never stay too long in his own village, because he will become a deadly danger to his own relatives. Indeed, nganga are often at the margins of the kinship organization; in many respects, they are nomadic figures, not clearly tied to a specific locality.

This paradoxical emphasis on intimacy and distance is paralleled by an equally precarious balance between *secrecy and publicity*. The intimacy of the relationship between nganga and client is reinforced by a sphere of secrecy. Healing sessions will often take place indoors, in the presence of only those people who are directly involved (notably relatives). And, of course, the nganga will be extremely secretive about the knowledge that enables him to perform so well. However, this emphasis on secrecy is balanced by a need for at least some publicity: indeed, nganga can only attract clients if they acquire a certain reputation.[13] Especially in recent times, nganga have become increasingly aggressive in advertising themselves and their capabilities. This advertising is done in the most literal way. Whereas, for instance, during the beginning of my research in East Cameroon in the early 1970s, nganga were somewhat marginal figures who lived at the outskirts of the village, keeping a somewhat low profile, this certainly does not apply any longer. A more modern type of nganga has emerged, sporting modern attributes such as sunglasses and a wide array of books on "Eastern" magic, who often adorn their houses with shrill signs (*astrologist*, *Rosicrucian*, etc.). Such modern nganga are also very aggressive in approaching potential clients, warning them about dangers they alone can see, admonishing them that they have to purify their compounds, and straightforwardly accusing close relatives of causing all the clients' troubles. In many respects, the nganga have become aggressive entrepreneurs, avidly looking for publicity.[14]

A crucial aspect of the relationship between nganga and client are finally the *interdictions*. It is especially this aspect that turns the support by a nganga into some sort of Achilles' heel. Just as the nganga's professor will always have imposed certain rules on the nganga when he was still a pupil, the nganga himself will always condition his support to the client. He can only heal or armor if the client respects certain interdictions. These can be of a very practical nature, for instance, the obligation to pay the nganga for his services (there are many stories of clients who, although empowered, refused to pay up and were destroyed by the very nganga whose help they sought). But they can also take the forms of warnings—such as the nganga in the story above, who warned Mimbang not to take the road yet. The more general moral of the numerous stories of how people were destroyed for not respecting the interdictions seems to be that the nganga, and witchcraft in general, can give additional power but will make one extravulnerable at the same time. Just as acquiring a second pair of eyes—the very first stage of any initiation into witchcraft—will make the client see but will simultaneously enhance his "visibility" to all other witches, support in the world of witchcraft may reinforce the politician—this is why it is thought to be indispensable by so many African politicians—but will expose him as well to new dangers. The outcome of Mimbang's story—who, in the end, was destroyed by the very witchcraft powers by which he tried to empower himself—summarizes a moral common to many witchcraft stories. There is a basic circularity to the witchcraft discourse—protection against witchcraft is to be found with the nganga, who is, however, himself a superwitch and draws his clients inexorably into the spirals of witchcraft—which makes it so hard to escape from it.

Such an enumeration of basic principles in the role of the nganga risks giving a static image, which is, of course, highly misleading. It is clear that the witchcraft world is rapidly changing. Ever since the beginning of colonial anthropology, there have been long debates over whether witchcraft is on the increase or not (see Douglas 1970). Even nowadays, with the general panic about a supposed proliferation of witchcraft, it is hard to prove that this is indeed the case. What is clear, however, is that, especially during the last two decades, witchcraft is coming more and more out into the open. In the 1960s and 1970s, in Cameroon as elsewhere in Africa, talking too openly about witchcraft was not done: it was seen as a "traditional" aspect that hardly fit the conception of "young States" that were destined to quickly modernize society, supposedly unencumbered by traditional ballast (Rowlands and Warnier 1988). But this conception has rapidly changed over the last decades: witchcraft is now very much present in the public sphere—in the newspapers, on the radio and TV, and certainly on Radio Trottoir (the grapevine).

It is tempting to explain this change with the contrast between the colonial and the postcolonial state; in general, it is certainly true that the present-day regimes tend to take witchcraft much more seriously than did their colonial predecessors. However, this contrast should not be exaggerated, because there is no radical discontinuity. The colonial state certainly had the pretense to address this difficult issue "rationally," starting from the commonsense premise that witchcraft did not exist and, therefore, could only constitute an imaginary crime. However, in practice, such a positivist attitude was extremely difficult to maintain. A very tricky but recurrent question was what to do with a witch doctor who had killed an alleged witch, supposedly in order to protect his client. The dilemma to the state's judiciary apparatus was—and still is—that convicting the witch doctor seemed to mean that the authorities were protecting the witches, whereas letting him get away with it meant condoning murder. In nearly all colonial archives one can find substantial files containing drawn-out discussions about this issue.[15] No matter how "rational" colonial authorities wanted to be, they found it extremely hard to maintain a categorical standpoint. What was at stake already in these colonial debates was the question about what kind of knowledge is valid: in principle, Western medical or judicial knowledge denies the validity of the nganga's expert knowledge. But in practice, even the colonial authorities found it extremely hard to stick to this categorical vision.

Morris and 'Primary Colors': Two Stories About American Politics

Does it make sense to try and compare these "witch doctors" to our modern "spin doctors"? An obvious objection is that witch doctors always emphasize secrecy, whereas spin doctors, as public relations experts, make their living by publicity. Someone such as Morris, for instance, goes to great lengths to emphasize the open and scientific character of his knowledge, notably his sophisticated polling technique. However, in practice the difference between the two is not that great.[16] The above may have shown that witch doctors need at least some sort of publicity to establish their reputation, whereas it is equally clear that spin doctors, for their part, use publicity in a most obfuscating way.

The precarious balance between secrecy and publicity is, for instance, central to Dick Morris's story. Morris has a long history with Clinton. He was called in twice, in 1978 and 1982, to help Clinton win the Arkansas governorship. But he was dismissed both times as soon as this goal was achieved. However, in 1994, he was called back once more, when Clinton, now president, seemed to be politically completely outmaneuvered by the Republicans: after a disastrous election by which the latter took over Congress, Clinton's chances to be reelected for the presidency seemed to be nil. In his last book—*Behind the Oval Office* (1997)—Morris tries to show how he helped Clinton to stage his comeback. It is the story of an indeed-surprising resurrection: in 1994 nobody would have dared to predict that Clinton would win the 1996 election with such a landslide victory over Bob Dole.

Morris describes how his work for Clinton was, at first, an absolute secret. He had a code name, Charlie. The White House aides only knew that they had to pass on this Charlie with high priority to the president whenever he was on the phone, but they had no idea who he was. After about nine months (April 1995), the inevitable happened: the press found out who "Charlie" was, and Morris began to work under his own name. From this time on, he was increasingly in the limelight and it is clear, from the book, that Morris really liked this. However, it is also clear that the increasing publicity finally led to his downfall. At the end of August 1996—just before Clinton's triumphant reelection—the *Star* tabloid published an article on Morris's affair with a prostitute in Washington, intimating that he had discussed his work for the president with her and even had made her listen in to phone conversations with Clinton. Morris insisted that he only had given the horn to "the prostitute" to show that he was really talking to the president. This quite pathetic assertion is as characteristic for the tone of the book as his consequent refusal to give this woman, whom he must have frequented for several years, a name other than "the prostitute."[17] Despite such attempts at self-justification, Morris was immediately sacked after the story appeared in the press.

The main aim of Morris's book is to try and prove that Clinton's remarkable resurrection was staged by him through scientific and highly rational techniques; in other words, that he was not the magic man "inside Clinton's head" or a modern Rasputin, as the press sometimes suggested. Indeed, Morris emphatically refuses to refer to himself as a spin doctor.[18] He calls himself a consultant, and he is constantly stressing that he added "substance" to Clinton's campaign: that he was not spinning policy choices made by others but contributing in very substantial ways to Clinton's political course.[19]

The key word in all this is *polling*. Morris seemed to have elevated polling to a real art. On each decision, he was constantly polling in order to measure the public's reactions. He explains that only a limited sample—his fixed quota is no more than eight hundred interviews—is enough to measure the public opinion on condition that this sample is drawn according to complex rules of selectivity (the principle of the "focus group"). What was new was that he polled in order to *anticipate* the effects of possible policy choices. His great example was the way Hollywood tests out the public's reaction to different denouements of the same film plot, basing its final choice on these reactions. Similarly, Morris's polling would have helped the president to make the right choices. Hence, Morris's claim to "substance": his polling would have had a decisive influence on Clinton's policies.[20] The following quotation can give an impression of the scale on which Morris was polling:

> Every night at the height of the budget crisis we polled to measure the public's reactions. Our interviewers started phoning at seven in the evening and continued until one the next morning, eastern time, to catch West Coast voters before they went to bed. At about four in the morning, I would awaken to the sound of my fax machine as it spit out the poll results that had been collected only a few hours earlier. Each morning at seven-twenty, I called George (Stephanopoulos) with the data from the previous night's interviewing so he could report to the daily seven-thirty meeting that Leon (Panetta) held with the top White House staffers (which I never attended). When the president was awake, he'd take my call, so he could start his day with a summary of the latest polling information. (1997:183)

In retrospect, the advantages of such elaborate polling are quite clear: Clinton succeeded much better than the Republicans in following public opinion. The disadvantages are equally clear. The costs of polling at such a scale were enormous. Morris himself describes how, from time to time, Clinton got really angry because of the constant fund-raising he had to do. The enormous expenditure for polling was one of the main reasons for this. The real bill was only presented after Clinton's reelection, when his position became seriously endangered because of strong indications of unethical fund-raising.[21]

After all this "scientific," hard-boiled stuff, the end of Morris's book is pathetic, not to mention lachrymose. Morris is deeply grateful that the president, who has just brutally sacked him, calls and requests Morris not to be "angry" with him. Morris is touched by this, saying meekly that he hopes their relationship "has developed a new dimension" and that he "desperately wants it to continue." Apparently so much humility lifts Clinton as well to a higher level of morality. Morris lets him have the final word of the book, which is *forgiveness*.

Primary Colors (1996) is an anonymous and therefore all the more captivating novel about the inside of the campaign of a certain Stanton in his bid to become the Democratic candidate for the presidency. The similarities to Clinton and his close collaborators (including Hillary, here called Susan) are so obvious that the novel created considerable commotion in Clinton's environment: had one of his intimates fallen for the temptation to wash dirty linen in public? Only after a few months was it discovered that the true author was not an intimate but Joe Klein, a journalist from *Newsweek*, who was clearly very well informed about what was going on inside.

The story is told by Henry, an African American, who becomes Stanton's (Clinton's) campaign manager. Henry has some links with black politics (apparently his grandfather played an important role in the black-consciousness movement). However, that is not where his heart is; rather, he seems to be obsessed with the excitement of the political game, although he is at the same time horrified by its amorality. Indeed, the main theme of the novel seems to be the amorality of politics and the passions and violence it evokes. Stanton equates with Clinton in every respect. There is his voracious appetite both for food and sex: he is constantly "sucking in" doughnuts, and he repeatedly emerges from his office zipping his pants or buttoning up his shirt, not even bothering to cover up the most unexpected sexual escapades. There is also his deep passion for politics as such. For instance, when his campaign is faltering he is "suffering from severe human-contact withdrawal. He would devour every employee in every television station, lingering over their personal stories and their problems, hungry for the sort of campaigning he'd done in New Hampshire" (286). Stanton is sleazy and charming at the same time. But first of all he is a political animal.

His antipodes in the novel turn out to be both moral and pure. This is very clear for his main political rival, Governor Picker, who more or less by accident becomes the obvious candidate for the Democrats. Originally, Picker is only supporting another candidate who, however, dies after an acute heart attack (triggered by a nasty tackle by Stanton during a telephonic radio interview). Picker is clearly reluctant to join the race himself, but he is more or less taken by the tide. He pursues an apparently apolitical and improvised campaign, full of seemingly naive gestures. As Stanton comments: "It's like he's not, like he never was, a politician. He doesn't have the instincts any more, the little things we do to cut into each other. You saw that, right? He isn't playing the game at all, not in any way. It's absolutely strange" (422). It is clear that Stanton is rattled by all this, all the more because the seemingly naive campaign of Picker threatens to catch him off guard. Significantly, one of Picker's most amazing declarations is that he will even abstain from polling.

The other antipode is Libby, the "dustbuster," whose morality comes as some sort of surprise. She has a strong personality and presence and often uses foul language—her dialogue in the book is rendered mostly in capital letters—and she is brought in to save the campaign when the first of Stanton's discarded lovers turns up to raise a scandal. Libby expertly solves this by pulling the woman's lawyer by his lapels over his desk, holding a gun against his groin ("Well, mister: YOU ARE FUCKED") until he confesses how he rigged the tape of Stanton's telephone call to the woman, inserting more juicy details to shock the public. As an experienced dustbuster, Libby is also sent to rake up the muck needed to stop Picker's triumphant campaign, which indeed she does in her own manner. However, she cannot stomach the casualness with which the Stantons decide, without a moment of hesitation, to bring the sordid, private details she dredged up on Picker into the press. Apparently she had thought that some of the old idealism—it turns out that she worked with the Stantons already in 1972 during the George McGovern campaign—was still there. After divulging a final sordid detail on Stanton's birth, she storms out of the room and commits suicide.

Despite such moral obstacles, Stanton's campaign continues, in the end even victoriously. The ambivalence in the book is that precisely because of his amorality, Stanton is such an enticing figure. The end is symptomatic. Henry is so shocked by Libby's suicide that he refuses to go on working for Stanton's campaign. He toys with the idea of going back to a romantic affair with another campaign collaborator (one ignominiously discarded by Stanton). But in the end and despite all this, he seems to be persuaded again by Stanton to come back to the campaign.[22] Clearly he is bewitched by politics.

Spin-Doctors and Witch-Doctors: Magic Versus Science?

As was mentioned before, this comparison may seem to be an audacious one. It is not only that the spin doctors' obsession with publicity appears to be the opposite of witchcraft and its secrecy. There is also the contrast that somebody such as Morris goes to great lengths to demonstrate the scientific character and the accountability of his methods, precisely because he wants to show that he is not some sort of a magician. However, the preceding summaries of the two spin doctor stories may have indicated already that there also are clear convergences. As was indicated earlier, the aim of this contribution is certainly not to try and demonstrate that witch doctors and spin doctors are "just the same." My intention is rather to show that there are striking parallels in the ways in which their "expertise" influences politics— parallels that risk being overlooked by current (and comfortable) oppositions between, supposedly, the occultism of African politics and the transparency of politics in the West. After all, the press's tendency to depict spin doctors as modern medicine men and a secret source of power behind the political leaders is not all that surprising.

First of all, there are striking correspondences in the language used. To quote a few examples: when Morris was taken aboard again by Clinton in 1994, he defined his task as "turning the president's misfortune around," which demands first of all "a clear idea of how he had fallen" (Morris 1997:29). Clinton has to be "redefined" by "reaching into this candidate's issue basket and pulling out certain positions" (40). These are similar to words a nganga might use when describing how he makes his client go through a complete "confession" before being able to "reconstitute" his personality and "pull out" the dangerous accretions causing him to disintegrate. Also strongly reminiscent of a nganga is Morris's verbose insistence on his good intentions. Nganga as well will always insist that their professor has bound them to use their secret powers only to heal, precisely because they are such suspect figures. However, like the nganga, spin doctors have an aura of amorality. They also can switch sides at any moment. Morris, for instance, worked alternately for Republicans and Democrats. Indeed, in his book, he emphasizes repeatedly that one of his assets while working for Clinton was that he succeeded in maintaining such good relations with his former Republican clients. To him, such lack of ideological commitment is part of the job. "Like other consultants, I am often called a mercenary, which is fair enough. . . . I have worked for both Democrats and Republicans, which strikes people as the height of cynicism. I would refute that. I do have political convictions . . . but I am not an ideologue in search of a candidate."[23] In contrast, another famous—or notorious?—Clinton consultant, James Carville, emphasizes his deep ideological commitment to the Democratic Party. His 1996 book tries, in a sort of playful way, to confirm the worst stereotypes of Republicans. Yet, he is now mainly remembered for the fact that for the 1992 presidential elections, he ran Clinton's campaign, whereas his wife, Mary Matalin, was the political director of George Bush Sr.'s campaign. Their joint 1995 book—written along with a ghost writer—tries to show that being married while working for fiercely opposed camps did not create any major ideological problems. The ease with which such "political consultants" can change sides or even work for both sides at the same time indicates a lack of ideological involvement that makes spin doctors, like witch doctors, seem suspect or even evil. No wonder Morris's and also Carville's books have such a defensive tone.

The term *spinning* itself reinforces this suspect aura. This may be the main reason why both Morris and Carville refuse to call themselves spin doctors. Yet, the term has become central to their profession (and in their books). A whole idiom has developed around it: hence the expressions "to spin the press" and "spinning that line"; journalists are taken to the "spinning room," and so on.[24] Even though the term has now acquired implications of shrewdness or even nastiness, it still evokes a kind of fairy-tale association: "spinning straw into gold" is an obvious one. Indeed, even in its political usage *spinning* has retained references to fantasy and to conjuring up things that are not really there.

Primary Colors is full of similar, evocative language and images. Stanton "devours" people in his eager campaigning. Picker, Stanton's apolitical rival, surprises himself and the audience by concluding his first speech for a large audience by exhorting them to go and donate a pint of blood. He promises to do so himself immediately after his speech. This simple gesture again baffles the Stanton campaign staff, especially because it evokes an enthusiastic response. However, just like the powerful symbols and rules of the nganga, "blood" proves to be such a polyvalent metaphor that it gets Picker into all sorts of difficulties. Later on in the book, it turns out that one of the secrets

he is hiding—and which made him withdraw from politics at an earlier occasion—is that, during the liberal 1960s, he regularly used cocaine, which
aroused him so strongly that he even had a homosexual affair. Indeed, this is
the secret that Libby (Stanton's suicidal "dustbuster") succeeds in dredging
up by tracing Picker's former lover in a nursing home, where he is dying of
AIDS. Picker himself realizes, after having donated his blood, that he is not
even sure that his blood is not AIDS infected. Thus he feels forced, after a
tortured night, to call up the hospital and inquire with a distorted voice
about whether his blood has been properly checked. Just as in the world of
the nganga, everything that seems to be pure and salutary can turn out to be
deeply corrupted. The very language of the book, moreover, constantly emphasizes the direct link between politics and violence: the capacity of politics
to destroy people, which strongly recalls the violent undercurrent of the
nganga's role in African politics.[25]

Such convergences in language point to deeper correspondences. Paradoxically, it is often the apparent contrasts that shade into unexpected re-
semblances. A good example is Morris's obsession with polling. His plea that
he does not spin but that, rather, he is a man of substance (Morris 1997:40)
is based especially on the openness and accountability of his polling methods. Polling is the answer to all his doubts and questions. He even goes as far
as to let the public decide through polling what the president has to do during his holiday on Martha's Vineyard (the response is that he should not play
golf but, rather, do something simple, such as hiking). Clinton reacts furi-
ously; apparently he feels that polling is penetrating too deeply into his personal life. The parallel of this case with nganga, who are all the time decid-
ing on their clients' plans for travel—a particularly magic moment—is again
striking.

More important is the question of whether there is really such a contrast:
is this polling as scientific and accountable as Morris pretends? In many respects, polling has become the highest form of statistics, the basis of what
Michel Foucault called the *gouvernementalité*, linked to the modern state and
the self-disciplining of society after the *grand enfermement* (locking up) of the
last two centuries. However, in a recent, seminal article on the remarkable
conversion of the nineteenth-century geographer/ethnologist Alfred Wallace, Peter Pels has interesting things to say about the origins of statistics,
which may help to qualify their sacrosanct status in modern society: "Early

nineteenth-century statistics was also very much a *moral* science, insisting on the perfectibility or 'improvement' of society on the basis of accurate measurement of its raw materials" (see Peter Pels, this volume). For this lofty aim, both statistics and its nineteenth-century counterweight, spiritualism, were basically about acquiring an extravisionary capacity—a "super-vision," as Pels calls it. Indeed, in many respects, statistics have become the modern language of divination. Like the language of the nganga, statistics have acquired a sacrosanct status, although this status is open to very different interpretations and very hard to verify. Moreover, especially lately, statistics seem to serve also to come up with surprising, if not shocking results.[26]

No wonder that in practice, polling, as the most advanced form of statistics, is full of magic moments. Its practice itself is far from "open" and "accountable." People are called up, anonymously, very early in the morning. They are confronted with a rapid series of questions. Moreover, there is the magic of the sampling. Morris's defense of how he is able to predict the reaction of a nation of more than 200 million people from a sample of only 800 respondents is very ingenuous, but at least to some—Clinton included, who regularly accused Morris of "biased polling" (Morris 1997:301)—it is on the border between science and magic. More important is that, apparently, polling and secrecy go very well together. Clinton tried to keep Morris's role—and his very person—a secret for as long as possible. And Morris, despite his obvious liking for publicity, grudgingly admits that he functioned best when he was a complete secret. It is therefore questionable whether the supposed openness of polling is indeed the opposite of witchcraft's secrecy. In many respects, polling can be compared to the "seeing" of the nganga, with their "second pair of eyes." It is, indeed, some sort of super-vision but used in a context of secrecy.

It is especially in relation to this precarious balance between secrecy and publicity that the deeper implications of certain parallels between the role of witch doctors and spin doctors can become clear. In practice, for instance, Morris is forced to execute a kind of tightrope walk between secrecy and publicity, which again reminds of the ambivalence of the nganga. Already at the beginning of his book, he states that secrecy is characteristic for his method and that he always feared that "publicity could destroy me—as it ultimately did" (1997:28). This preference for secrecy is by itself quite striking for a public relations expert whose stock in trade is publicity. But especially the end of the book shows also that it was, indeed, the tension between se-crecy and publicity that placed Morris in an impossible position and even became the main reason for his undoing. "The prostitute" figures as some sort of catalyst in this entanglement. When a *Time* journalist called Morris to tell him that he wanted to put Morris's photo on the cover with the head-ing "The Man Inside the President's Mind," Morris was with the prostitute. As usual, when there was an important telephone call—at least that is what Morris says—he asked her to go stand on the balcony. He needed a long time to persuade the journalist to tone down the cover: they finally agree on a cover showing Morris sitting on Clinton's shoulder with the text "The Man Who Has the President's Ear." Morris called Clinton, who accepted: "That's OK; you do have my ear." In between the two conversations, Mor-ris went to the balcony to tell "the prostitute" that he was sorry it was taking so long and to bring her a drink. And this is when the *Star* people shot the photograph that would become Morris's undoing (1997:322–23).

The figure of Leon Birnbaum, "the pollster" in *Primary Colors*, expresses this tension between secrecy and publicity in different ways. He is the only figure in the novel who remains a complete secret. He has absolute author-ity—the results of his polls are the final truth—but he is a curiously marginal figure: unemotional and very distanced. He speaks in a light way and appears invulnerable. In many respects he seems to be a better nganga—more capa-ble of handling the paradox of how to deal with publicity but remain himself a secret—than Morris does. Indeed, at the end of the book Morris turns out to be a pathetic sort of nganga. After his ultimate exposure, when the press divulges the secret of "the prostitute," he is completely at the mercy of his client. Clinton sacks him on the spot. And Morris feels that he can only de-pend on the president's "forgiveness." No sensible nganga would ever let a client come so close to him.[27]

All these difficulties in finding a proper balance between secrecy and public-ity can serve to highlight a general correspondence between witch doctors and spin doctors. The activities of both serve to draw a screen around power. The true sources of the politicians' power are shrouded in the secrecy of the expert's know-how. Despite all formal emphasis on openness and account-ability in American politics, the sources of power—the reasons for the suc-cess of the victorious and the failure of the losers—become as much hidden as in the witchcraft-infested politics of postcolonial Africa. The spin doctor, just like the witch doctor, functions as a screen between the voters and the politicians.

Morris's account of how he succeeds in bringing Clinton back to the middle of the political spectrum—through his complicated maneuvering with polling, "triangulation," and a growing emphasis on "substance" and "values"—points to the deeper reason for the latter's spectacular comeback.[28] In 1994, the Republicans succeeded in depicting Clinton as some sort of an extremist who was threatening the very basis of American society with his irresponsible spending, his health care reform plan, and so on. In a sense they succeeded in diabolizing him. However, after 1994, Clinton—or was it Morris, using the information coming from his strenuous polling?—succeeded in turning around this powerful image. Increasingly, it seemed that not Clinton, but rather the Republican leadership—people such as Newt Gingrich—were the real extremists, with their attacks on basic entitlements of American citizens and the strong presence of fanatical fundamentalists among their close collaborators. This was one of the main reasons for the Republican debacle two years later. All this manipulating and mirroring of images shows how important the imaginary is, in Western politics as much as in postcolonial Africa. However, as Bayart (1996:166) paraphrases it very aptly: "l'imaginaire, principe d'ambivalence"—the imaginary, whether invoked by the discourse of witchcraft or by the so-called scientific methods of polling, always introduces ambivalence and, therefore, the possibility of reinterpreting or even turning around the images involved.

Indeed, in many respects what is announced as scientific knowledge often turns out to be as "imaginary" as the fantasies evoked by the witchcraft discourse. In his last book—fantastic in every sense of the word—Michael Taussig (1997:144) introduces, quite unexpectedly, in the middle of his exploration of the "magic of the state" through the visions of his "spirit queen" of the mountain, the figure of Paul Levy, a U.S. economist working for Merrill Lynch. Levy's task is to evaluate the economic performance of nations, where "politics is played out in the shadows, affecting economic growth in ways which can only be surmised" (ibid.). Taussig succeeds indeed in showing that the ways in which such an economist comes to his evaluations—basing himself on "hunches" about other people's "hunches"—is not that different from the way in which anthropologists feel their way through the visionary world of a "spirit queen." The economist's way of producing the kind of knowledge on which "such gargantuan enterprises as the ship of state rest" is as much part of the imaginary.

In each context, the imaginary introduces basic ambivalence, not only conceptually but also in a very material sense. A concrete parallel is, for instance, that both polling, however scientific it may be, and the kind of support a witch doctor can provide turn out to have their costs. Above we saw already that the witch doctor's interdictions always demand their toll in the end. We saw also that Morris's account already foreshadows the price Clinton had to pay for the polling Morris was imposing on him. All this polling may have served to "armor" Clinton, but later on, it turned out to be his Achilles' heel.[29] It was—at least according to some (see Note 21 above)—especially the costs of polling that forced him to the kind of desperate fund-raising that was to bring him difficulties after his reelection. Again, this paradox—a source of strength turns into a source of weakness—has more general implications. In Africa, witchcraft is seen as the secret behind a politician's success, but it can also be invoked to explain his downfall. A similar ambivalence is at the root of Morris's spinning. The same image of extremist that was behind Clinton's debacle of 1994—and which may very well have been developed with the help of Morris, then at the service of the Republicans—could be turned around and become the reason for Clinton's *retour en force* in 1996.

Behind all this ambivalence is the link—in both contexts—between the imaginary and secrecy. The reproduction of the images in which both witch doctors and spin doctors deal seems to require a kind of tightrope act between secrecy and publicity. And it is precisely because of this double capacity—both public and hidden, both highly visible and at the same time intimate or even secret—that these images become so ambiguous, lending themselves to constant reinterpretation and reversal.

Conclusion

The conclusion of all this can certainly not be that a spin doctor such as Morris is like a witch doctor, after all. The brief sketches above will have indicated that there are also, of course, important differences and specificities (see further Geschiere 1997). Comparing witch and spin doctors may serve, rather, to show the inadequacy of current terminology and the oppositions it implies between magic and science, transparency and occultism. Such oppositions seem to mask basic issues in politics in general, both in Africa and America: notably the central role of the imaginary, with all the ambivalence and playing with images it introduces; and related to this, the precarious and ever-changing balance between secrecy and publicity.

In two recent contributions, Mariane Ferme (1998, 1999) shows that Georg Simmel's seminal statements about *das Geheimnis* (the secret)—which produces "an immense enlargement of life" while "numerous contents of life can not even emerge in the presence of full publicity"[30]—apply to both African societies and Western democracies. Ferme shows—also in her seminal book (2001)—that in Sierra Leone, political language is always double: it is about things that happen in the daylight world, but these must be complemented by interpretations in terms of the secret side of politics. But she warns also, following Jürgen Habermas, that the same complexity characterizes—and even increasingly so—politics in Western democracies. Apparently, in the West as well, the "public place" is not that public or transparent. It is tempting to refer here to the Internet and all the ambiguities between transparency and concealment it has introduced. Precisely because of its extreme openness, the information highway offers possibilities for the ramification of more or less hidden networks on a frightening scale—for instance, for the circulation of more extreme forms of child pornography. It is ironic that our information age is beset by fears of the expansion of hidden conspiracies on a global scale.[31]

All this may indicate that there is, indeed, some urgency in surpassing the worn-out oppositions between magic and science—between the occultism of African politics and the transparency of the West—and the unilinear vision they imply. The problem is that, in practice, they serve to maintain a highly one-sided view of Western politics: as said before, the more witchcraft-ridden African politics are said to be, the more transparent, by implication, the West appears. The convergences between witch and spin doctors may highlight that common, basic issues of power and the struggle to control it are at stake. The increasing role of spin doctors in Western democracies seems to confirm that power, precisely because it is always closely related to the imaginary, is marked by a deep ambivalence between publicity and secrecy. How this balance is worked out in practice varies, depending on the context and the moment. Yet, the omnipresence of such issues means that a nganga-ish reading of the stories of Morris and his colleagues can highlight alternative reasons—different from those advanced by the publicity industry itself—why spin doctors seem to play an indispensable role in "modern" politics. Paradoxically, publicity and the art of juggling images are inextricably intertwined with concealment and the secrecy that is crucial to any exercise of power. Therefore, the more important publicity becomes as a key moment in politics, the more important experts of revelation—such as the nganga or the spin doctors—can make themselves.

SEVEN

The Magical Power of the (Printed) Word

MARTHA KAPLAN

This chapter considers the magic of flags and the magic of the printed word in the British colonial state of Fiji. Asserting the power of ritual in the making of history, it engages more general questions about magic and power and the need of the state for familiars. Let us begin with two ethnographic sightings of books and flags in Fiji.

First, when studying the history of so-called cargo cult in Fiji, I was prepared to hear of secret books in which prophecies of returning ancestors, or secrets of the sources of cargo, might be found. The lost book, or the secret book is one of the stock ingredients of anthropology's formulaic cargo cult. And indeed, in Drauniivi Village, home to the Vatukaloko people, descendants of a prophet-leader (Navosavakadua of "Tuka movement" fame: see Burridge 1969; Worsley 1968; M. Kaplan 1995), there is a book, a beautiful bound book, kept carefully by a village intellectual. Rumors of its existence reach quite far beyond the village—I was asked about it by old gentlemen from inland districts miles away. It's actually written in longhand, its contents, largely concerning the origin places, migrations, and marriages of ancestor gods. The book was begun in 1917, by a Vatukaloko man, as a counternarrative to the inquiries and records keeping of the colonial government's Native Lands Commission. The Native Lands Commission records, in original longhand, and with printed summaries keyed to maps, are housed in Suva, Fiji's capital. Clerks in the offices of the Native Lands Commission, and other Fijians as well, call them Fiji's bibles.

Second, my interest in the history of prophet-leader Navosavakadua and his Tuka movement was shared, in the 1980s, by another eccentric prophet, a Fiji citizen of South Asian descent, who sought to create a narrative of Fiji as nation that could encompass and link its diverse peoples, notably the descendants of Pacific Islanders and of South Asian indentured laborers. Mr. Harigyan Samalia's national rituals included numerous flag-raising ceremonies. His ritual and elaborate cosmology were coherent but ultimately utterly marginal in the field of ritual politics in 1980s independent Fiji. What might interest us here is a fragment of Mr. Samalia's discussion with John Kelly and me in 1984, in which he prophesied the return of god to earth, probably in the form of a returned Navosavakadua: "He returns each time in different forms. His next incarnation will be as a Fijian, to found the new Kingdom on Maqo Island in the Lau Group. The living God will arise from earth, flowers will sing, dogs will speak like humans. Fifteen thousand flyers have been distributed prophesying this."

In both cases, the point is not to see Vatukaloko book-holders, or Mr. Samalia with his innovative flag-raising ceremonies and fifteen thousand printed flyers, as exotic, magic-wielding others but rather to consider the ways in which books about ancestor gods and landholding have come to have mana in a Fijian village and in the Fijian state and how the printed word (in the form of publicly distributed flyers) has come to figure in the efficacy of a prophet's vision.[1] This is not a simple matter of an oral tradition of magic now rendered mechanically in paper and ink (after all South Asia has a deep textual tradition). Instead, in these two ethnographic vignettes, and in Fiji now more generally, the power of the flag, the book, and the printed word come most urgently from their histories of colonial use. Flags and the printed word were key aspects of the magic of the colonial state.

The chapter has four sections. Following this introduction, the second section, "On Magic and Power," discusses interpretive issues concerning magic and power, building on Stanley Tambiah's approach to ritual in his article "The Magical Power of Words" (1985a). Briefly noting the literature on the power of printed words, and on the power of pomp (including flags) in empires, it argues that the magical qualities of these two sorts of phenomena are usefully understood via a theory of ritual in history making and via an additional new concept, the state familiar. Next, in the lengthy third section titled "State Familiars in the History of Fiji," printing and flags are discussed in detail as magical entities in the complex history of colonial Fiji. The concluding section considers ever-present interpretive problems of trajectory. It rejects the premise that magic should be understood as an element of the traditional, the premodern, the past surviving into or contesting a nonenchanted present, asserting instead that our present has its own enchantments.

On Magic and Power

Following Tambiah (1985a:18–19) this chapter does not seek to emphasize a difference between magic and religion or ritual. As Tambiah has noted (1985a:84), and as Keith Thomas (1971), Carlo Ginzburg (1983a), and others have variously shown, in European history categories such as magic, witchcraft, ritual, religion, and science emerge in complex competitions to define the real, to routinize and institutionalize cosmologies, and to wield power. In intertwined ways these categories also emerge in the centuries of colonial encounter (see, e.g., M. Kaplan 1989), culminating for anthropologists in classic nineteenth- and early-twentieth-century social evolutionary schemes such as Sir James Frazer's. From Frazer, Emile Durkheim, Bronislaw Malinowski, and Edward Evan Evans-Pritchard, anthropology has received a tradition of embedding magic in arguments about difference. Of course, as the introduction to this volume also affirms, there is something of a countertradition within anthropology, in which we can also read in these classics both respect for magic and the idea that we might find it here "at home," for example, in capitalism, as we find in Marx. It is argued here that several modes of representation, communication, persuasion, and coercion that colonial Europeans thought of as rational, technical, and utterly different from magic can in fact be well understood as magical.

Does magic have real power? Is magic real? There are many ways to approach this issue. First of all, we could indeed consider whether magic is real. Magic could be real because it is technically, materially efficacious. Or it could be materially efficacious only after it is socially real. Its social reality could be a matter of shared belief, or in Durkheim's sense, where religion is real because the totem refers to social facts, a matter of fact by connection to real social groups and relations. (In either such case, the material efficacy would follow from a social commitment.) Or it could be both materially efficacious and socially real. Or of course it could be neither materially efficacious nor socially real. In this sense, one could restrict the sense of "magic" to fraud or delusion. But if magic is so sharply circumscribed, there are all sorts of things that we cannot begin to understand. I think that the effort to weave a net to keep the magical separate from the real will inevitably produce its own uncanny remainders. I would rather allow the real and the magical a space to mix. I myself am sure that magic is socially real, and I would like to see a magical dimension to all sorts of techniques and entities that are implausibly efficacious from an outside point of view. But at the very least, this chapter proceeds with the assumption that magic is socially real and that it therefore has power in society, that in cultural (Tambiah's cosmological) contexts, people can use magic to make individual lives and to make history, to routinize narratives and build institutions. Magic is one of the means of domination, of possession, and sometimes also of struggle for autonomy.

Of course it is also important to keep in mind the issue of the question itself. What does it mean, what are the consequences of asking whether magic is real? Who, historically, has asked this question? The social evolutionary ranking of magic as less real, less efficacious than science or the delineation of traditional enchantment versus modern, disenchanted rationality are part of wider projects of colonial knowing and classifying. These self-designations of disenchantment may be ironically inaccurate. To complete our theoretical preliminaries, let us turn to another ethnographic example, the first instances of printing magic in colonial Fiji, then note some of the literature on print and flags, in colonial and other settings, and then turn to find a term, the *state familiar* that suggests their uncanny powers.

STATE FAMILIARS

In the Beginning was the Word—or maybe the Flag and the Word, in the history of powerful magical entities in early nineteenth-century colonial Fiji.

Great was the astonishment and delight of the people as they saw the marvels of the Mission press. The Heathen at once declared it to be a god. And mightier by far than their mightiest and most revered deities was that engine at which they wondered. In the midst of the barbarous people it stood, a fit representative of the high culture and triumphant skill of the land whence it came; and, blessed by the prayers of multitudes across the seas, and of the faithful ones who directed its might, that Mission press began, with silent power, its great and infallible work which was destined to deliver beautiful Fiji from its old and galling bonds, to cleanse away its filthy stains of crime, to confer upon its many homes the blessings of civilization, and enrich its many hearts with the wealth of the Gospel of Jesus. (Rev. Thomas Williams 1858:222)

Wesleyan missionaries came to Fiji in 1835 from the London Missionary Society. Initially they had Bible translations (the Gospel according to Saint Matthew) printed in Tonga. They got their own press, the first in Fiji, in 1838 and proceeded to produce translated New Testaments, alphabets, books of sermons, and catechisms. By 1858 they had published (in London) for overseas consumption *Fiji and the Fijians*: volume 1, *The Islands and Their Inhabitants*, volume 2, *Mission History* (see Calvert 1858; Clammer 1976).

Did Fijians believe the mission's printing press was a god? Let us avoid Marshall Sahlins versus Gananath Obeyesekere territory here. If nothing else, however, surely Fijians recognized worship when they saw it and recognized that the missionaries believed in the press as a magical and efficacious instrument of their god's and their own project. Maybe the missionaries didn't praise it so lavishly in daily use, when oiling and inking and damning rusted parts. But note how they used the printed word, not just to convert (almost all of Fiji by 1854; of course Fijian agency needs to be thought about here too—see Sahlins 1985; Toren 1988; M. Kaplan 1990) but also to extract money from the Missionary Society and Wesleyans at home, via such vivid, persuasive printed invocations.

But perhaps, one could argue, these missionaries are "other" enchanted exotics. They are nineteenth-century messengers of god, temporal others, who like spatial others are different, prior, and predictably prone to magic. No wonder that, in collusion with Fijian prophets, they have left a legacy of secret books and alternative bibles.

But the bibles are not held at the headquarters of the Methodist Church in Fiji. The best-known "bibles" of Fiji are held in a government office, the Native Lands Commission. They record something that is (to the recorders and many other colonial and postcolonial commenters on the matter) disenchanted, rational, and material, namely, titles to land. Fiji became, by 1854, largely Methodist. In 1874 it was given to and taken by the British Empire; it became colonial.[2] And in the beginning of the colonial state were flags and words, magical vehicles of power, "state familiars." Let us consider them.

It is useful to take as a powerful clue the colonial and postcolonial preoccupation—with books, printed words, and symbols of power such as flags— shown by people like the Vatukaloko and Mr. Samalia. When Mr. Samalia raised flags and distributed flyers in his idiosyncratic attempt to construct his own state, he recognized the effective power in those vehicles or technologies, the way they enabled the making of a colonial state. This leads to more general questions about what printing and flags are and do in colonial societies and the nature of their magic, how it works.

There is a deep and complex literature on the printed word tied to arguments variously about the market, the state, the public sphere, and "modernity" in Europe and the United States; for example, Lucien Lefebvre and Henri-Jean Martin (1929) 1997; Benedict Anderson 1983, 1991; Robert Darnton 1979; Thomas Gustafson 1992; Adrian Johns 1998; and Michael Warner 1990. Gustafson in particular usefully describes a history of U.S. critiques of British language use, during the revolutionary period, in which colonial American critics found British language to be a corrupted public discourse filled with lies and worried about how to secure their own truth. Often drawing on John Locke, the U.S. revolutionaries wanted to create a transparent, truthful language and legal and political system. Many believed that such "truthful languages" could exist. On the one hand, this gave a tremendous impetus to an American public sphere of literate expression of opinion (see also Warner 1990). And on the other hand, like Mr. Samalia in Fiji, or the Fijian villagers keeping secret books, the colonial American followers of Locke described by Gustafson diagnosed a key aspect of British hierarchical, colonial practice: the power they derived from controlled deployment of glorified, distinguished, ennobled, and thereby mystified words and other symbolic forms.

Yet, unfortunately for the optimistic followers of Locke, the Americans of Gustafson's history who thought their goal was to replace corrupt language with free, truthful language, the British may well have operated most successfully through most of Empire because of their conscious use of powers to render language unarguable, their skills with the manipulation of magical technologies of pomp. As Barney Cohn (1996) observed long ago in "Command of Language, and the Language of Command," British colonial language-learning in India willfully asserted hierarchical relations. From Cohn (1987, 1996) and David Cannadine (2001) come details of the self-conscious use of pomp, and ritual, in colonial states. In places like Fiji, colonial governors were not unaware of the existence of a public sphere (colonial Fiji had its secular newspapers, with lively letters to the editors), but they did not and could not seek legitimacy there. In fact they quite scrupulously sustained the distinction between this mere public sphere and their own official documents. Fijians have diagnosed this aspect of colonial power in their "secret books," the hidden books in remote villages that mirror the restricted colonial minute papers and resulting archives that enhanced and belonged to centers of colonial authority. (They have diagnosed it as well in their use of flags and rituals surrounding them, in countercolonial and counternational projects from the 1880s to the present.)

Printed words, therefore, were routinely used by the British in places such as Fiji as carefully nurtured and guarded augmentations to their power, intimately controlled and exercised. Presses were tended, their products circulated and archived. So too, as we shall see, flags were carefully raised and lowered, saluted and acknowledged, ranked visibly. Focusing on these powerful, magical entities and processes, we can give them a name. We could call them totems or spells, or "rituals and routines of rule" (e.g., Corrigan and Sayer 1985), but John Kelly and I have suggested a term that works even better. With an allusion to the cats and broomsticks of witches, literal vehicles of power, we propose the simultaneously playful and occult: *state familiar*. To develop the concept, let us turn to a history of changing state familiars in Fiji.

State Familiars in the History of Fiji: Flags, Words, and Property

The flag is what many Fijians talk about when referring to Cession Day, October 10, 1874, as "Na vakarewa na kuila" (the raising of the flag by the British). But the colonial documents and histories equally date the colony of Fiji's inception to words, to the signing of the Deed of Cession. Here is how it happened, that magical creation of a new polity, via ritual means, according to the dry prose of official historian R.A. Derrick, in his book that was "Printed and published in the colony of Fiji at the Government Press, Suva," in 1946 (revised edition 1950).

> His Excellency Sir Hercules Robinson was accompanied by Commodore Goodenough, Consul E.L. Layard, the Honourable G.L. Innes (Attorney-General of New South Wales), and Captain Chapman and other naval officers. The party was received in the Council Room by the King and his Ministers, attended by Ma'afu, Tui Cakau, Ratu Epeli, Tui Bua, Ratu Savenaca, and other high chiefs. Wilkinson, the interpreter, read the Chiefs' resolution of 30th September and a translation of the Deed of Cession. Two copies of the Deed in English were on the table; and when the signatures to these had been completed, His Excellency signed and sealed both, and handed one to the King. . . .
>
> The public ceremony of hoisting the flag took place on the lawn in front of the Council House, where the official party gathered at the flagstaff to hear His Excellency declare Fiji a possession and dependency of the British Crown. The flag of the Cakobau Government was lowered and the Royal Standard was raised, while the crew of H.M.S. Pearl manned yards, and a salute of twenty-one guns was fired from the warships. The guard of honour—consisting of naval ratings and a company of Fijian Constabulary—presented arms as the Pearl's band played the National Anthem; the marines fired a *feu de joie*, and cheers were given for Her Majesty the Queen, and for his Excellency. Sir Hercules Robinson then called for cheers for Cakobau, Vunivalu and Tui Viti, and for the Commissioners; and the ceremony ended with general handshaking and congratulations.
>
> A proclamation issued immediately made it known that Fiji was a possession and dependency of the Crown. (Derrick [1946] 1950:249–50)

And from then on, everything that was official and real in the colony was made real via the printed word. If it wasn't "gazetted," it didn't officially exist. And one of the things that was official and real was the colonial state itself. Another thing was property, quite valuable property, such as land, whose ownership is enshrined in bibles. Let us go back further in Fiji's history, to think about flag power and printed word power in the making of state and property in Fiji.

FLAGS AND WORDS OF OWNERSHIP: CHANGING RULES

Told as a history of Europeans in Fiji,[3] Cession marks the transition from an era of policy and property rights established by ships' captains and consuls, with warships, guns, and flags, to a colonial state in which flags shared a place as state familiars along with gazettes. From 1801 to 1874, Americans and Europeans who were not missionaries also came to Fiji. In the earliest decades, they were shipwrecked or seeking water and supplies. Those who remained for a time were beachcombers, or, until about 1815, they sought sandalwood, desirable in trade with India and China. To get the sandalwood, captains paid local chiefs, who organized their people to cut the wood, exercising right or coercion over people and the territories where the sandalwood grew. From the 1820s on, ships came for cargoes of beche-de-mer (sea cucumber) to sell to Manila merchants for the China trade. Here again local chiefs provided labor and access to fishing areas and sites for sheds for curing the beche-de-mer. By 1840 there were thirty resident foreigners at Levuka with their Fijian wives and families. Whereas early on whites got land through service to chiefs or via marriage, from 1840 on land "sales" became more common. In the 1860s a world cotton boom (partly due to the U.S. Civil War) sent floods of settlers into Fiji, especially whites from Australia and New Zealand, avid for land and labor, as did an 1870 gold rush. In 1871 there were close to four thousand resident Europeans (Derrick 1950; Routledge 1985; Records of the Cakobau Government, Ad-Interim Government and CSO minute papers, National Archives of Fiji, Suva).

Europeans and Americans wanted things from Fiji. They wanted sandalwood, beche-de-mer, and later, land and labor to grow cotton, copra, sugar, and other crops. And they wanted their rights to such things established. Over and over, they expressed this right as establishing order in the face of disorder, law over savagery, possession over chicanery. "I know my boundaries," settlers began their testimonies. And testimony is a key term. Throughout the nineteenth century, Europeans and Americans described what was for them a key scenario, over and over in Fiji. Its pattern went thus (as narrated by the European and American authors): Fijians commit an infamous act (e.g., they take possession of a wrecked ship and kill the shipwrecked survivors or strip them of everything, or Fijians burn down a beche-de-mer processing shed or steal from a trader or planter, or a Fijian chief sells land to a planter for trade goods and then he or other Fijians begin to use the land, claiming they had never agreed to alienate it).[4] Then a warship arrives (generally American or British) and the captain investigates the outrage, gathering testimony; renders a written judgement; and authorizes and carries out reprisals. Examples are HM brig *Victor* (Captain Crozier), which visited Lakeba in 1836 "to inquire into the murder of four of the crew of the British brig Active" (Derrick [1946] 1950:65) or the U.S. Exploring Expedition in 1840, in which Commander Wilkes negotiated a treaty with Tanoa, the Vunivalu of Bau, and also "inquired into the attempted seizure of the ship Charles Doggett, nearly 6 years before" (ibid.:91).[5] The ships, floating agents of the European powers, carried guns, of course. They also sailed under flags.

By the 1840s the floating agents and their flags came ashore. England, France, Germany, and the United States, increasingly conscious of each other's encroachments in the Pacific, had begun to establish consuls in places such as Fiji. In 1840 John Brown Williams, a U.S. vice-consul in New Zealand, was appointed U.S. "commercial agent" to Fiji. In 1845 he became U.S. consul in Fiji, in 1849 he "settled at Laucala point where he erected a flagstaff and built a house" (ibid.:96). In March 1857, when the US sloop of war *Falmouth* was at Laucala, the crew set up a new flagstaff at the consulate "and in the presence of chiefs and people from Rewa hoisted their ensign with impressive ceremonial" (ibid.:136). In 1857 Great Britain appointed a consul for Fiji, previously served by a consul based in Tahiti and Apia.

Increasingly, the consuls and the continually visiting ships ruled on issues of property. Williams of the United States was almost farcical in his practices, registering his own title deeds with himself and by himself. But what is worth noticing is that all the settlers sought to register their title deeds, seeking to claim European law in support of their claims to ownership. In so doing, they invoked the powers of American and European warships on their own behalf. And these ragtag settlers also transformed themselves, from flotsam and jetsam of empire to beings entitled to the protection of flags and warships.

This history of visiting, floating flags and more permanent local flags figures in crucial ways in the events that led to cession, to the events that made Fiji a British colony. Put far too simply, Cakobau of Bau, a powerful chief of a powerful kingdom, laid claim to the novel title Tui Viti (King of Fiji) and headed several 1860s and 1870s chiefly-planter governments.[6] But Cakobau was hounded by debts, some for ships he had contracted and some created and made real by the curious, magical powers of floating and consular flags. It was a combination of U.S. consul Williams and the authoritative captains of U.S. warships who decreed that Cakobau, as paramount of Bau and/or as self-styled King of Fiji, was responsible for thefts from Williams's property by unidentified Fijians during a fire at a July 4 celebration in 1849. (Williams himself had accidentally set fire to his own compound with his homemade fireworks.) Williams claimed losses worth U.S.$5,001.31, and when the USS *St. Mary* (Captain Macgruder) visited Fiji in 1851, Williams got the captain to authorize him to demand the money from Cakobau himself. In 1855 the captain of the USS *John Adams* found Cakobau liable for U.S.$30,000. In 1858 the US corvette *Vandalia* (Commander Sinclair) arrived to settle the claims fixed in 1855 by Boutwell of the USS *John Adams*. Cakobau was summoned on board, attended by a missionary, and signed an agreement to pay U.S.$45,000 within a year. Faced with no source of money, he took up the offer of the new British consul to offer Fiji to Queen Victoria. As historians of Fiji know, this offer was turned down. He then turned to a flash outfit, the Polynesia Company, and sold them land (see Brewster 1937). In part because the United States was busy with the Civil War, it was not until 1867 that the USS *Tuscarora* arrived to renew the threat and to once again cause Cakobau to contemplate the protection of the queen. And thus, eventually, Cession, the words, and the flag.

THE MAGICAL POWER OF THE PRINTED WORD IN COLONIAL FIJI

Looking simply at official practice, colonial Fiji was an extraordinary panopticon: extraordinarily literal and concrete, actually looking everywhere, selecting and permanently establishing a version of customary rights (see M. Kaplan 1989; N. Thomas 1990). Paternalist first governor Sir Arthur Gordon was determined to protect Fijians from exploitation by guaranteeing them their lands and shielding them from plantation exploitation. To make the colony pay, the Colonial Sugar Refining Company was brought in from Australia and allowed to become the colony's monopsony sugar miller. The Deed of Cession also guaranteed settlers rights to property. In the course of ordering the ownership of land, the entire colony was surveyed and allotted. In 1880, the Lands Commission began to evaluate claims to land by Europeans, scrutinizing the titles registered by the consuls (these records yield the persistent settler testimony "I know my boundaries"). In 1890 the Native Lands Commission inquired into Fijian landholding, the commissioners moving from province to province to take testimony, cross-examine, and survey boundaries. Eventually, every inch of land in Fiji was accounted for, mapped and keyed to printed volumes. The formation of the commission was announced by notice in the *Fiji Royal Gazette* on November 13, 1880, and every subsequent appointee was gazetted, as were all government officers, ordinances, regulations, and official policies.

The Lands Commission has at times claimed that its records achieve completion and reflect absolute truth. They do nothing of the sort, but those who wield them speak easily of their biblical authority. In 1985 the Native Lands Commissioner told me that when there was a dispute over land, or a succession dispute, he took the volumes from the office and read them to the people to tell them the truth of the matter. "These matters can't be reopened," another official told me, "they are written in stone, Fijian bibles." There is a small but fiercely polemical tradition in Fiji scholarship of debunking the certainties of the Lands Commission records, showing, importantly, the translation into Fijian practice of reified colonial categories of ownership and kinship units (e.g., Clammer 1974; France 1969), documenting the hegemony of a colonial orthodoxy. Small wonder then that alternative genealogies and claims to land, held by hinterland village intellectuals, were organized in book form, or that Mr. Samalia, convinced of the power of the gazetted word, put his family's money to use to buy newspaper space to gazette his own versions of truth and polity.

Flags and Books in One Corner of Fiji and in the United States As Well

This chapter has been most concerned with state familiars at the inception of Fiji as a colony. The power of floating flags and of words, printed especially, helped make the colonial state what it was. There is, as noted briefly above, another, long story to be told of colonially controlled printed words that routinized the chiefly-colonial state and of many books kept and flags raised in contestation over the colonial state. Here only some of its contours are suggested, via three quick examples.

The first is a history of a court case in colonial Fiji in 1901, where Indian "coolie" plantation laborers diagnosed the power of the printed word in colonial courts and attempted to subvert it to their own ends.

An overseer named James Montague Kemmis testified in court (having been sworn in on a Bible) that a group of laborers doing roadwork assaulted him and beat him badly. Afterward, he recounted:

> Some one called out "Let us put him in a bag and throw him in the big drain." Jokhan Khan said to me "You kiss this book + promise you will not summons any of us + we won't beat you up anymore on those conditions." The book he referred to was a pocket book in my belt. He saw I could not get it out as he took it out himself. He held the book up to me, kneeling beside me + made me repeat that I would not summons any of them if they let me off then. Khan Mohomed took the book from Jokhan Khan + said "You must kiss the book for me too." I did so. I could promise that I would not summons them because I knew that someone else would.[7]

Indians in Fiji encountered the Bible less in the hands of missionaries than in the hands of court officers (see Kelly 1999b on indentured laborers and the law in colonial Fiji). The Bible's power in colonial courts, its role in authorizing truth and consequences in colonial law, its role, in short, as a familiar of the state, was clearly manifest to the indentured men who sought to pirate the power of the printed word for their own, very particular act of resistance. Ultimately, in this court case, they failed to "turn" the familiar to their own uses.

Second, in Drauniivi Village in 1984, flags figured constantly in narratives of the history of the colonial state and challenges to it. People referred to 1874 and the inception of the colonial state as "Na Vakarewa na Kuila" (the raising of the flag). But alternative movements had their flags as well: in the book carefully held by the village intellectual, there is a handwritten account of another flag raising (December 15, 1914) when, in Drauniivi itself, a flag was raised on behalf of the Fijian anticolonial leader Apolosi Nawai and his "Fiji Company." Such flag raisings by and for Apolosi occurred throughout Fiji's hinterlands in the 1910s and 1920s, until he was imprisoned and deported from the islands as a purveyor of "disaffection." But the most significant flag I encountered in Drauniivi (and Fiji) in the 1980s was brought to Drauniivi by the eccentric prophet, Mr. Samalia. He wrote to the Vatukaloko people of Drauniivi asking them to build a flagpole and promising to bring them their ancestor Navosavakadua's flag. And he did, or at least he brought them a flag with a Hindu Diwali lamp on it, which he believed was their ancestor's flag. In Drauniivi, the people raised it on the flagpole they had built

for the occasion, and the 1980s postcolonial state of Fiji was enough persuaded of the magic of flags that it dispatched members of Special Branch
(police who deal with "Disaffection") to investigate. Interestingly, although
Special Branch investigated, impelled by the rumor of the raising of a flag,
nothing much came of their investigations. Alternative flags, perhaps more
than secret books, retain the magical power to threaten Fiji's well-en-
trenched postcolonial state but only to a certain limit: focusing the gaze of
panoptic authority, provoking the state to take a real look.

Third, in the United States, the problem with the national flag in the late
1990s was not people's raising alternative flags so much as people's stealing
and burning the Stars and Stripes, in defiance of state power and government policy. At the start of the Gulf War in 1990, students burned flags on
college campuses, provoking local politicians to grandstand with calls for
new (or enforced) flag protection statutes.[8] Following terrorist attacks on the
World Trade Center and the Pentagon in September 2001, Americans took
to displaying the flag, like an amulet, on houses, on cars, and on T-shirts and
baseball caps, both as a healing and defiantly antiterrorist device. On occasion in the United States, books get banned, and sometimes burned too, as
though burning the witch's cat would burn the witch, and as if burning the
book would burn the ideas. In both cases, the burning protests and the protective laws (especially against flag burning) bear out the magical powers
these familiars have in everyday U.S. citizens' lives, as did the extraordinary
proliferation of flags on bodies, cars, and buildings post–September 11, 2001.

Wondering why Fiji citizens don't seem to burn their flags, but rather have
hoisted alternative ones, led me to think about what they do burn, and this in
turn led back to the Word. Special Branch did little to punish the Vatukaloko
and Mr. Samalia for raising flags alone, but they (or military confreres) beat
and tortured a Fiji citizen, Anirudh Singh, who burned a copy of Fiji's 1990
constitution (the constitution put in place by a military coup) on Diwali night
on October 18, 1990.

Conclusion: The Magical Power of the Printed Word

In conclusion, I'd like to return to questions of magic and power. First, let us
consider the reality of the state familiar. A skeptic might say of Cakobau's

cession, "Where's the magic? It wasn't the flags that enforced the debt, it was the guns," and the same could be said of Anirudh Singh's constitution burning, that the incitement was met by brute force. Yet, in discussing Trobriand canoe building, in "The Magical Power of Words," Tambiah argues that magical words and practical activity are joined in complementarity. Alternating spells and carpentry, the Trobriand ritual is "an imaginative, prospective and creative understanding of the very technological operations and social activities the Trobrianders are preparing to enact" (1985a:50). In parallel, I would argue that the flag familiars, hoisted or struck, were essential aspects of the technological operations and social activities of warships or consuls. On ships, for example, guns were possessed and fired in relation to social relations signified and practically organized via flags, which totemically signified membership, rights, and shared social space. Flags were saluted with guns; while a flag still flew, a ship was to be defended; and white flags called for cessation of firing. Equally, the power of words to create and authorize truth in colonial courts, to constitute and order, via gazettes and constitutions, emerged in the constant practical colonial uses of the Word: lands commissions, civil and criminal courts, police inquiries, gazettes, and published ordinances. The compelling magical reality of the flags and books is harder to see for those outside of the social and cosmological context, the historical period, and the locations described in this chapter. But, following Tambiah, to investigate this social and cosmological context is to reveal magical efficacies that have real effects, in this case in making history in an emerging colonial context.

Second, let us consider some last thoughts on the printed word as ritual or magical language, with some musing on the different arguments of Maurice Bloch and Stanley Tambiah. In colonial Fiji, the point of gazetting, or printing the "results" of inquiries of the Lands Commission, was to fix official hierarchies, land boundaries, and titles to property (to name only a few of the things gazetted). This desire to fix, and the practice of fixing via printed words, might bring to mind Maurice Bloch's (1989:43) sense of ritual as an "extreme form of traditional authority." How useful will we find Bloch's analysis? For Bloch, the forms of ritual language and practice (chanting, singing, dancing, use of archaic language) are repetitive, stereotyped, impoverished in meaning. They suppress argument rather than engage discussion, thus promoting the authority of the officiants. Nothing could seem more appropriate for thinking about the colonial gazette, or the published report of the Lands Commission. Indeed, you cannot argue with a gazette. And, in Fiji, it is very hard indeed to argue with the records of the Lands Commission. To challenge the 1990 constitution, it was a matter of all or nothing: accept it or burn it. And colonial and postcolonial officials certainly have benefited from the closing of communications, the censuring of arguments in official printed forms. This is not the first note on the sinister, reifying power of colonial publication; one thinks immediately of Edward Said on the claims to authority of the Orientalist scholars or of Barney Cohn on the colonial census in India. And like Cohn, in particular, I am interested in emphasizing the practical effects of this magic in the life of the colony, its contribution to the making of colonial rule.

Cohn quotes Lord Lytton, Governor-General of India: "The further East you go, the greater becomes the importance of a bit of bunting" (1987:661). It was of course Lytton's colonial state that loved the bunting and more especially its durbars, state spectacles, a third quintessential colonial state familiar. Many colonial states, and states more generally, set out quite deliberately to constitute unquestionable, monological utterances, using means of asserting their finality that merit being called magical.

On the other hand, in agreement with Tambiah, I do not want to see colonial magic as all powerful. For Tambiah (in "A Performative Approach to Ritual" [1985b]), rituals may take opposite turns "to the right when ritual media lose their semantic component and come to serve mainly the pragmatic interests of authority, privilege and sheer conservatism" (166) and to the left when "there is a deliberate attempt to coin new doctrinal concepts and mold new rituals bursting with meaning attached to the contents of the acts per se. In such times of promise and hope the semantic meanings of words uttered and object-symbols and icons matter terribly" (165). Thus, for Tambiah, ritual or magic may uphold authority or overturn it. The book kept in Drauniivi, an alternative to the printed "bibles" of the Lands Commission, takes a fixed text (John 1:1, "In the Beginning was the Word, and the Word was with God, and the Word was God") and remakes its meaning. "In the Beginning was NaVosa [Fijian for 'the Word,' but also the name of their ancestor Navosavakadua, the anticolonial prophet] and Navosa was with God, and Navosa was God." And surely Mr. Samalia found a way to argue with a gazette—he wrote his own. With more widespread effects, in Fiji and in India, the Gandhian branch of the Indian National Congress commissioned and published many reports of its own, carefully and with an increasingly standardized resonance, subtitling each "An Independent Inquiry." These alternatives draw on the force of state familiars to create their own powerful, or at least unsettling, magic.

Last of all, one can humorously equate Fiji's British with what Bloch called "an extreme form of traditional authority" (their printing equally or more extreme than the trance chanting of Bloch's Merina elders at circumcision rituals). This quite apt comparison derives its humor from the fact that the colonial British so clearly thought of themselves as the antitheses of tribal elders and would have hated this equation. But here it is important to insist again that the colonial British of a century ago are not somehow enchanted and "traditional" (or even "Ornamentalist" as Cannadine [2001] names them) to our current, putatively disenchanted "modern," or modern to our postmodern. There is plenty of magic at the core of "modernity" or "postmodernity." On the one hand it may be that new technological forms render printing more odd and susceptible to analysis. But, on the other hand, I suspect that we can continue to identify some of our own familiars if we try hard enough. The sites may change, but surely we also (as Clifford Geertz [1973:5] once put it) live in webs of meaning that we spin ourselves and vest magical potencies in our newest familiars too.

EIGHT

Ghanaian Popular Cinema and the Magic in and of Film

BIRGIT MEYER

Since the late 1980s, a booming video feature film industry has evolved in Ghana. Although established filmmakers both within and outside the state-owned Ghana Film Industry Corporation (GFIC) found it extremely diffi-cult to generate funds for film production, formally untrained persons of various backgrounds—from cinema projectionists to car mechanics—took ordinary VHS video cameras, wrote brief outlines, assembled actors (from theater, TV, or just "from the street"), and produced full-fledged feature films, which turned out to be tremendously successful in urban Ghana, and especially in Accra. Established professional filmmakers initially regarded the initiatives of private producers (who often acted as producers, directors, and scriptwriters all at the same time) and their use of the medium of video with suspicion. Yet when they noticed the extraordinary success that these productions had in Ghana and realized that screening these films in local cinemas could generate sufficient funds to sustain a viable video film industry, they also turned to film production in the video format. Moreover, in order to improve the productions made by self-trained filmmakers, the GFIC offered editing services and other forms of advice to filmmakers in exchange for the right to show the film in its own cinemas in Accra first. Gradually, production networks and systems of distribution evolved and since the beginning of the 1990s, each year has seen the release of about fifty video movies made by private and GFIC producers.

In the course of time, differences pertaining to technical standards of films made by formally trained and self-trained filmmakers gradually faded. And so did differences regarding their social position in the field of film production. This was due to the fact that in 1992, after eleven years of military rule, Ghana returned to a democratic constitution, which implied the liberalization and commercialization of the media and the opening up of the public sphere (see also Meyer 2001a). In implementing this shift, the state sold 70 percent of its shares of the GFIC to the Malaysian TV production company Sistem Televisyen Malaysia Berhad of Kuala Lumpur in 1996, and as a consequence the GFIC transformed into Gama Media System Ltd. As this foreign company focuses on TV productions and shows little interest in cinema, popular movie production has increasingly landed in the hands of independent producers (both self- and formally trained), who all are obliged to make it in Ghana's newly evolving "showbiz" market. In order to generate funds for the next film and a (usually small) income, filmmakers depend solely on the approval of the audience.

One distinctive, recurring feature of video movies concerns the emphasis put on the visualization of otherwise invisible occult forces and the fact that their narrative is usually placed in the framework of the Christian dualism of God and the Devil, the latter regarded as the leader of all "powers of darkness." These preferences do not primarily and necessarily reflect the convictions of the filmmakers but spectators' expectations. Exactly because of this emphasis on occult forces and their incorporation into the domain of the Christian Devil, popular cinema has been subject to severe criticism on the part of established filmmakers and intellectuals. Films made by the GFIC hardly, if ever, dealt with occult phenomena. Rather, those films tried to describe problems arising in the city as *social* (and this meant prosaic) problems, made a plea for development of the countryside, or sought to contribute to the valorization of the "Ghanaian cultural heritage." This stance still informs the curriculum of the National Film And Television Institute (NAFTI). Kofi

Middleton-Mends, a NAFTI teacher and actor, asserted (in an interview on October 16, 1996) that NAFTI discouraged students from making films about *juju*, as black magic is popularly called, and required them to make films meeting NAFTI's artistic and intellectual standards. Conversely, students told me that their teachers urged them to depict Ghanaian culture in a positive way, as a heritage to be cherished, rather than as something dangerous and to be gotten rid of (as is propagated by Ghanaian Pentecostalists [Meyer 1998b], who have a tremendous influence on popular culture, as will be discussed below). Looked upon from this perspective, movies made by private producers are often ridiculed and denounced as being imbued in "superstition"—an assault also leveled against their audiences. Moreover, occasionally these films are charged with representing Africans in inferior terms, thereby confirming racist distortions and subverting the development of "national pride."[1] Private video producers are accused of turning a medium meant to serve "development," "enlightenment," and "unity" of the nation into a vehicle for the expression of ugly matters that should have no place in modern, national culture.

In this chapter, I seek to show how a quintessentially modern medium like film, which has been used ever since colonial times to educate and enlighten people through images, has been appropriated in order to express people's concerns about the hidden presence of the occult in modern urban society. In this context it is important to realize that the invisible realm of the occult—magic—is not a domain by and in itself, standing in a taken-for-granted opposition to modernity. Rather than taking as a point of departure a reified understanding of magic, this contribution seeks to unravel the particular ways in which magic is being constructed by a cinematic-Pentecostal mode of representation and how this construction links up with other discourses. Magic, as this chapter will show, is always—even if it is negated—produced by particular, historically situated discourses that generate power and impinge on attitudes and behavior in different ways. Elsewhere I have shown (Meyer 1999a) how nineteenth-century Pietist missionaries affirmed that the local gods, spirits, and witchcraft that populated their prospective converts' imagination were truly existing realities yet recategorized them as "evil spirits" operating under the auspices of the Devil. In the course of time, missionaries and indigenous church leaders realized the pitfalls of diabolization, because in that way converts were still preoccupied with exactly those forces Christianity urged them to leave behind. If colonial discourse constructed those beliefs as superstitions to be left behind with the gradual increase of education, postcolonial discourse emphasized the positive, cohesive function of the old gods and spirits but was at a loss with regard to more uncanny matters such as witchcraft, juju, and all sorts of new occult forces—they were considered superstitions to be discarded through education. The temporalizing vocabulary of "leaving behind" certain beliefs and practices, which pervades all these discourses, constructs magic as a matter of the past. At the same time, none of the discourses proved able to fully contain those beliefs and practices categorized in terms of heathendom or irrational superstition. Magic, though constructed through discourse, refuses to be fully captured. In this sense, magic is a floating signifier, never fully absorbed by but rather haunting the discourses seeking to assign it a place, and proliferating and articulating itself in places where it is not supposed to be.

By casting invisible occult forces as Christian demons, popular movies offer a particular perspective, which clashes, as we shall see, with the perspective of the colonial and postcolonial state but resonates all the more with Pentecostalist views. It will be argued that the visualization of the dark, secret aspects lurking behind the surface of modern city life concerns an "enlightenment" in another sense than usually intended by modernist protagonists. In so doing, I find it useful to follow a distinction proposed by Michael Taussig during the conference on which this volume is based (see Introduction) between revelation and exposure. Whereas the notion of exposure is part of a hierarchical perspective affirming the superiority of scientific thinking, which unmasks magic as false and based on mere superstition, the notion of revelation criticizes magic from within, thereby leaving intact the idiom itself. Thus, contrary to the elite's expectations of the medium of film to promote superior forms of knowledge and behavior leading beyond magic, watching popular movies does not make people go beyond magical imagination toward increased levels of rationality but rather constitutes, or at least confirms, the domain of the occult at the very moment of its revelation. It brings light into the dark and, at the same time, contributes to establishing the domain of occult forces as part and parcel of modern city life (cf. Comaroff and Comaroff 1999; Geschiere 1997). I argue that it thus brings about a break with colonial cinema and realizes the magical potential of movies that is so often ascribed to this art form in the West.

Cinema in the Service of the Colonial State

The medium of film was introduced to Ghana by private businessmen,[2] who opened cinemas in urban areas and employed cinema vans to tour the countryside (especially the cocoa-growing areas) in the course of the 1920s.[3] The colonial authorities who, as the scarce archival sources show, critically monitored the screening of films in private cinemas through its censorship board, discovered the medium of film as a means to promote the colonial project rather late. The Information Services Department of the colonial government, which screened and produced films considered suitable for the local setting, was founded in 1940. The colonial administration opened a number of new cinema halls in Accra and other urban areas and made use of cinema vans that would organize film shows in the rural areas, where it would assemble people in outdoor spaces in order "to show documentary films and newsreels to explain the colonial government's policies to people in towns and villages free of charge" (Sakyi 1996:9).

An important aspect of this information service were propaganda films about the Second World War, which were produced by the Colonial Film Unit (CFU) in London (cf. Diawara 1992:3). After the war, the unit also started to produce educational films and a number of feature films, which were screened in Britain's African colonies. Contrasting the Western and African way of life, these films represented the former as an embodiment of "civilization" and the latter as "backward" and with "superstitious" customs to be left behind (cf. Diawara 1992:3; Ukadike 1994:44ff.).[4] Film thus was closely related to governmental and imperial interests and employed to create loyal subjects. Placing film in the service of "civilization," the CFU avoided screening films that criticized or ridiculed aspects of Western life, thereby denying Africans access to the whole field of Western cinematic representation (cf. Diawara 1992:1). At the same time, as independent cinema operators kept on showing Indian movies and certain Western films, film screening was never fully dominated by the colonial authorities; the latter were even obliged to at least partly give in to audiences' yearning for entertainment and show them their beloved Chaplin after a number of educational films had been screened.

The Gold Coast Film Unit, which was to produce local films, took up themes particularly relevant to the Gold Coast. These movies, too, were to serve colonial interests, and the attention was on "purposes of better health, better crops, better living, better marketing and better human co-operation in the colonies" (Middleton-Mends 1995:1; cf. also Diawara 1992:5). As these objectives were thought to be best achieved "on the native soil with native characters" (Middleton-Mends 1995:1), from 1948 onward the unit started training African filmmakers.[5] Similar film units existed in other parts of British colonial Africa, and their products were mutually exchanged and shown to audiences all over British colonial Africa.

In a very interesting publication, Peter Morton-Williams has presented the results of his research on the reception of so-called fundamental-education films by rural Yoruba, Ibo, and Hausa audiences in Nigeria, which he conducted for the Colonial Office.[6] "Fundamental education," the author explains, refers to attempts by the British colonial administration "to instil motives and the requisite technical skills to improve the material conditions of life, and to make it possible to apprehend, in some degree, the relationship of the rural community to the rest of the territory and to the world" (1953:xii). Next to brief descriptions of the content of thirty-four films (made by the CFU in England, film units in Africa, and commercial producers), which address topics from "clean cooking" to "the circulation of blood," his study provides detailed overviews of audience reactions to these films. Although this study focuses on Nigeria, I see no reason to doubt that these and similar films would have been shown in the Gold Coast as well and that audiences—also in urban areas—would have reacted in similar ways.

According to Morton-Williams, the bulk of the films fall into the categories of health films, farming films, and village development films. The basic message of all these films, of course, is a demonstration of the superiority of Western knowledge and of how clinging to certain "traditions" not only implies backwardness but also leads to ill health and poverty. Indeed, it may be concluded that the films sought to establish colonial authority on the basis of the *exposure* of existing beliefs, constituted as magical and superstitious, as false. That colonial films sought to speak to existing views and attitudes should not deceive us into assuming mere continuity between these views and attitudes in everyday life and their representation on screen. Clearly films incorporated them into a newly constructed domain of magic, which was constituted as modernity's other—an other called upon continuously in order to picture Western superiority. Magic, in this sense, was a necessary, albeit opposed, presence in colonial discourses on civilization.

Intended to serve public goals rather than offering mere private entertainment, these films were to convince audiences about the necessity of changing their behavior. The CFU would send cinema vans to tour the countryside from village to village; throughout the day the oncoming film show would be advertised by loudspeakers, in the evening a big screen would be erected, benches would be put down and a generator put on, and then audiences would be shown a number of educational films (usually explained by local instructors in the local language), with some shorter, more entertaining spots in between. In a context without electricity and far away from the big city, film shows were major events celebrating the superiority of Western technology. Literally bringing light into the dark, colonial film certainly resonates with Marshall McLuhan's famous dictum "the medium is the message." Although Morton-Williams observed that rural audiences rapidly accustomed themselves to the medium (thereby defying Western fantasies about primitive people taking film images for reality; cf. Gunning 1989; Moore 2000:3ff.), it appeared that in practice many films did not convey their intended message. This was due to the fact that it either failed to come across at all, or, if it did, was unacceptable and had no future impact on actual behavior. For instance, health films relating sicknesses such as smallpox and dysentery to natural causes could not convince audiences of the falsity of their own supernatural explanations. Watching educational movies thus would not lead to a decline in magical beliefs as envisioned by its producers. As audiences watched films on the basis of existing ideas and experiences, and were not prepared to accept the general superiority of the West, the expectation that the medium of film would set in motion processes of increasing "development" and "civilization" appears to be unwarranted.

Therefore one should be careful not to confound the intended message of colonial films with their actual impact. What can be assumed, however, is that cinema transformed urban and, temporarily, rural space into icons of the modern and generated a new public and a new colonial public culture, characterized by an entanglement of discipline and pleasure (cf. Barber 1997; Larkin 1998:99). Audiences, realizing the efforts made by colonial authorities to show their films even in the remotest village, understood that film was intended to implement colonial development schemes and educate people more than entertain them—an intention that also showed through the fact that educational films were always given priority over Charlie Chaplin.[7] As such, colonial film appeared as a medium and mediator of colonialism. Thriving on the opposition between Western knowledge and African superstition, the films represented magic and modernity as mutually exclusive. Here, attributed to the camera was the ultimate power of all pervasive vision and, figuring as "the mechanical eye of reason" (McQuire 1998), the capacity to expose false beliefs. Thus, in colonial film the camera was put in the service of a positivist, rational worldview and made to assert its power. In this way it became a key symbol of colonial power and of the superiority of science and rational behavior—and ultimately Western "civilization." Although audiences certainly understood these power claims, their unwillingness to let themselves be convinced by colonial films to change their behavior intimates that both the authority of the camera and the message became subject to contest by the colonized.

Popular Cinema Between the State and the Market

When the GFIC replaced the Gold Coast Film Unit after independence, state authorities continued to regard film as a powerful medium of "education" and "enlightenment" and as an appropriate means to "explain" institutions and policies to the people. As in colonial times, film was above all to serve public goals, albeit now redefined from a Nkrumahist perspective. Above all, film was to contribute to the emergence and consolidation of a national culture and identity. Although much emphasis was placed on Kwame Nkrumah's notion of the "African personality" and the need to retrieve cultural roots in the traditions of Ghana's various ethic groups, there was no room for representing matters such as juju, witchcraft, ghosts, and other occult forces. In line with the anticolonial critique, foreign films were held to distort and misrepresent African culture by representing it as "exotic" and to mislead Africans into adopting bad Western habits (Ukadike 1994:111ff.). The task of the GFIC thus was not only to produce information in the service of education and development and create counterimages to racial distortions but also to control the potentially bad influence of foreign films through their depiction of violence, sex, and racial prejudice. Due to a chronic lack of funds, in practice it proved to be difficult for the GFIC to live up to these expectations. Having produced a number of films in the immediate postcolonial period, the local cinema industry was virtually defunct in the beginning of the 1980s because of a financial and technological breakdown (partly due to the fact that the state had put more funds into television since its introduction in 1965).

Around this time, foreign films entered the country on a massive scale with the advent of video technology. Hundreds of small video centers and video libraries sprang up in the suburbs of the major cities, thereby turning film into a feature of mass entertainment. But video technology made possible much more than offering access to foreign films. Due to its easy accessibility, video technology was quickly appropriated by local people. Video enterprises were founded that recorded major family occasions, such as funerals and weddings, and eventually the first video feature filmmakers appeared on the scene and enticed the urban masses with local movies. The stance of the state toward video technology was ambivalent. Regarding foreign films as a serious, yet virtually uncontrollable, threat that would mislead Ghanaians into adopting bad Western habits, the Ministry of Information welcomed the revival of cinema brought about by private producers because they devoted so much attention to local affairs and were able to speak to a mass audience. At the same time, the state perceived the new video film industry as a challenge. And rightly so, for due to the new policy of liberalization and commercialization of the media and the relatively low budget and little technological expertise required for the production of video movies, video is a potentially democratic medium able to express alternative views in the public sphere (cf. Meyer 2001a).

Being convinced of the tremendous power of the moving image to influence the masses, the government—as is the case in any nation-state—therefore attempted to keep control over the consumption and production of locally produced video films. Not only was there (and is there still) a censorship board to watch and approve of any locally produced film, the Ministry of Information also met the video boom with a *Draft of the National Film and Video Policy for Ghana* (n.d., but probably drafted 1995), which asked (video) filmmakers to make movies in line with the established GFIC policies (cf. Meyer 1999b:100)—a mission that has not been easily matched with the financial need to appeal to popular taste. In 1999, the National Media Commission drew up a *National Media Policy*, which addresses the new role of media in the age of democracy and commercialization. It is important that the policy deliberately moves beyond a view of media as promoting "positive national identity and confidence" (National Media Commission n.d.:22) and is mainly concerned with the balance between the positive and negative effects of the globalization of information and communication on local culture (especially regarding the gap between the information rich and the information poor). Nevertheless, reminiscent of the earlier draft policy, it still is critical about the "poor technical, artistic and ethical standards with most of the current generation of films made in Ghana" (ibid.:12). According to the new policy, steps are to be taken in order that films are "in keeping with Ghanaian traditions and mores and promote desirable aspects of Ghanaian culture," entail "the extensive use of authentic national cultural forms and symbols," and "establish the common identity and shared interests of all African and black peoples and cultures everywhere" (ibid.:50). Along with the Film Censorship Board, the institution to safeguard these guidelines is the National Film Board. However, as film production now fully depends on audience approval, one can only wonder how far it will be possible to actually implement these aims.

Ghanaian filmmakers appear to be positioned between expectations of the state bureaucrats who expect media to "enlighten" people, on the one hand, and the need to sell their products in a market dominated by audiences, on the other. Especially the presence of Nigerian video films in the Ghanaian market, a development that took off in 1998, forms a serious challenge to Ghanaian producers. As Nigerian films easily eschew censorship both in Nigeria and Ghana, they give more room to transgression into evil and occult forces than Ghanaian films are able to (cf. Meyer 2001b). In interesting ways, Nigerian films replay themes addressed by Ghanaian producers already in the early beginnings of popular cinema, with its strong emphasis on occult forces. As a result of ongoing criticism on the part of artistic and academic elites, many Ghanaian filmmakers have felt somewhat insecure about magic in films. Yet, the recent popularity of Nigerian films has confirmed for them that the visualization of magic is the key trademark of popular film. More confidently than before, they keep pursuing these themes. The only difference with regard to earlier productions is the use of more sophisticated, computer-designed special effects.

The audiences of Ghanaian movies cannot simply be pinned down to a distinct social category. In fact, we are concerned here with a mass phenomenon, which encompasses the urban lower and (aspiring) middle classes, and—as the main language spoken in the majority of Ghanaian movies is English—cuts across ethnic divisions. A successful movie can easily be watched by more than thirty thousand people in Accra's various cinemas and video centers in the center and suburbs and become the talk of the town. Some years ago, many producers have started to sell their films as home videos without even showing them in the cinemas; often they organize spectacular sale sessions in the center of Accra (called "floating") during which they sell thousands of films. Even if films may increasingly be watched at home on video, they are still much talked about in public. A good film's story will be "broadcast" through mobile people such as taxi drivers, street vendors, and traders in Makola Market. Although the audiences as such are of multiple social and ethnic backgrounds, one recurrent pattern is easily discernible: for reasons to be given below, the instigation to go and watch a certain film or to buy the videotape for home consumption often comes from women, who drag their boyfriend or husband along.

Although it may be stated that Ghanaian video movies created new audiences, one could also argue the reverse. In fact, the new Ghanaian filmmakers completely depend on their audiences' approval, and in order to somehow make a profitable film, they have to ensure meeting spectators' expectations. Hence filmmakers do their best to visualize the elusive rumors, heartbreaking stories, and dramas of everyday life—all of which usually imply occult forces—circulating in town. As they by and large share the social background and experiences of their audiences, it is not difficult for them to lend their ear to what keeps people busy and project it back to them to see.

On Magic in Film

Most movies, in the same way as their audiences, take occult forces for granted and hardly ever question their reality. Only a few films introduce skeptics (just on the sideline) who are gradually convinced of the existence of magic through incontrovertible facts. In *A Mother's Revenge* (Ananse System Productions, 1994) for instance, there is a white woman who at first does not believe in the existence of ghosts yet by the end of the film asserts that such powers do indeed exist. Turning a white woman into an advocate of a worldview that grants reality to occult forces is of course highly symbolic, as Western people are usually regarded as representatives of a rational perspective on the world. Popular film contests precisely this perspective.

In order to examine the appearance of occult forces in films and to understand magic's relation with the camera, I will focus on two selected films—*Ghost Tears* and *Fatal Decision*—in which different invisible forces—ghosts (that is, spirits of the dead) and witchcraft—play a prominent role. During my research, these films were well known among Ghanaian audiences and formed a topic of animated debate. Although there has been a plethora of films produced later on, these films can certainly be regarded as paradigmatic, in the sense that they inspired many other productions. Before discussing and comparing the films' specific characteristics, I will briefly describe a number of distinctive features with regard to setting, plot, and moral geography of popular cinema in general.

First, popular films take as a point of departure the distinction between what people call the "physical" and the "spiritual" (cf. Meyer 1999a:157ff.). Although only the realm of the "physical" is visible to the naked eye, it is generally assumed that what actually happens in people's life is to a large extent determined by invisible, spiritual forces. The capacity to reveal what is going on in the realm of the spiritual and how it affects a person's life is a source of power. Presently, in Ghanaian society there is a market for this capacity, and Christian preachers, especially Pentecostal preachers—who are currently extremely popular in Ghana (e.g. Gifford 1994, 1998; Meyer 1998a, 1999a; Van Dijk 1997)—and native doctors compete with each other. As will soon become clear, the camera, too, takes part in this competition and the visualization of occult forces has to be seen in this context.

Second, popular films usually focus on domestic space and all the problems involved, rather than serving public goals as was the case with colonial cinema.[8] They share a similar setting in that the house of the main protagonists is located in one of the rich residential areas, which keep on expanding all around Accra. Tens of thousands of this type of mansion exist or are in the making.[9] In contrast to houses in the village or in the popular quarters, the houses in these areas are fenced with massive cement walls, which symbolize and emphasize the privacy of the house as a space confined to the modern nuclear family. The fence actually stands for the separation of the couple and their children from the extended family and their inclusion in a private domain difficult to penetrate. Yet, whereas in real life what is going on within the confines of the modern house remains invisible and, also in stark contrast to other quarters, virtually inaudible to outside observers, in the movies the camera follows the characters mercilessly, thereby enabling audiences to become eyewitnesses of what is going on in this secluded domain. The films show that devastating tensions are going on in the modern family. Located in a space beyond wider familial and social control, it becomes an arena for (undetected) horror and even crime.

Third, films represent modern life in the city—in a beautiful, well-furnished house, which is only inhabited by a caring husband, his loving wife, and their children, who all lead a Christian life—as ultimately desirable. And yet, this ideal is so difficult to attain because it is threatened from so many angles. Films thrive on a moral geography that opposes the village, which is the realm of the extended family, and the forces of nature, on the one hand, and the secluded house in the city, on the other. This is accentuated in *Ghost Tears*, where the wife accuses her husband and his girlfriend (the housemaid Esi) of still being stuck in the inferior village way of life. As in many other video movies, the village is here depicted as caught in a low stage of development from which people are to be uplifted. Very much in line with colonial film and in contrast to "high art" African films shown in the West, the village is also seen as an abode of the powers of darkness, which threaten to mess up life in the city. At the same time, films show how village and city are connected through social networks, with all the spiritual links entailed by them. Insinuating that forces from the village, or from nature, still intrude into people's life in town, popular films demonstrate that magic and modernity are completely intertwined.

Fourth, taking the relationship between husband and wife as a point of departure, many films show its destruction, which may even lead to the death of at least one of the spouses. Focusing on marital drama, with all the conflicts between the spouses and the extended family it entails, popular films highlight problems that are easily recognizable to the audiences. By bringing into the picture the nasty aspects involved in familial and marital relations, the films certainly have much in common with the genre of soap operas: they, too, reveal people's "dirty little secrets" and, by enticing audiences to keep on watching and discussing the latest film, generate "the dirty discourse of gossip" (Allen 1995:4).

Significantly, in films husbands are usually shown to be rather weak characters, who run after sexual pleasure, deceive and even "sack" their wife from the house because of a young mistress, and squander money. This echoes women's views about their current situation and turns the wife into the heroine of each film. She may be mistreated by her husband but appears as the embodiment of ultimate morality (and, often, as close to God as one can possibly get). As popular cinema conspicuously celebrates their female audiences' moral superiority (Meyer 1999b), it is no surprise that wives and girlfriends are so eager to make their partners watch Ghanaian films. Films are regarded as didactic devices illustrating dramatically how the failure of the husband to choose for his wife and children inevitably leads to unbearable troubles and how Christianity, especially its Pentecostal-charismatic variant, brings moral superiority and enduring success in modern, urban life. In marital conflicts, women sometimes stress their arguments by reminding the husband of a particular film.

Ghost Tears (Hacky Film and Movie Africa Productions, 1992)

Kwesi; his very rich wife, Dina; their baby, Yawa; and a girl from the village (Esi, Dina's cousin's daughter, who came to stay with the couple when she was a child), live in a very posh two-story building that conforms to the highest standards of modernity. Kwesi has a secret affair with Esi, who pretends that she is pregnant. The drama starts when Dina finds out about the affair and scolds them, referring to them as ungrateful "village people." One night, Esi drowns Dina in the bathtub. Kwesi marries Esi, and Yawa grows up without knowing anything about her true mother. Esi, however, treats the young girl cruelly. Yawa has to work hard until late in the night, and Esi is never satisfied. She does virtually nothing, just lounges on the sofa and watches TV.

When Yawa is working, the camera depicts the ghost of the dead mother weeping about her daughter's fate. Also, about ten years after Dina's death, Kwesi often thinks about his wife and dreams about happier times, when they visited very expensive places, such as Labadi Beach Hotel (the first hotel in town), gorgeously dressed in the latest African fashion, and listened to piano music while sipping cocktails. Kwesi is seriously concerned about the way Esi treats his daughter but is not able to change anything.

Yet one day, when Yawa has been sent to the market and has lost her money in a taxi, Dina appears before her. She gives Yawa ten thousand cedis for the lost three thousand cedis and tells her that she is Esi's auntie. She tells Yawa that she should greet her and lets her know that she will come and visit her some day: blood is blood. Having said this, she vanishes miraculously. Upon Yawa's return home, she tells her father what happened. He is shocked about the story and immediately expects this woman to be the ghost of his dead wife. But why now, after ten years? He is scared, and now he takes better care of his daughter.

One night, the ghost of Dina, dressed in the clothes in which she was murdered, enters the house without opening the gate: she just passes through and appears to Kwesi, who falls down the stairs in fear (a powerful scene, for the audience with whom I watched it screamed: "Jesus, the ghost!"). And this is also what Kwesi shouts before he wakes up and tells himself that this was "just a dream." Even Esi starts to get scared about all these things, but it is Kwesi who takes action. He stops drinking alcohol and talks to one of his friends in order to find out what he knows about ghosts. Kwesi tells him about his dreams and about the woman who appeared to Yawa at the market. Could this be the ghost of his wife who wants to take revenge? The friend asserts that since Dina knew that she died by accident—as Kwesi has told him—she would certainly have no reason to return as a ghost of revenge. This would just be an hallucination. But the friend does not go so far as to assert that ghosts as such do not exist. Kwesi interrupts him and says firmly what he wants to believe: ghosts don't exist.

Yet he continues to see Dina in his dreams, even during the day when he is stuck in the usual Accra traffic jam. One night, Yawa is called by Dina, who discloses her identity to her and tells her about the circumstances of her death. Again, the film leaves it open as to whether the ghost really appears to Yawa or whether this happens in a dream. Eventually we see Yawa weeping in her bed. Her father comes and takes her downstairs. Yawa asks about her true mother and, having taken a drink, he tells her the truth. Esi overhears this and runs downstairs to kill him by smashing his head with the bottle she finds on the table. Dina's ghost is present in the room and looks at the scene, without tears. Then Yawa, who is weeping in despair, gets up and strangles Esi until she is dead. At that moment we see the ghost leave the body of her daughter (suggesting she had gotten hold of her daughter's body to kill Esi), who remains behind, all alone and weeping.

This film was screened in the cinemas for weeks. Virtually everybody I spoke to knew this film or at least its story. The main attraction of the film, as I was told, lies in the fact that it makes visible a revenge ghost (not a technically easy task with video material, because special effects are much more difficult to realize than with celluloid, as I learned from the film editor Marc Coleman), thereby taking up a tremendously popular theme and giving it a visual dimension. Regularly, newspapers publish accounts about ghosts appearing to people who are not aware that the people whose ghosts these are had died or about ghosts living happily with a stranger far away from home until a relative shows up and discloses the ghost's identity.[10]

Kwesi desperately wishes that ghosts do not exist, yet in the course of the film he is forced to accept the contrary. By keeping secret the truth of Dina's death and, in addition, insulting her by marrying Esi and allowing her to maltreat Yawa, Kwesi calls the ghost's revenge upon himself. The revenge consists in the exposition of his and Esi's evil deeds to Yawa and, finally, their death. Ironically, while Kwesi is still contemplating the truth of ghosts, the ghost herself is revealing the truth surrounding her death. In this way, the ghost appears to be the sole entity able to bring about justice and teach Yawa about her roots, whereas her own father lets her grow up in a home which is based on a deception.

Therefore, the central message of the film is not simply that ghosts do indeed exist but rather that they punish evildoers and reveal truth, whereas people's lives in the visible realm of the physical abound with secrets and lies. The spiritual, as it represents itself through dreams, thus becomes a means for the establishment of truth. Here the camera is put in the service of the ghost's revelatory enterprise (as in the case of Alfred Wallace's photography: see Peter Pels in this volume). The audiences witness the quarrel that led to the murder of Dina, through the eye of the camera, and in the course of watching are made complicit in the ghost's struggle for justice and truth. By making the ghost visible and occasionally conveying her perspective, the eye of the camera offers audiences the extraordinary experience of penetrating the otherwise invisible.

The emphasis on ghosts, which formed a major theme of popular film in the early 1990s, has evoked protests from different groups in society.[11] The intellectual elite have complained that filmmakers should refrain from supporting the societal obsession with the living dead, which one could also find in popular newspapers and tabloids, and, rather, come up with films that would refrain from visualizing occult forces altogether. Criticisms were also raised from a Christian point of view, which regarded the emphasis on ghosts of revenge as a denial of the absolute power of God. It was asserted that rather than celebrating these embodiments of punishment, films should show that evil deeds would have consequences for the life of the person committing them and that they would eventually be judged by God. The production of films about the living dead diminished after these criticisms, but popular movies—far from accepting elitist criticisms—kept on picturing other invisible, occult powers, preferably in a Christian framework, or at least by representing occult forces as downright evil.

Taking up more or less explicitly Christian narrative forms, films since then have often been framed as "confessions"[12] and thus as media meant to make visible the hitherto-hidden machinations of "the powers of darkness." Although films offer audiences the possibility to take up different subject positions (for instance, that of the bad guy who destroys the moral order that the film seeks to defend), the most superior one among these is the perspective of the all-seeing God (cf. Meyer 1999b). When the characters in the film are still wondering why all sorts of mishap are troubling them, the audiences, assisted by the eye of the camera, already know who is responsible for all this. They have been enabled to penetrate the secret actions of evil persons, and have seen them visit shrines in the village or at the margins of the big city, and now wait patiently until these people eventually get the punishment they deserve.

Popular films thus deliberately echo Pentecostal views of occult forces as demons—a view that initially has been introduced by nineteenth-century missionaries and prevailed at the grass roots of mission churches, even at a time when church leaders started to regard these forces as mere superstitions (Meyer 1999a). In my view, one important reason for Pentecostalism's popularity lies in the fact that it recasts spiritual beings—the old gods and ghosts, witchcraft and magic, which have been haunting as floating signifiers even those who strove to move away from their sphere of influence—as part and parcel of Christian imagination and offers them as space in the realm of the powers of darkness. Popular films, by offering a visual dimension to this imagination, parasitically link themselves with Pentecostalism but at the same time contribute to an increasing entanglement of religion and entertainment (cf. Meyer 2002).

If popular film shifted away from dead people's ghosts, the role of invisible, occult forces in marriage dramas involving one man and two women certainly has remained a hot topic up to the present day. This is also the case in *Fatal Decision*, which can safely be regarded as the paradigm for the production of successful movies.

Fatal Decision (H.M. Films, 1993)

A well-to-do couple, the Mensahs, is married happily for twenty years, the sole trouble being that they do not have children. Eventually Sarah manages to convince her husband to take a second wife in order to have a baby. He marries Mona, who indeed gives birth to a son. From then on, Mona does her best to chase Sarah out of the house. First she tries to do so through witchcraft, and the camera follows her when she leaves her sleeping body behind in the bed, goes to the beach, and transforms herself into a vulture, one of the favorite animal shapes taken by witches. She stands in front of Sarah's bed and blows into her face. Sarah, while sleeping, experiences a tormenting dream, with much lightning and thunder. When she wakes up, her first words are "Thank you, Jesus, for giving me victory over my enemy!"

As this witchcraft attack has failed because of Sarah's spiritual strength, which is due to her Christian faith, Mona now plans a plot to show that Sarah is unfaithful to her husband. Unfortunately the latter believes Mona more than his first wife, who is sacked from the house. Miraculously, she has become pregnant after so many years (so the name Sarah certainly was chosen in analogy to the biblical Sarah, who could hardly believe that she could give birth at her age and then gave birth to Isaac), but the husband refuses to accept responsibility for the child. Sarah and her son, whom she calls Obimpe (Akan for "somebody does not want [you]," i.e., a child without a father) live all alone, under difficult circumstances, but never lose faith in God. Eventually Sarah dies from poverty, and Obimpe, a bright child and devout Christian, has to suffer in the house of a mischievous aunt. Sacked from the house, he is eventually invited to live in the house of the pastor, who appears to belong to the Pentecostal form of Christianity. Performing extraordinarily well in school, he receives a scholarship to study medicine in Europe.

Mona's son, in contrast, is a good-for-nothing. He and his mother have squandered all their riches, and the father is desperate about the whole situation. One day, Mona falls ill, and in the hospital she meets Obimpe, who has just returned home (significantly by Swiss Air, whereas he left Ghana by the much less prestigious Ghana Airways) as a doctor. Realizing that she is about to die, she confesses that she is a witch and is responsible for the sad fate of his mother. The old father begs his son for forgiveness, and they visit Sarah's grave and weep.

This film had enormous appeal because of its powerful narrative. Thriving on the contrast between the God-fearing Sarah and the witch Mona,[13] the film defends monogamous marriage and the Christian nuclear family. Compared to *Ghost Tears*, this film celebrates Christian values in a straightforward way.[14] This is made explicit in a scene when the pastor comes to announce Sarah's death to Mr. Mensah and admonishes him that taking a second wife was a "fatal decision," as a result of which his home and business were broken up—a message he does not like to accept yet one all the more endorsed by the audiences, especially women. I learned that women like this film tremendously because of its warning against polygamy and its appeal to wait patiently until God gives a couple the baby they and their parents long for so much.[15]

The pastor, of course, also plays a crucial role in taking care of Obimpe instead of his stubborn, misguided father who even fails to realize that he is married to a witch, another central theme in many films. Well-behaved, God-fearing, intelligent, and modest, Obimpe conforms to the image of the ideal son. The fact that eventually his ultimate dream of becoming a doctor is realized very much appeals to audiences, who pity him for being forsaken by his father and having to lead a miserable life. Watching this gives both hope and moral satisfaction, another important gift of popular films to their audiences.

For our investigation of the way in which magic features in popular films, the witchcraft scene is of special importance. The transformation from woman to vulture—made possible through special effects—is certainly as spectacular as the spiritual fight between Mona and Sarah. Blurring the boundary between dream and reality, between the realm of "the spiritual" and that of "the physical," the camera depicts things that are usually invisible to the naked eye. Completely in line with Christian imagery, and in contrast to *Ghost Tears*, in *Fatal Decision* magic is here the domain of the evildoers, who will perish in the end, while the camera is put in the service of penetrating and revealing the secret domain of people's engagement with occult forces. In this sense, here the camera is magic's fiercest enemy: following witches into their secret machinations and making their actions visible on the screen, the camera engages in a modern, mediated form of witch hunt, through which the guilt of the witch is established beyond doubt. In so doing, however, the camera also is very much complicit with occult forces, such as witches, because it confirms, and even proves, their existence. Indeed, the relationship between magic and the camera in popular film is paradoxical in that the latter confirms the existence of occult forces and defeats them at the same time. To return to Taussig's distinction once again, here the camera is engaged in the *revelation* rather than exposure of magic; it does not question the existence of occult forces as such.

In this context it is important to emphasize that *revelation* is a term that is frequently used with regard to what is achieved by popular films. This can be nicely illustrated through a conversation I had with the filmmaker William A. Akuffo and a scriptwriter (whom I only met once and whose name I do not know). Akuffo told us how incredibly difficult it was for him to produce certain scenes in which the workings of occult forces were to be visualized (during filming sessions, the light suddenly stopped working; actors refused to play in scenes in which they were to be prayed upon by a pastor, for fear of appearing to be possessed by evil spirits; later there appeared to be nothing recorded on the tape; etc.). The scriptwriter asserted that as films are "revelations of occult powers," evil powers would sometimes try to prevent the production of such films. So, in fact, even film production itself is placed in the context of the struggle between occult forces and the camera, which is in the service of divine power.

The obsession with the revelation of the powers of darkness is an enduring feature of popular cinema. Successful movies include some more or less explicit references to secret practices such as making juju (sorcery) and the visualization of otherwise invisible occult forces such as witchcraft, and they put the camera in the service of revelation. In so doing, popular movies offer audiences a superior form of vision—indeed a "super-vision" (see Peter Pels, this volume)—which affirms Pentecostal-Christian views and morals. Although there is a particular historically generated elective affinity between popular cinematic and Pentecostal modes of representation, it is important to realize that adopting "revelation" is above all a device that facilitates the depiction of the utmost transgression into evil and horror. Its adoption does not mean that producers are steeped in Pentecostal views. Although to them revelation offers the condition of the possibility of showing transgression, they also assert that similar things happen in Hollywood productions and lament that Ghanaian film should be denied by the censorship board the opportunity of making films replete with horror and magic. A case in point is the introduction of Bob Smith, a Ghanaian actor famous for his role of snake-man in *Diabolo* I through III (World Wide Motion Pictures, 1991, 1992, 1994; cf. Meyer 1995; Wendl 1999), as the "Ghanaian Christopher Lee."

Popular film, by democratizing and individualizing vision, goes beyond Christian practices of seeing, where vision is regarded as a special gift by God, which is only granted to the true believer. Through the medium of film, the revelation of magic through the eye of the camera becomes a common practice, and this indicates the complete subversion of the role of the camera in colonial film. Here, film technology clearly got turned on its head. Providing an extension of the human eye and showing occult forces at work, the camera claims the ultimate power of revelation. In popular cinema it certainly does not act as the "mechanical eye of reason" engrained in a positivist worldview that rules out occult phenomena as "superstitions" but as a mediator of a form of truth-knowledge that successfully transcends the boundary between the visible and the invisible, the physical and the spiritual, and enables people to share its perspective. Asserting that the visible world is dominated by invisible forces, video films paradoxically affirm that transparency is neither given nor achievable in the visible realm but always depends on the revelation of what lies beneath (cf. Ferme 2001).

The Magic of Film

It is interesting that both Western and African film critics and cinematographers often refer to the "magic" of film. They do so usually in passing, without deep reflection about the implication of this statement.[16] This expression seems to suggest in a somewhat evolutionary way that in modern, "disenchanted" societies, one can still find "survivals" of mythical-magical thought, or at least spaces allowing for regression into such thought. The magic of film, of course, consists in the capacity of images to conjure up virtual worlds and make its spectators part of it and "become a dreamer under their spell," as McLuhan ([1964] 1995:285) put it. Recently, Rachel Moore has explicitly addressed the magic of cinema. Taking as a point of departure Walter Benjamin's notion of the dialectical image, which draws on the creative power of commodity fetishism thriving on the murky borderline between mystification and understanding, she addresses the entanglement of magic and cinema. An embodiment of modern technology and, at the same time, allowing for a nostalgic retrieval of "primitive faculties" lost through modernity (2000:11), cinema has a curative magic of its own. And so, the "camera is our one magical tool flush with animistic power to possess, enchant, travel through time and space, and bewitch" (2000:163), thereby "joining the primitive to the modern" (2000:162).

These reflections are of immediate relevance to our understanding of the achievement of popular cinema. Indeed, right from the beginning of cinema, films visualized imaginations such as the ones evoked by gothic novels like Bram Stoker's *Dracula*, Robert Louis Stevenson's *Dr. Jekyll and Mr. Hyde*, Sir H. Rider Haggard's *King Solomon's Mines*, and Edgar Wallace's *Sanders of the River*, in which the occult breaks through and turns civilization into barbarism. Clearly, as the Introduction to this volume also argues, the claim that magic has been superseded by modernity is ideological rather than real. Patrick Brantlinger has linked the upsurge of the occult with British imperialism and shown that many gothic novels deal with an encounter with another culture—he therefore calls their genre "Imperial Gothic"—and thrive on the anxiety that "Western rationality may be subverted by the very superstition it rejects" (1988:227). The novels as well as the films made out of them are racist (cf. Ukadike 1994:35ff.) and, at the same time, seriously question as well as lament the supposedly disenchanted character of modern society.[17] Here the magic of film thrives on the magic in film: a dream performance in which the fantastic and the real merge in unexpected ways.

Over and again the magic in American and European films—and, for that matter, in other genres (see the Introduction to this volume)—has been the magic of a noncivilized Other, modeled after the "backward primitive" or the "mysterious Oriental" encountered at the periphery of the colonial empire, who threatens to subvert the rationality of the Westerner and is cast as the "primitive" object of nostalgia. Against this background, it is understandable that Ghanaian film critics and professional filmmakers are highly critical of films in which Africans are still associated with magic and prefer to show how, on the contrary, European attitudes subvert African dignity and warn about the devastating influence foreign films have on African audiences. Yet, in attempting to decolonize cinema, ironically, they tend to reproduce rather some of the paternalistic attitudes toward film as a means of education in pursuit of public goals that also motivated colonial cinema. Manthia Diawara has stated that colonial cinema denied Africans the full cinematic heritage of the West, because of the fear that "backward people" would not be able to distinguish between truth and falsehood of filmic representation (1992:1), between reality and fantasy.[18] Hence, as we saw, colonial authorities did not like to screen films that challenged Western superiority, and they even let people sit through a number of educational films before showing them Chaplin.[19] Films were to serve colonial interests and entice people to learn and progress, to move toward increasing levels of rationality and self-control, leaving behind the stage of "superstition." As, according to the British colonial authorities, these goals could not be achieved by merely screening Western films, they found it necessary to limit access to Western cinematographic repertoires and make specific films for solely African audiences.

In similar ways, the postcolonial state sought to control citizens' access to films through the GFIC and the censorship board. Although these projects never were entirely successful (Indian films, for instance, were for view in privately owned cinemas), they pinpoint the power of the colonial and postcolonial state to control the production and circulation of moving images. This power was only threatened with the arrival of video technology and eventually subverted by the liberalization and commercialization of the media. Realizing the entertainment value of Satan and his demons, popular movies parasitically adopted the Pentecostal mode of revelation and thus offered visual space for depicting magic, the floating signifier that keeps on haunting and gliding through the discourses that seek to capture and pin it down.

Against this background, the stance toward video movies of those critics who still regard people's struggle against occult forces as a "superstition" that forms a stumbling block to development, or as an attitude that should not exist, let alone be visualized in film, appears to be quite problematic. For in this way these critics not only speak from a statist perspective; they also deny film a central (and perhaps defining) feature, namely, the performance of magic as a way to cast doubt on modernity's dominant claim of disenchantment and to point toward the actual entanglement of magic and modernity. To me, it looks as if private video producers, in their urge to make products that appeal to popular taste, finally—and probably without consciously striving to do so—have moved beyond paternalizing statist cinema, which has been dominant in Africa ever since this medium was introduced. Whatever one thinks about magic *in* film, its presence certainly contributes to the emergence of the magic *of* film, which transposes audiences in the border zone of the realms of the physical and the spiritual, where much more may be revealed— and learned—about everyday life in an African city than through any "realistic," educative style of representation stuck in the opposition of magic versus modernity.

NINE

Dr. Jekyll and Mr. Hyde

Modern Medicine Between Magic and Science

JOJADA VERRIPS

In the modern Western world . . . there are many elements of ambivalence in public attitudes toward science and the scientist, which are expressed in much irrational and some relatively rational opposition to his role. The obverse of this is that there is a strong non-rational element in the popular support of the scientist. He is the modern magician, the "miracle man" who can do incredible things. Along with this in turn goes a penumbra of belief in pseudo-science. Scientists themselves are, like other people, far from being purely and completely rational beings.

—TALCOTT PARSONS, *The Social System*, 1951

In May 1997 the following message by David Obeng could be read in the *Ghanaian Digest* on the Internet: "The Ghanaian Public is reeling with shock over the news that a respectable looking Doctor has shown symptoms of being a vampire and may have been responsible for the deaths of three patients who have died under his care within only six months of his service with the hospital." According to a nurse who caught the man, an American gynecologist, in flagrante delicto, he was licking the fresh blood of a patient who was delivering a baby. She alarmed colleagues, and they too saw how the "revered doctor" drank the blood of the woman in labor. However, before the man could be arrested, he had flown home.

Dr. "Jekyll" once again turned out to have another identity, that of a terrible Mr. "Hyde," this time manifesting himself as a vampire in Ghana, where trust in biomedically trained doctors and Western drugs has been propagated as a central feature of enlightenment and development ever since colonial times. Whether this story is true or not is less important than the fact that it has cropped up, for it confronts us with a highly ambivalent and apparently very widespread attitude of the general public toward the representatives of science in general and of the medical profession in particular. The story of the American vampire doctor in Ghana does not stand by itself. Variations of it have been told for decades in the modern Western world, for example, Robert Louis Stevenson's gothic novel that also has been made into several films. And it seems that there will be no end to this long storytelling tradition, which reflects a highly ambivalent attitude toward doctors. On the contrary, there still is a large number of books, comics, and (videos) movies in which mad doctors of old—such as Mary Shelley's Frankenstein and H.G. Wells's Dr. Moreau—and more modern ones—as the Mantle brothers of David Cronenberg's movie *Dead Ringers* (1988)—figure, claiming to be scientists but seriously sinning against the scientific and ethical codes of their profession (cf. Tohill and Tombs 1994:17–25). If the modernist claim that the modern world is disenchanted is right, one might at least expect a slight decrease in the production and consumption of these figments of the imagination, but this is evidently not the case. That they still are so popular reflects how firmly the general public witnessing the developments on the medical front seems to be in the grip of a long-standing and deep fear of doctors (cf. Ten Have and Kimsma 1987), who are portrayed and perceived as kinds of dangerous witch doctors or modern magicians tinkering with the borders between life and death.

Of course, the assertion that *magic* and *modernity* do not exclude each other is not very original. Nor is it original to assert that *magic* and *science* do not represent two mutually exclusive ways of dealing with the world and that the former is disappearing rapidly because of the expansion of the last, as some supporters of the *Entzauberung-der Welt* hypothesis claim. Such criticisms have been raised already by different scholars (cf. Gijswijt-Hofstra 1997; Verwey 1998). Not so long ago I myself tried to demonstrate that animistic, anthropomorphic, and magical-mythical ways of thinking about the material environment and technological acquisitions are not only widespread among the Dutch population but also on the increase (Verrips 1994).[1] A striking feature with regard to this apparent growth of magical-mythical thinking about the technological acquisitions of the times is that their anthropomorphic and animistic representation by laypersons appears to be increasingly appropriate. For, on the one hand, more and more technical products contain organic material, such as, for instance the biochip, whereas, on the other, a growing number of scientists talk about the possibility of developing very advanced electronic devices that differ very little from human beings.

In this contribution I will further develop this theme with regard to the relationship between magic and modernity or, more precisely, magic and science. Particular attention will be paid to physicians' ways of thinking and acting. Many social scientists charmed by the secularization thesis and many medical practitioners themselves consider these academically trained doctors as spearheads of modern science in which there is no place any longer for animistic, anthropomorphic, and magical-mythical representations and practices. Although they would claim that their predecessors from previous centuries closely resembled the classical magician, medicine man, or witch doctor, they maintain that this would no longer be true with regard to the doctors who have taken care of patients since the professionalization and rationalization of the medical discipline in the nineteenth century.[2] But this raises the key questions: Is this image indeed correct? Are contemporary, biomedically trained physicians free of magical-mythical thinking? Are their representations of the illnesses they claim to know and to be able to cure as scientifically objective as they want us to believe? In his classical study *The Social System*, Talcott Parsons, for example, emphatically draws attention to the occurrence of "pseudo-scientific" elements "in the technical competence of the medical profession" (1951:468). But he does not want to hear of the occurrence of "magic" in modern medical practice. "It is suggestive that pseudoscience is the functional equivalent of magic in the modern medical field. The health situation is a classic one of the combination of uncertainty and strong emotional interests, which produce a situation of strain, and is very frequently a prominent focus of magic. But the fact that the basic cultural tradition of modern medicine is science precludes outright magic, which is explicitly nonscientific" (ibid.:469).

Magic is for Parsons a ritual based on the notion that the supernatural forms a system, which is based on knowable laws that can be manipulated in order to achieve concrete goals in the same way as the scientifically established laws pertaining to our empirical reality (1951:375). He talks about "pseudoscience" occurring if one fills gaps in empirical knowledge with "*scientifically inadequate* empirical beliefs," which, by the way, do not need to be completely "*non*-empirical" (ibid.:359). For supernatural interpretations and magical treatments of illnesses one has to look, according to Parsons, to "nonliterate societies," where a little bit of "proto-scientific" knowledge may exist but where magic prevails. Furthermore, one could come across, for example, in traditional China and the Middle Ages, much of what he calls "health 'superstition' in the sense of pseudo rational or pseudo scientific beliefs and practices" (ibid.:433). Though he admits that this kind of superstition has not yet disappeared in our modern society, it is crystal clear to him where one has to look for it, that is, in nonacademic, popular circles, not to say lower classes of society. A typically classical evolutionist perspective.

A similar conclusion is reached by Keith Thomas in his seminal study *Religion and the Decline of Magic*. He remarks:

> Indeed the role of magic in modern society may be more extensive than we yet appreciate. . . . If magical acts are ineffective rituals employed as an alternative to sheer helplessness in the face of events, then how are we to classify the status of "scientific" remedies, in which we place faith, but which are subsequently exposed as useless? This was the fate of Galenic medicine, which in the sixteenth century was the main rival to folk-healing. But it will also be that of much of the medicine of today. (1973:799)

For Thomas there is no doubt that the differences between modern, scientifically oriented physicians, on the one hand, and premodern, magically thinking, and acting healers, on the other, are less profound than one is inclined to believe. A sharp boundary between science and magic is difficult to draw, especially for a modern patient: "Usually he knows no more of the underlying rationale for his treatment than did the client of the cunning man. In such circumstances it is hard to say where 'science' stops and 'magic' begins" (ibid.:800; see also Stivers 1982:126).[3] Although Thomas's view is less evolutionist than the one developed by Parsons, he nevertheless seems to position the blurring of boundaries between magic and science in nonscientific circles.

A few years ago the Dutch sociologist Marijke Gijswijt-Hofstra published an article on recent medical-historical research in which the role of "belief" and "magic" in healing processes is highlighted. This article is interesting for several reasons, but I want to deal with just one. According to Gijswijt-Hofstra, one has to be careful with an all-too-quick perception of magic and belief as the antipodes of what one considers to be science. "For such a strategy prohibits a clear view on the internal rationality of 'belief' and 'magic' as well as on their part in 'science'"(1991:124). Though the processes of rationalization and medicalization have been going on for already more than a century, it is still a question for her to which degree these processes have led to "a pushing back of 'belief' and 'magic' . . . , not only on the demand side but also on that of the supply" (ibid.:132). According to Gijswijt-Hofstra, there has not yet been much research conducted on the degree to which "religious and/or magical ideas" form part and parcel of the range of thought of contemporary medical doctors.[4]

In this contribution I will try to shed light on this issue by concentrating on the kind of anthropomorphizing imagery physicians preferably use in describing, analyzing, and interpreting illnesses and on how this imagery colors their therapies. I will try to show that a closer inspection of medical metaphors and their effects on treatment can help us better understand why doctors may be considered as pseudoscientists of some kind, much closer than they want to admit to the "unscientific" health experts nearby and far away in space and time, from whose perspectives and practices they vehemently distance themselves (cf. Van Vegchel 1991).[5]

Moreover, I want to address the fact that there still seems to be no end to the production and consumption of popular representations of physicians who come to believe that they are endowed with life-creating potentialities or of doctors who every now and then transform themselves into wild men or women giving in to death and destruction. The number of (science fiction [sci-fi]) novels, comic strips, and (videos) movies—to name just a few genres—in which modern versions of derailing doctors figure next to the classical examples is still great and very much in vogue with a broad public.[6] I think that such products of the imagination in which scientists, that is, physicians, come to the fore as types of creators, suffering from megalomania (cf. Bann 1994), or as destructors, threatening the lives of innocent people (cf. Geduld 1983), are not groundless. They, at least, invite us to further explore their possible origin, especially because they are diametrically opposed with the image or self-image of the physician as the prototypical representative of a radically rationalized and professionalized scientific community.[7] One of the sources of the image of doctors as "lunatic creators" nowadays seems to lie in their tremendous efforts to prolong the lives of patients by implantations of dead and transplantations, including xenotransplantations, of living matter. Another one seems to be their recent endeavor to create living beings out of human tissue after the rather successful cloning of plants and animals. The background of the image of doctors as life-threatening destructors is, I think, the fact that some of them became the killing accomplices of totalitarian despots and regimes.

Thus, in this chapter I shall pay attention to the sources of the image of the physician (1) as a mad creator of life, or descendant of Frankenstein, (2) as pseudoscientist, and (3) as destroyer of human life.

Physicians as the (Re)builders of Human Beings, or How Dr. Frankenstein Is Still Alive and Kicking

This source of the image of the physician consists of physicians' activities in the area of im- and transplantations, on the one hand, and in that of reproduction, on the other (cf. Helman 1988). For ages doctors have been engaged in the implantation of all sorts of dead material in sick or not properly functioning bodies, for example, dentures, artificial arteries and eye lenses, silver pegs and pieces of ivory in order to keep broken arms and legs together, tantalum brain plates and ceramic ossicles, titanium hips and valves of plastic, pacemakers, and so on. They made great progress in creating a kind of bionic being, as we know them from sci-fi novels and sci-fi movies and about whom the old Greeks already talked in some of their myths (e.g., the Greek myth of Pelops, who got an ivory shoulder). These achievements in replacing living material by dead matter are at the same time a source of both respect and fear and are articulated in a great number of highly (ambivalent) collective fantasies woven around the representatives of medical science. But along with doctors, there are also other scientists who nourish this kind of fantasy, for example, the men and women who are busy with the development of artificial intelligence. Some of them indeed have remarkable ideas about the future of the human body. Ruth Mourik, who studied the viewpoints of a number of scientists affiliated with the Massachusetts Institute of Technology, with regard to the relationship between technology and being human, reported, for example, the following statement by one of them:

I think bodies will disappear, slowly but they will. The whole idea of the body will disappear. First of all, what is interesting about a person are the bits, the information. Bodies are temporary, they are pretty bad machines. They are still better than what we can make right now. And in a sense they last for a long time but not very long. They wear out, they have got a lot of problems. . . . The body has no value; it is just implementation of technology. What is interesting is the information process. (1996:52)[8]

According to Bruce Mazlish (1993) we are on the eve of abandoning what he calls the "fourth fallacy," that is, the idea that there exists a discontinuity between humans and machines.[9] Other scholars, for example, the information scientist Joseph Weizenbaum, think that all this is nonsense (cf. Weizenbaum and Haefner 1992:114). Anyhow, one is forced to conclude that the ever expanding efforts of medical scientists to prolong the life of their patients by implanting dead matter into their bodies form an important source of the ongoing production of popular representations of doctors as "mad magicians." Equally important for this ongoing production are the replacements of badly functioning organs, such as hearts, livers, and kidneys,[10] by "new" ones coming from both human beings and animals,[11] as well as everything they have to do to get these "spare parts" (cf. Dowie 1989).

For the last decade, all sorts of "urban legends" are told in the United States and Europe about the theft of organs, especially corneas and kidneys, by an "organ mafia" consisting of physicians eager to cut and villains who cleverly profit from the shortage of donor organs (cf. Scheper-Hughes 1996; Sharp 2000:307).[12] These legends also circulate in the Netherlands and create "an eerie sphere around transplantations, which are already perceived with suspicion by many persons ('they pull the plug a bit earlier when they need your organs')" (Burger 1995:40). Just like a certain type of horror movie, these legends reflect both a widespread mistrust toward and a fear of the activities of doctors (cf. Carroll 1990:210; Brunvand 1986:97–98).[13] Recently the experiments of specialists with regard to the production of, for example, bone and skin implantations with human cells and their talk about the possible breeding of complete organs in "clean rooms" supply new food for the popular imagination.[14] In this connection, one should not forget the new medical practices in the realm of procreation (cf. Davis-Floyd and Dumit 1998), such as, for example, in vitro fertilization, and, *last but not least*, the high expectations of some doctors concerning the possibilities of cloning, that is, the breeding of genetically identical persons out of the cell tissue of a human being, for instance, with the goal of creating a storehouse of "spare parts." All these phenomena form a rich breeding ground for both fear-reflecting and fear-inspiring popular fantasies, alloys with a high Frankenstein component.[15]

The optimism of many physicians with regard to the possibilities of growing all sorts of organic tissue, building blood vessels, repairing genetic material, manipulating procreation processes, and cloning humans contrasts sharply with the messages about mistakes made by them,[16] illnesses that they themselves help generate, side effects of surgical operations and drugs they cannot control (cf. Moerman 1979),[17] ignorance concerning many diseases, and the inability to keep operation rooms and intensive care wards free from dangerous bacteria. These negative sides of modern biomedical practices are not without effects; they contribute to the decision of many people troubled by ailments to look for help elsewhere, for example, in the alternative medicine circuit. But apart from this, these negative sides keep alive the idea among a broad public that physicians are ambiguous experts, able to transform from Dr. Jekyll into Mr. Hyde or to become a kind of Doctor Frankenstein tinkering with human life and powerless in front of his own horrendous freakish creations.

Instead of interpreting these popular perceptions of doctors nowadays (as well as in the past) as another proof of a lack of sound and appropriate knowledge of the medical profession (as Parsons, for example, would do), one could also see them as particular ways in which a general nonacademic public expresses its observations of a series of undeniable dark sides to this vital profession. Whereas physicians themselves tend to talk about these dark sides in a supposedly objective and scientific type of language, applied heavily in the case of such notorious cures as leukotomy and lobotomy, folk versions tend to deal with them in myths and fantasies, which are not simply expressions of false consciousness, as professionals and scholars like Parsons and others would claim, but rather should be regarded as another type of discourse on the very same phenomena. In the next section I will deal in a more detailed way with this blurring of boundaries between medical science and folklore or popular culture. I will also try to show that doctors, just like anyone else, are prisoners of language in representing what goes on in human bodies and how this not only influences their medical practice but also contributes to their image as pseudoscientists.

Physicians as Warriors Against Evil in Human Beings

In his book *Body Myths* (1991), Cecil Helman shows in a fascinating way how laypeople took possession of the scientific "germ theory" developed by medical researchers and transformed it into what he calls "germism."

> In the everyday use of the term, "germs" have become a potent symbol, embodying within them a whole cluster of meanings and memories, of ways of being and ways of interpreting many of the phenomena of everyday life. This lay, metaphorical use of Germ Theory, taken out of its original medical context, is what I would term *Germism*. Its origin lies in a collage of folk traditions and diluted science, in bits of bacteriology blended with magical thinking. It is a way of talking, but also a way of thinking—a set of beliefs, perhaps even a sort of folk religion, whose images are drawn from the discoveries of Pasteur, Koch and Lister, but with only a slight understanding of scientific cause and cure. (Helman 1991:30)

In the past laymen used concepts such as *spirits* and *demons*, and metaphors such as *insects*, *swarms*, and *dogs* (cf. also White 1991; Martin 1991; Sibley 1995; Leibovici 1998), to designate dangerous elements in their environment. But nowadays, according to Helman, they use the representations of bacteriologists as metaphors for all kinds of evil, big and small, by which they feel threatened, as well as for explaining how this evil might expand. Meanwhile a large metaphorical folk discourse has grown in which the idea of becoming "contaminated" or "infected" by "bacilli" and "viruses" plays an important role. I think that Helman's observation concerning the manner in which medical discourse on contagious microorganisms has become a rich source of metaphors for the scientific and nonscientific public is to the point and relevant.[18]

Yet what I miss in his thought-provoking essay is a thorough examination of the metaphors used by physicians themselves, their imagery with regard to how human beings can fall ill and regain their health. He constantly speaks of the "Germ Theory (of modern science)," "(models of medical) science," and "(language of) bacteriology" without saying very much about the ways doctors express themselves, about the characteristics of their language. In so doing, Helman intimates that the scientific discourse of physicians might be of a totally different nature than the discourse of laypeople, who utilize the models of the former "in a distorted, diluted form" in order to come to grips with a world they otherwise would not understand. This physicians' scientific discourse itself would not be characterized by a lack of under-standing and "magical thinking." It would be unfair, however, to assert that Helman does not say a word about the kind of metaphors used by doctors. He remarks, for example, "the Germ Theory of modern medicine—and its noisy step-child named Germism—have always carried with them the im-agery of war, of attack and counter-attack against an unseen enemy" (Helman 1991:34–35).[19]

Having said that, Helman leaves the issue. Yet its further examination could have led him to interesting insights, for instance, that physicians in their study of microorganisms, such as bacilli, bacteria, viruses, cells, and their possible approach in order to remove physical afflictions, not only to a large extent use anthropomorphic representations but also particular perfor-mative models occurring in their social environment.[20] They very often rep-resent the microorganisms as kinds of human beings who can get involved in a fight to the bitter end.[21] It is striking that medical researchers frequently utilize "macrometaphors" and see a human body as a society consisting of good and evil beings, whereas laypeople use "micrometaphors" and perceive a society as a body full of malevolent microorganisms.[22] On close examina-tion, one is not confronted with two totally different ways of representing things but rather with similar universes of discourse, that is, metaphorical ones. Such discourses neither are totally true nor always present a distorted or mythical image of what we consider to be reality (cf. Hufford 1982; Ver-rips 1996; Sibley 1995:122). If one looks at it in this way, one realizes that Helman's sharp distinction between scientific and nonscientific thinking should be less rigid.

Recently G.W. Van Rijn–Van Tongeren published a fascinating study *Metaphors in Medical Texts* (1997) in which she shows how important anthro-pomorphizing and using war metaphors are in the work of physicians who do research on the origin and development of all sorts of diseases, for example, cancer, an ailment very often applied metaphorically in order to disparage human beings, their thinking, and their acting (Sontag 1979).[23] Cells are evidently perceived by many medical researchers as "human beings," with a plethora of human characteristics.[24] These cells form societies with each other; some of them, that is, cancer cells, "behave aggressively," for they *invade, colonize,* or *carry on war* (Van Rijn–Van Tongeren 1997:66ff.).[25]

It is striking that physicians not only use the performative model of the warrior in order to obtain and present an image of the course of micro-processes within the human body but also for their own role as therapeutists. They see themselves, just like the healthy cells, as fighters or soldiers, who by killing malevolent opponents or building a good defense system try to protect the body that is under attack.[26] In other words, the use of war metaphors is not only limited to cells but it also encompasses doctors. A performative model, which also plays an important role in representing their activities, is that of the hunter who is after harmful game that has to be killed in order to restore balance in nature.[27] With regard to physicians' "war" against cancer, they sometimes speak of launching a "magic bullet," or *Zauberkugel,* a powerful combination of antibiotics and toxic reagents that at once will end the devastating "actions" of tumor cells (ibid.:72; see also Helman 1991:35). Though the search for this magic bullet started a long time ago, it has not yet been found.

This brings us to the defective nature of the knowledge of cancer and how to treat it, as well as of several other fatal diseases, as it has been accumulated so far. Though it cannot be denied that the whole of representations concerning cancer has been improved on the basis of scientific research, due to their strong anthropomorphic and metaphorical character these representations remain in a certain sense magical-mythical and do not differ from the representations of laypeople in essence but only in their empirical precision. Indeed, the medical representation of microorganisms causing cancer as kind of minuscule beings with malevolent intentions and behavioral patterns shows a remarkable resemblance to the popular myths about cancer.[28] In the last case it concerns a *macroscopic* representation of (or view on) the cause of fatal physical decay, in the first a *microscopic* one. That there exists no fundamental difference between the two perspectives seems to be a consequence of the undeniable fact that physicians, just like everyone else engaged in the exploration of the unknown, are prisoners of their language, ergo of symbols, imagery, and metaphors (cf. Verrips 1996; Lupton 1994:54–71; Sharp 2000:315). Because illness and disease are matters of life and death, it is not surprising that this imagery and these metaphors very often are borrowed from such violent domains as hunting and war and that these domains also function as the sources for the performative models physicians use to characterize the performances of cells and themselves in relation to these cells.[29]

On the basis of all this, I conclude that the view (even acknowledged by, for example, Parsons) that the medical scientific discourse bears a hybrid character cannot be denied. It does not consist of a constellation of purely scientific, objective representations—*whatever that may be*—but of a mixture of scientific, pseudoscientific, and magical-mythical notions and ideas. In any case, it is a partial metaphorical ensemble, which undergoes constant transformation. With each new medical discovery, something else will be veiled.[30] In other words, doctors and especially the ones engaged in medical research are caught in an intricate dialectic of revealing and concealing at the same time. The process of revealing what is going on in (sick) bodies is characterized by the fact that out of all the sensory experiences, the visual one has come to play a dominant role, which pushed the other ones, such as the senses of touch and hearing, to a subordinate level. Though the stethoscope still functions as an important symbol for the medical profession, microscopes, X rays and cameras, scanners, and screens, in short instruments to make invisible things visible, are much more important now. In a sense "scrying" is not decreasing but increasing in our modern world. Divination and speculation (from the Latin word *speculum*, mirror, and related to the Latin word *specularia*, windowpane) on the basis of observations through "glass" and "liquid crystals" is flourishing as never before (cf. Verrips 1998). If one realizes the fundamental role these materials play in revealing otherwise hidden "realities," one is struck by the family resemblance between crystal gazing and looking through lenses and at screens.[31] For in both cases "glassy" materials are used to achieve more knowledge and deeper insights.

This is not to say that there are no differences between the two types of speculators (in the sense of spy and researcher), but the correspondences at certain points are greater than one frequently is prepared to admit. There exists no radical and principal gap between the perspective of magicians or "wild thinkers" and (medical) scientists. If one furthermore realizes that both the crystal gazer and the medical scientist tend to anthropomorphize what they believe to have observed, the familial resemblance becomes still stronger. But it is exactly this tendency or more generally the impossibility of avoiding metaphors that implies partial concealment of aspects of that which is observed, seen, or visualized. However, as part of this inescapable fact, doctors often consciously strive to conceal or keep secret what they discovered with respect to the bodies of their patients. According to the German philosopher Peter Sloterdijk (1992:538), in this respect an analogy with a secret service agent is appropriate.[32]

That laymen started to think in a germistic way cannot be properly understood if one does not take into consideration the fact that physicians themselves use metaphorical discourses with regard to illnesses and therapies. In other words, the metaphorical jump in lay discourse from the so-called scientific microlevel to the societal macrolevel was made possible by a similar jump in medical discourse but then in the reverse direction. In this context the question arises to what extent physicians contributed to the rise of "xenophobic metaphorism," that is, the "germistic" view of society as an entity/body full of *Fremdkörper* threatening its order (cf. Helman 1991:37). Unfortunately, I did not have the time to do extensive research with regard to this question. However, if one thinks of the role physicians played in the rise and spread of the medically colored language of the German National Socialists, who were much inspired by the performative model of the physician, and of Nazi doctors who used a germistic type of discourse, then this hypothesis seems to be rather plausible. Let me try to illustrate this.

Physicians as "Warriors" Against Evil in Society, or How Dr. Jekyll Can Transform into Mr. Hyde

At the end of the nineteenth century, it was rather common in scientific circles in America and Europe to talk about the right of the state to sterilize particular persons in their own interest or that of the nation and even to kill them. The idea that one could keep a population healthy and strong by means of sterilization, for example, of the mentally ill, as it was defended and propagated by racial hygienists and eugenicists, was widely accepted by all sorts of politicians within and outside Europe. Due to their efforts, laws were designed and accepted that made the sterilization of specific categories of people possible. In Germany such laws were accepted in 1933. However, Switzerland and Denmark had acted earlier, for there sterilization laws were already introduced in, respectively, 1928 and 1929, whereas Norway, Sweden, Finland, Estonia, and Iceland followed the Germans (Proctor 1988:97). In 1997 these laws and how they were implemented all of a sudden became front-page news in the Netherlands, because a Swedish journalist published a few articles in which he raised the issue of why the sterilization policy in his country was not properly dealt with in school and history books.[33] America, where eugenicists and racial hygienists were rather influential, had enacted sterilization laws at the beginning of the century. And long before the National Socialists came to power, German scholars thought of America as a guiding country that should be followed without hesitation (ibid.:97–101).

It is important to realize that (a) the sterilization laws of the Nazis, which after 1933 were frequently tightened, were not unique at all and (b) scientists, especially doctors, contributed a lot to their implementation. They developed the theoretical or scientific foundations and the criteria for the selection of persons who might be sterilized, as well as the technology. Especially these foundations and criteria have later been qualified as nonsensical, serving no other purpose than providing politicians with a pseudoscientific legitimization for the implementation of a reprehensible population policy. But one should not forget that the doctors and a lot of persons following in their wake were totally convinced of the fact that everything done on the basis of the sterilization laws was scientifically correct and sound. In Germany the sterilization of people on the advice of and by doctors took place on a uniquely large scale. According to estimates, the total number of people sterilized during the Nazi regime amounts to 400,000.[34]

Along with sterilization, the admissibility and social profits of euthanasia were much-discussed topics in scientific circles at the end of the nineteenth century. Some scientists were of the opinion, as I have already remarked, that the state had the right to end the lives of particular citizens. In 1920 this viewpoint was propagated in Germany by the jurist Karl Binding and the physician Alfred Hoche in their book *Die Freigabe der Vernichtung lebensun-werten Lebens* (Release to destroy lives not worth living):

> in which they argued that the principle of "allowable killing" should be ex-
> tended to the incurably sick. . . . The right to live, they asserted, must be
> earned and justified, not dogmatically assumed. Those who are not capable
> of human feeling—those "ballast lives" and "empty human husks" that fill
> our psychiatric institutions—can have no sense of the value of life. Theirs
> is not a life worth living; hence their destruction is not only tolerable but
> humane. (Proctor 1988:178)

Through the publication of this kind of book, an extensive discussion was started concerning the question as to whether euthanasia was to be allowed or not. Especially the rising National Socialists appropriated with eagerness the perspectives of such scholars as Binding and Hoche. And we know where this adoption of their "scientific" notions and ideas led in the years to follow. The destruction of the lives of feeble-minded and seriously handicapped children and adults first, and the lives of homosexuals, Gypsies, political opponents, prisoners of war, and Jews somewhat later.[35] According to Ervin Staub, a reversal of medical ethics was of crucial importance for this horrific development: "Killing became a kind of healing—of the nation, the group, the collectivity, the race" (1989:122).

> A bureaucracy was established. Questionnaires haphazardly filled out . . .
> were used to select victims. Overdose of drugs, injections, starvation, and
> eventually gassing were used. Doctors filled out the questionnaires, made
> the selection, and did the actual killing, establishing many of the procedures
> later used in killing Jews. . . . The medical system was placed in the service
> of killing (ibid.).

Instead of asserting that a reversal of medical ethics occurred, one could also say that Nazi doctors did expand in a bizarre way the medical practice applied at a microlevel, that is, within a body, with regard to microorganisms causing illnesses, to the macrolevel of society, perceived by them as a social body full of sickness-causing elements that had to be killed before they got a chance to totally corrupt it. Since the end of the nineteenth century and certainly after the Nazis came to power, an increasing number of doctors had made the jump from the treatment of health-threatening bacilli, viruses, bacteria, and so on within individual bodies to the treatment of sick people or people deemed to be ill—as if they were a kind of dangerous microorganism—in the body social. In other words, to use Helman's terminology, they fell under the spell of germistic thinking and acting. The idea that particular categories of people, for example, Jews, represented malevolent microbes forming a serious obstacle to a sound development of society was already in circulation at the end of the nineteenth century.[36] After that, the idea gradually spread in Germany among both physicians and laypersons. After the Nazis came to power, the medicalization of social issues gained momentum and, fully in line with this, the radical extermination of thousands and thousands of unwanted citizens.[37] In a sense they performed a big operation on their own society, which they perceived as suffering under the attack of several very dangerous creatures who had succeeded in penetrating it and settling in different corners. What I want to emphasize in this connection is that the performative model of the Nazi doctors was that of the warrior, whereas that of the politicians and their followers was that of the physician (cf. Forgacs 1994).[38] Hitler saw himself, for example, as the big healer of the German people and was represented on posters in this way (cf. Proctor 1988:51). I think that this combination of metaphorical perspectives is a very dangerous one, for which we have to be always on our guard.[39]

The American psychoanalyst Richard A. Koenigsberg showed in a number of publications (1975, 1977, 1995) that in Nazi Germany a coherent collective fantasy came into existence, which was shared by a great number of citizens and can be summarized as follows: "The nation is a living organism; this organism is suffering from a 'disease,' the source of which is a particular class of persons lying within the body of this organism; in order to cure this disease, and thereby to 'save the nation,' it may be necessary to 'remove' this class of persons from within the body of the nation" (1977:15).[40] According to Koenigsberg this type of fantasy is not unique, for it also cropped up elsewhere in the world with similar dreadful consequences.[41] He emphasizes the fact that the people who develop or adopt such a fantasy and start to remove "sick elements" from their society do not consider themselves murderers at all but instead the faithful servants of the public interest and, I would add, in many cases also excellent practitioners of medical science. Koenigsberg, however, compares them with exorcists who try to cast out evil (ibid.).

Many physicians, and not only German ones, demonstrated before and during World War II that just like Dr. Jekyll they had a second, very destructive personality. In showing that dark side they (again) nourished all sorts of skeptical and suspicious notions and ideas about the scientific and ethical integrity of doctors in general. In this connection Lifton's observation with regard to the medical doctors who were active in Auschwitz is interesting. According to him they were able to continue with their work, that is, with driving people to their death, by engaging in what he calls "doubling": "This is a process whereby two opposing selves are created, one of which is responsible for evil. The two selves seem encapsulated, walled off from each other to avoid internal conflict" (Lifton, as paraphrased by Staub [1989:143]).

Whether this view is correct or not is less relevant than the fact that Lifton presents Nazi doctors as Dr. Jekylls and Mr. Hydes. That physicians still figure to such a large extent in all sorts of popular fantasies as specialists who do not save people's lives but instead seriously impair or even kill them has, at least according to me, everything to do with the destructive role played in this century by doctors within and outside Europe, but especially in Germany, who claimed to serve science.[42] Along with the fact that their science presents a less precise picture of the reality they study and try to manipulate than they themselves want us to believe—which I see as a direct outcome of their dependence on language or metaphors—their science has frequently been used in a destructive way, especially in cases where physicians used their metaphorical language about microprocesses in the body for macroprocesses in their society.[43]

Epilogue

In this chapter I have dealt with three facets of biomedical perspectives and practices that play an important role in the maintenance of popular images of medical professionals as dangerous scientists not to be trusted: (a) the (metaphorical and mythical) nature of their knowledge of microprocesses in the human body, (b) their ability to play—often together with politicians—a destructive role in keeping all sorts of social bodies "healthy," and (c) their activities in the realm of building or rebuilding people and the creation of life. Especially the latter two facets still speak to the imagination and are in my view the main sources of the fact that a lot of people see the shadows of Frankenstein, the weird creator, and the alter-ego of Dr. Jekyll, Mr. Hyde, the crazy destroyer of life, always looming behind the backs of physicians. I do not think that this ambivalent perception will decrease with a further growth of medical knowledge; on the contrary. The more specialists claim to know about life and death, the greater the chance that laypeople will perceive them as types of modern "technocratic exorcists," busy with delivering individual and social bodies from of all sorts of "evil," from both microorganisms and death, and—hence, unavoidably—making a great number of mistakes. And, likewise, the greater the chance will be that laypeople figuratively cannot and literally will not follow them any longer and will start looking for other healers, for example, modern shamans. In any case, the entanglement of magic and science will increase rather than decrease with new developments in the medical field and become ever more intricate.

TEN

Spirits of Modernity

Alfred Wallace, Edward Tylor, and the Visual Politics of Fact

PETER PELS

> Up to the time when I first became acquainted with the facts of Spiritual-
> ism, . . . I was so thorough and confirmed a materialist that I could not at
> that time find a place in my mind for the conception of spiritual existence,
> or for any other agencies in the universe than matter and force. Facts, how-
> ever, are stubborn things. My curiosity was at first excited by some slight
> but inexplicable phenomena occurring in a friend's family, and my desire
> for knowledge and love of truth forced me to continue the inquiry. The
> facts became more and more assured, more and more varied, more and
> more removed from anything that modern science taught or modern philos-
> ophy speculated upon. The facts beat me. (Wallace [1874] 1896:vi–vii)

This is how Alfred Russel Wallace, pioneer anthropological fieldworker, and
coauthor with Charles Darwin of the modern biological principle of natural
selection, described his "conversion" to Spiritualism in the preface to the first
edition of *Miracles and Modern Spiritualism* (published 1874).[1] In classic Ba-
conian fashion, Wallace tried to empirically prove the capacity of ancestral

spirits to manifest themselves among the living. At first glance, his empiricism appears a necessary but hardly sufficient strategy in a late-nineteenth-century intellectual environment where conversations with the deceased were regularly regarded as survivals of primitive superstition. However, Wallace's account also warns us against hasty generalizations about late-nineteenth-century intellectuals' conceptions of the trajectory of "modernity": apparently, some could be "converted" from Enlightenment empiricism to a belief in spirits and come to think that modernity includes miracles and spirit possession.[2]

Wallace's opposition of the material and spiritual is, of course, not very unusual: despite regular condemnations of modern civilization as materialist, invocations of the spiritual are not something foreign to it—they are, at the very least, a staple of its romantic menu. Even more, the "spirit of capitalism" (Weber 1958) or the "spirit of consumerism" (Campbell 1987) can serve as a reminder to social scientists that even the most material of social practices are often thought to need interpretation in immaterial terms, terms pointing to a history of Protestant spirituality that shaped and continues to shape what we understand by the modern. Nor does the spiritual necessarily imply something before or beyond reason: the dialectics of increasing human knowledge, subjective or objective, have classically been described in terms of *Geist*—which can be translated as "mind" as well as "spirit" (Hegel [1807] 1977). Yet, such invocations of the spiritual in the *singular*—the spirit of the nation (rather than its matters of state), or the spirit of the law (rather than its letter)—usually do not make room for an empirically established miraculous intervention in this world. The genealogy of modern miracles and spirit manifestations must rather be sought in more subaltern movements of spirit possession—such as, for example, the Methodists' "experimental" religion, where personal religious assurance and authority were produced by the direct experience of and communion with the Holy Spirit (Davies 1963; Garrett 1987:74ff.). The "secular Methodism" of phrenology (Cooter 1984:chapter 6)—the art of reading character from the bumps on someone's head—transferred this experimental "direct communion" to the level of human interaction, and, as we shall see, linked it to Spiritualism's communion with the spirits of the dead.

Popular Christianity retained worries about whether the spirit concerned was Holy or "false" and satanic (Davies 1963:7; Garrett 1987:133), and this suggests that miraculous spirit communion tends toward a conception of spirits in the *plural*. Modern European musings on plural spirits, however, generally define them as "other." If one checks a library for titles that carry the word *spirit*, singular, one finds that they predominantly refer to works on European history and society in the spirit of Montesquieu, Hegel, or Max Weber. In contrast, spirits in the plural mostly signify studies of the "rest" rather than the West. This tendency, however, fails to do justice to the historical role of spirit possession in the formation of modern conceptions of the self. In one of the first major accounts of modern Spiritualism, Emma Hardinge Britten's *Nineteenth Century Miracles*, the genealogy of modern spirit possession is not only traced to esoteric and to some extent marginal predecessors of modern occultism (Britten 1883:89–90) or to a folklore of hauntings and ghosts (ibid.:92–99). The "telegraphy" of spirit communion is also found in such culturally central movements as John Wesley's Methodism or the both scientifically and politically influential work of Franz Anton Mesmer (ibid.:91; cf. Darnton 1968). That some of these movements have been described ex post facto as marginal to the development of the spirit of modernity does not necessarily prove that they were, but it does identify them as sites of political contest about the proper constitution of the modern.

Ethnology or anthropology—the "counterscience" that dissolves our singular conceptions of humanity and thereby poses the most general questions about it (Foucault 1970:379)—has always been more intimately concerned with spirits in the plural, even if, as noted above, its general tendency was to locate them in other places than its own.[3] Alfred Wallace's empiricist defense of the existence of spirits points to a specific case of anthropology's dealing with both the singular and the plural spirits of modernity: the debate between Wallace and Edward Burnett Tylor over the cultural significance of modern Spiritualism in the broader context of nineteenth-century doctrines of human evolution. Wallace aimed at Tylor, among others, when he wrote that the assurance of spiritual facts became more and more removed from the "speculations" of "modern science" and "modern philosophy." Thus, Wallace's spirits—developed, in part, from his plebeian background as well as his Malayan fieldwork—were juxtaposed with a more "armchair" and elite science and philosophy, represented by Tylor's presumed "psychic unity of mankind." A dominant and singular "mind" stood juxtaposed with an unruly multitude of spirits.

The debate between Wallace and Tylor about spiritualism must, therefore, be read against the background of specific relations of power. With both Wallace and Tylor, the interface between the spiritual and material was, as I hope to show, at the same time a way to distinguish what counted as publicly acceptable knowledge. Because the definition of what knowledge was publicly acceptable was based on how it was properly produced (for Wallace, by domestic experiment; for Tylor, by being modeled on statistics), the debate was about different constructions of public culture as well. In outlining the social and historical significance of this debate, I am guided by Michel Foucault's proposition that the modern soul is not the substance imprisoned in a sinful body of Christian theology but "the element in which are articulated the effects of a certain type of power and the reference of a certain type of knowledge" (1979:29). This "reality-reference" is the *effect* of a "political anatomy" that paradoxically emerges in the guise of a constraint, "the prison of the body" (1979:30). In a similar way, Tylor's mind and Wallace's spirits, although discursively positioned as the *causes* of or constraints on human evolution, have to be understood as effects of specifically modern types of power/knowledge.

However, I do not want to give the impression—often associated with the early work of Foucault—of discourse produced by a monolithic (carceral or panoptic) type of power. The first two sections of this chapter discuss Wallace's scientific career and his involvement in Spiritualism, as a way of situating the debate in specific class, gender, and race relations, and this will bring out the political and economic struggles needed to understand it. These struggles were translated into specific idioms of modern knowledge and authority. On the one hand, the third and fourth sections of this chapter discuss the extent to which Wallace and Tylor shared a number of discursive themes: the morality of social and cultural reform, empiricism, and the emphasis on a visualist conception of admissible evidence. On the other, they show that these staples of nineteenth-century empiricism were less an issue of "truth" than an issue of cultural politics (cf. Ludden 1993). The class, gender, and race issues that informed the debate were translated, through the idiom of moral empiricism, into two different, yet related types of power/knowledge: the panoptic vision of Tylor's statistical classifications and the more experiential one of Wallace's domestic experiments. Thus, the struggle over the proper ways to conjecture (or divine or reveal) invisible or occult causes of human evolution can be interpreted as a struggle over the proper *publicity* of science: in Tylor's case, a public revelation of progress on the basis of a certain kind of exclusive scientific expertise, and in Wallace's, one that situates it in a more democratic and domestic interior. In conclusion, I hope to show that this causes us to question our stereotyped interpretations of the occult, public science, and the position of anthropology.

Alfred Russel Wallace: Scientific Entrepreneur and Social Reformer

Alfred Russel Wallace (1823–1913) was the third son of a man "of independent means" who lost his fortune, and Alfred's childhood and education were marked by financial difficulties. His brothers and sisters were, from an early age, forced to learn a profession and earn their own living, and Alfred was, after leaving school at fourteen, sent to London to live with his brother John, an apprentice carpenter. John and Alfred spent most of their evenings at a "Hall of Science," a "kind of club or mechanics' institute for advanced thinkers among workmen, and especially for the followers of Robert Owen, the founder of the socialist movement in England" (Wallace 1908:45). There, Wallace was introduced to "secularism or agnosticism" and the writings and work of Owen, which was the probable source of his democratic epistemology—"a definition of knowledge as open to anybody" (Barrow 1986:146).[4] Shortly afterward, he joined his other elder brother, William, to begin his education as a land surveyor, and as most land surveyors were amateur geologists, he began a largely autodidactic education in science as well. An elementary introduction to botany was a "revelation" that induced him to study "the system that underlay all the variety of nature" and to start noting his thoughts about it. By the time he came of age, Wallace notes, "I was absolutely nonreligious" (1908:59, 102, 107–9, 120).

At twenty-one, he was left to fend for himself and went on to teach English at a school in Leicester, where his self-education continued, among other things through reading Alexander von Humboldt's *Travels* and Thomas Robert Malthus's *Principle of Population*. In Leicester, a lecture introduced him to mesmerism and led him to try whether he could induce the mesmeric trance on patients himself, with marked success (Wallace 1908:124). Wallace had already read George Combe's *Constitution of Man* and other works on phrenology, the doctrine that the brain is the seat of the mind and that the mind can be divided in different "faculties" located in different parts of the brain. He became interested in phrenomesmeric phenomena: the exciting of the different mental "faculties" by touching the "organs" on the skull that corresponded to them, while the patient was in trance (see Kaplan 1975). Wallace bought a phrenological bust to determine the positions of the organs and experimented at home, finding, to his surprise, that a few seconds after touching an organ, the patient in trance "would change his attitude and the expression of his face in correspondence with the organ excited." He found the effect "unmistakable, and superior to that which the most finished actor could give" (Wallace 1908:126).

The materialism of Wallace's thinking at the time is evident from the fact that he thought mental suggestion or telepathy could not explain these phenomena, because when he once accidentally touched an "organ" different from the one he thought he had touched, the patient displayed the effect corresponding to the organ rather than to Wallace's expectations. The experiments convinced him that the scientific disdain about mesmerism was unjustified and should not be preferred above observation and experiment by "as sane and sensible" other men (Wallace 1908:127; see also Darnton 1968; Kaplan 1975), a good example of Wallace's democratic epistemology, here informing his opposition to the scientific establishment.

It was also at Leicester that Wallace met Henry Walter Bates, who fired him with an enthusiasm for entomology (the collection and classification of insects), and when Wallace, after two years, went back to surveying, the two men kept up a correspondence about botany and zoology, exchanging views about evolution and the origin of species and becoming more and more determined to visit the tropics on a collecting expedition (encouraged by their reading of Humboldt's *Travels* and Darwin's *Beagle* journal).[5] The two men determined on the Amazon, hoping to pay for their expenses during the voyage by collecting and selling botanical and zoological specimens, and set sail from Liverpool in April 1848. They worked together for two years and then separated, Bates remaining on the Amazon for seven years, while Wallace returned to England in 1852, losing most of his collections through being shipwrecked on the way home. This loss occasioned that, after writing an account of his voyage (Wallace [1853] 1972), he set off immediately afterward on another collecting expedition, resulting in his highly successful *The Malay Archipelago* (Wallace [1869] 1962).

Bates and Wallace are examples of a distinct type of Victorian scientific career, both starting as independent entrepreneurs rather than being employed, as were Charles Darwin, Thomas Huxley, and Joseph Hooker, by a government institution such as the navy. Whereas the latter were enabled, by their contacts with the Victorian establishment, to secure such relatively safe positions,[6] the former had to struggle their way up by their own initiative, reinforcing, to some extent, their association with working-class culture by having to restrict themselves to a very modest and low-cost way of life. Nevertheless, Wallace got to know, after his return to London in 1853, some of the major scientists of the day.[7] He managed to obtain free passage to Singapore through the help of Sir Roderick Murchison, President of the Royal Geographical Society. Wallace chose the Malay Archipelago for this new expedition, prompted by what he read and saw of its natural history in London and by the opportunities for safe travel offered by the establishment of European rule in the Dutch Indies and Sarawak (Wallace 1908:169).

At Ternate, in the Moluccas, Wallace hit upon the idea of natural selection and wrote the paper that would provoke Darwin to write *The Origin of Species*. Wallace's impulse, Darwin's reaction, and the decision of Charles Lyell and Joseph Hooker to have both Wallace's paper and an extract from Darwin's older work read together at the Linnean Society on July 1, 1858, are well known (Bowlby 1990:319–32; Loewenberg 1957; McKinney 1972). Less well known is the fact that both Wallace and Darwin derived the idea of "natural" selection from ideas about *human* and *artificial* selection. They were decisively influenced by Malthus, whose *Essay on the Principle of Population* ([1798] 1970) was based on a quantification of the knowledge of human nature. Darwin thought of natural selection on the basis of the model of artificial selection in the breeding of domestic animals (Bowlby 1990:338). And this is how Wallace says he hit upon the principle while suffering a bout of fever in Ternate:

> One day something brought to my recollection Malthus' "Principles [*sic*] of Population" which I had read about twelve years before. I thought of his clear exposition of the "positive checks to increase"—disease, accidents, war,

and famine—which keep down the population of savage races to so much lower an average than that of more civilized peoples. It then occurred to me that these causes or their equivalents are continually acting in the case of animals also; and as animals usually breed much more rapidly than does mankind, the destruction every year from these causes must be enormous. . . . It occurred to me to ask the question, Why do some die and some live? And the answer was clearly, that on the whole the best fitted live. (Wallace 1908:190)

The "disease, accidents, war, and famine" cited above are all topics that in the 1830s and 1840s came under the scrutiny of a new breed of British statisticians (Malthus foremost among them). In the decades to follow, this generation and its pupils slowly turned "statistics"—originally, the qualitative intelligence needed for statecraft—into the present-day practice of quantitative calculation (Cullen 1975; Stagl 1995). Ian Hacking (1990) has shown how this *social* development—the accessing and regulation of society by means of a novel form of intelligence gathering—was the necessary condition of a majority of the revolutions in nineteenth- and twentieth-century science. Early nineteenth-century statistics was also very much a *moral* science, insisting on the perfectibility or "improvement" of society on the basis of accurate measurements of its raw materials—both animal and human, both "savage" and "civilised" (Pels 1999b:151). We see that both Darwin and Wallace came to their revolutionary conception of evolution through statistical thinking (that is, Malthus's concept of population), coupled with musings about the improvement of domestic livestock (in Darwin's case) or the lack of improvement among "savages" (in Wallace's case; cf. Kottler 1974:152). It is crucial to realize this, for it is the possibility of "improving" animals or humans that allowed them to think beyond the immutability of species and races that was still a major assumption of biology at the time. Moreover, because they both based their idea of the "fitness" of species or races on the positive *utility* of their organic structure and habits in relation to their environment, they used, as we shall see, a concept of survival that was radically different from that later employed by Edward Tylor and some of his colleagues.

On Wallace's return to London in 1862, he started to enhance his reputation by writing a great number of papers on botanical, zoological, and anthropological subjects, which earned him the Royal Medal of the Royal Society in

1868 and the Gold Medal of the Société de Géographie in 1870 (G.T.B. [1853] 1889:xxi). The scientific establishment, however, seemed to have had difficulties in accepting this all-too-working-class genius, because his application for the secretaryship of the Royal Geographical Society, which his friendship with the scientific elite of Darwin, Huxley, Sir John Lubbock, Lyell, and John Tyndall should have secured him, was turned down. He was jilted by the woman he wanted to marry and lost most of his Malay expedition earnings through unfortunate financial manipulations (F. Turner 1974:92). It is in this context that his interest in Spiritualism, present ever since he had first heard about table rapping and mysterious apparitions while in the East, grew. His experiences, from the first séance he attended in July 1865, more and more tended to make him into one of the most famous advocates of the new wave of spirit materializations that occurred from the late 1860s on.

Before turning to Wallace's Spiritualism, it should be noted that Wallace's working-class associations, latent Owenism, Malay fieldwork, and democratic epistemology created a problem that supported his conversion to Spiritualism. *The Malay Archipelago* concluded with the statement that a "perfect social state" of individual freedom and self-government was found among communities of savages, while English society was, despite its physical progress, in a state of social barbarism (Wallace [1869] 1962:455–57). This had been anticipated in a famous paper of 1864,[8] in which Wallace argued that the "single homogeneous race" that would be the end product of human evolution would know no inferiors or nobler specimens:

> Each one will then work out his own happiness in relation to that of his fellows; perfect freedom of action will be maintained, since the well balanced moral faculties will never permit any one to transgress on the equal freedom of others. . . . Mankind will have at length discovered that it was only required of them to develop the capacities of their higher nature, in order to convert this earth, which has so long been the theatre of their unbridled passions, and the scene of unimaginable misery, into as bright a paradise as ever haunted the dreams of seer or poet. (Wallace 1864:clxix–clxx)

Wallace's image of a nobly savage past mirrored in an equally noble egalitarian future upset, of course, the hierarchical schemata of evolutionism. It drew forth a sympathetic reply from John Stuart Mill, who persuaded him to join the campaign for land nationalization, reinforcing Wallace's links to British socialism (Wallace 1908:319–29). Thus, Wallace displayed the link between socialist thought and occult inspiration evident throughout the nineteenth century (see Webb 1974).

Class, Domesticity, and Heterodox Medicine in Victorian Spiritualism

Wallace's first experience with Spiritualism was in 1865, when a séance at a house of a friend "with none but the members of his own family present," all "highly intelligent and well-educated persons," resulted in taps and motions from a table. In September of that year, he visited the public medium Mrs. Marshall in London, but he preferred to research the phenomena in his own home. His first attempts were not very successful, until, in November 1866, Wallace's sister discovered the mediumistic gifts of another lady in the house,[9] after which impressive shows of spiritual force followed (Wallace [1874] 1896:133–37). In that same year, his first defense of Spiritualism was published as a pamphlet ("The Scientific Aspects of the Supernatural," reprinted in Wallace [1874] 1896:33–125) and distributed among his scientific friends, most of whom read it, in the words of Tyndall, "with deep disappointment" (quoted in Wallace 1908:336).

When this pamphlet was republished in the first edition of *Miracles and Modern Spiritualism* in 1874, Wallace added a section called "Notes of personal evidence" ([1874] 1896:126–43), which was not included in the original essay because "I had not then witnessed any such facts in a *private* house, and without the intervention of *paid* mediums, as would be likely to satisfy my readers" ([1874] 1896:126; my emphasis). The formulation indicates the crucial role that domesticity played in British Spiritualism, especially for the middle-class or upper-middle-class audience to whom Wallace addressed the pamphlet. The oppositions public and private, and paid and unpaid, strongly influenced the definition of reliable evidence (as we shall see further below) and relied upon a British middle-class definition of the "female sphere" that diverged from the more radical feminist varieties of Spiritualism developed in the United States.

"Modern Spiritualism" had, after all, started in the United States when the Fox sisters discovered in March 1848 that the spirit of a murdered man communicated with them through raps and taps (Wallace [1874] 1896:152–53). The movement spread quickly and reached England in the early 1850s in the shape of two female American mediums and Harriet Beecher Stowe (Britten 1883:129, 137; Owen 1989:19). In the United States, the movement was allied with radical—individualistic, abolitionist, and feminist—critiques of society. Ann Braude has shown how, through the trance-speaking medium—the definition of which depended on "female" receptivity to possessing spirits—female opinion leaders could emerge who had previously been barred from speaking in public (Braude 1989). In Britain, although one of Spiritualism's first converts was the octogenarian socialist Robert Owen, the movement would shed much of this American radicalism, which in England was often negatively associated with "free love" principles and a critique of marriage (Braude 1989:117ff.; Owen 1989:35). Moreover, the development of Spiritualism as a whole, both in the United States and in Britain, tended more and more to depart from its radical roots and from the trance speaking in which so many subversive ideas could be uttered, toward "spirit materializations": the establishment of physical proof of spiritual presences, a development that was associated with the ("male") control of mediumship under test conditions and the emergence of the far more elitist occultism of Theosophy from 1875 on (Braude 1989:176–77; Washington 1993).

As Alex Owen has argued, although social class was in itself not an indicator of mediumship in Britain, it defined its sphere of operation. The Spiritualist vocabulary of *public* and *private* (or *professional* and *domestic*) mediumship was determined by an ideology of separate spheres, which implied the definition of private and domestic as a "natural" domain of women, to which female receptivity, care, and religiosity were to be applied, and which was distinct from the masculine public sphere (Owen 1989:49). This also led to a distinction of forms of mediumship on a class basis:

> Although believers chose not to express this directly, public mediumship was associated not only with the working classes but also with middle-class assumptions about lower-class morality. The rationale that working-class mediums needed to earn a living and might therefore be more tempted to resort to legerdemain if their gifts deserted them or failed to come up to scratch merely cloaked other class-based anxieties. Certainly, amongst more

affluent believers and researchers there was built-in resistance to the idea
that a "lady" could possibly stoop to fraud. Although this was by no means
true, private mediumship remained closely associated in spiritualist minds
with middle-classness, uplifting moral imperatives, and the sanctity of the
family circle; public mediumship remained associated with the working
classes and less sublime inducements. (Owen 1989:51)

Thus, although Spiritualism had a large following among English "plebeians" and continued to feed socialist rhetoric and organizations (Barrow
1986; Webb 1974), Wallace was more concerned to present his spiritual facts
to an audience that had modified Spiritualist radicalism with (upper-) middle-class domestic respectability.

This was also the result of a drive toward organization that, although
bound to fail because of the anarchistic nature of Spiritualist individualism,
was especially strong during the decade that Wallace became acquainted
with it. London, the Bloomsbury area in particular, had gained the lead over
former Spiritualist centers such as Yorkshire, Lancashire, Edinburgh, and
Dublin. In 1863, James Burns established the Burns Progressive Library and
Spiritual Institute at 15 Southampton Row, just off Bloomsbury Square, and
he started publishing *Human Nature* in 1867, followed by the widely read
Medium and Daybreak in 1870. The *Spiritual Magazine* and the *Spiritualist*
were other initiatives of the period (Owen 1989:23–24). Several attempts at
national organization, largely dominated by men, were made, although
women's rights continued to be integral to the Spiritualist program. The increasing pressure of the critique of the medical establishment in the 1870s
(denouncing mediumship as psychological abnormality) forced Spiritualists
further on the defensive, and the establishment of the Society for Psychical
Research in 1882 (which Wallace joined, although his interests had shifted
to land reform and the campaign against vaccination) marked the submission
of the—predominantly female—mediums to male-imposed test conditions
(Owen 1989:38).

However, despite this literal "domestication" of Spiritualism in Victorian
society, many of its radical elements were retained in modified form. The
democratic epistemology of Owenism remained in force, as is clear from
Wallace's statement that the "cardinal maxim of Spiritualism is, that every
one must find out the truth for himself" ([1874] 1896:230; see also Barrow
1986:146–212). Spiritualism also continued its alliance with the "Puritanism

of the body" and the medical holism that was characteristic of phrenology and mesmerism (Leahey and Leahey 1983:94), and it provided a running critique of the medical profession and its pretensions to authority. Wallace himself was a vegetarian and a leader of the protest against vaccination, and he continually deplored that the neglect of mesmerism in surgery led doctors to rely on poisonous drugs as anesthetics. Another phrenomesmerist and Spiritualist anthropologist, John William Jackson, wrote that the heterodox view of medicine was based on a "return to Nature":

> Homeopathy reduces the drug dosage to vanishing point. Hydropathy, kinesipathy and mesmerism wholly ignore it. While all combine to reject the murderous lancet and the cruel blister [*sic*]. This is only saying, in other words, that the orthodox or established system is eminently analytical and disintegrative. . . . It attacks the disease through the patient, generally wounding the latter in the process of destroying the former (quoted in Barrow 1986:163–64).

Jackson was one of the foremost propounders of the relevance of phrenology for ethnology, arguing that the identification of different racial forms of the skull, and thereby of the different psychic "faculties" of races, could form the basis of ethnological classification (Jackson 1863). Like Wallace, he wrote about the way in which mesmerism could explain many of the realities behind so-called primitive superstitions (Jackson 1858; Wallace 1872a; 1896:216). Both criticized the as yet only briefly established medical profession for undue assumptions of authority, and both, therefore, found themselves in opposition to an anthropology that was dominated by this medical establishment.[10] Jackson, however, was always a marginal figure, and he devised an almost cabalistic polygenism, in which the future would turn the "castes" of present-day humanity into a hierarchy of mutually supporting but distinct races, a vision appealing to many leading members of the Anthropological Society of London (Pels 2000). In contrast, Wallace's 1864 paper, although presented at the Anthropological Society, wasn't much liked by its members (Kottler 1974:149), probably because its monogenism was much closer to the ideas of the scientific elite of the Ethnological Society of London. Whereas Jackson's phrenomesmerism and Spiritualism tended toward reactionary racism, Wallace's was progressive and egalitarian, and as much directed at social reform as the majority of Victorian scientists had been.

The Spirit Hypothesis and the Morality of Victorian Science

To some extent, anthropology and Spiritualism shared a similar intellectual background. Phrenology, in particular, had been crucial for the development of the ideas of Auguste Comte and Herbert Spencer. Spiritualism's direct ancestor, phrenomesmerism, became suspect for established science shortly after its emergence in the 1830s,[11] but the phrenological idea that mental faculties could be *located on* the skull was not pushed into the sphere of the occult until the late 1860s, and occasionally resurfaced to inform developments in physiological theory (Cooter 1984:21). To Comte and Spencer, the biological determinism suggested by phrenology—that an individual's capacities were situated in the head and largely immutable—was a materialist warning against the optimism of social reform. But among working-class theorists such as Robert Owen, or middle-class climbers such as George Combe, phrenology often developed into a kind of biological *pragmatism*, building on the thesis that once the natural givens of individuals, for which they could not be held responsible, were known, a judicious remaking of their nurture was possible—and this made phrenologists into some of the most forceful advocates of education (Cooter 1984:135ff.). Whereas for some, therefore, phrenology was an argument for the immutability of organisms and species, for others—Wallace foremost—it directed attention to the *relationship between* organism and environment, a relationship that could be captured in the concepts of survival of the fittest, natural selection, and the mutation of species.

This distinction between determinism and pragmatism also had a methodical side: for Edward Tylor, the determinist pupil of Comte and Spencer, the emphasis of method lay with a totalizing *classification* of species, objects, customs, and stages of evolution. During his self-education, Wallace had also become convinced of the value of classification, but "not as a metaphysically complete system, but as an aid to the comprehension of a subject" (Wallace 1908:109). Thus, for Wallace, classification was not a totalizing metaphysics but a pragmatic feature of research, and the classification of mental faculties by phrenology gave him an invitation to experiment with mental faculties before accepting them as given. In this sense, "experiment" was another aspect of Wallace's democratic epistemology: rather than determining the status of objects from a specific, classifying subject position, he *engaged with* them in order to find out about this status. This is part of the morality of empiricism, of the reformist implications of being "beaten by the facts": like many early-nineteenth-century British reformers, Wallace insisted that correct "information" and "facts" were themselves powers in the world, capable of convincing one of the necessity of improvement (cf. Pels 1999c:104–6).

The goal of reform was clearly formulated in Wallace's famous 1864 article, which argued that natural selection was not sufficient to explain human evolution. Prophesying the development of humans toward a "single homogeneous race" of equals, the original article ended with the liberal fantasy quoted above. His mediumistic researches suggested to Wallace that such a future could not be attained without spiritual intervention. Some years later he hypothesized that the consciousness, the large brain, the hand, the external form, and the organs of speech of human beings could not be explained by natural selection's principle of present utility and relative perfection. The mere observation of artificially selected wheat, milk cows, or seedless bananas would fail to show that these species had been produced by human intervention. Therefore, the hypothesis of an even higher intelligence—a spirit—guiding the laws of human organic development was not contradictory to science (Wallace 1869:204–5).

When he published these views in more detail in the following year (Wallace 1870), Darwin lamented Wallace's "retrograde metamorphosis." To the *Saturday Review*, the introduction of "some occult or spiritual agency or force in nature and man" meant "parting company with science." Many reviewers tried to seriously refute Wallace's arguments, while others displayed insecurity about their own position by resorting to ridicule and reductio ad absurdum. Some, like Lyell, Charles Kingsley, the *Edinburgh Review*, and much of the popular Christian press, approved of Wallace's reasoning. E. Claparède's quip that for Wallace, "man was God's domestic animal" stuck despite the fact that Wallace tried to argue that intelligences other than God—other spirits—could have been active in human development (all quoted in Kottler 1974:156–59).

Wallace's invitations to his scientist friends to investigate Spiritualist phenomena met with a less ambiguous refusal. His neighbor, medical doctor and pioneer psychologist William Carpenter, showed up once at a fairly inconclusive and unspectacular séance. When Carpenter later ridiculed Spiritualism by attributing it to "unconscious cerebration" (indicating a rather unhealthy state of mind), Wallace retorted by pointing out that Carpenter should not argue against the "refusal" of Spiritualists to have their practices tested when he himself refused to thoroughly investigate them (Wallace [1874] 1896:279–80). Wallace also invited John Tyndall, with a similar result (Kottler 1974:172; Wallace [1874] 1896:279). Thomas Huxley, who had investigated the American medium Mrs. Hayden in 1863, refused Wallace's invitation by saying that he had no time for such an inquiry and took no interest in the subject "if the folk in the spiritual world do not talk more wisely and sensibly than their friends report them to do" (Huxley 1900:420). Most of Wallace's colleagues echoed Darwin's reaction to a report by Huxley about a seemingly fraudulent séance that "the same sort of things are done at all the séances" (quoted in Huxley 1900:421). Only Edward Tylor seems to have been sufficiently disconcerted to go out and investigate at some length—and he had pressing reasons to do so.[12]

George Stocking has provided us with the story: Tylor had been toying with the concepts of fetishism, animism, and spiritualism in the years before publishing *Primitive Culture* (1871), not knowing exactly which one to apply to his "rudimentary definition of religion" (Stocking 1971a:89–91; Tylor 1873:1:424). He seems to have had previous experience with Spiritualism, having attended a séance in 1867, but he held to the opinion that "even supposing the alleged spiritualistic facts to be all true, and the spiritualistic interpretation of them sound," it would still be true that "modern spiritualism is a survival and a revival of savage thought, which the general tendency of civilization and science has been to discard" (quoted in Stocking 1971a:90). Wallace was much incensed by this, to him both callous and contradictory, statement of theoretical superiority and wrote a very critical review of the first edition of *Primitive Culture*, arguing against Tylor's way of classifying phenomena, "well-established cases of abnormal mental phenomena" in particular:

> [These phenomena] can thus be grouped into classes, and this fact, of each one forming an item in a group of analogous cases, is supposed to preclude the necessity of any attempt at a rational explanation of them. This is the method very largely adopted by Mr. Tylor, who in treating of the beliefs,

customs, or superstitions of mankind, seems often to be quite satisfied that he has done all that is required when he has shown that a similar or identical belief or custom exists elsewhere (Wallace 1872a:69).

Wallace mentioned, as an example of the advantage of such "rational explanation" over Tylor's arbitrary classifications, the explanation that mesmerism can give of the way in which powerful mesmerists can make "sensitive individuals" believe they are were-wolves and use their influence "for bad purposes" (1872a:70). Predictably, Tylor pounced on this rather weak argument by saying that Wallace did not provide any critique of his "suggestions": "[Mr. Wallace] offers nothing like a reason why knavish sorcerers in districts of Europe, Asia, Africa and America should have all hit upon the device of imposing the same peculiar delusion upon their dupes; nor does he account for the fact . . . that in certain cases the supposed were-wolf is himself utterly persuaded of the reality of his own transformation, and goes to execution believing his offence." Tylor ignored, however, Wallace's argument against the arbitrariness of his classifications by misrepresenting Wallace's critique as an argument against the presentation of "copious and widely distributed evidence" (Tylor 1872a:343).

Wallace replied to this by outlining why the mesmeric influence on "sensitive," and thus deluded, individuals could not be compared to the objective observation of phenomena produced by mediums (Wallace 1872b). Whether this reply was a direct cause of Tylor's further investigations into Spiritualism or not, some months after his exchange with Wallace, he went to London to investigate the phenomena himself. Stocking shows how Tylor, after attending a number of séances, grudgingly admitted a "a prima facie case on evidence" for a psychic force that causes "raps, movements, levitations, etc." (Stocking 1971a:100). His ambivalence about Spiritualistic phenomena, however, seemed to have resulted not so much from having witnessed remarkable phenomena as from having heard "respectable"—upper-middle-class—people express the conviction that they had happened. According to Tylor's theory of mental evolution, Spiritualism was a "survival" that should not find believers among the middle and upper classes, only among the lower. For Tylor's "reformer's science," this psychic force was both theoretically and politically anomalous.

In the second edition of *Primitive Culture*, Tylor's doubts about psychic phenomena were suppressed and Spiritualism roundly denounced as a survival of animistic beliefs (Tylor 1873:1:141–56). Yet, even the formulations used in *Primitive Culture* betray an ambivalence within its scheme of mental evolution that seems fundamental to contemporary scientific politics. Tylor felt forced to class modern Spiritualism with "primitive" animism—the kind of arbitrary classification that Wallace was up against in his critique of *Primitive Culture* and in his earliest writings on botany. But Tylor also had to acknowledge that Spiritualism was not just a survival but an extraordinary revival of animism (1873:1:142). He even went as far as to recognize the anomalous status of Spiritualism within his progressionist scheme, because the former "is a truly remarkable case of *degeneration*" (1873:1:156; my emphasis), the possibility of which *Primitive Culture* was originally intended to argue out of existence (1873:1:chapter 2).

This ambivalence was part of the, far wider, ambiguity of the concept of mind (or spirit) in its relation to the material facts of empirical studies and in its consequences for Victorian morality. Wallace's 1864 paper was a (at present still insufficiently recognized) landmark in the history of anthropology because it argued that natural selection, from a certain point in the evolution of humanity onward, no longer applied to the human body but instead worked on the mind. This opening up of a space for strictly *mental* evolution subverted a number of more materialist approaches to studying human improvement, approaches that supposed it could be read directly from physiognomy (as in phrenology), or from comparative anatomy's measures of brain size, or that defined mental operations as the result of molecular change in protoplasm. Such scientific materialism had, in the first half of the nineteenth century, been closely allied to the cause of radical reform, but by 1870 the democratic ideology of the "Republic of Science" and the "humble and self-taught" scientist, whose heroes were John Herschel, Joseph Priestley, and Michael Faraday, was retreating in the face of a process of scientific professionalization (Shapin and Thackray 1974:6, 11). As the materialists' critique of Wallace's "occult" or spiritualist explanations showed, an explanation from material facts was still desired by the scientific elite to maintain the momentum of their critique of the theological and aristocratic establishments.

One solution, promoted by Lubbock and taken up by Tylor, was to take *material* culture as the major indicator of mental and moral evolution. But the equation of material culture, mind, and morality that provided both Lubbock and Tylor with the classifications that "marked out" survivals for "destruction" (Tylor 1873:2:453) was essentially *negative*, based on a "survival of the *un*fit," rather than on Wallace's and Darwin's positive idea of the survival of the fittest (Stocking [1968] 1982:97). Tylor's reaction to modern Spiritualism showed that this approach could not determine what exactly was a survival, and what a revival, without resorting to classificatory decree. Wallace recognized the arbitrariness of reasoning from technological evolution to the existence of spiritual survivals, and he was not the only one to doubt whether material and moral progress went together. In a way similar to Wallace, the Duke of Argyll had already criticized John Lubbock's defense of "progressionism" by the comparative method: the demonstration of a "crude level" of technological knowledge in primeval times was no ground for inferring a comparably low degree of moral and intellectual life among "savages," nor did it warrant the assumption that the more coarse and vicious a custom, the older it was (Gillespie 1977:44). Similarly, Wallace argued in *The Malay Archipelago* that Britain was in a state of "social barbarism" in total contradiction to the material progress it had made. Granted such an argument, it remained possible that modern times were actually morally degenerated.[13]

Argyll, an important member of the establishment that both Tylor and Wallace felt they were up against, did not draw the conclusion that British society was barbaric. Unlike Wallace and Tylor, he was not interested in letting scientific facts "prove" the necessity for reform. Predictably, Lubbock never engaged directly with Argyll's critique of the arbitrariness of his progressionist classifications and instead accused him of theological prejudice (Gillespie 1977:49). The imputation of religious prejudice was also a political move meant to counter the unsettling possibility that mind could not be reduced to matter: if "savages" had as high a morality as the "civilized," and if man's "noblest" inventions were his first (as both Wallace and Argyll claimed), the materialists were faced with the possibility that "mind" had suddenly appeared, full blown and in possession of all its faculties, when humanity first embarked on its evolutionary process. This was a critique that the new scientific elite, only barely established and still fighting against the theological establishment's hold of the major educational institutions, could not openly face.[14]

However, we should also note the difference between Wallace's adoption of "degenerationism" and that of Argyll and other scholars allied to the religious and aristocratic establishment. Lubbock's imputation of religious prejudice to Argyll, though unjustified as far as his arguments went, may have been correct: Argyll's attempt to defend degenerationism was, of course, in line with the desire to retain a space for Divine intervention in human progress, a desire he shared with comparative philologists such as Max Müller. With the latter (and a host of colonial administrators in India that Argyll ruled when he was secretary of state for the colonies) he shared, for instance, a view of Hinduism as a degenerated or stagnated version of the lofty ideals of Vedic religion, which were thought to be similar to original revelation (understood in Christian terms). The difference with Wallace's way of thinking about mind and spirit comes out when we compare Argyll's view of "degenerated" India with the appearance and impact of an East Indian spirit in a séance attended by Wallace: this spirit, given his knowledge of a higher level of existence, commanded respect instead of denigration, and contributed to the moral lessons that the spirits were able to communicate to the living (Wallace 1908:340–41, 345; see also Wallace [1874] 1896:226). Thus, Wallace's again turns out to be the more democratic morality, in which, regardless of birth or Bible, even Indian spirits could contribute to human progress and criticize modernity's barbarism.

In contrast with both Christian and occult "spiritualists," "materialists" stressed a different morality, one more directly allied to the politics of "Science." The argument that mental evolution could be read from technological progress was an indirect legitimation of the scientific establishment that pretended to produce that technology. More important, it was made in a context that transformed a formerly radical and more or less democratic set of scientific conventions into the claim to authority of a professional elite, an "intellectual aristocracy" (Annan 1955). The former opposition between "honesty" and (mostly theological) "prejudice" underpinning the critique of the ossified Oxbridge establishment by many bourgeois scientists in the first half of the century—it is echoed in Lubbock's exchange with Argyll—was now transformed into a more hierarchical conception of intellectual progress and expertise.[15] "Culture," that "complex whole" (Tylor 1873:1:1), was presented as an effect of these expert operations modeled on "the statistician's returns":

The fact is that a stone arrow-head, a carved club, an idol, a grave-mound where slaves and property have been buried for the use of the dead, an account of a sorcerer's rites in making rain, a table of numerals, the conjugation of a verb, are things which each express the state of a people as to one particular point of culture, as truly as the tabulated numbers of deaths by poison, and of chests of tea imported, express in a different way other partial results of the general life of a whole community. (Tylor 1873:1:12)

The Tylorean perspective has not for nothing been described as intellectualist: by incarcerating the plethora of material facts as "data" in the slots of a classificatory scheme, it turned this scheme of intellectual progress from an effect of an expert technology of classification into the cause of the data itself. Tylor's "reformer's science" (Tylor 1873:2:453) presumed a spirit of modernity—a rational, psychic unity of humankind—in order to purify it of unwanted survivals. As we have seen, this could function to keep out hypotheses and theories from quarters—"amateurs," workers, women—that were critical of elite morality and (especially medical) science. But the shift from an early Victorian morality of scientific honesty to a more exclusive professional expertise was not a direct expression of class or gender struggle, for this expertise was crucially inflected by techniques of the revelation of public truths that betray a specific politics of perception (see Van Dijk and Pels 1996).

A Victorian Politics of Perception: Spiritualism and Visualism

In the past three centuries, Europe's encounter with magic has nearly always resulted in a rethinking of its perceptual repertoire. The eighteenth-century reception of shamanism led Herder and Goethe, among others, to speculate upon the way in which hypersensitive people, artists, and other geniuses were able to perceive in ways not represented, or representable, in hegemonic scientific discourse (see Flaherty 1992). Today, again, encounters with South American shamans and African sorcerers have led scholars to upset received ideas about perception and representation (Taussig 1993b; Stoller 1989). And Alfred Wallace, too, felt he had to introduce his first, 1866, defense of Spiritualism by an argument about a "higher sense than vision" unknown to most of us mortals. This typifies the late-Victorian "frenzy of the visible" (Jean-Louis Comolli, quoted in Jay 1993:147). Wallace underscored the Victorian hierarchy of perceptive faculties by restricting discussion to this unknown higher sense than vision and ignoring the role of the "lower" senses and of visceral perception in spirit possession in general and the Spiritualist séance in particular. As we shall see, Tylor did the same.

In *Miracles and Modern Spiritualism*, the argument about perception was developed after Wallace denounced the theoretical fallacy of assuming that because Spiritualist phenomena run counter to our knowledge of the laws of nature, they cannot exist. He argued that the physical phenomena that occur during a séance can only be explained by presuming invisible intelligences, which was only "another and more striking illustration than any we have yet received of how small a portion of the great cosmos our senses give us cognisance" ([1874] 1896:43). He compared the force exerted by these intelligences with light, heat, electricity, and magnetism (all "modes of motion" of a space-filling "ether") to show how these "diffuse and subtle" forms of matter can act upon "ponderable bodies" and become known to us only by their effects.[16] The fact that we do not know this higher sense is no argument, Wallace wrote, because likewise the "faculty of vision" would be "inconceivable" to a race of blind men. "It is possible and even probable that there may be modes of sensation as superior to all ours as is sight to that of touch and hearing" ([1874] 1896:44–45). The subject of divination, in particular, allowed Wallace to elaborate on this. The clairvoyance that is at the basis of divination led him to suppose a "new sense" that amounts to "a kind of rudimentary perception, which can only get at the truth by degrees." Again, he states, "If ordinary vision were as rare as clairvoyance, it would be just as difficult to prove its reality as it is now to establish the reality of this wonderful power" ([1874] 1896:68–69).

The supremacy of vision is best represented by Wallace's conviction that "spirit-photographs" were "the most unassailable demonstration . . . of the objective reality of spiritual forms" ([1874] 1896:188). These photographs first appeared on the Spiritualist scene in the early 1870s and were supposed to demonstrate that the rarefied perception of invisible spirits by mediums was real because a photographic plate could capture these forms. Wallace could not believe that these photographs had been tampered with; such a "wicked imposture" was beyond the respectable mediums that produced them

([1874] 1896:195). Photography, indeed, was "a witness which cannot be deceived, which has no preconceived opinions, which cannot register 'subjective' impressions; a thoroughly scientific witness," and on the basis of the evidence it provided, Wallace declared that, to him, the phenomena of Spiritualism did not require further confirmation ([1874] 1896:211).

Visualism—"second sight," clairvoyance—is still an important element of present-day occultism, but recent investigators such as Paul Stoller (1989) and Michael Taussig (1993b) tend to look for a comprehension of occult phenomena in what Wallace called the "lower" senses: smell, taste, hearing, touch, or a kind of "inner," visceral perception. Before Victoria, Herder found the *Ur*-sensitivity of shamans and artists in "language, tone, movement, portrayal, proportion, dance: and that alone which tied everything together—song," in short, in aural/oral sense-perception (quoted in Flaherty 1992:138). But in the Victorian period, the eighteenth-century definition of a positivistic sense of vision was glorified in authoritative practices such as panoptic statistics, comparative anatomy, and photography. Wallace's emphasis on vision as the royal road to fact was therefore in itself fairly orthodox. However, it is important to realize that the Victorian "frenzy of the visible" encompasses multiple modes of vision, and, even more, that Wallace's specific version was one that anticipated the experiential mode of sight sought out by protomodernists such as Claude Monet and Odilon Redon (Jay 1993:154–57). This becomes particularly clear when contrasted with Edward Tylor's own sense of "super-vision," which, like Wallace's clairvoyance, was a faculty ranking higher than ordinary sight.

Wallace's rejoinder to Tylor was printed in the same issue of *Nature* in which Tylor eulogized Adolphe Quetelet, the Belgian father of statistics and a major contributor to its growth in Britain (Tylor 1872b). Although Tylor was to suggest the use of quantitative statistics himself only at a much later stage (Tylor 1888), the early 1870s were the heyday of statistics in British society, when William Hunter was commissioned to do the first all-India statistical survey (Hunter 1885:1:viii), and Florence Nightingale had provoked sufficient interest in the subject to have British statesmen apply it in practice (Woodham-Smith 1955:passim). Epistemologically speaking, statistics had its roots in the visualist "diagrammatic reduction of thought" of Ramist philosophy (Fabian 1983:116; Stagl 1990, 1995). By the 1870s, statistics had moved away from its original, more qualitative conception—one that was close to the ethnography-by-questionnaires of German scientific expeditions to east Asia, and that was adopted by James Cowles Prichard, Tylor, and other anthropologists in the (predecessors to the manual) *Notes and Queries in Anthropology* (Hodgkin and Cull 1854; Slezkine 1994; Vermeulen 1995). As we have seen, there was a close correspondence between the argument of Tylor's *Primitive Culture* and the gathering of intelligence through statistics: both relied on a form of classification of items in order to bring them under the sway of a "complex whole" of measurement.

Although Tylor's classifications in *Primitive Culture* were primarily qualitative, and he would not start counting customs until his 1888 paper, his show of respect for Quetelet in 1872 demonstrates his sensitivity to the magic of enumeration and explains his invocation of the "statistician's returns" in the second edition of *Primitive Culture*. He also invoked its mercantile roots: "It might, perhaps, seem practicable to compare the whole average of the civilization of two peoples, or of the same people in different ages, by reckoning each, *item by item*, to a sort of sum-total, and striking a balance between them, much as an appraiser compares the value of two stocks of merchandise, differ as they may both in quantity and quality" (Tylor 1873:1:31; emphasis mine). Statistical reasoning was, indeed, pioneered by European merchants trying to control their overseas trade, by itemizing the objects they exchanged, the manpower they needed, and the exchange value of both (see Pels 1997:174). "Item by item," statistics and ethnography allowed the classifier to visually reduce material facts to the slots of a tabular space (cf. Fabian 1983), an account book epistemology that allows one to *see*, at one glance, the extent of their serial equivalence. Wallace's critique of Tylor's classifications was directed at this world of statistical equivalences, a world of homogeneous time-space where Spiritualism lost all the potential for experimental rupture that it possessed for Wallace. The visualism—more precisely, the "panopticism," or super-vision—of statistical accounting was crucial to the epistemological move that Wallace disputed.

Empiricist vision recurs in the last sentence of Tylor's unpublished "Notes on Spiritualism": "Seeing has not (to me) been believing, & I propose a new text to define faith: 'Blessed are they that have seen, and *yet* have believed'" (Stocking 1971a:100; emphasis in original). As George Stocking brings out, the sentence covers up a paradox in Tylor's dealings with Spiritualist phenomena, for although it asserts an empiricism of direct observation with which Tylor was wont to associate himself, the rest of his notes on Spiritualism clearly show that he tended to give far more weight to hearsay coming from "respectable" witnesses—which confirms that his classifications were, indeed, derived from a similarly hegemonic class ideology. In fact, during Spiritualist séances, there was very little to *see*, because the spirits mostly communicated through trance, raps, talk, touch, and an occasional shoving of tables in the dark. What doubts Tylor had about a "genuine residue" in Spiritualist phenomena that could not be explained away as either hysteria or fraud was based on hearsay or on perceptions through touch or sound rather than vision. Indeed, there is one remarkable passage in Tylor's notes that compresses a number of the processes discussed above and shows the use of discussing the "politics of perception" of these debates. It indicates the importance of mainstream medical opinion—the misogyny of "hysteria"— in Tylor's interpretation of Spiritualism; it shows his reliance on middle-class respectability; but it also shows a form of perception that was almost completely suppressed by the hegemonic hierarchy of the senses but that nevertheless nearly abolished the positivist distance that Tylor wanted to keep from his object of study (by, among other things, privileging vision or supervision). During a session with William Staunton Moses, an unpaid medium, and a gentleman on top of that, Tylor notes: "I think [Moses' trance] was genuine, & afterwards, I myself became drowsy & seemed to the others about to go off likewise. To myself, I seemed partly under a drowsy influence, and part consciously shamming, a curious state of mind which I have felt before & which is very likely the incipient stage of hysterical simulation" (Stocking 1971a:100).

Was this "hysteria" or a form of perception that did not meet the criteria of admissible evidence of male middle-class society? Tylor indicated that this was not his first time to experience such a state of drowsy shamming, or (partly) involuntary fraud. What one person would interpret as the incipient stage of hysterical simulation, another could perhaps perceive as a sign of the potential for skilled revelation and concealment that a trickster or shaman draws upon (see Michael Taussig, in this volume). Whatever the case may be, there is a remarkable correspondence between Tylor's experience and the way in which a number of anthropologists in Africa represented an experience different from their "scientific" expectations of reality. Be it an oncoming trance leaving an awareness of an invisible presence (Gibbal [1988] 1994:81), a mysterious paralysis removed by reciting a charm (Stoller 1989:46), or a mysterious illness successfully cured by African healing (Van Binsbergen 1991), all these experiences depend on an "inner," visceral perception, a way of being moved or touched on the inside by an unknown or at least invisible influence.

Such inner tactility or visceral perception is an important part of medical practice.[17] Many cures need to be initiated by inferring a disease from (talk of) tactile and visceral effects (e.g., "Does this hurt?"). Similarly, the Spiritualist séance largely employed communication through trance, the senses of touch, and the aural/oral senses. This points out an important dimension of the contemporary understanding of the occult. Although the process of marginalizing the notion of knowledge of the occult was already well under way (helped, of course, by the emphasis on the visibility of reliable knowledge), it was not until *after* Wallace's discussion with Tylor that "occultist" movements such as Theosophy defined themselves exclusively in terms of an esoteric or *secret* knowledge (Blavatsky 1888; Braude 1989:178; Waite 1891).[18] The use of *occult* by the *Saturday Review* in its critique of Wallace's spiritual speculations, therefore, does not refer to an established category of esoteric knowledge that twentieth-century scholars tend to classify, after the fact, as "marginal" or "deviant" (Tiryakian 1974). As the debates outlined above have shown, Spiritualism did not claim secret knowledge, and it merited public engagement and criticism by scientists, even if the outcome of this engagement was to push its findings into a private, domestic, and subjective sphere that made them marginal to authoritative knowledge production in Victorian society. At the time, *occult* could still mean "hidden from sight" and this reference to the invisible had, around 1870, a far more ambiguous relation to established knowledge than had the marginalized secrecy of twentieth-century occultism.[19]

Wallace's comparison of the spirits' higher intelligence to the forces of light, heat, electricity, and magnetism shows that he tried to situate his reasoning within the common scientific practice of conjecturing invisible causes or forces from the perception of visible, minute effects (compare this to Carlo Ginzburg's view [1983b] on medical semiotics, historiography, and divination). Calling this practice "Zadig's Method" of "retrospective prophecy," Thomas Huxley accorded conjecture a legitimate place in the scientific pantheon (T.H. Huxley 1881). It becomes immediately obvious that Tylor's classifications, too, were ways to reason from perceived effects toward invisible causes of human progress. Ignoring, for the moment, their vast differences, one might complement Wallace's sequence of invisible forces—light or heat waves, electricity, magnetism and "spirits"—with Tylor's conceptions of the progress toward a rational psychic unity of mankind and the mental diseases that stood in its way (be it "hysteria," individual and feminine, or "fraud," collective and lower class). In a sense, Tylor's notion of progress was undergirded by causes of human development that were equally "occult"—although his careful avoidance of spiritual terms indicated that for him, the spiritual and the occult were threats to the desired hegemony of materialist naturalism. Yet, even Tylor's notion of culture can be regarded as taking part in the late-nineteenth-century reaction to naturalism and its attempts to develop a non-Christian, modern sense of spirituality (F. Turner 1974:3).

In other words, what remained occult in Tylor's scheme of explanation was the rational spirit of modernity and the reasons for its absence—the reasons why something could be classified as a survival. This shows that the politics of perception in the Wallace-Tylor debate largely concerned the legitimacy of conjecture. Conjecture was an embarrassing aspect of medical science, especially where the visual rigor of comparative anatomy's lancet had to give way to the tactile, intersubjective, and visceral perceptions that were needed to start healing a living person. To the heterodox, the lancet was murderous because they distrusted the conjectures of the powers that wielded it. Wallace's admiration for the camera—an eye without inference—also shows distrust of conjecture and a desire for a more immediate super-vision than human perception can provide. Medical science authorized Victorian anthropology and psychology—in fact, the three sciences were not even institutionalized as separate professions at the time, and this indicates why it was such an important arena for the struggle over the proper production of scientific knowledge.[20]

But Wallace and Tylor were not trying to heal living bodies or uncover the structure of dead ones. Their object was more profound, for their different forms of super-vision were trying to undo the barrier that separates human beings from a direct knowledge of past or future. By clairvoyance or panoptic classification—by consulting the spirits of the deceased, or the spirit of reason, about the future—both Wallace and Tylor tried to abolish the invisibility of time. Their sensory politics supported two different forms of distinctly modern divination (cf. Ginzburg 1983b). Their technologies of experiment and classification also revealed two distinct modern temporalities: the hegemonic "homogeneous, empty time" of technological progress, as opposed to the time "(ful)filled from the present" that "flashes up" in a moment of danger: a messianic, experimental, and miraculous rupture of the flow of everyday life (see Benjamin 1977:253, 258).

Conclusion

I have refrained from judgments about the truth of Wallace's Spiritualist experiments in order to bring out the sociohistorical contests that are needed to understand his and his opponents' most simple observations. Although Wallace was naive, an honest foil to fraud, I hope to have shown that the classification of his Spiritualism as the mental aberration of an otherwise brilliant scientist—the common reaction beginning with Darwin and continuing to the present day, and one that relegated this brilliant mind to scientific obscurity in its later years—was somewhat arbitrary, at least when compared to Tylor's thick-headed empiricism and classificatory urges (later demolished by Emile Durkheim ([1912] 1915:64ff.]). The emergence of personal, small-scale spirits in mid-nineteenth-century Britain, regardless of the kind of truth or temporal vision that such entities are used to endorse, challenges the idea—fed by Tylor's intellectualist heritage of mental progress—that they are no longer effective means of "explanation, prediction and control" in a modernizing and expanding world (Horton 1971).[21] On the contrary, Spiritualism marks the emergence of a distinctly modern spirituality that, failing to convince the public scientific establishment of its claim to attention, blossomed in the more private practices of late-nineteenth-century occultism. Organizations such as the Theosophical Society (1875) and the Order of the Golden Dawn (1888) mark the defeat of Wallace's efforts to claim a public presence for spiritual intervention, as much as they signal the start of the development of New Age thinking centered on the modern spirituality of realizing the potential of the human self (Heelas 1996).

The spiritual person who, in New Age thinking, has to liberate him- or herself from the indoctrination exerted by mainstream society through the ego (Heelas 1996:18–19) was to a considerable extent prepared by debates such as the one between Wallace and Tylor. The invisible can only be taken on trust (Shapin 1988:374), and for both our protagonists this meant that the spiritual became a test of the kind of social relationships on which they thought this trust could and should be based—the "interior" against which their visions of public acceptability could be contrasted. For Wallace, this interior consisted of the domestic sphere of experiment, where personal experience, the visibility of experimental manifestations, "honest" individual (but class-based) testimony, and suspicion of scientific fashion and orthodoxy determined what could be taken as trustworthy—as "fact"—and we have seen that Tylor, too, confessed that he was temporarily swayed by this form of authority in his private notes on Spiritualism.[22] This domestic space of experiment was a locus classicus of the public performance of seventeenth-century science, but it was displaced, in the course of the nineteenth century, by "a new privacy" of science screened off by the "visible display of the emblems of recognized expertise" (Shapin 1988:404). In the twentieth century, the personal and domestic sociality of trust claimed by Wallace would continue its career in the sphere of the occult rather than in that of established science (Bennett 1987:89; Heelas 1996:21).

In contrast, Tylor claimed trustworthiness precisely on the basis of such a scientifically "expert" interior, modeled on the specialist operations of the statistician (but before such operations became a fully quantified staple of social scientific practice). This expert interior was suspect to the likes of Wallace, who thought the public scientific realm was dangerously close to being a system that hid the private prejudices and speculations of the powerful. For Tylor, however, the knowledge produced in the domestic realm should remain private, because its trustworthiness was fatally undermined by the threat of (mostly feminine) physical or psychological disorder or (lower-class-based) social malfunction, that is, fraud. Both ways of constituting an interior of knowledge production derived from a similar cultural complex that combined, in an often uneasy tension, the technologies of the self that underlay Wallace's claims to individual freedoms with the technologies of domination allied to Tylor's reasons of statecraft (the original sense of statistics). Here we find, then, the political anatomies that produced the effects of, on the one hand, a multitude of unruly spirits (women, workers, even East Indians) and, on the other, the monolithic spirit of powerful modernity—and turned both into the causes of modern "improvement."

Yet, the preceding paragraph could easily be read in support of an understanding of temporal progress, of a teleology of modernization that makes plural spirits into the private, if rebellious, citizens of a secularized divinity of reason. Can that system of homogeneous, empty time be closed and the "whole monstrous farrago" of magic (Tylor 1873:1:133) be brought under control? Tylor himself was uncertain; he could only "hope" that if the belief in witchcraft reappeared in the civilized world, it would "appear in a milder shape than heretofore" (1873:1:141), and he shared this anxiety about the containment of magic with many of his contemporaries (Pels 1998b). Here, we might note a potential for rupture and rapture, for miracle and play, that spirit possession and cultural anthropology seem to share (cf. Kramer 1993:240ff.; see also Taussig 1993b and this volume). In Fritz Kramer's study of African art and spirit possession, he suggests that anthropological fieldwork can produce "an experience of being truly overwhelmed and moved which accords precisely with the *passiones* of the African alien spirit hosts" (1993:243) and, we might suggest, with Wallace's willingness to be "beaten" by the "facts" of Spiritualism. Indeed, one can trace the notion of fieldwork *rapport* between ethnographer and people studied—this experiential experiment—to the earlier use of the term to designate the dominance of the mental suggestion by the hypnotist or mesmerizer, extending beyond the actual session to posthypnotic suggestion (Hansen 1989:151; *Oxford English Dictionary*, vol. 13, 191 [1989]).

Leaving aside who exactly mesmerizes whom, Kramer's remarks put an aspect of Spiritualism that was largely ignored by its historiographers into striking relief. In the late 1830s, the first phrenomesmerist mediums often embodied a "negro" spirit (Kaplan 1975:41), at the time that T.F. Buxton's Niger Expedition had led to the formation of the Aborigines Protection Society (the parent of the Ethnological Society of London) as a way to sustain the Whig and Radical momentum of the campaign for the abolition of the slave trade (Rainger 1980; Stocking 1971b). It is also striking how often North American mediums produced the spirit of a native American "Indian" girl, encountered by both Tylor (Stocking 1971a:passim) and Wallace (during the latter's séances with William James in the United States). It seems, therefore, no coincidence that—shortly after the Great Mutiny had revolutionized British visions of India—a British (male) medium visited by Wallace materialized East Indian, "Mahomedan and Hindoo" spirits (Wallace [1874] 1896:226, 1908:340–41). This spiritual alliance between subordinate groups in British society—plebeian intellectuals, workers, women—and the spirits of the colonized became a practical reality when the Theosophical Society moved to India to search out its mysterious Indian "Masters" and become an important contributor to Indian nationalism (Van der Veer 2001:55ff.; Washington 1993). A posthypnotic suggestion, perhaps, flashing up in moments of danger? Whatever the case may be, given the overwhelming power and violence of modern technologies of domination and their singular spirit of reason, we can regard such interventions of "other" spirits in modernity as being little short of miraculous.

ELEVEN

Viscerality, Faith, and Skepticism

Another Theory of Magic

MICHAEL TAUSSIG

Underlying all our mystic states *are* corporeal techniques, biological methods of entering into communication with God.

—MARCEL MAUSS, "Les techniques du corps," 1960

The sorcerer generally learns his time-honored profession in good faith, and retains his belief in it more or less from first to last; at once dupe and cheat, he combines the energy of a believer with the cunning of a hypocrite.

—EDWARD BURNETT TYLOR, *Primitive Culture*, 1871

My aim in this chapter is as follows: to tackle the vexatious problem of faith as in religious and magical faith by means of (1) highlighting the fact that faith seems to often coexist with skepticism, that (2) such faith may even require skepticism, that (3) there is a deep-seated public secret as to the existence of a trick that allows this (perhaps necessary) coexistence to function, that (4) this usually involves some physical substance or object that exists in relation to the insides of the human body, and that thus, finally, we may conclude (5) there is a relation between faith and skepticism, no less than between faith and viscerality, that has escaped notice in some classic illustrations of magical healing made famous, indeed iconic, by an earlier anthropology, in that the success of such ritual lies not in concealing but in revealing trickery and that this is the peculiar mix of craft and *mysterium tremendum* that lies at the basis of magical efficacy, theories such as that of Claude Lévi-Strauss's referring such efficacy to purported structuring, of Edward Evan Evans-Pritchard's use of E.B. Tylor's idea about some combination of statistical reasoning involving the category versus the particular, or theories of symbolic and metaphoric potency, notwithstanding (Evans-Pritchard 1937; Lévi-Strauss 1967). The real skill of the practitioner lies not in skilled concealment but in the skilled revelation of skilled concealment. Magic is efficacious not despite the trick but on account of its exposure. The mystery is heightened, not dissipated, by unmasking and in various ways, direct and oblique, ritual serves as a stage for so many unmaskings. Hence power flows not from masking but from unmasking, which masks more than masking. Max Horkheimer and Theodor Adorno no less than Friedrich Nietzsche were correct in discerning magic in Enlightenment, and this is reinforced when we consider the texts on shamanism and magical healing by Claude Lévi-Strauss and Evans-Pritchard as themselves shot through and empowered by the magic they ostensibly transcend (Horkheimer and Adorno 1969). Let me now flesh this out, beginning with what for me stands as the ur-scene of conjuring and viscerality on the part of the sorcerer.

Uttermost Parts and Humbuggery

"Frequently the chief object of a raiding party, in the perpetual clan warfare of the Ona," writes Lucas Bridges on the basis of many decades of intimacy with these legendary people at the turn of the century in Tierra del Fuego, "was to kill the medicine man of an opposing group" (Bridges [1949] 1988:264).[1] Raiding was a constant preoccupation, as therefore, was sorcery, so we can conclude that magic and sorcery were of considerable importance in this "uttermost part of the earth," as Bridges entitled his extraordinary memoir.[2] Indeed, he felt he had to decline the invitation of his Ona friends to become a medicine man, or *joon*, saying "No! I would not become a *joon*, to be blamed, maybe, for a fatal heart attack a hundred miles away" (Bridges [1949] 1988:264).

Yet it was curious how the fear of magic coexisted with humbuggery. The first of Ona superstitions, according to Bridges, was "Fear of magic and of the power of magicians, even on the part of those who, professing that art, must have known that they themselves were humbugs. They had great fear of the power of others" (Bridges [1949] 1988:406).

"Some of these humbugs were excellent actors," notes Bridges, and it will be useful to follow him in his description of what he calls "acting" and observe the focus, if not obsession, with the "object," an object withdrawn from the interstices of the living, human, body.

> Standing or kneeling beside the patient, gazing intently at the spot where the pain was situated, the doctor would allow a look of horror to come over his face. Evidently he could see something invisible to the rest of us. . . . With his hands he would try to gather the malign presence into one part of the patient's body—generally the chest—where he would then apply his mouth and suck violently. Sometimes this struggle went on for an hour, to be repeated later. At other times the *joon* would draw away from his patient with the pretense of holding something in his mouth with his hands. Then always facing away from the encampment, he would take his hands from his mouth gripping them tightly together, and, with a guttural shout difficult to describe and impossible to spell, fling this invisible object to the ground and stamp fiercely upon it. Occasionally a little mud, some flint or even a tiny, very young mouse might be produced as the cause of the patient's indisposition. (Bridges [1949] 1988:262)[3]

Reading the state of the soul from the bodily exterior, reading insides from outsides in relation to the human body and especially the face, has a long history in Western and Middle Eastern traditions of physiognomy.[4] But here at the Uttermost Part some things are different; the practitioner seems not to read external signs so much as look through them into the body, and he uses objects, inert and alive, as proof of such discernment and the therapy entailed.

As an aside be it noted that a salient feature of physiognomy are the eyes, and those of the medicine man, perforce an expert in physiognomy, are no exception. Take those of the great medicine man Houshken. He was over six feet tall and his eyes were exceedingly dark, almost blue-black. "I had never seen eyes of such color," muses Bridges, and he wondered whether Houshken was nearsighted. Far from it. For not only was the man a mighty hunter, but it was said that he could even look through mountains.

These are the sort of eyes that can look through the human body, as was brought out when Bridges allowed another famous medicine man, Tininisk (who twenty years later became one of Father Martin Gusinde's most important informants), to begin inducting him into the ways of the medicine man. Half-reclining naked on guanaco skins by the fire sheltered by a windbreak, Bridges's chest was gone over by the medicine man's hands and mouth as intently, said Bridges, as any doctor with a stethoscope, "moving in the prescribed manner from place to place, pausing to listen here and there." Then come those eyes again, those eyes that can see through mountains, the mountain of the body. "He also gazed intently at my body, as though he saw through it like an X-ray manipulator" (Bridges [1949] 1988:263).

But it's not only the eyes that allow this. For might there not be a certain potential, at least, for transparency of the body, for a certain instability of flesh involved in bodily flowing and becoming animal?

The medicine man and his helper stripped naked. The medicine man's wife, one of the rare women healers, took off her outer garment, and the three of them huddled and produced something Bridges thought was of the lightest gray down, shaped like a puppy and about four inches long with prick ears. It had the semblance of life, perhaps due to the handlers' breathing and the trembling of their hands. There was a peculiar scent as the "puppy" was placed by the three pairs of hands to his chest, where, without any sudden movement, it disappeared. Three times this was repeated, and then after a solemn pause Tininisk asked whether Bridges felt anything moving in his heart or if he could see something strange in his mind, like in a dream?

But Bridges felt nothing and eventually decided to abandon what he had found to be a fascinating course of studies because for one thing, he would have to frequently lie, "at which I was not very clever," and for another, it would separate him from his Ona friends. "They feared the sorcerers; I did not wish them to fear me, too" (Bridges [1949] 1988:264). Yet, although his desire to learn magic waned, it never completely left him.

When he later met up with the famous Houshken, about whom he had heard so much, Bridges told him he had heard of his great powers and would like to see some of his magic. The moon was full that night. Reflected on the snow on the ground, it cast the scene like daylight. Returning from the river, Houshken began to chant, put his hands to his mouth, and withdrew a strip of guanaco hide three times the thickness of a shoelace and about eighteen inches long. His hands shook and gradually drew apart, the strip stretching to about four feet. His companion took one end and the four feet extended to eight, then suddenly disappeared back into Houshken's hands to become smaller and smaller such that when his hands were almost together he clapped them to his mouth, uttered a prolonged shriek, and then held out his hands, completely empty.

Even an ostrich, comments Bridges, could not have swallowed those eight feet of hide without a visible gulp. But where else could it have gone but back into the man's very body? He had no sleeves. He stood stark naked in the snow with his robe on the ground. What's more, there were between twenty and thirty men present, but only a third of them were Houshken's people and the rest were far from being friendly. "Had they detected some simple trick," writes Bridges, "the great medicine man would have lost his influence; they would no longer have believed in any of his magic" (Bridges [1949] 1988:285).

Houshken put on his robe and seemed to go into a trance as he stepped toward Bridges, let his robe fall to the ground, put his hands to his mouth again, withdrew them, and when they were less than two feet from Bridges's face slowly drew them apart to reveal a small, almost opaque, object, about an inch in diameter, tapering into his hands. It could have been semitransparent elastic or dough but whatever it was, it seemed to be alive, revolving at great speed.

The moon was bright enough to read by as he drew his hands apart, and Bridges realized suddenly the object was no longer there. "It did not break or burst like a bubble; it simply disappeared." There was a gasp from the onlookers. Houshken turned his hands over for inspection. They were clean and dry. Bridges looked down at the ground. Stoic as he was, Houshken could not resist a chuckle, for there was nothing to be seen. "Don't let it trouble you. I shall call it back to myself again."

By way of ethnographic explanation, Bridges tells us that this curious object was believed to be "an incredibly malignant spirit belonging to, or possibly part of, the *joon* (medicine man) from whom it emanated." It could take a physical form. Or it could be invisible. It had the power to introduce insects, tiny mice, mud, sharp flints, or even a jelly-fish or a baby octopus, into the body of one's enemy. "I have seen a strong man shudder involuntarily at the thought of this horror and its evil potentialities" (Bridges [1949] 1988:286).

"It was a curious fact," he adds, that "although every magician must have known himself to be a fraud and a trickster, he always believed in and greatly feared the supernatural abilities of other medicine-men" (Bridges [1949] 1988:286).[5]

Viscerality and the Gay Science

At this juncture I want to draw your attention to several things that shall pre-
occupy me in this chapter, as they may stimulate and even instruct us as to the
sleight of hand demanded by powerful knowledges recruiting the "inside-out-
ness" of the body in the process of staring down fate. First, there is the mirroring of what comes out and goes back into the healer's body with what is
meant in other circumstances to occur with the patient's body, with the enemy's body, or with a novice healer's body during preparation for becoming an
experienced healer. In other words, these feats displayed are among what we
might allude to as the "primary mechanics" of the shamanism in question.[6]

Then there is the exceedingly curious object that is said to be a spirit belonging to or to be actually part of the body of the medicine man; it appears
to be alive yet is an object all the same; it marks the exit from and reentry into
the body; it has a remarkably indeterminate quality—the fluffy puppy of
down, the weird elasticity of the guanaco strip, the semitransparent dough or
elastic revolving at high speed, all in some way acting like extensions of the
human body and thus capable of connecting with and entering into other
bodies, human and nonhuman.

I also want to draw your attention to the sudden appearances and equally
mysterious disappearances of these objects, no less than to an emphasis on
movement, most notably bodily movement, meaning not only the place of
the body in space, nor simply rapid extension of limbs in what is almost a
form of dance, but also very much a movement of egress and ingress, of insides into outsides and vice versa combined with a movement of sheer becoming, in which being and nonbeing are transformed into the beingness of
transforming forms; to the metamorphosing capacity of curious unnamable
animated objects to become more clearly recognizable but out-of-place
things such as baby octopi or mud or a flint in the body of the enemy, a capacity not only for change but of an implosive viscerality that would seem to
hurl us beyond the world of the symbol and that penny-in-the-slot resolution called meaning.[7]

Above all at this point, I want to draw attention to the skillful display of
magical feats and tricks and to wonder about their relationship to the utterly
serious business of killing and healing people, the very point of this chapter.
This combination of trickery, spectacle, and death must fill us with some

confusion, even anxiety, about the notion of the trick and its relation to both theater and to science, let alone to truth and fraud. We therefore need to dwell upon this corrosive power creeping along the otherwise imperceptible fault lines in the sturdy structure of language and thought, splicing games and deceit to matters of life and death, theater to reality, this world to the spirit world, and trickery to the illusion of a world without trickery—the most problematic trick of all. Here one can sympathize with Friedrich Nietzsche in *The Birth of Tragedy*, where he writes that "all of life is based on semblance, art, deception, points of view and the necessity of perspectives and error" (1968:23), no less than with the attempt by Horkheimer and Adorno to position not Eve and the tree of knowledge of good and evil but shamanism and its magic as the true fall from grace onto the first faltering steps of Enlightenment and what has come to be called science, imitating nature so as by this "deception" to control nature, including human nature, transforming trick into technique and knowledge into power/knowledge (Horkheimer and Adorno 1969:3–43).

Following Nietzsche, I take there to be two somewhat separate points here, one being his often-repeated assertion about the long-term well-being provided by error and untruth in human and social life, the second being the injunction for us not to labor under the illusion of eliminating trickery on the assumption that there is some other world out there beyond and bereft of trickery, beyond and bereft of what has come to be latterly known as power/knowledge and the artistry associated therewith, but to practice instead our own form of *shamanism*, if that's the word, as philosophy and as search for *understanding*, if that's the word, and come up with a set of tricks, simulations, deceptions, and art or appearances in a continuous movement of counterfeint and feint strangely contiguous with yet set against those weighing on us.[8] It is something like this nervous system, I believe, that Nietzsche had in mind with his Gay Science, a "mocking, light, divinely untroubled, divinely artificial art" built around the idea, if I may put it this way, that exposure of the trick is no less necessary to the magic of magic than is its concealment (Nietzsche [1886] 1974:37).

"To describe any considerable number of tricks carried out by the shamans, both Chuckchee and Eskimo, would require too much space" (Bogoras 1904–9).

The word *shaman* is taken as the name for one of the several classes of healers amongst the Tungus of Siberia, and from its very inception, the naming and the figure of the shaman on the anthropological stage was profoundly insinuated in the vigorous display of trickery by means of startling revelations about ventriloquism, imitations of animal spirit voices, curtained chambers, mysterious disappearances and reappearances, semisecret trapdoors, knife tricks, and so forth, including—if *trick* is the word here, and why not?—sex changes by men and women (Bogoras 1904–9:433–67). By the last quarter of the twentieth century, so-called shamans came to be thought of by anthropologists and by laymen as existing everywhere throughout the world and throughout history as a universal type of magical and religious being, and the trickery tended to be downplayed as the mystical took center stage. The term itself had become early on diffused throughout Western languages, thanks to the Siberian ethnography, the phenomenon thus joining an illustrious company of colonially derived native terms such as *totemism* and *taboo* and even *cannibalism*.[9]

Hearken to the wonderful tricks presented by Waldemar Bogoras for the Chukchi shaman of Siberia, Bogoras's 1904 monograph thus constituting a solid contribution to the veritable birthplace of "shamanism" as a Western discovery, if not invention, of a universal type of man or woman able to presence the world of the spirits.[10] Bogoras was fascinated, for instance, by the shamans' skill in ventriloquy and the creation by this means of soundscape so complex and multiply layered that it seemed like one was immersed in a spirit world. He took pains to capture the trick of voice throwing on a phonographic record and was surprised that he could do so. Another form of trick was performed by a shaman wringing her hands to make a large pebble reproduce a continuous row of small pebbles on top of her drum. Bogoras tried to trick her into revealing her trick but was unable to. Another of her tricks was to rip open the abdomen of her son to find and remove the cause of illness. "It certainly looked as if the flesh was really cut open," he writes. On both sides, from under the fingers flowed little streams of blood, trickling to the ground. "The boy lay motionless; but once or twice moaned feebly, and complained that the knife had touched his entrails" (Bogoras 1904–9:433–67). The shaman placed her mouth to the incision and spoke into it. After some moments she lifted her head, and the boy's body was quite sound. Other shamans made much of stabbing themselves with knives. Tricks are everywhere. As Bogoras concludes, "To describe any considerable number of tricks carried out by the shamans, both Chuckchee and Eskimo, would require too much space" (Bogoras 1904–9:433–67). Yet can we resist mentioning a couple more?

> Upune, for instance, pretended to draw a cord through her body, passing it from one spot to another. Then suddenly she drew it out, and immediately afterward pretended to cut it in two and with it the bodies of several of her children, who sat in front of her. These and other tricks resemble to a surprising degree the feats of jugglers all over the world. Before each performance, Upune would even open her hands, in the graceful manner of a professor of magic, to show us she had nothing in them. (Bogoras 1904–9:433–67)

The greatest trick was not that of being able to descend and walk in the underground but to change one's sex, thanks to help from the spirits, a change that could well eventuate, at least in the case of a man, in his taking male lovers or becoming married to a man. Such "soft men," as they were called, were feared for their magic more than unchanged men or women (Bogoras 1904–9:447).

"A peculiar state of mind": "It would be wonderful if a man could talk with animals and fishes."

"It is perfectly well-known by all concerned," writes the eminent anthropologist Franz Boas toward the end of his career, that "a great part of the shamanistic procedure is based on fraud; still it is believed in by the shaman as well as by his patients and their friends. Exposures do not weaken the belief in the 'true' power of shamanism. Owing to this peculiar state of mind, the shaman himself is doubtful in regard to his powers and is always ready to bolster them up by fraud" (Boas and Hunt 1930a:121).

At the risk of being odiously pedantic, allow me to try to catch this slippery fish of Kwakiutl shamanism by itemizing its contradictory components as they come across here in Boas's rendering. I am aware that all I demonstrate is the more you try to pin this down, the more it wriggles, and this is I guess my labored point, to watch the figure of logic emerge as a vengeful force of pins and points bent on restraint.

1. All concerned know that a great part of shamanistic procedure is a fraud.
2. Yet shaman, patient, and friends all believe in shamanism.
3. Moreover, exposure of shamanism's fraudulence does not weaken belief in it.
4. But contrary to Points 2 and 3, the presence of fraud does make the shaman doubt his or her worth.
5. Point 4 has the effect that the shaman resorts to (further) fraud.
6. Now start with Point 1 again.

And after close study, Stanley Walens states that anthropologists "have often wondered why it is that the natives do not complain that the shamans are performing tricks and not real cures. They have found it difficult to explain the seeming paradox that while Kwakiutl shamans are admired for their abilities at legerdemain, if a shaman bungles one of these tricks, he is immediately killed" (Walens 1981:24–25).

"Unlike his more mystical and more spiritual counterparts," writes Irving Goldman, contrasting Kwakiutl with arctic shamanism, "the Kwakiutl shaman relies heavily on elaborate tricks in his public demonstrations. He devises hidden trapdoors and partitions, and uses strings to cleverly manipulate artificial figures. He is in appearance the modern magician" (1975:102).

At this point, let us pause and cast an eye over the strategies one might pursue to understand the fraudulent as not only true but efficacious, the trick as technique.

One could find relief in Boas's statement that not all but only a (great) part of the shamanistic procedure is based on fraud and hope that the lesser part may turn out to be the more important.

One could plunge into the heady waters of interrogating the meaning of *belief* as in "still it is *believed* in by the shaman as well as by his patients," thus forcing the issue about the difference between belief as in a personal psychological state, versus belief as in "tradition" as some sort of cultural "script" (the British "intellectualist" approach to magic versus the French à la Emile Durkheim and Lucien Lévy-Bruhl), and so forth. One would also want to ask questions such as to what extent is belief ever an unflawed, totally confident, and uncontradictory thing anyway? How much does one have to "believe" for shamanism to work? And so on (a well-worn path, actually).

One could play the E.B. Tylor maneuver taken up by Evans-Pritchard that because what we might call scientific procedures of verification or falsification of the efficacy of magical healing are either not available, not practiced, or by definition inapplicable, there is always a way of explaining failure away (e.g., bad faith or ritual error on the part of the healer, a stronger sorcerer at work in the background, unstoppable malevolence on the part of a too-powerful spirit). This argument is usually packaged with another: that this infamously "closed system," about which so much has been written as regards Africa, is in some yet to be plausibly connected way associated with the yet to be explained belief that although any particular shaman may be fraudulent, shamanism is nevertheless valid (believed in, plausible, worth a shot?). As in the modern police system, it takes more than a few bad apples to render the barrelful bad, as the New York Police Commissioner is fond of saying.

Or one could do something still more interesting, even fruitful and original, and substitute for the word *fraud* the word *simulation* or *mimesis*. This has remarkable fallout poetically as much as philosophically and is uncannily resonant with the ethnographic record itself—as we shall later see. With this, perhaps, our fish would stop wiggling and start to swim, a manner of "resolving" contradiction I find preferable to that of pins and points.

Boas's intimate knowledge concerning this "peculiar state of mind" came from his four-decades-long relationship with his Kwakiutl informant George Hunt and the ten thousand pages of material they published, plus several thousand more existing in manuscript form.[11] Their weighty conversations about Hunt's shamanic experiences began in 1897 and reached a peak in the 1925 *auto*biographical text of Hunt's published in Kwakiutl and in English in 1930 as "I Desired to Learn the Ways of the Shaman," a text delivered from obscurity by Claude Lévi-Strauss in a famous essay entitled "The Sorcerer and His Magic," being an attempt to provide what must now seem more of an expression of faith as in structuralism, than an explanation of faith as in magic, the point being that Hunt, known at the beginning of the 1930 essay as Giving-Potlatches-in-the-World, becomes by his own admission a famous shaman not so much despite as because of his profoundly skeptical attitude.[12]

In fact, over the twenty-nine years from 1897 to 1925, Hunt had given Boas no less than four accounts of his experience in becoming a shaman, and it was for Boas remarkable how the last account—the one that became published as "I Desired to Learn the Ways of the Shaman"—eliminated what Boas called all the supernatural elements in the earlier versions, in which Hunt vividly described his mysterious fainting fits as a child; finding himself naked in the graveyard at night; the visits by immensely powerful spirits such as the killer whale named Tilting-in-Mid-Ocean, who told him how to cure the chief's sick boy the following day; how the feather-down indicative of disease just appeared of its own accord in his mouth as he was sucking out the disease; how killer whales accompanied his canoe; how he ate of the corpse of the shaman Life-Maker; and so forth. Most of the time, it seems, in the early versions, he was falling unconscious, passing out into these other realms, while in the last version, that of 1925, Hunt takes the position, as Boas puts it, that "his only object was to discover the frauds perpetrated by shamans" (Boas and Hunt 1930a:121). Small wonder then that confronted with contradictions such as these, and resolute to the facts at hand, Boas, unlike the fledgling field of British social anthropology, in the pioneering hands of Bronislaw Malinowski, with his simplistic yet powerful functionalist formula relating part to whole, for instance, never came up with a general theory or picture of Kwakiutl society.

At one point Boas commonsensically notes that the skepticism displayed by Kwakiutl people toward magic should be seen as a political defense because Indians did not want to come across to whites as irrational and so would fake a critical attitude toward shamanism. (How things have changed!) Hence at one stroke we could dismiss questions concerning the place of skepticism in faith and simply view such perplexity as mere artifact of another sort of fraud—or is it mimesis?—namely, that of Indian self-representation to whites at that time and place. But then of course another hypothesis intrudes, that if fraud is an essential part of (Kwakiutl) shamanism, or at least of its "greater part," as Boas elsewhere states with much vigor, and if skepticism exists alongside such fraud, then it probably wouldn't require much effort, if any at all, to "adopt" (as Boas puts it) a skeptical attitude toward shamanism when talking to whites, and this would hold true for two connected reasons. The first is that skepticism is part of the greater part and that the Indian is merely being honest and nonfraudulent and is in fact giving "the native's point of view" in admitting to the fraud, and the second is that insofar as one is being fraudulent vis-à-vis the white interlocutor, presumably one has had much practice with fraud and skepticism in discussing shamanism with fellow Indians anyway.

And what are we to make of the fact that Hunt's scathingly skeptical 1925 autobiographical account of shamanism comes not at the beginning but after forty years of friendship with Boas and that it is the earlier, not the last, versions that are the credulously mystical ones? Given that their friendship would have become more intimate and trusting over the years, does this not tend to contradict Boas's attempt to interpret the veracity of his Indian informant, where he observes that the Indian is likely to stress skepticism with whites so as to appear rational? Wouldn't the later version be more likely to be more honest and less concerned with creating a good—that is, rational— impression?[13]

In any event, the colonial relationship through which such epistemically sensitive and imaginative activity as shamanism is to be conveyed inevitably becomes no less part of our object of study than the activity itself. To get to the truth about shamanism, we start to realize, means getting to the truth of an intercultural relationship objectified by means of autoethnographic intercultural texts such as the fourth version over three decades of "I Wished to Discover the Ways of the Shaman."[14] But this is most definitely not to say that the pervasive influence of colonialism accounts for skepticism with regards to the autoethnography of magic. On the contrary. The magic at stake here first and foremost concerns the way in which the colonial presence provides yet another figure to be caught in the legerdemain of revelation of concealment.

Perhaps an outline of Hunt's meteoric shamanic career, as he presents it in his final, 1925, text, will assist us here, although the comforting sense of a career does scant justice to the zigzagging through contradiction that is entailed. First let us dwell on the fact that from the very first line of his forty-one-page account, he presents himself as the arch-doubter, yet wants to learn the ways of the shamans.

The tension here seems so crucial, so carefully highlighted, that it would surely not be unfair to venture the hypothesis that learning shamanism means doubting it at the same time and that the development of such a split con-sciousness involving belief and nonbelief is what this learning process is all about. "I desired to learn about the shaman," he starts off, "whether it is true or whether it is made up and whether they pretend to be shamans." His doubting is all the more striking given that the two shamans with whom he is involved were also, as he states, his "intimate friends."

His first step is to be the target of a shaman's vomited quartz crystal dur-ing a public healing ceremony. He himself, we might say, becomes a display object, a ritual within a ritual, a trick not unlike the trick with the concealed feather down in the mouth that he later learns for healing. Next he appears as a powerful shaman in the dream of a sick boy, the son of a chief, whose dream acts as a detailed script full of technique for the subsequently effective cure he practices on the young dreamer, and with this his fame is ensured, his name is changed, and a succession of shamanic competitions ensue as he travels the land in search of truth and technique in which he exposes other shamans as fakes or at the least puts the healing efficacy of their techniques in grave doubt, such that they are convinced that he possesses a secret more powerful than their own.[15]

From the outset, he not only privately doubts shamanism but goes out of his way to publicize the fact. It seems culturally important to do this, making it clear that he is "the principal one" who does "not believe in all the ways of the shamans, for I had said so aloud to them" (Boas and Hunt 1930a:5). And in case you assume he is unique in either his doubting or in giving voice to his doubting, he lets you know that one of the first persons he meets after the quartz has been shot into him asks, "Have you not felt the quartz crystals of the liars, the shamans, the one that they referred to that was thrown into your stomach?. . . . You will never feel it, for these are just great lies what the shamans say" (Boas and Hunt 1930a:5). And the head chief, Causing-to-be-Well, the next person with whom he speaks, similarly disabuses him: "They are just lies what the shamans say."

Just about everyone, so it seems, revels in declaring shamans to be fakes and rarely lets an opportunity slip to insist on this elemental fact. What's more, as if in keeping with what we might call this sadomasochistic attitude of loving skepticism toward truth and authenticity, each time Hunt, known here as Giv-ing-Potlatches-in-the-World, serves as a target of opportunity for the revela-tion of this fakery, his desire to learn the ways of the shamans redoubles. One really has to admire his enthusiasm—no less than that which the accomplished shamans bring to bear to the task of revealing their secrets.

Take the case of the famous Koskimo shaman, Aixagidalagilis, he who so proudly sang his sacred song,

> Nobody can see through the magic power
> Nobody can see through my magic power.

But when Giving-Potlatches-in-the-World (Hunt) cured the patient whom Aixagidalagilis was unable to cure, and did this through his *pretense* of trembling and through his *pretense* of sucking out the bloody worm of disease (I am merely emphasizing here what he says in his text), then Aixagidalagilis implores him not so much to reveal "the secret," although certainly that, too, but first he says—and implied by this, the ontological status, the reality, if you will, of the technique employed—"'I pray you to have mercy and tell me what stuck on the palm of your hand last night. Was it the true sickness or was it only made up?'" (Boas and Hunt 1930a:31). It seems like a wrenching pathos here, an almost childish pleading, surfacing with a terrible anxiety as to whether or not the technique is a trick.

To which Giving-Potlatches-in-the-World responds, again striking the appropriate ontological concern but disturbing its gravity with what seems like a rather mischievous, rather nasty, bit of teasing, "Your saying to me is not quite good, for you said 'is it the true sickness, or is it only made up?'" Note that this is the very same Giving-Potlatches-in-the-World who has just finished singing his sacred song on completing his successful cure in front of the assembled throng, humiliating Aixagidalagilis:

> He tried to prevent me from succeeding, the one who does not succeed.
> Ah, I shall not try to fail to have no sacred secrets.

(This string of double negatives must tell us something crucially important about the curious transparency of the secret in the shamanic cure, no less than in the sacred.)

And having been bettered, Aixagidalagilis then pours out his secrets. "Let me tell you the way of my head ring of red cedar bark," he says.[16]

Truly, it is made up what is thought by all the men it is done this way. Go on! Feel the thin sharp-pointed nail at the back of the head of this my cedar bark ring, for I tell a lie when I say that the alleged sickness which I pretend to suck out from the sick person. . . . All these fools believe it is truly biting the palm of my hand. (Boas and Hunt 1930a:31–32)

Secrecy is infinitely mysterious here because it is allied with and able to create what we might call the sacredness of a hiddenness within the theatricality that mediates between the real and the really made up, with no less importance than that which mediates between trick and technique and therapeutic efficacy, and what is equally crucial is that not only do the established shamans, once they lose out in competition, beseech him for the secret of the technique, but in doing so they seem even more concerned with telling him theirs. In fact their predisposition to confess their secrets is amazing. The secret teaching of shamanism has thus a peculiar confessional, post hoc belatedly historicist turn to it, secrets revealed after they're no good, secrets discarded after they've failed to maintain the tension of reality as really made up.[17]

This curious excavating mechanism of confession proceeds in passionate and intricate detail about how the deception was achieved. Nothing seems without pretense anymore, other, of course, than this exposure itself (and the double-headed serpent with the head of a human in its middle; for more about this, see below). "It would be wonderful," Aixagidalagilis says at one point, "if a man could talk with animals and fishes. And so the shamans are liars who say they catch the soul of the sick person, for I know we all own a soul" (Boas and Hunt:1930a:32).

It is his daughter, Inviter-Woman, who then tells us what happened to this cynical manipulator that is her shaman-father, of the great unholiness that befell herself and him when, on account of his shame, they fled the haunts of men and in their wandering came across a creature lying crossways on a rock, which they recognized as the double-headed serpent, with a head at each end and a large human head in the middle. Seeing this they died, to be brought to life by a man who told them he would have brought them good fortune, but because she was menstruating they would have trouble until they died.[18] And from then on they were driven out of their minds. She was laughing as she told this, and then she would cry, pulling out her hair, and her father, the great pretender, died crazed within three winters. And the moral? "Now this is the end of talk about Aixagidalagilis who was believed by all the tribes to be really a great shaman who had gone through (all the secrets). Then I found out that he was just a great liar about everything that he did in his shamanism" (Boas and Hunt 1930a:35).

Thus, we might say, shamans might be liars, but menstruation and double-headed serpents are not without a decidedly nasty potential. And surely this is one of those tales that not only belies the satisfaction of a moral or any other system but delights in exploiting the idea of one? This we might with truth call a "nervous system," not only in which shamanism thrives on a corrosive skepticism but in which skepticism and belief actively cannibalize one another so that continuous injections of recruits, such as Giving-Potlatches-in-the-World, who are full of questioning are required. They are required, so it would seem, to test and therewith brace the mix by serving not as raw material of doubt positioned to terminate as believers, nor yet as cynical manipulators, but as exposer vehicles for confession for the next revelation of the secret contained in the trick that is both art and technique and thus real and really made up.

Technique is thus revealed as trick and it behooves us to inquire further into this momentous distinction—recalling, as an aside, how fundamental a role the passage from trick to technique is in Horkheimer and Adorno's argument regarding the role of mimesis in the extraordinarily pivotal role of (what they refer to as) shamanism in Enlightenment and modern technology.

Here we are indebted to Stanley Walen's reading of shamanic tricks as technique in the Boas-Hunt texts, because of his pointing out the awesome magic of mimesis in which the practitioner sets up a performance, which, through its perfection, spirits will copy. This follows from the fact that the Kwakiutl believe their world is mimetically doubled in several ways, that "animals and spirits lead lives exactly equivalent to those of humans. They live in winter villages, perform dances, wear masks, marry, pray, and perform all other acts that humans perform." When the shaman sucks disease from the human body, the spirits are there, sucking too. In this way magic involves what Walens calls "the magnification and intensification of a human action to a greater level of power" (Walens 1981:24). Hence he can claim that there is no real paradox involved in shamanism, because the tricks turn out to be models or scenes for the spirits to follow, and it is the spirits who ultimately supply the cure. It is as if the paradox is an artifact of Enlightenment, of the way of looking at human and social phenomena that comes with a disenchantment of the world and that therefore, so the stream of thought goes, spirits are to be explained rather than providing the explanation. It is thus devastating, I think, to read Walens when he tells us that the shaman is at all times dependent on the spirits and that "Kwakiutl pay no attention to the thoughts of the shaman while he is performing the act because the spirits effect the cure using the shaman as their instrument and the shaman's thoughts are irrelevant to the efficacy of his cure" (Walens 1981:25).[19]

Nevertheless, how would this explanation help us understand the continuous anxiety about pretense and the continuous excavation of fraud through revelation of the (failed) secret? Could it be that the shaman is not only tricking the human but also the spirit world—on whom he or she is dependent? What sort of "dependency" is this, you might ask?

And here something innately carnal takes center stage, something bodily tied to the mimetic faculty defined as "the nature that culture uses to create second nature," as when Walens points out that the "critical part of the cure is the fluidity, skill, and physical perfection with which the shaman performs his tricks, for it is the motions of the tricks (reinforced by their exact duplication by the spirits) that effect the cure" (Walens 1981:25).[20]

Although at times he refers to the reciprocation of humans and spirits as responsible for effecting the cure, it should be pointed out that it is mimesis that is at stake and not some form of instrumentally conceived mutual aid contract. "The characteristics of the physical movement made by the ritualist are of the greatest importance," he says, "for the particular qualities of the movement he makes during the performance of the ritual will be repeated exactly in form, but with greatly increased power by the spirits" (Walens 1981:25).

There is this immensely suggestive feature left hanging here, along with perfection and skill, and that is *fluidity*. "As long as the shaman performs his actions fluidly," insists Walens, "the spirits are conjoined by cosmic forces to use their power to cure" (Walens 1981:24). And whatever fluidity is, it is the opposite of *bungling*. "The shaman who bungles his tricks," Walens goes on to say, "forces the spirits to perform actions that are as disjointed, undirected, and destructive as his." Not only does this bungling not result in a cure, but, far worse, it actually kills people by unleashing what Walens refers to as "uncontrollable chaotic power on the world." For this reason, the bungler must be immediately killed before he or she can do greater damage (Walens 1981:25).[21] This puts Giving-Potlatches-in-the-World's desire to learn the ways of the shaman in admirable perspective.

This reminder about flow and its immense importance in building the simulacrum that is the trick that is technique has the merit of sensitizing us to the play of metonymy within and extending beyond metaphor, in other words, to a certain play of "bodiedness," contagion, and physical connection as the co-component of the mimetic alongside the idea, the symbol, the distanced visual or quasi-visual dimension of things. There are terms and dichotomies aplenty for this, testimony, if such be required, to our studied and probably necessary incapacity to put the "language" of body into language per se; Jakobson's metaphor versus metonymy, Nietzsche's Apollinian versus Dionysian, Sir James George Frazer's homeopathic versus contagious forms of sympathetic magic, Walter Benjamin's aura versus tactility, Gilles Deleuze and Felix Guattari's rhizomic "logic" becoming animal, and so forth.

Whatever we might mean by sacredness, and its attendant dangers and rites, it surely has a great deal to do with such dichotomies uniting yet dividing spirit from body, such that the *flow* in technique in Kwakiutl shamanism, it should be noted, bears heavily on the ability of soul/body to be dislocated (spirit-caused illness) or on the implosion via mystical force of Otherness into the body of the victim (sorcery). Hence flow directly implicates not one but several bodies and energies flowing into and out of one another, across borders accessed by dream, surrealism, and animal visitations such as the toad or the wolves come down the beach vomiting foam over the body while the others lie dying on account of the holocaust brought by white society in the form of smallpox, reducing the Kwakiutl population by an unbelievable 80 to 90 percent from 1862 to 1929 (Masco 1995:55–56).[22]

The flow is between animals and humans—as from the very beginning of Kwakiutl time when the original ancestors took off their animal masks and skins to present their human selves. The flow is also from the clothes, presumably of the white people, the flow of the pox. "After we had stepped from our canoe," recounts Fool, describing how he became a shaman, we found much clothing and flour. We took them and ten days later became sick with the great smallpox. "We lay in bed in our tent. I was laying among them. Now I saw that all our bodies swelled and were dark red. Our skins burst open and I did not know that they were all dead and I was laying among them. Then I thought I also was dead." Wolves came down to the beach, whining and howling, licking his body, he recounted, vomiting foam, which they put into his body. They tried hard, he explains, to put foam all over my body, continuously licking him and turning him all over. When it was all licked off, they vomited over him again, licking off the scabs of smallpox in the process. "Now I saw I was lying among my dead past nephews" (Boas and Hunt 1930b:41–42).

The flow may be no less interior than exterior, as in getting certain insides outside so as to disappear again inside the healer's body, first requisite being a type of diagnostic anatomy as in the searching of the chest, the mighty theater of the unknown.

> For a long time he felt of the middle of the chest. I heard Aixagidalagilis say that there was no sickness in the middle of the chest. Then he felt of the right hand side of the chest. He had not been feeling long before he felt of the left hand side of the chest. Then he pointed with his first finger to the place where the heart of Wawengenol was beating. Then the shaman spoke and said, "I have now found the place where the sickness is" [and] he put his mouth to the place where was beating his heart. Four times he blew at it and then he sucked. (Boas and Hunt 1930a:25)

And then maybe the sickness is dispatched by being swallowed by the healer. Or else the intestines and not the chest shall be the focus, as with the female shaman Helagolsela at Nimkish pressing down with both hands on the lower part of the ribs of the poor female patient, pressing so strongly that she went to the backbone, passing over the navel as she groaned in the pain of it, coming down inside the crotch, repeating this over and over again so it sounded as if her intestines were boiling. She had now gotten the sickness to go downward to collect at the rectum from where it would be defecated, she said, blowing for a long time from the stomach to the inside of the crotch. This is done by these shamans for men or women, for headache or for urinary obstruction—this sickness called "blocked up inside" (Boas and Hunt 1930a:35–37).

As with the very concept of the mimetic and its magic, let alone the degree to which spirits themselves can be fooled, is there not a crucial secret here in that although the shaman pretends to suck out disease and demonstrate the success of this action with a fake worm or piece of down supposedly retrieved from the insides of the patient's body, the spirit is supposed to actually extract something—such that we might say that the trick "tricks" (calls, encourages, seduces?) first and foremost the spirit so as to become fluidly efficacious technique? Is it here where imitation in being fraudulent ensures realness and works its wonderful magic? "We might say," says Walens elsewhere, "that the Kwakiutl play games as much with the spirits as with their human opponents" (Walens 1981:26).

In this regard it is illuminating to read the vicissitudes of Boas's translation of the Kwakiutl name of the stupendously important Winter Ceremonial of the Kwakiutl, when the spirits emerge in their fullness from November well into the following year and take over the life of the villages, the ceremonial in which humans impersonate the spirits, enact the myths pertaining to the origins of human acquisition of supernatural powers from some fifty-three human-animal doubles such as Wolf, Killer Whale, Eagle, Thunderbird, and Man Eater ("Cannibal Dancer").[23]

Its name, *tsetseqa*, meaning "fraudulent" or "to cheat" (as well as being synonymous with *to be good-minded* and *happy*), is curious, says Boas. "For instance, when a person wants to find out whether a shaman has real power or whether his power is based on pretense, he uses the same term meaning 'pretended, fraudulent, made-up' shaman. Even in the most serious presentations of the ceremonial, it is clearly and definitely stated that it is planned as a *fraud*" (Boas and Hunt 1930a:172; my emphasis). In *The Mouth of Heaven*, Irving Goldman tries to mitigate this curiousness by arguing that Boas's translation is crude. It should, claims Goldman, using Boas's posthumous grammar, mean "imitated" (1975:102).

Here, I think, fortuitous as it may be, we have located the core of the riddle, especially when one notes that Boas had, according to Goldman, "in an earlier stab at translation" suggested that the stem of the word for the winter ceremonial, *tseka*, meant "secrets."

There is a certain anxiety, even pain and craziness, here, as Goldman heatedly insists that to imitate is not necessarily to secularize. Who said it was? What's the problem? All these words start to swim in multiple and multiply conflicting configurations of overlapping associations and streams of reversible meanings:

> fraud
>
> simulation
>
> exalted
>
> imitation
>
> secret
>
> happiness
>
> sacred

From here on, the philosophical ground becomes steep and slippery and perhaps only fools dare go further, as the impenetrable mysteries of representation and reality, within Western philosophy alone, not to mention Kwakiutl, emerge with all their force.

Yet if there is a moral, it might be this: that the real novice in "I Wished to Discover the Ways of the Shaman" was Boas and, beyond him, by implication, the "science of man" he came to spearhead and the momentous historical moment of modernity that spawned this science. This, of course, very much implicates us too and yet gives us the choice provided by this insight. For the point of the text as I read it (and as is amply confirmed by Boas's later commentary) is not that Boas as a neutral observer and recording angel somehow lucked out and found the one unique Enlightenment individual ready to challenge hocus-pocus and give the inside story to our Our-Man-from-New York, nor even that there seems to be a ready supply of such skeptics, but that the text in itself, an artifact of the fledgling science of anthropology, especially one given over to Giving-the-Natives'-point-of-View, is an utterly perfect instance of the confession of the secret, the very acme of the skilled revelation of skilled concealment. In other words, this text is not so much about shamanism as it is shamanic in its conformity to the cannibalistic logic of having to have ever-fresh recruits for ceaseless confession, such that in its very skepticism lies its profound magic, and Lévi-Strauss can quite inappropriately conclude that at the end Giving-Potlatches-in-the-World seems to have lost sight of his fallacious technique and, by implication, has crossed the threshold from skepticism to faith, from science to magic. The problem arises in not having taken with enough seriousness the necessity for skepticism in magic as relayed through rituals of exposure and unmasking and, second, in not having seen the text "I Desired to Learn the Ways of the Shaman" as in itself just this very ritual transposed into textual form and readied as science by the anthropologist. Leaving this text as raw material in the mode of Boas's textual realism, or recruiting it as does Lévi-Strauss for the purpose of validating structuralism, misses the point but also the invitation that such ritual offers—that it lives as magic and makes claims even on us in its request for a reciprocal response composed in equal measure of confessional responsibility and judicious and intricately moving medleys of skepticism and faith, continuously deferred through the opening and closing of the secret.

For we have our tricks to develop too, "the trick of the floating quartz crystal," we might call this, involving a heightened sensitivity to fluidity, mass, and movement, no less than to ecstatic moments of appearance and disappearance of objects inside and between bodies as when the liberated quartz crystal vomited out by the shaman Making-Alive enters the body of our friend here, Giving-Potlatches-in-the-World. "Now this one will be a great shaman, said he" (Boas and Hunt 1930a:4) suggests a certain fluidity of performance with identities, if not with the logic of becoming itself, the song leaders beating fast time as Fool looks upward, watching the quartz float around in the cedar beams, while Making-Alive staggers like a drunk around the fire in the middle of the house in front of a great mass of onlookers. For might we not say that the reality of shamanism hangs on the reality of this fragment of flickering light in tumbling stone, passing between intestines through streams of vomit, lost for the moment in a graceful float up there in the cedar rafters?

There are many issues here, but keep your eye on the quartz crystal floating free. For who knows how short or long a time it stays up in the air heavy with the tension of bodily interconnection? The quartz is a trick and the trick is a figure and the figure of the trick is one of continuous movement and metamorphosis in, through, and between bodies, carrying power one jump ahead of its interpretation. The language of true or false seems not just peculiarly inept here but deliberately so.

At one point, struggling to understand the place of theater and spirit impersonation in the Winter Ceremonial, Goldman seems to be stating that mimetic simulation is a way of keeping hidden things hidden while at the same time revealing them, of keeping secret things secret while displaying them. "The ceremonies deal with the secret matters that are always hidden and can be experienced, therefore, only in a simulated form" (1975:102).

I can think of no deeper way of expressing my thesis regarding the skilled revelation of skilled concealment.

Dancing the Question

> Indeed, skepticism is included in the pattern of belief in witchdoctors. Faith and skepticism are alike traditional.
>
> —EVANS-PRITCHARD, *Witchcraft, Oracles and Magic Among the Azande*, 1937

Witchcraft was ubiquitous in Zande life when Evans-Pritchard, fondly remembered in anthropological circles as EP, did fieldwork there in the very south of the Sudan in the watersheds of the Nile and Congo Rivers in the early 1930s, and it was witchcraft, oracles, and magic that were the focus of interest of his first publication about these people in a book that through the sheer brilliance of its writing and intellect came to define the field of study of magic, and much else besides (Evans-Pritchard 1937). Yet at the outset, it should be emphasized how curiously unclear this ostensibly transparent book actually is when any particular point is examined, how certainties dissolve into ever more mystifying contradictions magically dispelled, momentarily as it were, by the author's self-assured explanations of the multifarious aspects of magical phenomena. I take this to be striking confirmation of how magic begs for and at the same time resists explanation most when appearing to be explained and that therefore in its unmasking, magic is in fact made even more opaque, a point given a special twist here through the technique, or is it a trick?, of (what Clifford Geertz has called) EP's "transparencies" (Geertz 1983:62–80). It is then to the issue of technique and trickery and the use of tricks to out-trick other tricks that we need to pay attention, not to further the mystifying effects of unmasking that the Enlightenment, transparency, project, seems to assume, but to lay foundations for something along the lines of that gay science Nietzsche proposed as its critical, masquerading alternative, or even what Benjamin seems to have often had in mind as ploys of demystification and reenchantment in his Marxist-inspired search for a critical language of social forms and political power drawn both from Jewish mysticism and from Christian theories of allegory in European, Baroque drama.

Now, witch doctors are those persons, generally male, whose task it is to divine the presence and identity of a witch in this witch-infested Zande land and heal the sicknesses arising therefrom. They form corporations with group secrets, and initiation into the group is long and arduous. These secrets are the knowledge of medicines and what EP calls their "tricks of the trade," principal of which is the actual extraction by hand or mouth from the body of the victim of witchcraft objects such as bits of charcoal, splinters, black beetles, or worms. There are plenty of other tricks too, such as vomiting blood, extracting worms from one's own person, resting heavy weights on one's chest, and shooting black beetles and bits of charcoal from one's leg into the body of somebody else, even over large distances, but no trick is as secretly guarded, in EP's narrative, as that of extracting the witchcraft object from the body of the sick. Whether we are to call these tricks or techniques, I for the moment leave for you to decide. (That is pretty much an EP sort of sentence, in both senses of the word.)

The doctors would not divulge their secrets to EP, who decided entering into the corporation would be counterproductive and so instead paid for his Zande servant, Kamanga, a gullible man with profound faith in witch doctors, to undergo initiation so as "to learn all about the techniques of witchdoctors."[24] Evans-Pritchard was able to learn even more by using the secrets elicited by Kamanga to play on rivalries between doctors, but he felt sure that certain things, especially the extraction of witchcraft objects, would not be told to Kamanga, because he had acted straightforwardly, as he puts it, in telling the doctors that Kamanga would pass on all he learned to EP. "In the long run, however," EP adds, striking a militant note, "an ethnographer is bound to triumph. Armed with preliminary knowledge nothing can prevent him from driving a deeper and deeper wedge if he is interested and persistent" (EP 1937:152).

But what would happen if it turned out that the secret lies in there being no secret and that this is what will always resist the wedge of truth no matter how interested or persistent, or, for that matter, white, the wedge might be?

To the extent that the secret can be and is revealed, I would like to suggest that revelation is precisely what the secret intends; in other words, part of secrecy is secretion and this is especially the case with what I call the "public secret," that which is known but not generally articulated or, to put it another way, thus bringing out its quality of paradox, it is that which it is known not to know, and so this talk of wedges and driving deeper and deeper is beside the point, or, rather, is the intended and labored drama of the secret's make-believe, which, in this case, EP's remarkable text fulfills remarkably well. The play of the secret in the colonial relationship, itself often a highlighted version of Enlightenment staging, often functions this way with the public secret being displaced by the notion of the secret, the penetration of which serves to demonstrate both the pugnacity and cleverness of the truth seeker.[25]

We are a long way from Nietzsche's gay science, in which "We no longer believe that truth remains truth when the veils are withdrawn. . . . What is required for that is to stop courageously at the surface, the fold, the skin, to adore appearance" (Nietzsche [1886] 1974:38). But like most of us, EP just has to get to the bottom with his wedge driving deeper and deeper—his aim is to expose the exposure of the witchcraft object extracted through the surface, the fold, the skin, as if penetrated by surgical incision. What's more, his obsessive search for truth here is uncannily mimetic with that of the doctors whose secrets he is intent on uncovering: "It would, I believe, have been possible by using every artifice to have eventually wormed out all their secrets, but this would have meant bringing undue pressure on people to divulge what they wished to hide" (Evans-Pritchard 1937:151). Yet in fact, as we shall later see, he has no scruple in applying such pressure and does so in a most devastating way.

And while the anthropologist dives deep, let it be noted, the witch doctor brings the secret to the surface, counterposed movements destined to meet in making the pages of the monograph, a triumphant conjunction of movements through which the anthropologist is drawn into a ritual scheme, neither of his own choosing nor understanding—that in telling the witch doctors his servant is to reveal to him the secrets they tell to him, he is thereby fulfilling to the letter the need for unmasking that is actually demanded by the secrets of their magic. In other words, there is this sort of oblique ritual of exposure of the secret within the witch doctors' ritual, which the presence of the anthropologist has here drawn from its otherwise obscure existence.

Such rituals of exposure, amounting to meta-rites of secretion of the secret, thus account for the ubiquitous "trickery" and also the skepticism alongside faith in witch doctors, and they seem especially pronounced among the Azande at the time of EP's stint there. It was not uncommon for young nobles to expose witch doctors by tricking them—an activity EP refers to as "testing" and as "playing a joke." He also cites how a commoner friend of his, Mbira, once placed a knife in a covered pot and asked doctors to divine what lay within. The three doctors danced in the fierce sun the better part of the day, trying unsuccessfully to ascertain the contents, and, grabbing the opportunity, one sought out Mbira in his hut and pleaded he be secretly told the answer and thus avoid humiliation, but Mbira refused, calling him a knave (1937:186). Only a people imbued with a measure of skepticism could indulge in such activities, EP points out (neglecting to wonder at the witch doctors' motivation in agreeing to participate in such tests), and yet Mbira believed firmly in every kind of magic, was himself a magician of standing, and consulted witch doctors when he had a problem. But I want to go further and ask why a sincere or even just your middling sort of skeptic would want to indulge in such sport, given such skepticism? And the answer, I submit, has a good deal to do with the need for rites of exposure built into rites of magic in order to strengthen magic itself.

There is in EP's book a dramatic moment of great poignancy concerning rites of exposure, and as an aside, I would like to note how postmodern this 1930s straight-from-the-hip text is, how it has sneaked into the canon for other than what it is, you might say, with its powerful, personal, anecdotal form of analysis; its steady layering of exemplification; its studious, almost manic aversion to theory in place of storytelling; its constant swerving away from what is supposed to be the point; and, above all, the way its chaos not merely passes for a seamless argument, regarding the explanation of witchcraft, for instance, but is indispensable to it.

Far be it for me to expose such exposure, no matter how close I may appear to be to EP that memorable day he out-tricked the trickster when his servant, Kamanga, under the tutelage of his instructor, Bogwozu, was about to wipe the body of a sick man (another servant of EP's) with the poultice of grass prepared by Bogwozu. This, we are told, is standard medical practice. It is wiped over the abdomen of the patient with the aim of extracting an object of witchcraft, which, if extracted, is shown to the patient, who is then likely to recover. But it was this technique that, to EP's chagrin, the witch doctors stubbornly refused to impart to Kamanga because "they were naturally anxious that" EP "should not know their trade secret" (1937:230). It was a complicated state of affairs, made even more so by the fact that Kamanga himself stubbornly held to the belief that there was no trickery involved in this technique. Now I want you to concentrate on the complexity of this situation in its various shadings of gullibility and trickery, faith and skepticism.

First, the anthropologist tricks the witch doctor:

When the teacher handed over the poultice to his pupil I took it from him to pass it to Kamanga, but in doing so I felt for the object which it contained and removed it between my finger and thumb while pretending to make a casual examination of the kind of stuff the poultice consisted of and commenting on the material.

It was a disagreeable surprise for Kamanga when, after massaging his patient's abdomen through the poultice, in the usual manner of witch-doctors, and after then removing the poultice, he could not find any object of witchcraft in it. (1937:231)

Then, the exposure:

I considered the time had now come to stop proceedings and I asked Kamanga and his teacher to come to my hut a few yards away, where I told them that I had removed the charcoal from the poultice, and asked Bogwozu to explain how it had got there. For a few minutes he pretended incredulity and asked to see the object, since he said that such a thing was impossible, but he was clever enough to see that further pretence would be useless, and, as we were in private, he made no further difficulty about admitting the imposture. (1937:231)

There is something awesome in the anthropological authority exposed by this combined exposure of trickery and gullibility, the anthropologist giving away his tricks of the trade like this, interposing himself between the teacher and the pupil, the disease and the patient, the event and the reader. We can read this with moralizing energy as yet another crass instance of colonial power flexing Enlightenment muscle against primitive magic, staging its own rites of scientific method right there in the heartland of magic, and we can at the same time marvel at the imagination and daring it might have taken to do this.

We could also read this a quite different way, coinciding with the first reading, that the anthropologist was doing little more than the culturally appropriate thing. For just as Mbira took delight in ridiculing witch doctors as described above, so the anthropologist was following a well-worn path, although there are no instances described of Zande's being as sneaky or as daring as EP in actually removing the key to the trick midway through the healing of a sick person. After all, it is one thing to test a doctor's powers. It is another thing to trick him.

In any case, whether this anecdote is viewed as staging Enlightenment triumph or Zande ridicule, the point to consider here is whether or not the anthropologist was himself part of a larger and more complex staging in which exposure of tricks is the name of the game and that what we are witness to via the text is an imaginative, albeit unintended and serendipitous, rendition of the skilled revelation of the skilled concealment necessary to the mix of faith and skepticism necessary to magic.

Finally, we have to consider the effect that the teacher's confession and the revelation of trickery had on the young pupil:

> The effects of these disclosures on Kamanga was devastating. When he had recovered from his astonishment he was in serious doubt whether he ought to continue his initiation. He could not at first believe his eyes and ears, but in a day or two he had completely recovered his poise and *developed a marked degree of self assurance which if I am not mistaken he had not shown before this incident* (1937:231; emphasis mine).

In short, evidence that suggests unmasking adds to, rather than eliminates, the mysterium tremendum of magic's magic.

We see this also in what I can only call studied exercises in unmasking that hardly appear as such on account of the viewer who, constantly on the lookout for "tricks," fails to see that this same viewer is instead party to the skilled revelation of skilled concealment. For example, Kisanga, "a man of unusual brilliance," told EP how a witch doctor begins his treatment:

> When a man becomes sick they send for a witchdoctor. Before the witch-doctor comes to the sick man he scrapes down an animal's bone and hammers it till it is quite small and then drops it into the medicines in his horn. He later arrives at the homestead of the sick man and takes a mouthful of water and swills his mouth round with it and opens his mouth so that people can look into it. He also spreads out his hands to them so that every one can see them, and speaks thus to them: "Observe me well, I am not a cheat, since I have no desire to take anything from any one fraudulently." (1937:191–92)

"Some training in trickery is essential," writes the anthropologist in that confidence-restoring tone that talking about other people's trickery seems to always instill.

> In the first place, the Zande has a broad streak of skepticism towards his leeches who have therefore to be careful that their sleight-of-hand is not observed. . . . If the treatment is carried out in a certain manner, as when the *bingba* grass is used as a poultice, he will be frankly suspicious. But if the witch-doctor sits down on a stool and calls upon a third person to cut *kpoyo* bast and make a poultice of it, rinses his mouth with water, and holds his hands for inspection, suspicions will be allayed. (1937:232)[26]

It is hard not to feel these ostentatiously demonstrative acts of denial are saying the very opposite and that everyone knows (and enjoys) that. It is also hard to believe that the anthropologist is alone in detecting skilled conceal-ment of trickery as when he writes, "If you accompany a witch-doctor on one of his visits you will be convinced, if not of the validity of his cures, at least of his skill. As far as you can observe, everything which he does appears to be above-board, and you will notice nothing which might help you to de-tect fraud" (1937:232–33).

He is so busy looking for concealed trickery, he doesn't realize that he might be a privileged witness of the skilled revelation of such and that the secret of the secret is that there is none or, rather, that the secret is a public secret, being that which is generally known but cannot generally be articulated. This is not a question of seeing more or seeing less or seeing behind the skin of appearance. Instead it turns on seeing how one is seeing. Whatever magic is, it must also involve this turn within the known unknown and what this turn turns on, namely, a new attitude toward skin.

There are, however, by EP's reckoning, three ways by which faith manages to live with and overcome skepticism concerning witch doctors. One is what was noted by E.B. Tylor by way of probabilities wherein one says that even though most doctors are fake, there are some who are not, and it is often the case, says EP, that a Zande never knows whether any particular doctor is a cheat or not and hence faith in any particular practitioner is tempered by skepticism. There is, in other words, a rock-steady ideal of the truly endowed witch doctor who can divine and cure the evil effects of witches, and now and again the ideal is actualized despite the fact that many, probably the great majority, of practitioners are faking it. Let it be noted that the probability of the ideal being actualized increases the farther you go from home; the magic of the Other is more truly magical, and faith lies in distance and hence difference.

The second modality wherein faith triumphs is by way of substances, of which there are two: herbal medicines; and the human body, as with the body of the witch, inheritor of witchcraft substance, *mangu*, and as with the witch doctor's medicine-laden body in motion, dancing the questions.[27]

It is deferment that these apparently dissimilar explanations for the coexistence of faith with skepticism have in common, a continuous and relentless deferral—a position and flow of intellection that stands in marked contrast to the driving of the wedge, a driving itself driven by the quest for the catharsis of the triumphant revelation of the secret and of the supposed "principles" hidden behind the social world's facade. The explanation through probabilities and the logic of the particular versus the general in its very quality of being tautologous is by definition a deferral, referring us back to where we started in the middle of the problem of magic's truth, which is a truth continuously questioning its own veracity of being. Circular reasoning and doublings back are the movements of intellection here, not the wedge. Deferral also lies here in the power of the "stranger effect," meaning that truth lies in a never attainable beyond and that cheating is merely the continuous and expected prelude to the mere possibility of authenticity, for behind this cheat stands the receding shadow of the real in all its perfection, but it is strange and never homely or destined for homeliness for all of that. Authenticity is that beyond that is permanently below the horizon of being.

As for medicines, in many ways the bedrock of the entire system of witch doctoring, subject to careful instruction over years of training and to much secrecy as well, deferral could not be more obvious on account of the massive, world-consuming tautology on which the medicines rest; namely, that not only do they serve as the basis for faith in witch doctoring, as EP's text tirelessly informs us, but the medicines are themselves the quintessence of magical power, and so we end up with no end in sight but that of tracing an endless circle in which magic explains magic. It is medicine that ensures magical power, as in accuracy of divination. "Thus my old friend Ongosi used to tell me," the anthropologist informs us, that "most of what the witchdoctors told their audiences was just *bera*, just 'supposition': they think out what is the most likely cause of any trouble, and put it forward, in the guise of an inspired oracle, as a likely guess, but it is not *sangba ngua*, the words of medicine, i.e. it is not derived from the medicines they have eaten" (1937:184).

To become a witch doctor, one must learn the medicines and partake in the communal meal thereof with other doctors as well as be taken to the source stream in the watershed of the Nile and Congo rivers, where, in caves, some of the more powerful plants are to be found. There are many magical things about medicine, beginning with the fact that medicine connects the interiority of the body with exterior substance; indeed it is with medicine that the very force of corporeality and metonymy—as opposed to metaphor—is best established, medicines being the fluid flow by which the exterior penetrates the interior to fundamentally empower the soul of the doctor-in-training.

The novice must hold his face in the steam of the cooking pot but with his eyes open so that the medicines will eventually allow him to see witches and witchcraft. The medicines are served in a highly ritualistic way, with the server offering the spoonful of medicine from the cooking pot to the mouth of one man, only to quickly remove it as he goes to swallow it by offering it to another. Incisions are made on the chest, above the shoulder blades, and on the wrists and face, and medicine is rubbed in (1937:210–11). The medicines are spoken to as they are being cooked and as they are rubbed into the novice's body. As soon as a novice has eaten medicine, he begins to dance.

Medicine must be paid for; otherwise it may not work, and payment must be made in sight of the medicine. "Purchase is part of the ritual conditioning of the magic which gives it potency," we are told, and this seems to imply some almost humanlike mentation and capacity for retribution on the part of the medicine itself, as much as of a dissatisfied vendor. Evans-Pritchard tells us of a witch doctor placing money—an Egyptian piaster—of his own on the ground when treating a patient, explaining "that it would be a bad thing if the medicine did not observe a fee, for it might lose its potency" (1937:209). At one point, EP refers to this exchange as a gift.

If angered, a witch doctor can use magic to remove the magic of the medicine he has sold to a novice by taking a forest creeper and attaching it to the top of a flexible stick stuck in the ground to form a sort of bowstring, to which he brings a few drops of the magic of thunder such that the medicine will roar and sunder the creeper, the top half flying on high, the lower staying in the earth. As the top half flies, so the medicine flies out of the novice (1937:213–14). It is of some importance that this is one of the very few instances of Lévi-Straussian metaphoric or Structuralist magic, or of Tambiah's analogic formulas, present in the magic of witch doctoring. By far the bulk of the instances supplied in this long text referring to witch doctors are, to the contrary, metonymic and what we might call visceral and concern flows and interruptions to flows of physical connectedness.[28]

In any event, it cannot be gainsaid that here we have anything but profoundly powerful instances of magic explaining magic in a circular, albeit staggered, manner and that this is the movement of deferral par excellence, in which the very idea of a secret behind a facade is not just plain silly but sign of another sort of philosophic despair, even illness, that we have to associate with the will to knowledge.

Nowhere does this question of deferral intrinsic to the mix required of faith and skepticism find more dramatic epistemological expression than in the witch doctors' séance of divination. "A witch-doctor does not only divine with his lips, but with his whole body. He dances the questions which are put to him," states the anthropologist in what must be the most exquisite description of dance in anthropological writing, comparable to those of Maya Deren (Deren 1970; Evans-Pritchard 1937:154–82).

He dances the questions. His body moves back and forth in the semicircle bounded by the witch doctors' upturned horns filled with medicines. He kicks up his leg if annoyed by the slackness of the chorus of young boys and may shoot black beetles into them. The spectators throw their questions about what aspects of the witchcraft bother them. Back and forth, question and answer, another circle is being traced as the doctor leaps and swirls through the heat of the day for hours on end as the answer is ever more refined through clever elimination of alternatives and leaps of intuition. Gongs and drums resound. Back and forth go the questions and the answers as the public secrets of envy and resentment are aired in this flurry and fury of intellect and bodies in motion.

The dancing is ecstatic and violent. The dancer slashes his body, and blood flows. Saliva froths around the lips. The medicines in the body are activated by the dance, just as the medicines in their turn activate dancing, these medicines of divination. When a question is put to a particular doctor, he responds by going up to the drummers to give a solo performance, and when he can dance no more, as if intoxicated, he shakes his hand bells to tell the drummers to cease and, his body doubled over, looks into the medicines obtained in his upturned horns on the ground and he voices his oracular reply. He dances the question, and the dancing is spectacular. "The dance of the Zande witchdoctors," writes the anthropologist, "is one of the few performances I have witnessed in Africa which really comes up to the standards of sensational journalism. It is weird and intoxicating" (Evans-Pritchard 1937:162).

Here trickery is deferred, transmuted into theater where theater meets the magic—the weirdness and intoxication—of a ritual. The various dichotomies of trick and technique, intellect and intuition, secrecy and public secrecy, are deferred by a series of other epistemic efficacies given in a body dancing the question under an open sky. This is most definitely neither a question of replacing mind by body nor of sense by the senses but of giving to the skilled revelation of skilled concealment a density and fluidity almost sufficient to dispel the craving for certainty that secrecy inspires. It is this revelation of the already known, the public secret, that the witch doctor dances in his dance of faith and skepticism.

And while the secret magnifies reality and creates a vivid sense of mysterious other worlds of magic and witchcraft, sorcery and religion, the public secret provides the reservoir of the secret's secretion bound as that is to the skin of the secret, announcing the existence of secrecy through marvelously ritualized permutations of concealment and revelation concerning the known unknown, a species of knowledge no less political than it is mysterious, if not mystical.

This is all the more impressive in the Boas and Hunt record of the Kwak-iutl, wherein the shaman's performance of healing provides the model for the spirit helper and, so we are told, the success of this spiritual mimesis depends on the fluidity and perfection of the shaman's movements. That these movements are tricks and fraudulent seems common knowledge and a most powerful instance not only of the public secret but of that most elusive trick of all, the magic of mimesis itself—at heart, a fraud, yet most necessary for that ceaseless surfacing of appearances we defer to as truth.

Turning Tricks

All along I have been asking myself, what, then, is a trick? What is not a trick? What for instance is the opposite of a trick? What sort of technique is a trick? Is reality the opposite of a trick? Why would such a silly proposition seem intuitively right on? Is reality *highlighted* by trickery? I keep thinking of the way a trick highlights nature's mysteries by *defying as well as displaying* them—the trick of an acrobat or a diver performing twists and somersaults and backward flips, or a cardsharp pulling aces. I think of these tricks as requiring inordinate skill, inordinate technique, inordinate empathy with reality. Would this put the trick on a par with technology? What then of magic? Would magic then mean a supreme level of technique, so rarefied and skilled that it passes from "mere" technique to something else we might dignify as magic or even sacred—as with a musician or even a short-order cook, for example? Here magic and technique, as in scientific technique, flow into one another, magic, we might say, being the highest form of science.

Translations of quotations throughout this volume are the work of the individual chapter authors unless otherwise noted.

INTRODUCTION

The editors of this book originally intended to write this introduction together, but other commitments forced Birgit Meyer to withdraw after extensive discussions of its general argument. Birgit Meyer also provided many of the ideas formulated in the section on Max Weber. I am also indebted to Gerd Baumann, Peter Geschiere, Peter van Rooden, Patricia Spyer, and Peter van der Veer; to the participants in the seminar Magic and Modernity at the University of Wisconsin, organized by Florence Bernault; and to Vincent Crapanzano, Brad Weiss, and another (anonymous) reader at Stanford University Press for their comments on an earlier version of this text. They are, of course, not responsible for any of the book's remaining imperfections.

1. This case runs parallel to the media conspiracy in the Netherlands that, in the 1950s and 1960s, tried to cover up the scandal of the Dutch Queen Juliana's occult leanings, her pacifism, and her possible divorce from her husband, Prince Bernhard—a scandal that was also made public by the American press. The Dutch monarchy, as well, easily survived this assault on its privacy and secrecy, to the extent that the present Queen Beatrix has successfully proclaimed a moratorium on leaks to the press of the more politically unwelcome of her private opinions.

2. Cf. Cannadine 1983; I owe many of these insights to discussions with Rafael Sanchez (see Sanchez n.d.).

3. The distinction between exposure—unmasking false appearances—and revelation—uncovering a viable perception of the world—was first made by Michael Taussig during the conference on which this volume is based. The usefulness of the distinction is shown by Birgit Meyer (in this volume). Moreover, the chapter by Taussig (in this volume) makes clear how ambiguous the distinction in fact is. See also the section on Marx's theory of commodity fetishism.

4. The following section is inevitably selective and incomplete in its dealings with the history of anthropological theory; it lacks, e.g., a discussion of the work of Lévi-Strauss. My purpose is less to provide a comprehensive overview than to argue for a different perspective on the history of the anthropology of magic and witchcraft, whose thrust will, I hope, be tested against the parts of the anthropological canon that this introduction fails to discuss.

5. This conception seems to have been adopted by Benedict (1934).

6. This fusion produced, in 1875, the avatar of modern occultism, Helena Petrovna Blavatsky's Theosophical Society (Pels 2000; Washington 1993).

7. The term *occultism* was first used by the Theosophist A.P. Sinnett in 1883 (*Oxford English Dictionary*, vol. 9, 681 [1989]).

8. Frazer directly inspired William Butler Yeats's construction of Celtic magic in the context of the Order of the Golden Dawn (the most important early modern occultist organization next to Blavatsky's Theosophy; see Gould 1990); his work persuaded Margaret Murray to reinvent "witchcraft" as a secret fertility cult, and it can therefore be said to have indirectly inspired the modern Wiccan movement of Gerald Gardner (Baker 1996; Simpson 1994).

9. Again, I select "classical" British anthropology to bring out a certain tendency, well aware of less prominent but also very different approaches to magic and witchcraft in contemporary France or America (but see the later discussion of Hubert and Mauss).

10. Next to Heelas (1996), Hanegraaff has provided the most comprehensive study of the New Age to date (Hanegraaff 1996). Although providing much insight, it is kept within the sphere of the study of religion and therefore does not discuss how the anthropology of magic is related to the New Age (but see Hanegraaff 1998).

11. See Meyer (1992, 1998a, 1999a); Pels (1998b, 1999a:237ff.); Shaw (1997); Taussig (1993b, 1997); Thoden van Velzen (1995); and Wiener (1995).

12. I thank Vincent Crapanzano for pushing me to clarify this point. For some reflections on the modern notion of the occult, see Pels 2000:18–19.

13. Even more than his fellow mystery writers (discussed earlier), Dickens was heavily involved in phrenomesmerism, an important predecessor of modern occultism (Kaplan 1975; see also Peter Pels, this volume).

14. Here, one should again note the use of metaphors of scientifically imponderable entities: Durkheim's *electricity* is comparable to Frazer's *ether*, and both are comparable to the use of such metaphors by contemporary occultists and psychologists (see earlier in this chapter; and Pels, this volume).

15. The Ghost of Christmas Present shows Scrooge "great round, pot-bellied baskets of chestnuts, shaped like the waist-coats of jolly old gentlemen, lolling at the doors, and tumbling out into the street in their apoplectic opulence. There were ruddy, brown-faced, broad-girthed Spanish Onions, shining in the fatness of their growth like Spanish Friars; and winking from their shelves in wanton slyness at the girls as they went by, and glanced demurely at the hung-up mistletoe" ([1843]

1971:89–90). And so on: Dickens's language wallows in a still life of almost aggressive objects of desire, like the still lifes that have elsewhere been theorized as belonging to the world of the fetish (Foster 1993). I have discussed this in an earlier essay, on which these paragraphs draw (Pels 1998a).

16. Pietz's argument that, in Marx's view, fetishism as a functional epistemology is epitomized by the monetized transactions of financial markets (Pietz 1993:149) seems to be especially relevant in the context of present-day, globalized "casino capitalism."

17. I have discussed, in another essay, the historical provenance of Occidental object relations in general, and fetishism in particular, in terms of this ambiguity of the exposure of false appearance and the revelation of functional understandings (Pels 1998a).

18. This sequence of the exposure of commodity fetishism, subsequently reinforced by the reliance on and revelation of a fetishized commodity, exemplifies Michael Taussig's notion of the complementarity of faith and skepticism in understanding the working of magic (in this volume).

19. See Appadurai 1986:31 for references; although the Baudrillardian critique of Marx may not be completely justified (see Pietz 1993).

20. I should add that this by no means exhausts Benjamin's relevance for understanding the magic of modernity, especially in his thinking about "magical philology" and his thoughts about a miraculous, messianic temporality distinct from the "homogeneous, empty time" of progress, ideas on which I cannot elaborate in this introduction (but see the reference to the latter concept in Pels, in this volume).

21. I have considerably modified Talcott Parsons's original 1930 translation of this famous passage (Weber 1930:181–82); see later discussion in the chapter.

22. Goethe was one of those who employed the new ethnographic knowledge of shamanism, especially in his portrayal of Faust (Flaherty 1992:166ff.).

23. One might say that the term *stahlharte Gehäuse* evokes the Kafka of *Die Verwandlung* (The metamorphosis)—the story of a man who suddenly finds himself caught within the scaly body of an insect—rather than the Kafka of *Das Schloss* (The castle)—a man encaged by the bastions of bureaucracy.

24. In fact, Weber seemed to have preferred the trajectory of modernity of a predominantly Puritan country such as England to that of the Lutheranism characterizing his own.

25. It would be fascinating to research the extent to which Weber's notion of genius was indebted to German Romantic images of the "shamanistic" artist, emerging from the work of Herder and Goethe.

26. These two options also help to explain the very different receptions of Weber after World War II: on the one hand, the suspicion of German scholars, for whom the political use of *charisma* was far too reminiscent of what went wrong after the Weimar Republic; and on the other, the appreciation of U.S. modernization theorists, who only saw an optimistic belief in the possibility of institutionalizing rational authority.

27. This equally applies to notions such as witchcraft, shaman, totem, and mana but, interestingly enough, to a much lesser extent to notions such as taboo, fetish, or the occult.

CHAPTER I

1. A copy of the letter is in my possession.

2. Here, I am drawing on Jacques Derrida's (1981) concept of dissemination as scattering and dispersal. Also relevant here is Homi Bhabha's concept of hybridization. This is commonly misunderstood as mixture and fusion, but in my reading it means a contingent and contentious conjoining of incommensurable positions and knowledge.

3. This debate was cut short as, according to the text, the Christian and Muslim representatives were unwilling to pursue it to its completion, prompting Dayanand to say that he was denied consideration of the remaining questions by "the shifts and subterfuges of paid priestcraft" (Prasad 1889:209).

4. So firm was the belief in the efficacy of the sacrificial fire that when an editor of a newspaper suggested that McDuggal's powder, instead of butter, be used as a disinfectant, the Arya Samaj responded: "We pity this knowledge of the Editor with respect to the Hom [*homa*] philosophy of the Aryas. . . . We will simply ask the learned Editor to state what obnoxious gases there are in the atmosphere and how does McDuggal's powder clean the atmosphere of them. The truth is that he believes this powder to be a disinfectant at the most because it is so regarded by English Science. The ancient Scientific world with him has no existence" (*Arya Patrika* 1886:6).

5. The militant wing's argument that the nationalization of education demanded a Vedic curriculum and the description of the curriculum of the Gurukul school appear in Arya Pratinidhi Sabha 1899. See also Jones 1976:90–93, for details on the dissension in Arya Samaj.

CHAPTER 2

Research for this article was carried out in several periods between 1988 and 1993 in southern Mozambique.

1. Rui de Carvalho, "Filho por Filho," *Media Fax* (Macondo), no. 1041 (June 26, 1996). Maconde is a social group from northern Mozambique (District of Mueda, Province of Cabo Delgado). This group was strongly represented in the armed forces throughout the country (both during the liberation war and in the postindependence government).

Throughout this chapter the term *traditional* is not being used in its conventional sense. Rather, it is used to depict societies and belief systems that are not necessarily static and retrograde but in a state of constant change and adaptation to new situations.

2. Please refer to the previous note regarding the use of the term *traditional*.

The war between the government and the rebel forces started in 1977 with the creation of the Mozambique National Resistance (Renamo) by the Rhodesian Central Intelligence Organisation (CIO).

3. Samora Machel became president of Frelimo in 1969 following the death of Eduardo Mondlane, the first president and the founder of the movement. Machel proclaimed Mozambique's independence from the Portuguese in June 1975. He died in a plane crash in South Africa in 1986.

4. Communal villages (Aldeias Comunais) were established with communal modes of production and were aimed at a socialist development of the rural areas. This program has been criticized by several authors. See Geffray and Pedersen 1986; Geffray 1990; Clarence-Smith 1989.

5. Chirindja, in an interview conducted in the Locality of Munguine in April 1993. I conducted the interview in Ronga.

6. In 1992 the government promoted the establishment of the National Association of Traditional Healers, in which diviners and spirit mediums and other spiritual healers took part (Honwana 1996). Likewise, a research group to study the forms of integration of "traditional" political authorities into local government was established by the Ministry of State Administration.

7. Only in 1981 were Renamo's previously vague objectives elaborated in a manifesto and political program with its goals set out in very broad terms: basically its position was against communism and in favor of free market economic policies (Thomashausen 1983).

8. Andre Matsangaissa, Renamo's first president, died in combat. He was replaced by Afonso Dhlakama, who signed the peace accord with Frelimo in 1992.

9. Matsanga is a popular name given to Renamo soldiers. It is a short form of the name Matsangaissa, Renamo's first president.

10. I had several interviews with Sitoe in Manhiça during May and June 1993.

11. The Nguni were a dissident group of the Zulu Kingdom in Zululand (part of what is now South Africa) who migrated north. The Ndau are a group from central Mozambique and are part of the Shona-Karanga group that includes several other groups across the Zimbabwe border.

12. Tsonga is the linguistic group of southern Mozambique that comprises the Shangaan, Ronga, and Tswa groups.

13. Ngungunyane was the last Nguni king. He was defeated by the Portuguese in 1889.

14. Various authors have given attention to this issue. Sundkler (1961) and West (1975), who have studied the Zionist phenomenon in South Africa, have both detected strong similarities between the Zionist prophets and the ancestral mediums and diviners. These authors refer to analogies in the experience and training of the Zionist prophets and the mediums and diviners and to a measure of overlap in their

respective functions. Kiernan (1994) in turn argues that among the Zulu, Zionists have fused the Bible and healing into a single, coherent system of meaning. See also Comaroff 1985, on Zionist Churches in Botswana. On religious syncretism, see also Stewart and Shaw 1994.

15. As I have shown elsewhere, this is at the heart of the conflicts between the Zionists and the tinyanga (Honwana 1996).

16. Rui de Carvalho, "Filho por Filho," *Media Fax* (Macondo), no. 1041 (June 26, 1996).

CHAPTER 3

1. Originally published in the *Atlantic Monthly*, "The Coming Anarchy" has since been "translated into over a dozen languages and reprinted constantly" (Kaplan 2000:xv).

2. For accounts and analyses of the war, see Abdullah and Bangura 1997; Hirsch 2001; Reno 1998:113–45; P. Richards 1996; Zack-Williams 1997.

3. Many of those who write about the civil war in Liberia, for instance, make much of Liberia's long historical connections with the United States—not, usually, in order to explain the conflict's cold war roots but to underscore the journalist's own sense of the incongruous.

4. It should be noted, however, that Goldberg's blanket statement that "the terrorists of the Revolutionary United Front are the bad guys" (2000:13) criminalizes the thousands of children and teenagers who have been targeted as fighters, abducted, traumatized, and drugged by the RUF leadership and who constitute most of the RUF's fighting force (Sommers 1997). It also fails to confront the fact that for the kamajos, "doing what they can to stop [the RUF]" (ibid.) has included summarily executing children and youths whom they arbitrarily suspect of being RUF fighters.

5. For a similar conjunction of these representations, see the following Listserv item:

Liberian General Dressed to Kill.

The Defense Intelligence Agency writes that an unusual leader has risen up among the warring factions in Liberia's endless slaughter. He's "Gen. 'Butt Naked,'" the DIA says in a memo to the Senate Foreign Relations Committee. "Gen. 'Butt Naked' is a prominent ULIMO-Krahn commander who led several offensive skirmishes against the NPFL in Monrovia during the April-May fighting," the DIA says. "His 'nom de guerre' probably comes from his propensity for fighting naked. He probably believes that fighting in this manner terrorizes the enemy and brings good luck or, in the Liberian context, good 'juju.' Belief in magic is widespread in Liberia and accounts for some of the outrageous behavior of Liberian fighters of all factions." . . .

Meanwhile, Hill folks were wondering where the good general pins his ribbons. (*Observer News*, posted on "Leonenet," December 8, 1996)

6. John Hirsch, the U.S. ambassador to Sierra Leone from 1995 to 1998, however, has spoken out in criticism of "The Coming Anarchy" (2001:17, 105).

CHAPTER 4

I would like to thank all the participants of the Magic and Modernity conference, and particularly Birgit Meyer, Peter Pels, Gyan Prakash, and Patsy Spyer, for their contributions to my thinking here. I would also like to thank Katharine Brophy Dubois, Fernando Coronil, Monique Dubois-Dalcq, Paul Eiss, Aims McGuinness, David Pedersen, Steven Pierce, Setrak Manoukian, and Anna Wexler for their helpful comments on earlier drafts of this article. Finally, I am deeply indebted to Erol Josué, whose friendship and generosity lay its foundation.

1. See Trouillot 1995, esp. chapters 2 and 3, on the silencing of aspects of the Haitian Revolution both inside and outside of Haiti. See also Hurbon 1988; and Dayan 1995; and Buck-Morss 2000. Gilroy 1993 has argued that there is a need to rethink the history of slavery as part of "the intellectual heritage of the West as a whole" and as an integral part of the production of modernity. Such a project, he notes, requires "fresh thinking about the importance of Haiti and its revolution" (49).

2. See Geggus 2002: 81–92 for the most detailed examination of the sources surrounding the Bois-Caïman ceremony; see also Dalmas 1814; Dumesle 1824: 88; Rachel Beauvoir-Dominique, "Investigations autour du site du Bois Caiman," http://www .anvcities.com/koridobaskya (2002).

3. Such stipulations were already present in the Code Noir of 1686, which made *attroupments* of slaves illegal, especially in "isolated places"; see Sala-Moulins 1988. See Desmangles 1992 for a description of colonial policy and Vodou in colonial Saint Domingue.

4. In 1891, Leon Emmanuel lamented the lack of proper archives as a source for Haiti's exploitation by other countries. "Our lost treaties, exiled in the hands of a few old collectioners greedy for documents, rarely see the light of day." This absence undermined the diplomatic power of Haiti, he argued, suggesting powerfully the connection between the lack of archives and the lack of political power. See his preface to Leger 1891:A.

5. One British writer used Madiou's work (which he had bought in Haiti) to laud Toussaint-Louverture and the Haitian Revolution but also pleaded for Christian missionizing of the Haitians, who, he said, practiced "the idolatrous dances of their ancestors" in "horrid," serpent-worshiping ceremonies. See C.M.B. 1850:125–27.

6. When the Second Republic was installed in France, one of its first actions was to abolish slavery. This was accomplished through the intervention of the abolitionist Victor Schoelcher, who convinced the minister Arago of the necessity of emancipation by reminding him of the history of the revolts of the 1790s and arguing that if slavery were not abolished, the slaves would rise up once again. See Schmidt 1994.

7. The same language, and the same correlation, would once again emerge in the 1980s, as Haitians were pegged as the source for AIDS. See Farmer 1992 and Dubois 1996.

8. See Chef of the Gendarme D'Haïti, General Correspondence, RG 127, Entry 170, Box 2, Folder 86, National Archives, Washington, D.C. On the repression of "Voodooism," see Entry 166, Box 2, Folder 18. On Batraville, see Gaillard 1983.

9. The information about Josué's life, and his quotations, are drawn from a series of interviews done with him in Paris in 1996 and 1997.

10. On the dechoukaj, see Dayan 1988; Mintz and Trouillot 1995. Note that Duvalier's absorption of the networks of Vodou was only one part of the "total absorption of civil society," including the Catholic and Protestant Churches, which opportunistically encouraged the murders of priests after the fall of the regime. Laennec Hurbon has explored in detail the complex ways in which practitioners of Vodou relate to "magic" and "sorcery," which are often seen as a kind of "other" within the religion. The use of "black magic" for individual ends is itself often condemned by those who practice Vodou, who see it as an instrumentalization of the power granted by the lwa. See Hurbon 1988. Hurbon has also suggested compellingly that the practice of magic within Vodou develops in relationship to the stereotypes, both within Haitian society and beyond, about the religion, as visions of its "dark" possibilities become incorporated into certain practices. He has also noted some of the economic and social causes and effects, notably among the urban middle and upper classes, of the instrumentalization of Vodou. See Hurbon 1995.

11. Deren argues that the available descriptions of the Bois-Caïman ceremony, notably the sacrifice of a black pig, mark it as a Petro ceremony. Deren 1953:62. Metraux 1959 also notes the New World origins of Petwo and the presence of revolutionary slogans in songs. Brown 1991, 252–57, addresses the ways the function and performance of possession responded to New World conditions.

12. Stoller 1995 has argued that the Hauka possession rituals of Niger also carry a "cultural" and "embodied" memory of the history of colonialism; Stoller pursues questions raised earlier by Taussig 1987, which suggests that rituals of healing could be a realm through which the violent history of colonization was remembered and reworked.

CHAPTER 5

Research for this paper at the Algemeen Rijksarchief in the Hague and the Koninklijk Instituut voor Taal-, Land-, en Volkenkunde in Leiden was funded by the National Endowment for the Humanities, the Southeast Asia Council's Small Grants Program, and the Luce Foundation. I also thank Cornell University's Southeast Asia Program and the International Institute for Asian Studies for institutional support, and the University of North Carolina at Chapel Hill's University Research Council for a grant that funded a research assistant. For inspiring discussion and critical readings, I particularly want to thank James Hevia, Sylvia Hoffert, Carol Mavor, Laurie Maffly-Kipp, Birgit Meyer, Peter Pels, Sarah Shields, and Patsy Spyer.

1. For excellent discussions of the novel, see Beekman 1996; Nieuwenhuys 1978; and Pattynama 1998.

2. Van Dale's authoritative Dutch-English Dictionary (*Groot woordenboek Neder-lands-Engels* [1986, 1991]:1281) actually lists the phrase *stille kracht* under *stil* but translates it as "silent or invisible forces."

3. Like the author of a series of magazine articles on "Magic in the Indies" (Hitzka 1930), I use the term *magic*, in speaking of colonial Indonesia, as a virtual synonym for "hidden force," to refer to a multitude of practices involving what Europeans judged to be beliefs in the supernatural—various forms of sorcery, the possession of amulets, divination and fortune-telling, involvement with spirits, and so forth.

4. There were, of course, some differences too. If colonial-era anthropologists writing about magic invariably find it necessary at some point to mention the falsity of magical belief, they differ from other authorities writing about native practices in their efforts to account for the sometimes surprising efficacy of magic. In addition, they seek to explain why, if based on error, magic has persisted—and why such practices should continue.

5. If, as many have argued, anthropology was ineluctably implicated in colonial power (Asad 1973; Stocking 1991; Pels and Salemink 1994), the relationship between ethnological knowledge and administration was much more overt in the Netherlands Indies (Ellen 1976; Fasseur 1993). Moreover, a number of the best-known works of Dutch ethnology were written by men who developed their theories while engaged in more practical work in the colonies (such as A. Nieuwenhuis, a medical doctor, and A. Kruyt, a missionary).

6. My source for what follows is mail rapport 514, in V. 13 April 1922 No. 119, Ministry of Colonies archives, Algemeen Rijksarchief, the Hague. At the time of these events, Damsté had served in the colonial administration for twenty-seven years and was two years away from his retirement, at the age of forty-nine. Kuys, on the other hand, had entered the civil service only three years before.

7. Most commonly, balians do heal, though in a broader sense than biomedical doctors do because their purview includes disturbances in social relations and the natural world, as well as individual afflictions. Some balians specialize in childbirth, others in finding lost objects, still others in mediating conversations with the dead. Many Balinese think that balians have the ability to harm as well as cure, and they may be hired for that end too. To provide their services, some balians go into a trance; others consult texts and mix herbal remedies. For more on balians see Connor, Asch, and Asch 1986; and Lovric 1987.

8. This was all Damsté said about the letter in his report. However, he included a copy in the dossier he sent to the governor-general, which was forwarded in turn to the minister of colonies. The letter itself (written in a dense Malay, the language colonizers

and colonized used to communicate with one another) is rather more complicated than Damsté's summary suggests. It simultaneously deploys images of disorder that are calculated to arouse official attention (and that suggest that its writer appreciated the value of some official visions), and it critiques Nang Mukanis's claims from a perspective located within Balinese discourses about power. (For more on these, see Wiener 1995; see also Note 22, below.) Damsté's interpretation of the letter clearly plays a role in his subsequent actions, although his reading tends to elide ways in which his point of view and the writer's might not coincide.

9. Damsté evidently took pride in his handling of this episode. In 1924 he published a version of his report as one of a series of short pieces detailing matters relevant to the administration of Bali or addressing Balinese cultural affairs (Damsté 1924).

10. The colonial state's position on sorcery has had significant consequences for both anthropologists (Ellen 1993) and present-day Indonesians (Slaats and Portier 1993).

11. See Hekmeijer 1918:articles 545, 546, 547; see also Lemaire (1934), who compares the Netherlands Indies Penal Code with that of the Netherlands, which lacks these articles, and provides some background on the grounds for their addition. Apart from the provisions just discussed (which were the most heavily punished), these articles also prohibited wearing amulets when called to testify as a witness in a court of law, because amulets could nullify the dire consequences of violating oaths, which were administered by religious authorities. In addition, they outlawed fortune-telling and dream interpretation. Enforcement of this last provision appears to have been sporadic, since fortune-telling was a widespread leisure activity, even among Eurasians and Europeans. Only if such practices led to unrest or were pursued as a profession for profit did the government bother interfering with them.

12. For instance, he noted, amulets played a major role in burglary. Professional thieves made amulets from the dirt and a piece of shroud from certain graves in order to break into houses while people slept. Others also implicated amulets in crimes of this sort; a police museum in Surabaya housed a collection of such amulets (Meijer 1935).

13. Kohlbrugge, who was in the Indies for eleven years before and after the turn of the twentieth century, asserts that various uprisings in Java during that time could be traced to persons trafficking in esoteric knowledges and amulets (1907:32–35). According to Soeriokoesoemo (1919:161), both administrators and journalists tended to favor such ideas.

14. Apparently, the haji's disaffection began when he refused to sell a substantial portion of his rice crop to the government (which was attempting to stockpile rice in the event of shortages) and was informed that if he didn't comply, it would be taken by force. Short accounts of the Garut affair appear in several discussions of the growth of Indonesian nationalism, primarily because investigators briefly entertained the idea that the haji might have been involved in a conspiracy organized by the na-

tionalist organization Sarekat Islam. See, e.g., Shiraishi 1990:113–14; and van de Doel 1994:380–81. Such sources pay little attention to the government's inquiry into amulet sellers, including one supposedly delegated by Sarekat Islam. By contrast, amulets and those who sold them received considerable attention in contemporary colonial newspapers, such as the *Bataviaasch Nieuwsblad* (July 1919) and the *Soerabaiasch Nieuwsblad* (July 8–August 18, 1919). Soeriokoesoemo, a leader of the short-lived Javanese Nationalist movement, wrote a brilliant response to the Garut affair, in which he presents the government's obsessions with the danger of amulets as a kind of fetishism, suggesting that the authorities, not the Javanese, are the ones "infected" with the "amulet-bacillus" (1919). He argues that officials should not focus on the invulnerability conferred by amulets (which, in any event, are a feature of Javanese life) but on the conditions under which people live if they want to explain disaffection. See Sears for more on Soeriokoesoemo, who she claims tended to mediate between Javanese custom and Dutch contention (1996:139–43, 157–63).

15. Furnivall (1944:229–428) provides an extended discussion, van de Doel (1994:164–71) a more recent one. Among other effects, the policy resulted in the expansion of the colonial state throughout the archipelago, often justified as protecting local populations from their own ruling classes. The new policy had the combined support of church groups and capitalists (who saw in it opportunities for developing new markets). Everyone dates the inception of the policy to an influential article that appeared in 1899; scholars disagree, however, in specifying precisely when the Ethical Policy ceased to inform administrative decisions (see Ricklefs 1993:161–62), and the policy itself always was contested.

16. This is all the more the case because some influential "ethicists" argued that providing native elites with a formal education would best develop the population as a whole, allowing advanced ideas to trickle down to the masses from above.

17. Consider anthropological attempts to distinguish among magic, religion, and science. By proclaiming magic "false science," as early anthropologists such as Frazer did, hence distinguishing magic from science as false from true, anthropologists opened the possibility of finding disconcerting similarities between them—and ultimately of relativizing science.

18. The two divides that interest Latour drag with them a host of other familiar pairs—such as male vs. female, reason vs. emotion—that also played a part in discourses about magic in the Indies. This is too complex a subject to do justice to it here, though I allude to it briefly in my concluding remarks. For more on gender in Indies magic, see Wiener n.d. and Beekman 1996. Here let me note that some administrators blamed the persistence of magical beliefs among native members of the colonial civil service, and within the native population generally, on the wives of native officials, "who day in, day out consult their books, their spirits, their dukuns [healer/magicians], their dice and cards and give a bad example with respect to this to the lower classes" (Jasper 1904:132). Recall the wives of the district head and judiciary member encountered by Kuys in Nang Mukanis's house.

19. For this phrase, see T. Richards 1993. In thinking about the archive, I am indebted to conversations with James Hevia. See also Hevia 1998.

20. His preoccupations with such systems suggests that Damsté had an agenda beyond that of informing the governor-general about some unpleasantness in Bali, namely, to convey the need for improvement.

21. The letter irresistibly recalls a host of Indies novels where anonymous missives serve as the medium through which secrets are brought to the attention of principals, including *The Hidden Force* (Couperus [1900] 1985). In the latter, the main character, Resident van Oudijck, learns that he may have a son by a youthful indiscretion with a Javanese woman.

22. As suggested above, this letter provides insight into new Balinese subject positions produced through colonial rule. Internal evidence suggests its author was an aristocrat who, like one of the Balinese officials, had attended Dutch schools. What seems to have alarmed him about Nang Mukanis, however, was the healer's claim that he was a seat for divinity, Betara Widhi. This was indeed a bold—even dangerously arrogant—claim, within the framework of both prevailing and emergent theological positions. To analyze this intriguing document in the detail it deserves would, however, take me too far afield.

23. Since in this instance purification involved iconoclasm, it raises questions about the role missionaries played in shaping such discourses and practices, especially given the well-known hostility to "magic" in the Protestant denominations that predominated in the Netherlands. This is difficult to determine, however. Missionaries were not as central to the civilizing mission of the Dutch in the Indies as they were in other colonial formations. Even though Dutch religious parties were important in electing the coalition that instituted the Ethical Policy, many Indies policy makers maintained that missionaries could cause political unrest, particularly in Muslim areas, and also—for historical and political reasons—in Bali. Throughout the colonial period the government primarily licensed missionary work in "heathen" or "animistic" areas in the so-called outer territories, those regions of the archipelago beyond Java and Bali, although there was some activity in these core areas as well (Kipp 1990; Furnivall 1944:218–20, 378–81). On the whole, secularism dominated colonial policy and practice. Apart from official policy, the sense one gets in reading about colonial Indonesia is that most Europeans resident there, including administrators, were not especially observant Christians. Missionaries did, however, make important contributions to ethnography. Such works (e.g., Poensen's 1879 article on amulets) evince little trace of an explicitly theological hostility to "superstition" or magic, although their tone may be amused and mocking, rather like Damsté's.

24. *De Locomotief* May 22, 1908.

25. Perhaps Indonesians sometimes engaged in their own demonstrations of power. In an article concerning the audacious theft of curtains from the home of the resident of Madiun, Onghokham (1978) fails to mention the use professional Javanese thieves made of amulets and spells. This was, however, common knowledge

among Javanese and no doubt contributed to the impression this incident made on them, especially because many wondered if Europeans could be affected by Javanese magic (see Habbema 1919:314).

26. No Balinese, incidentally, would see in the burning of these decorative paraphernalia anything but an act of shockingly malign destruction. From a Balinese perspective, only by burning his house shrines (which would not be in the middle of a compound) could the Dutch destroy the sources of Nang Mukanis's power.

27. This is not to deny that some Indonesians were indeed disenchanted; some were, which was in part why they regarded themselves as "modern" (see Anderson 1990; Shiraishi 1990). But isolated pedagogic performances had little to do with this. Graduating from Dutch institutions of higher education was more germane, though by no means conclusive.

28. Now that Bali is the center of extensive tourist and handicraft export industries, and increasing numbers of Australians, Americans, and Europeans spend time there (or even set up residence), it has become an equally productive object of narratives of magic and mysticism. See, e.g., Iyer 1988:56–58. Such processes began between the wars, when international tourists first invented Bali as an island paradise. Filmmakers in the 1920s even produced a film about Bali entitled *Goona-Goona*, although this film represents sorcery as a purely Balinese affair rather than something that might potentially affect non-Balinese as well. More to the point is a novel by Fabricius (1948), based on a visit to Bali in the 1930s. It is, however, written from the perspective of a Dutchman born in Java.

29. For more on guna-guna tales in the Netherlands Indies, see Wiener n.d.

30. What brought this story to public attention was an account published in the premier Orientalist journal in 1872, by General J. van Swieten, at the time a member of Parliament. (He was shortly to be recalled to active duty to command the Netherlands Indies Army in the interminable Aceh War.) Van Swieten begins his contribution by noting that a recent performance in the Hague by Herne and Williams—well-known British spiritualists—had recalled the 1831 incident to the minds of a number of former colonial agents. Their mistaken impressions of that event, says Van Swieten, moved him to publish what he knew of it, in an effort to set the record straight (1872:492).

31. In fact, Jasper reviewed *The Hidden Force*. Not surprisingly, he thought the book excessively imaginative, and he glossed what Couperus terms "the hidden force" as "fanaticism among natives." Nonetheless, he found much to admire in the novel, ranging from descriptions of life in the Indies to the character of the Resident, though he found it implausible that such a man would meet the fate that Couperus describes (Jasper 1901).

32. Note, of course, that such complaints and the distinctions on which they were based themselves belonged to the infamous process of "inventing" native tradition.

33. Unlike the colonial terrors and fantasies associated with South American Indians (Taussig 1987), the threat most present in the colonial imagination of the Indies

was not the "wild men" (of Borneo, e.g., though these are regarded as sources of danger and cure by their Muslim neighbors [Tsing 1994]). Instead, Dutch colonizers were anxious about those Indonesians most intimately involved in their lives, those whose nearness and familiarity should have made them trustworthy: lovers, servants, and aristocrats incorporated into the state apparatus through the Native Civil Service.

34. A remarkable number of writers quote this line from Shakespeare's *Hamlet*. For an example of such an argument (and of such quoting) see Kalff 1925.

35. *Soerabaiasch Nieuwsblad*, no. 149 (June 29, 1916):section 2, 2. The passage is quoted in a magazine article about hidden force appearing later that same year, by an author who signed himself "Converted" (Bekeerde 1916:714–15).

36. For a "low culture" example from around the time of Nang Mukanis's arrest, see Van Wermeskerken (1922). The title of his novel, translated into English, is *Haunted House: A Novel of Hidden Force and Indies Superstition*. For discussions of some of this literature, see Nieuwenhuys 1978 and Beekman 1996.

37. Kohlbrugge (1907) offers a wealth of such explanations: e.g., fears about the use of sorcery by discarded mistresses were really expressions of unacknowledged guilt over violating one's own moral code.

38. According to Kerremans (1923), the impressionable nature of women put them particularly at risk.

39. Of course there was more than climate involved in theories about the dangers European rationality faced in the Indies. One vector for the transmission of "native mentalities" affected mainly European children—namely, Indonesian servants, especially nursemaids, who passed along tales about spirits and who often practiced magic. This too is a theme that concerned Dr. Kohlbrugge. See also Stoler 1995.

40. Hybridization, of course, worked in the other direction as well. Some Indonesian intellectuals educated in colonial schools made their own use of some of this Indies culture.

41. See, e.g., the memoirs of Romein-Verschoor (1971:64–66). See also Peter Pels (this vol.) on Alfred Wallace.

42. Significantly, however, hidden forces only worked on colonizers as individuals and in spaces removed from the networks (the imperial archive) that provided the grounds for their self-confidence about reality and truth.

CHAPTER 6

Many thanks first of all to Peter Schrader, who suggested the title (which posed a real challenge for me because I liked it so much while it proved quite hard to fill it in), and second to Achille Mbembe, who used his usual *nganga* talents to point out which books to pick from the vast literature on Clinton and how to relate them to the secrets of African politics. Furthermore, I would like to thank Ralph Austen, Misty Bastian, Paul Brass, Bambi Ceuppens, Mamadou Diouf, Cyprian Fisiy, Pierre Halen, Janet Roitman, and Patricia Spyer for their suggestions, which were, as the subject requires, both unsettling and stimulating. Moreover, I profited greatly from the occasion to discuss a first draft at a seminar of the CERI (Centre d'études et des recherches internationales, Paris), where notably the discussant, Denis Lacorne, and—*évidemment*—Jean-François Bayart gave most enlightening comments. And, of course, special thanks to the editors of the present volume, Birgit Meyer and Peter Pels (also the organizers of the conference where this paper was subsequently presented), for their visionary comments.

1. As we—like many others—emphasized in earlier publications (Fisiy and Geschiere 1990, 1991), Western terms such as *witchcraft, sorcery*, or *sorcellerie* are highly unfortunate translations of African concepts with a much broader spectrum of meanings. The problem is especially that these Western terms have a predominantly pejorative tenor, whereas the corresponding African notions often refer to both negative and positive aspects of the occult. A more neutral term such as *occult forces* might therefore be preferable. However, terms such as *witchcraft* or *sorcery* have been appropriated on an ever wider scale by the African public. Nowadays, it is in these terms that the general fear for the occult is discussed in the press, on the radio, on TV, or through the grapevine. This is why Fisiy and I have chosen to maintain these terms even though their translations—as is true for most translation in this field (see Pels 1999a; and Meyer 1999a)—have most confusing effects.

2. See Bayart 1996:134–35; many more references could be added (see, for instance, particularly striking ones on President Bongo of Gabon in Cinnamon 1996; and Péan 1983); see more generally Geschiere 1997. Cf. also Achille Mbembe's recent and visionary *On the Postcolony* (2001).

3. As work along similar lines by Pierre Halen (1994) convincingly shows, such terminological convergence is never gratuitous: it is especially in the use of such key words that the ambiguities of seemingly self-evident perspectives come to the fore.

4. The conference was on recent transitions in African politics (Violence and the Politics of Participation—organized by Mamadou Diouf, Catherine Newbury, and Pearl Robinson). The fact that Brass, as an expert on ethnicity and communalism, notably in South Asia, was a relative outsider to this field made his comments all the more stimulating.

5. Yet, Malinowski ([1935] 1966) pointed already in the 1930s to similar instances of convergence, when he emphasized that "magic" was not an earlier stage in development but rather a way of thinking (or rather of doing) present in all societies. Significantly, he mentioned advertisement and politics—that is, the areas that later on were to become central to the publicity industry—as fields where magic is of prime importance in Western society. It is also striking that, nowadays, the popular press in the West has no difficulty at all in identifying "spin doctors" as "witch doctors." On the contrary, some journalists seem to relish doing so: consider, for instance, an article in the respectable British newspaper *The Independent* (*Independent on Sunday*, "Real Life" [April 4, 1998:3] on Michael Sitrick, who describes himself as an expert in "the art of spin": "In LA they call Michael Sitrick the leading witch doctor in the hot new

Hollywood industry of crisis management. Sitrick's boutique, or image rescue firm, operates as a rehab [rehabilitation] clinic for the reputation of stars; and like any good California rehab, the treatment is reassuringly expensive." The rest of the article is about Sitrick's advice on how George Michael should have handled his "coming out" on CNN-TV after he had been caught in the act with another man at a public toilet (with thanks to Bambi Ceuppens for sending me this article). In many similar articles in the press on the cutting edge of the publicity industry, references to witchcraft or magic seem to come as something more or less self-evident.

6. See the book by his private *astrologue* (astrologist), Elizabeth Teissier, *Sous le signe de Mitterand* (1997) and many articles on Jacques Pilhan, *le montreur d'ours* (the "bear-leader"), first of Mitterand and then of Jacques Chirac (see, for instance, *Libération* July 3, 1998). Cf. also Mitterand's confidences in Benamou (1996—notably 99).

7. Good examples of such "Othering," creating an implicit and all the more comfortable contrast with Western politics, are the recent articles and commentaries on African politics in the Dutch quality journal *NRC Handelsblad* by Kurt Lindijer. Cf., for instance, the article and the commentary on developments in Nigeria after dictator General Sani Abacha's death (NRC Handelsblad [July 9, 1998]:1 and 7); African politics are described as being dominated by "autocrats, in the tradition of former tribal chiefs" (but can Hausa history be equated with "tribal chiefs"?); this is related to other characteristics: politics are about persons, not issues, and "what counts in a land like Nigeria is not what you are but what you seem to be." This is exactly why the role of spin doctors is becoming ever more important in Western democracies. Precisely because the contrast with "our way of doing things" remains implicit, it appears to be all the more self-evident—with thanks to Peter Pels for drawing my attention to this article.

8. The two Mimbang men were not from the same family. In the early 1960s, François Mimbang had to step aside to give the mayorship to Pierre Mimbang. Since then, open hostilities have existed between these two as well.

9. This Bantu area of closely related languages stretches roughly from the Douala-Mombasa line to the southern tip of the continent.

10. A striking aspect of the role of witchcraft in more modern sectors—in politics but also in sports or in modern forms of entrepreneurship—is that men seem to acquire a dominant role. Although in the local setting, women play at least as important a role in witchcraft rumors as men—as the Maka of southeast Cameroon say, "women were the first to go out" (that is, leave their bodies at night to fly away to meet their fellow witches)—women seem to become marginalized when new forms of power or riches are at stake. The same applies to the nganga. Locally, there are at least as many female as male nganga. But, the more modern type of nganga, which emerged especially over the last decades—for instance, the nganga who are performing as expert witnesses before the state tribunal or who are consulted by modern politicians or businessmen—are mostly men (see Geschiere 1997). The world of the nganga is becoming a men's world, just as is African politics in general. This is why I will speak in the rest of this section of nganga as men ("him" and "his").

11. Cf. Geschiere 1997; Meyer 1999a; de Rosny 1981; and many other authors on the close relationship between witchcraft and kinship in most parts of Africa.

12. Many nganga also exhibit transvestite traits; again this seems to emphasize that they are beyond "normal" oppositions (such as the one between men and women).

13. Cf. Taussig's seminal characterization of witchcraft as a "public secret" (Taussig 1993b:85; see also Ashforth 1996 and Ferme 1999a and 1999b; and, of course, Simmel 1923). I will return to this very important aspect below.

14. Similar stories about the increasingly high profile of *inyanga* or *sangoma* come from South Africa (see, for instance, the *Weekly Mail* [April 16 to 23, 1992]; and more generally Ashforth 1996 and Niehaus 2001).

15. See, for instance, Archives Nationales Yaounde, files 2 AC 906 and 7 (from 1928) and 2 AC 898 (from 1950) for debates on this issue in French Cameroon; and National Archives, Buea, file Aa 1934 (16) for similar discussions in Nigeria and British Cameroon; see also Fields 1982.

16. Cf. Alisdair MacIntyre's irreverent but highly effective attack (1981:74–87) on the claim to "scientific expertise" by "managers" (whom MacIntyre characterizes as "the dominant figures of the contemporary scene"—74). In his view, the social sciences' claim to produce "law-like generalization with strong predictive power" is based on a philosophical confusion with a long history. However, if this claim is unfounded, the very idea that there can be a managerial science is clearly wrong (MacIntyre even speaks of a "deceptive and self-deceptive histrionic mimicry of such [that is, natural sciences'] technology" [85]). Hence there is good reason to distrust any claim to scientific expertise of any manager (many thanks to Vincent Crapanzano for drawing my attention to MacIntyre's brilliant analysis of modern "experts").

17. Morris's relation with the prostitute may have been so stable because, as other sources maintain, Morris was in for special sexual activities, notably of the S and M variety, in which the prostitute was specialized (thanks to Denis Lacorne for bringing up this point).

18. Apparently, to Morris there is a strict opposition between "spinning" and "being scientific." Interestingly, Sitrick, the "leading Hollywood witch doctor" with his "rehab clinic" referred to before, makes the caesura somewhere else; to him "the art of spin is not an arcane science or a black art. . . . It is, rather, a rational discipline" (*Independent on Sunday* [April 19, 1998:2]). For Morris, who is certainly identified as a spin doctor by the press, spinning seems to be close to magic, whereas for Sitrick it is its opposite. Apparently the conceptual oppositions in this field are open for discussion.

19. There is the same ambivalence in the book, published three years later, by George Stephanopoulos (Morris's great rival for Clinton's favors). Stephanopoulos's book (1999), written after the start of the Lewinski affair, is pervaded by deep disappointment with Clinton, but it is also an attempt to get even with Morris. Even so, the book confirms the core of Morris's story (for instance, the idea that Morris functioned far better as long as his identity remained a secret). Striking also is

Stephanopoulos's preference for magical terms to depict Morris, for instance, as "a political shaman casting a spell, enraptured by his own ecstatic dance" (360). But like Morris, Stephanopoulos seems to resent any characterization of himself as a spin doctor. The aim of his book seems to be also to provide himself with a moral perspective. Somewhat in contrast with this is his true predilection for the word *spinning*, which he uses in the most striking variations: e.g., "I couldn't . . . change the subject, or even spin myself" (79); he refers to "counterspin techniques" and "legitimate spin options." Most intriguingly, the answer to all this is for him "zen-spinning" (72)!

20. This is what makes Garry Wills in the *New York Review of Books* (1997) underline that Morris's role underwent a spectacular change after his return to the Clinton machine in 1994. In the earlier Arkansas elections, his role had been limited to campaigning (as opposed to governing). But in 1994, his contribution became much more substantial—indeed to such a degree that he participated, as Wills put it, in both campaigning and governing. Wills is clearly suggesting that in such a context, spin doctors are no longer just auxiliaries but more and more determine policy choices. Cf. the general surprise in Britain when Blair made his spin doctor a minister.

21. Ralph Austen (oral intervention at ASA panel, Columbus, 1997) doubts that polling was such a drain on Clinton's finances. (He reproached me for letting myself be "spun by Morris." But isn't there a clear parallel with witchcraft's vicious circle, mentioned above: everybody involved with spinning, even those who study it, becomes "spun," just as any dealings with witchcraft inevitably mean that you become drawn into it.) Garry Wills (in his review of Morris's book in *New York Review of Books* 1997:4) directly relates the costs of polling to Clinton's reckless campaigning for money. Cf. also what Morris himself says about this: "Clinton complained bitterly at having to raise this much money. . . . 'I can't think. I can't act. I can't do anything but go to fund raisers and shake hands. You want me to issue executive orders. I can't focus on a thing but the next fundraiser'" (1997:270).

22. In the book, it remains more or less open whether Henry is indeed giving in to Stanton (this in contrast to the film, which opts for a much more definite ending). In general, the film (by Mike Nichols) is strikingly faithful to the book: most dialogues come directly from it (only Libby's lines during her surprisingly moral outburst, just before her suicide, are mostly new, making for a sentimental and hardly credible moment in the film). Lacking, however, in the film is all the technical information about how the campaign is run, how the press is spun, etc., which makes the book so interesting. The film becomes more of a psychological drama, with the campaign an interesting background.

23. Morris 1997:6. Similarly, Jacques Pilhan, the *montreur d'ours* quoted earlier, saw no problem in working first for Mitterand and, then, for his successor, Chirac (cf. *Libération* [July 3, 1998]).

24. Cf. Stephanopoulos 1999—note 19 above—on "counter" and even "zen spinning."

25. Cf., for instance, the complaint of Gabonese peasants that their politicians should "stop killing them" with their witchcraft (Cinnamon 1996); for them, in any case, politics, witchcraft, and violence are very hard to distinguish from each other.

26. This might be directly related to the fact that researchers are increasingly in need of press coverage in order to be sure of continued funding. In the Netherlands, for instance, over the last few years, we had a series of reports that, on the basis of intricate statistics, came up with the most amazing results—for instance, that the Netherlands was the fourth most unsafe country in the world (!)—which, therefore, received broad press coverage. No doubt, it will be possible to mention scores of similar examples from other Western countries. All this clearly shows how much the wish to "score" is stimulated by the importance—in the Netherlands, but no doubt elsewhere also—that funding agencies (and especially university boards) now attach to resonance in the press.

27. Cf. what was said above on the tension between intimacy and distance in the nganga role.

28. In Morris's jargon *triangulation* means finding a third viewpoint to surpass the deadlock between Democratic and Republican positions that had led to Clinton's debacle in 1994. (In his usual euphemistic way, Morris characterizes his idea of triangulation as an attempt to "change, not to abandon, the Democratic party" [Morris 1997:80].) In this context he advocated that Clinton put ever more emphasis on (American) values in order to get rid of his leftist reputation and show that the Republicans did not have the monopoly over such values (cf. what is said in the text that follows about turning Clinton's extremist image around and placing, instead, the Republicans in the position of extremists—I owe special thanks to Denis Lacorne and Jean-François Bayart for emphasizing this aspect).

29. It would be tempting to continue the parallel and try to include also the subsequent spectacular developments around Clinton that are now known as "the Lewinski affair." Brad Weiss (one of the readers for this collection) suggested, very interestingly, that this whole affair could also be read as an unexpected outcome of the tension between publicity and secrecy. Unfortunately, my "expertise" in American politics and society is too limited for this. And, of course, there is no dearth of daring explanations for this whole affair. The aim of this article is just to highlight some intriguing parallels between witch and spin doctors in politics, and Clinton's presidential campaigns provide fertile material for this.

30. Cf. Simmel 1923:272. It is interesting that in the same passage, Simmel already takes his distance from any unilineal conception of a historical development from secrecy toward increasing openness: "The historical development of society is in many respects characterized by the fact that what at an earlier time was manifest, enters the protection of secrecy; and that, conversely, what once was secret no longer needs such protection but reveals itself"—(Wolff 1950:331). Cf. also Ferme's concise statement that "the effect of secrecy on social actors is to make them 'radiate' in their

knowledge, without actually giving them away"—a striking characteristic of the performance of both witch and spin doctors.

31. Cf. Jean Comaroff 1997 on the increasing fear of hidden, satanic networks and child abuse in the West.

CHAPTER 7

I acknowledge research permission from the Government of Fiji and particularly thank the late Mr. Jone Tuiwai of Drauniivi Village and Miss Margaret Patel and staff at the National Archives of Fiji. This chapter was written for the conference "Magic and Modernity," Research Centre Religion and Society, University of Amsterdam, June 1997; I thank organizers, participants, and also volume reviewers, for their comments. As always, I thank John Kelly, noting that this chapter draws on our ongoing discussion of ritual begun in the 1980s (see Kelly and Kaplan 1990). Of course responsibility for arguments and interpretations in this chapter is mine.

1. For more on the Vatukaloko, see M. Kaplan 1995. On Mr. Samalia, see M. Kaplan 1995:chapter 7; Kelly and Kaplan 2001.

2. It actually became chiefly-Christian-colonial, as high chiefs from coastal and island kingdoms signed the deed of cession. Cakobau of Bau, for decades styled king of Fiji, had benefited in part from missionary 1830s creation of a standard Fijian for translation and publication that although diverse in origins was known as Bauan (see Calvert 1858:223–24; Clammer 1976:19–22).

3. This history need not be told from a settler/colonial perspective, as Routledge (1985), and most importantly, Sahlins (e.g., 1985) have shown. Most of my own writing focuses on Fijian history making and the intersection of Fijian and British ritual politics. Here, however, I am focusing on the agency of Europeans in order to track the magic they brought with them. Over time, of course, Fiji's colonized and colonizers came to borrow, steal, scrutinize, sometimes subvert—and sometimes share—various powerful forms with each other.

4. Note that one might write this scenario from a different perspective, where Fijians have always had the ritual political right to foundered vessels and to consume in sacrifice "men with saltwater in their eyes"; where Fijians coerced by a chief whose authority they did not acknowledge to gather beche-de-mer might resist that chief by burning a beche-de-mer shed; where alienation of rights to land did not rest with chiefs, who in general had the power to *lewa* (rule) and to grant use rights but not "ownership" of land.

5. Wilkes's treaty as summarized by Derrick ([1946] 1950:91) called for protection and respect for foreign consuls and foreigners conforming to law, required that foreign vessels be received into ports and harbors, required protection for crew and property of wrecked vessels, and so on. My favorite provision is the final regulation, which required that the Regulations be printed and a copy furnished to the master of

every vessel visiting the islands, a practical requirement that also had the effect of engaging the chiefs in the practice of colonial printing magic.

6. Much more could be said of Cakobau's polities and flags. His flags especially led a turbulent life, often in contest with settler and consular state familiars (see, e.g., Brewster 1937).

7. This story and all quotations are drawn from the records of the Fiji Supreme Court, Criminal case #6 of 1901, which are housed in the National Archives of Fiji, Suva.

8. Indeed, when an earlier draft of this chapter was written in early July 1998, right before U.S. Independence Day (July 4), my local newspaper led its editorial page with "Who took Old Glory?" admonishing the unknown persons who stole an American Legion post flag (*Poughkeepsie Journal* July 1, 1998:8A); while the more august *New York Times* (July 3, 1998:A20) included several letters debating what constitutes flag desecration. More recently, since September 11, 2001, both newspapers have run multiple stories on the prevalence of flags on U.S. bodies, houses, and cars and on profits made by flag-making factories in China.

CHAPTER 8

The data on which this chapter is based have been assembled in the course of a research project taking place in the framework of the research program Globalization and the Construction of Communal Identities, sponsored by the Netherlands Foundation for the Advancement of Tropical Research (WOTRO). For their comments on earlier versions of this essay, I would like to thank Peter Geschiere, Peter Pels, and Jojada Verrips.

1. For instance, the Ghanaian film critic Audrey Gadzekpo wrote: "And when other nations do get to view us through the lens of our present crop of budding filmmakers, I am afraid they may be tempted to conclude that Ghana must be a nation of superstitious, contentious people whose men have libidos that are way out of control" (quoted in Middleton-Mends 1995:6).

2. The history of cinema in Ghana has hardly been a topic of research. Next to Ukadike's (1994) and Diawara's (1992) invaluable overviews on African cinema, in which they also deal with the Ghanaian situation, there are only two unpublished theses about the GFIC (founded in 1957) and its predecessor, the Gold Coast Film Unit (established in 1945) (Mensah 1989; Sakyi 1996).

3. According to Mensah, the first feature film was shown to a paying—and, of course, well-to-do and educated—audience at the Palladium Cinema in Accra in 1922 (Mensah 1989:8). The owner of this cinema opened more theaters in other parts of the country. The films shown in this period were silent movies from India; because they were shown in "chapters," it took a number of nights to complete the whole epos. At the beginning of 1930, a number of mobile cinema exploiters started

to show films in cocoa-growing areas, where people, at least after harvest time, had sufficient funds to pay for this new form of entertainment (ibid.). In the 1940s a number of Lebanese businessmen also ventured into film and opened a number of theaters, above all in Accra, Kumasi, and some important towns in the cocoa-growing areas.

4. Diawara has qualified the Colonial Film Unit as "paternalistic and racist." Wishing "to turn back film history and develop a different type of cinema for Africans because they considered the African mind too primitive to follow the sophisticated narrative techniques of mainstream cinema," their films turned out to be "boring and clumsy" (1992:4).

5. Yet, due to a serious lack of funds, during more than thirty-five years only thirteen celluloid feature films were made by the Film Unit and, later, the GFIC, in some cases in collaboration with European producers (Sakyi 1996:96).

6. These films differ in length (between ten and forty-five minutes), and many of them convey their message through a story. Usually a number of films were shown, with fragments from, for instance, Chaplin films in between. I assume that with regard to message and story line, these films are quite similar to feature films.

7. Chaplin, of course, countered the self-image of the West created by colonial film. As Morton-Williams indicates, audiences were wild about his films: "the responses to the old Chaplin films in particular being no less hilarious than that of the audience they were made for" (1953:37).

8. I am not sure why domestic space is so privileged in popular cinema. On the one hand, audiences, especially women, are certainly concerned a great deal with matters of the house. On the other hand, the recent fascination with Nigerian video movies, which also address issues such as corruption and crime on the part of those in power, shows that Ghanaian audiences are eager to watch this type of film. A number of Ghanaian filmmakers told me that they were reluctant to take up political issues or events of immediate public relevance, because they feared problems with either the censorship board or the people involved in these issues and events.

9. In Ghana it is considered of utmost value for a man to construct a house. This is *the* symbol of a successful life (see Van der Geest 1998). Whereas until the 1960s and 1970s a successful man was expected to, and actually would, build a house is his hometown or village, where he would eventually retire, nowadays there is a trend toward building houses in Accra.

10. Stories concerning ghosts who seek revenge for evil done to them during their lifetime build on existing cultural concepts. In Akan, Ga, and Ewe culture, power is attributed to the victims of bad, violent deaths, and rituals have been developed to keep control over these forces by relegating them once and for all to the realm of death or, if they keep on appearing to living people, establishing a shrine for them. Yet, in the context of the city, where the circumstances leading to a person's death are not (made) transparent, these forces remain untamed, thereby threatening to blur the boundary between life and death. There is an ongoing debate about the truth of ghosts and the nature of dreams, which is taken up by many movies.

11. Many filmmakers told me that, after the boom of ghost films, such as *Ghost Tears*, *A Mother's Revenge*, *Step-Dad*, and *Suzzy*, in various journals one could find letters to the editor which complain about why filmmakers should just focus on "Ghost-ghost-ghost"; didn't they have better stories to tell? These criticisms incited filmmakers to look for new stories.

12. "Confession" holds a central place in the Pentecostal churches. In contrast to Catholicism, where confession takes place in a secluded space between the priest and an individual sinner (Pels 1999a:107–9), Pentecostal churches celebrate *public* confession, where born-again Christians tell spectacular stories about their experiences in the realm of "the powers of darkness." In many respects, this form of confession resembles Akan, Ga, and Ewe practices of confession (for instance, in the case of witchcraft), which also took place in public. At the same time, Pentecostal confession certainly forms part of a corpus of modern technologies of self (see Pels ibid.), in the sense that Pentecostalists are encouraged to continuously investigate themselves about their involvement with occult forces relegated to the "past" and the domain of evil and eventually come up with a story (Meyer 1998b). This public form of confession is carried a step further by popular cinema, where unbounded, anonymous audiences can now shiver about the evil committed by certain people before they turned on the right path.

13. For the Ghanaian public, well grounded in the Bible as it is, it is clear immediately that the film takes up the biblical story about Abraham, Sarah, and Hagar, Abraham's second wife and mother of his first son.

14. This is all the more interesting because the producer, Hammond Mensah, is a Muslim. As a member of the Ahmadiyya order, he stresses the similarity between Ahmadiyya's understanding of Islam and of Christianity and has no problems with making films for a Christian public.

15. In fact, plenty of films are devoted to the theme of the young couple who remains childless, the husband's liaisons (often instigated by his mother) with other girls, the poor wife's prayers, and, finally, her well-deserved reward.

16. But see Tyler ([1947] 1971) and Powdermaker (1950), who each emphasized the magic of dream creation taking place in Hollywood.

17. This reminds of the fierce debates about Jean Rouch's documentary on the Hauka-possession cult in Ghana, *Les maîtres fous*, which depicts Africans portraying their white overlords in a barbaric way. Whereas some spectators regarded the film as racist, others noticed that this cult implied a deep anticolonial critique because it questioned the very order that lay at the base of the civilizing mission (cf. Kramer 1987:137; Ukadike 1994:50ff.).

18. In the West, one finds similar paternalistic doubts about the ability of the so-called masses to not let themselves be lured into the magic of film and become unable to distinguish between fantasy and reality (cf. Starker 1989; Verrips 2001).

19. I have not yet been able to find out whether and to what extent films such as *King Solomon's Mines* have been shown to an African public during colonial times. I

would not be surprised if watching these films would have been restricted, both because of the racism and the doubts about Western rationality. In any case it is clear that not many Africans had access to films anyway. Ukadike mentions in passing that African men had the opportunity to watch this type of film when they took part in the First World War in France.

CHAPTER 9

I am most grateful to Birgit Meyer and Peter Pels for their constructive and inspiring comments on an earlier version of this chapter.

1. Magical-mythical is used in the sense of empirically not exact but nevertheless based on the assumption that the reality (to which representations called magical-mythical refer) can be influenced and manipulated.

2. Himmelman, e.g., observes for the past the existence of a "fine line between professional medicine, folk belief and religious ideology" and how they were not "as clearly separated as they are today" (1990:197).

3. See in this connection Vyse, who scorns physicians with medical degrees who promote "quack therapies" such as the "therapeutic touch": "Therapeutic touch is closer to magic than it is to medicine; yet it is being promoted by respected health-care professionals. If we cannot trust the medical establishment to promote scientifically valid treatments, how are we to choose a rational course of medical treatment?" (1997:208).

4. In a review of a volume of essays about health, illness, and healing in the Netherlands from the sixteenth to the beginning of the twentieth century, De Blécourt points out that the authors indeed pay a lot of attention to the religious aspects of healing in the early modern times but not in the nineteenth century. Therefore, he advocates research on the ways in which "notions about health and healing developed in a religious context in the nineteenth and twentieth century" (De Blécourt 1993:220).

5. See Van der Geest for the importance of metaphors and metonyms in connection with the "magical" attraction of medicines (1990a). He also points out how metaphorical language in medicine can lead to mystification. "The use of difficult terms of the Western physician has its parallel in the enigmatic metaphors used by healers in other cultures" (1990b:228).

6. In this connection I want to mention the films of the Canadian cult-director Cronenberg (see Rodley 1993). They teem with remarkable doctors who defy the image of the perfectly normal healer. In *Crimes of the Future* (1970) there figures a mad dermatologist; in *Shivers* (1975) Dr. Emil Hobbes, creator of a rare type of parasite; in *Rabid* (1976) Dr. Dan Keloid, who uses radical surgical techniques; in *The Brood* (1979) Dr. Hal Raglan, an expert in "psychoplasmics"; in *Dead Ringers* (1988) the twin brothers Elliot and Beverley Mantle, rather bizarre gynecologists (cf. Frank 1992). The last film can be interpreted as a modern version of Robert Louis Stevenson's *Dr. Jekyll and Mr. Hyde*.

According to Tudor, who wrote a cultural history of the horror movie, the mad doctor who misuses science for nonscientific goals played an important role in the genre before 1960. Afterward (medical) science was presented as a source of the totally unexpected, e.g., of strange diseases and of epidemics (Tudor 1989:152ff.). See also Carroll 1990:210.

7. This is a positive image that also crops up in countless popular novels on doctors.

8. The film *AI* by Spielberg deals in a fascinating way with their endeavors. See Hersbach for the way in which after the American Civil War all kinds of "images and metaphors of machine-men complexes" circulated "that drew on recent developments in physiological explanation in which divisions between human and machine, body and self are increasingly difficult to locate" (1997:25).

9. In this connection, the following remark of the Dutch "future specialist" Polak is interesting: "The electronic man becomes more and more like a car, with replaceable spare parts; worn-out and diseased internal and external organs, vital for a good functioning of the body-motor, will be repaired or exchanged. The hospital becomes a garage, the physician a mechanic, the patient an electronic composition. At a particular moment the question will arise: what of this electronically prepared and repaired human being is still human and what machine?" (n.d.:93). For essays on the changing relations between body and technology, see Featherstone and Burrows 1995. The developments in this field are tremendous. In 2001, e.g., German researchers succeeded for the first time in constructing a functioning bioelectronic circuit by connecting two living neurons and a microchip.

10. Right now interesting research is being done, e.g., by anthropologists, with regard to issues such as the kind of identity persons who underwent an organ transplant think they have or will develop (see Wiebel-Fanderl 1997).

11. An animal that is becoming increasingly important as a supplier of kidneys is the pig. All sorts of pharmaceutical industries are working hard to grow genetically manipulated pig organs, which can be implanted into human beings (cf. Velander, Lubon, and Drohan 1997). It appears that so-called xenotransplantations will become the new fashion due to an increasing shortage of human donor organs (cf. Aan de Brugh, *NRC Handelsblad* [February 22, 1996]). Only in 1999 did the implantation of heart valves of pigs in humans occur in the Netherlands. The use of pig hearts then was still forbidden, but the government has prepared a discussion on the negative and positive sides of this use. For an interesting volume on gene technology in general and reactions of the public, see Lundin and Ideland 1997.

12. See also Scheper-Hughes 2000a and 2000b. Striking is the fact that sick people often seem to have no problem in accepting the organs of people they would otherwise avoid, keep a distance from, or even discriminate against.

13. One should not underestimate the role of the media in this. Documentaries about the theft of organs everywhere in the world are rather regular news items. An example: in 1996 the German weekly *Stern* published a report with the following headlines: "Thousands of people have been murdered in Argentina and Columbia in

order to sell their eyes, kidneys, heart, and liver. But only now the unscrupulous doctors and their helpers are being investigated" (April 9, 1996:9). See Haraway 1997 for a concise exposé of the way in which particular projects, such as the Human Genome Diversity Project—which had as its goal to collect hair root, white blood cell, and cheek tissue samples from indigenous groups on six continents—might give rise to all kinds of stories in which what she calls "technoscience" becomes associated with "realms of the undead, vampires, and transgressive traffic in the bloody tissues of life" (248–54).

14. "De mens en zijn reserve-onderdelen," *Vrij Nederland*, nos. 26, 27 (April 19, 1997).

15. See Dowie for a fascinating prognosis of the developments in the realm of organ and tissue transplantations at the end of the twentieth century as well as a thought-provoking overview of the bright and dark sides of human organ transplantation (1998:chapters 11, 12). An important source of worries and fears is also formed by the question, who in the near future will have the right to make decisions with regard to biotechnological issues (Pott 2000)?

16. A poignant case with regard to side effects in which doctors made one mistake after another is "the scandal of the blood," which took place in France in the 1980s. Although they knew that the blood they were giving hemophilia patients was contaminated with the HIV virus and that this could lead to AIDS within due time, they did not stop giving it to them (*NRC Handelsblad* [June 27, 1992]).

17. Especially in the realm of mental illnesses, horror stories with respect to operations occur. Lobotomy and electroshocks are two examples of notorious and much disputed biomedical cures in the recent past used by psychosurgeons. These brain operations, instead of improving the situation of their patients, as doctors thought they would, were based on scanty knowledge and often had devastating effects, as is vividly shown in the movie *One Flew over the Cuckoo's Nest*. The "high priests" of psychosurgery, the Portuguese António Egas Moniz (who even received a Nobel prize for his destructive operations on human beings) and the American Freeman, liked to pose as objective scientists who really knew what they were doing, whereas they evidently did not. See Van Soest 1982a, 1982b; and Pressman 1998.

18. A striking example is the use of the term *virus* in the computer world. Sometimes computer specialists are represented, e.g., in advertisements, as doctors (see the ad by CMG Information Technology, in *Volkskrant* [August 22, 1998]). A few years ago a Dutch journalist compared the British boulevard press itself, which published one alarming article after another on a certain "meat-eating" bacterium (streptococcus Group A), with a contaminating bacillus.

19. Helman also refers in another place to "the imagery of war" as used by physicians (1991:46) but without elaborating on it. See also Stein 1990:997; and Lupton 1994:61.

20. See Zulaika 1988 for a brilliant exposé on and application of the concept performative model.

21. See, for a humorous example of this way of representing microorganisms, De Jager 1991. De Jager is a pseudonym for Van der Hoeden (1891–1941), a famous Dutch bacteriologist.

22. It is an old convention among social scientists to understand society in analogy with a healthy or ill body. In that sense they do not differ much from people all over the world who learned to perceive their society as a body, a theme about which Mary Douglas has said a lot of stimulating things. The movie *Osmosis Jones* by Peter and Bobby Farrelly, released in 2001, represents a fine example of representing the body as a society. In this popular product of the imagination, microorganisms are represented as good and bad guys involved in a huge fight with each other.

23. In Dutch there are a plethora of terms of abuse in which cancer is referred to. Furthermore, tuberculosis, typhoid fever, pest, syphilis, and cholera play a dominant role (cf. Heestermans 1989:41ff.). It is striking that more recent illnesses are not yet used much as insults.

24. "The following sections of metaphorical expressions have been found in the texts . . . : -cells have a life cycle and lifespan -cells have children, parents, and family -cells have their own metabolism and must be nourished -cells have human abilities and attributes -cells show different modes of behavior -cells take initiatives, perform actions and are able to do things spontaneously -cells are able to recognize things. On the basis of these metaphorical expressions the following basic conceptual metaphor can be formulated: *cells are human beings*" (Van Rijn–Van Tongeren 1997:66).

25. For the importance of anthropomorphizing in science in general, see the work of Guthrie, who remarks: "As Nietzsche and others point out, anthropomorphism is inescapable since we can avoid neither human interests nor human senses" (1993:164). Not only "microbiologists, neuroscientists, and other laboratory biologists . . . anthropomorphize" (171) but also "sociologists and anthropologists including Spencer, Durkheim, Radcliffe-Brown, and A.L. Kroeber, in a tradition going back at least to the Greeks, credit society or culture with a life, purpose, and will of its own" (175). For the way surgeons use military metaphors in describing their work, see Hirschauer 1991:281.

26. "The war metaphors can be divided into two main groups, based on the choice of strategy to stop the invaders: either attacking the tumour cells or boosting the host's defence system" (Van Rijn–Van Tongeren 1997:71–72).

27. Recently the Dutch publisher B.V., located in Rijswijk, published a translation of a book by McCormick and Fisher-Hoch with the title *The Virushunters: The War Against Contagious Diseases*.

28. A remarkable fact is that advertisements in such journals as *Science* and *Genetic Engineering News* rather often contain anthropomorphic representations of cells, proteins, and viruses. See Fleising 2000 for a fascinating essay on the use of biblical and magical images in advertisements for careers in biotechnology and products related to biotechnology.

29. This does not mean, however, that other metaphors and performative models would not also be used. One also uses mechanical metaphors, e.g., machine and motor, and the performative model of the repair or mechanic (cf. Van Rijn–Van Tongeren 1997). In the last decades, the application of metaphors borrowed from the computer domain for a better understanding of the functioning of the human brain and nervous system has been expanding rapidly. However, according to Smith Churchland, it is an open question as to how useful the computer metaphors for the development of theories about the workings of brain and nervous system function really are: "Metaphors can certainly catalyze theorizing, but theories they are not" (1986:408).

30. See Van Rijn–Van Tongeren 1997:91 for the way in which the use of war metaphors with regard to cancer leads to "incomplete" and "biased" interpretations and therapies.

31. It would be interesting to make a systematic study of the ways in which medical researchers are represented in advertisements in professional journals. It struck me, when I skimmed through certain of these journals, that these researchers not only often stare into glass bowls, just like crystal gazers, but also are contrasted with scryers by the advertisers. Of course, one could say that these are "inventions" of ad makers, but this would not be a convincing argument for putting this parallelism or analogy aside as irrelevant. See Frank, who cogently shows how modern medicine has become dependent on video screens: "Real diagnostic work takes place away from the patient: bedside is secondary to screenside" (1992:83).

32. For Sloterdijk, doctors and agents of secret services strongly resemble each other in practice and language. The former spy into the bodies of their patients in order to discover their hidden secrets, whereas the latter try to figure out what certain members of the social body who are considered to be dangerous are doing. He also pays attention to the particular metaphorical discourses used by physicians. See Sloterdijk 1992:537–43.

33. See Noordman 1989 for this kind of law in the Netherlands.

34. "The sterilization of 400,000 people required an enormous effort from Germany's medical profession. Doctors competed to fulfill sterilization quotas, sterilization research and engineering rapidly became one of the largest medical industries. Medical supply companies . . . made a substantial amount of money designing sterilization equipment. Medical students wrote at least 183 doctoral theses exploring the criteria, methods, and consequences of sterilization" (Proctor 1988:108–9).

35. It took a long time before the study of these atrocities was taken up seriously, at least in Germany. The work by Mitscherlich and Mielke, *Medizin ohne Menschlichkeit* (1960), was indeed already published in 1948, but only in a limited edition for the national organization of doctors. Though the amount of literature on the horrendous activities of Nazi physicians is still not impressive, there are several well-documented studies available right now. See, for instance, Proctor 1988; Staub 1989; Burleigh 1994; Bastian 1996; and Klee 1997.

36. The metaphor of the Jew as *parasite, bacillus, poison,* or *vermin* predates the Nazi period: as early as 1895 Hermann Ahlwardt, member of the German parliament, labeled Jews "beasts of prey" and "cholera bacilli," as part of an effort to halt Jewish immigration (Proctor 1988:379 n. 165).

37. Proctor speaks about the "medicalization of anti-semitism" (1988:194).

38. In his review of Peter-Ferdinand Koch's book *Menschenversuche: Die tödlichen Experimente deutscher Ärzte,* Groeneveld says: "Physicians were no longer busy healing people, but they changed into 'biological soldiers' with the authority to cross borders" (*NRC Handelsblad* [May 4, 1996]).

39. Every now and then the representation of organizations or society as an ill body in need of an operation by a medical specialist crops up in advertisements. In 1997, e.g., the Dutch province North Holland, together with a number of transport companies, published an ad with a photo of a naked male body onto which a map of the province was projected. The city of Amsterdam was at the place of the heart, and all kinds of roads led to it, e.g., a new road for buses only. The construction of this road was represented as "a kind of bypass operation," and the ones who took care of it as "cooperating (medical) specialists." In the same year an ad of the municipal transport company of Amsterdam with a cartoon of surgeons appeared in which people were asked to help this organization to become healthy again. See also the cover of *Stern,* no. 45 (October 30, 1997), which shows a naked lady with a map projected onto her body, demonstrating the occurrence of cancer in Germany.

40. In this connection, Koenigsberg's publication of 1975 is particularly relevant, for therein he shows where exactly in *Mein Kampf* and in his speeches Hitler makes remarks about the country as a living organism; the disintegration, the disease, and the consumption of the national body; etc. In order to get a clear picture of Hitler's xenophobic, germistic discourse, it is useful to consult Koenigsberg's work. The dictator also compared the Jews with vampires, who can be seen as the popular macro-representation of sexually transmittable diseases comparable with the scientific representation used by doctors of microorganisms causing these diseases (cf. Verrips 1992). It should be noted that Hitler and his henchmen were often perceived by their opponents in a similar germistic way; they were seen, e.g., as contagious "cholera patients," who spread "the deadly microbes of Jew-hatred" (Krueger 1953:318). We are confronted here with a universal mechanism: the classification of adversaries as non-human in order to be able to more easily exterminate them (cf. White 1991).

41. A similar coherent fantasy to the one occurring in Germany existed for a long time in the former USSR. For there, too, certain people who were deemed to cherish incorrect political ideas were defined by physicians and politicians as being "seriously ill" and in need of a thorough psychiatric treatment (which often boiled down to sheer mistreatment) in an asylum. For the way in which psychiatry became a means of repression after the death of Stalin, see Bloch and Reddaway 1977.

42. See, e.g., the video movie *Ilsa: She Wolf of the S.S.* made by Don Edmonds. The method used by the Nazis to sterilize people in concentration camps with

radiation would after World War II be applied by Norwegian and American researchers on psychiatric patients. (*Volkskrant* [April 29, 1998].).

43. But see Proctor 1999 for an extensive sketch of the more constructive aspects of the medical practice during the Nazi period.

CHAPTER 10

The editors of *Etnofoor* kindly permitted me to republish the material used in an earlier version of this chapter (Pels 1995); I thank Vincent Crapanzano, Birgit Meyer, Brad Weiss, and the members of the Department of Cultural Studies and Comparative Literature of the University of Minnesota, for their comments.

1. *Conversion* was a term Wallace himself regularly used, although without explicit religious connotations. For some remarks on the contemporary relationship between religion and science, see Pels 1995.

2. The conversion of convinced materialists to Spiritualism was not an unusual occurrence in Victorian Britain (see Pels 2000:29–30).

3. I hope to deal with these issues at length in a book on anthropology and the occult. Elements of its argument can be found in earlier publications (Pels 1998b, 2000; Van Dijk and Pels 1996).

4. This democratic epistemology, however, derived not only from secular or agnostic roots: it can also be traced to the Methodist emphasis on the personal experience of salvation; the Society of Primitive Methodists (founded 1812), in particular, was an important contributor to the British Labour movement (Davies 1963:152).

5. Bates's and Wallace's early speculations on evolution were prompted by reading Robert Chambers's *Vestiges of the Natural History of Creation* ([1844] 1969), a hotly denounced phrenomesmerist forerunner of Darwin's *Origin of Species*.

6. "Relatively" safe, however, as Huxley, in particular, shows how insecure the position of an aspiring young scientist in the 1840s and 1850s could be (Huxley 1900:1:passim).

7. Among them was R.G. Latham, leading member of the Ethnological Society and at that time occupied with the ethnological exhibition in the new Crystal Palace (the exhibition hall in London that housed the Great Exhibition of 1851), for which he asked Wallace's advice on some Guiana figures; Latham also wrote a note on Wallace's linguistic materials from the Amazon (Wallace 1908:166).

8. According to Darwin, "the best paper that ever appeared in the *Anthropological Review*" (Kottler 1974:156).

9. That was Miss Nichol, the later Mrs. Guppy, who, with her husband, became famous for producing the first full-form spirit materializations (Wallace [1874] 1896:175).

10. Of the six presidents of the Ethnological Society from its foundation in 1843, five were trained as medical doctors (James Cowles Prichard, Sir Benjamin Collins Brodie, John Connoly, John Crawfurd, and Huxley). From its inception,

the Anthropological Society of London was led by James Hunt, M.D. When both merged into the Anthropological Institute in 1871, Thomas Huxley, M.D., was its first president.

11. Still, the young Spencer published one of his first writings in the phrenomesmerist journal *The Zoist* (Spencer 1844).

12. Kottler says that Tylor actually encouraged Wallace to research spiritual phenomena, but he fails to give evidence for this (1974:164), and given the situation sketched below, it is highly unlikely.

13. In his 1876 presidential address to the biological section of the British Association for the Advancement of Science, Wallace embraced the degeneration argument even more explicitly, in further support of his critique of natural selection in human evolution (Kottler 1974:160). Wallace's selection for the presidency shows that even then, his Spiritualism had not completely discredited him in the eyes of his scientific colleagues.

14. Tylor, for instance, was at the time of the publication of *Primitive Culture* still barred from taking up a post at an Oxbridge College because of his nonconformist background.

15. I have yet to come across a history of the nineteenth-century public discourse on scientific and social "honesty." The notion is ubiquitous in Huxley (Huxley 1900:passim); it is not only central to Wallace's understanding of reliable evidence but also a linchpin in his argument for why natural selection does not apply to human evolution (Kottler 1974:155; Wallace [1874] 1896:35). Its seventeenth-century roots, however, have been brilliantly dealt with (Shapin 1994).

16. Wallace extended these insights into a theory of natural phenomena that stressed that matter was an impossibility and that all phenomena in the universe were really manifestations of force that eventually boiled down to manifestations of the will of beings of superior intelligence (Kottler 1974:156).

17. For other uses of a metaphor of tactility in thinking about knowledge production, see Pels 1999a:20–29; Taussig 1993b:35; Van Dijk and Pels 1996.

18. On *occultism*, see the Introduction, Note 7. For a more detailed discussion of the social and historical circumstances of its emergence, see Pels 2000.

19. This is also shown by the key role that phenomena now often classified as "occult" played in the experiments that supported the late-nineteenth-century emergence of psychology (Hacking 1988, 1995; Hansen 1989; Leahey and Leahey 1983).

20. See previous note. William Rivers founded the first psychological laboratory and journal in Britain around 1900, after Rivers and Alfred Haddon had pioneered the practice of intensive anthropological fieldwork during the Torres Straits expedition, which was also largely devoted to psychological research.

21. This attitude is also implicit in the stereotype that spirit possession is something that happens in "Asia, Africa, Afro-America, . . . Latin America, . . . Oceania and historical and contemporary (chiefly Mediterranean) Europe" (Boddy 1994:409), that is, everywhere but in modern northern Europe and America.

22. Compare this to Durkheim's suggestion—tantalizing and worthy of elaboration—that mysticism and empiricism are two closely correlated ways of thinking (1974:67).

1. Note that Ona and Selk'nam are interchangeable names.

2. The epigraph to his book reads: "And ye shall be witnesses unto me both in Jerusalem . . . and unto the uttermost part of the earth" (Acts I:8). Not a bad epigraph for anthropology, either.

3. Note that Bridges spoke the Ona language, and when he describes speech as guttural he is not necessarily mistaken.

4. The discipline of physiognomics was not invented by the Greeks, writes Barton. In Mesopotamia from the first half of the second millenium B.C. onward, fragments of manuals have been found dealing with the prophetic significance of aspects of individual human bodies (see Barton 1994:100).

5. And note the story in Gusinde's more than one thousand pages of ethnography on the Selk'nam (based on fieldwork undertaken over four trips between 1918 and 1924) of how in 1919 a group of medicine men had been offered presents by Bridges's brother, Guillermo, if they could kill one of his dogs with magic. The medicine men refused, as they believed their magic to be of no use against white men or their dogs (Gusinde 1982:698–99).

6. It is with reluctance that I bend to linguistic convention and employ the all-too-universalizing term *shamanism*, as readers of my previous work will readily understand.

7. The phrase *Penny-in-the-slot* or something like it comes from Walter Benjamin's essay on surrealism, referring to a universe of dislocating, unstable, and carnal meaning as opposed to the penny-in-the-slot variety of predictable, mechanistic, semiotic, and other related meanings of meaning.

8. As regards the first point concerning error, "The falseness of a judgment is for us not necessarily an objection to a judgment; in this respect our new language may sound strangest. The question is to what extent it is life-preserving, species-preserving, perhaps even species-cultivating. And we are fundamentally inclined to claim that the falsest judgments (which include the synthetic judgments *a priori*) are the most indispensable for us. . . . To recognize untruth as a condition of life—that certainly means resisting accustomed value feelings in a dangerous way; and a philosophy that risks this would by that token alone place itself beyond good and evil" (Nietzsche [1886] 1989:11–12).

9. *Totemism* of course came in for a curious attempt at dismantling in the hands of Claude Lévi-Strauss, whose object, however, was not to emphasize the strange curving back of the North American Indian concept to find a useful place in Western European sensibilities but to elaborate totemism as a fictitious entity best understood

as but part of special sorts of classificatory systems using metaphor and opposition.

10. On the crucial importance of the eighteenth-century explorations in Siberia for the dissemination of the very notion of shamanism see Flaherty 1992.

11. Boas's texts on Kwakiutl society have been described by Walens as "one of the monuments of American cultural anthropology" (1981:7). Walens also points out in a footnote that the "degree to which the excellence of Boas' work is the result of the meticulousness and diligence of both men [Hunt as well as Boas] has never been amply discussed" (ibid.:9). Goldman describes these texts as "probably the greatest single ethnographic treasure [in existence]" (1975:vii).

12. On Kwakiutl names and naming: "The name is the essential ingredient of religious worth" (Goldman 1975:56).

13. This is hardly the place to make an extended analysis, but it needs to be observed that the Boas/Hunt mode of ethnography contains enormous problems for the interpretation of Kwakiutl culture precisely because the character of the relationship between the two men is not opened to analysis. Why did Hunt write? How did he see his task? What instructions did Boas give him? What did Hunt think he was doing telling a white man about the secrets of shamanism? Later research may uncover much in this regard, but the point is that these issues need to be faced up to in the actual Boas/Hunt texts themselves for them to be of real use in themselves.

14. I acquired this terminology of intercultural autoethnography from Mary Louise Pratt.

15. On a certain equivalence between secret and sacred, see Goldman: "In many places, however, the Hunt manuscript is more precise [than Boas's edited and published version] in rendering Kwakiutl meanings. For example, Boas characteristically converts Hunt's 'secret' to 'sacred'" (1975:86–87).

16. See the preceding note, concerning the equivalence between secret and sacred.

17. Note the implications of this for re-sorting Foucault's distinction crucial to his later work regarding transgression and confession—where he contrasts the transmission of bodily knowledge through a master-apprentice system ("ars erotica")—vs. the confessional, as with modern Western sexuality, as the secret which has to be spoken.

18. In his first major monograph Boas described this double-headed serpent, the Sisiul, as perhaps the most important of the fabulous monsters whose help was obtained by the ancestors and had therefore become the crest of a clan. To eat, touch, or see it was to have one's joints dislocated, to have one's head turned backward, and to meet with eventual death. But to those persons who had supernatural help, it may instead bring power (1895:371–72).

19. Even with his focus on mythology and ideas, Claude Lévi-Strauss makes the mistake of omitting this from both of his famous essays on magic, "The Effectiveness of Symbols," concerned with Cuna shamanism in the San Blas Archipelago off Panama, and "A Sorcerer and His Magic," most of which works through George Hunt's 1925 account of his shamanic experiences written down for Boas. In the Cuna case Lévi-Strauss expends his entire analysis, finding Structuralist closure in his assumption

that the sick person understands, both mentally and especially, bodily, the curing song sung in a specialized shamanic language—a most dubious proposition because the ethnography indicates that ordinary Cuna do not understand such language and that the song is intended not for the patient but for the spirits, providing, through words much the same sort of simulacrum Walens describes for the tricks practiced by the Kwakiutl shamans. It is curious how this error is made in both of Lévi-Strauss's essays, and the implications are immense, swinging the analysis away from metonymic, mimetic, and transgressive considerations to his reformulation of "totemism" as the logic of classification in accord with the semiotics of Ferdinand de Saussure and Roman Jakobson and a particular epistemology of "structure," series, and contradiction.

20. "The nature culture uses to create second nature" is a phrase I coined to define the mimetic faculty in my book *Mimesis and Alterity* (Taussig 1993b).

21. Cf. Boas on the reaction of the seal society when they notice a mistake in dancing or singing of the performer in the Winter Ceremonial; they jump from their seats and bite and scratch the person who made the mistake, who then pretends to faint, meaning that the spirit has taken the performer away. In fact, members of the seal society sit on the platform of the house or stand during the dances to be certain of discovering mistakes. If the cannibal dancer falls while dancing, it is said that in former times he was killed by the other cannibal dancers, often at the insistence of the dancer's father (Boas 1895:433–34).

22. Masco cites Robert Boyd's estimate of a close to 70 percent loss in the 1862 smallpox epidemic, from a population before then of 7,650 people. The precontact population is estimated as between 15,000 and 20,000.

23. Goldman (1975) gives a figure of fifty-three from Boas's report of 1895, and sixty-three from Edward S. Curtis, *The North American Indian*, vol. 10 (1915).

24. The approach differs from that of Frank Hamilton Cushing, who through bluff and trickery more or less forced himself into the priesthood of the Bow Lodge of the Zuni (see Cushing 1979:99–101).

25. The great geographical "discoveries" of European modernity, such as the discovery of the New World or of Machu Pichu, have something of this quality too.

26. Here, the word *leech* is an archaic English term for a "folk" healer. Like other terms used by Evans-Pritchard, such as *ensorcell* and *knave*, this term creates its own mystique, if not mystification, combined with an implicit notion that African medicine is on a developmental line that British society superseded. This is unfortunate and probably far from the author's intention.

27. I have not here analyzed the deceit wherein the witch doctor is supposed to cut a deal with the witch who caused the disease so that both will share in the fee for curing (see Evans-Pritchard 1937:191–93). Here the skepticism in the magical powers of the witch doctor is balanced by faith in those of the witch to cause and withdraw misfortune by mystical means and that these means reside in mangu substance inherited at birth in the body of the witch. The question begged by this account is, Why would there be a need for the elaborate performance of the witch doctor? Why

can't the doctor act more like a lawyer or peacemaker? Why the art? In the healing practiced by the people indigenous to the New World (if I may be so bold as to generalize), the answer lies readily at hand: the art is essential as the mode of establishing a mimetic model with the spirits. I know too little about Africa to comment, but I suspect the New World notion is applicable there, too, raising a totally different approach to the one of rationality and philosophy of science that has dogged British commentary on magic.

28. See Claude Lévi-Strauss, *The Savage Mind* (1966) and *Totemism* (1963), and S.J. Tambiah (1973), "Form and Meaning in Magical Acts: A Point of View."

Abdullah, Ibrahim, and Yusuf Bangura, eds. 1997. "Youth Culture and Political Violence: The Sierra Leone Civil War." Africa Development 22 (2, 3).

Abrams, Philip. [1977] 1988. "Notes on the Difficulty of Studying the State." *Journal of Historical Sociology* 1(1):58–89.

Adas, Michael. 1989. *Machines as the Measure of Man: Science, Technology, and Ideologies of Western Dominance*. Ithaca, N.Y.: Cornell University Press.

Adorno, Theodor W. 1951. "Thesen gegen den Okkultismus." In *Minima Moralia: Reflexionen aus dem beschädigten Leben*, 321–29. Frankfurt am Main: Suhrkamp.

Allaux, Gustave. 1860. *L'Empereur Souloque et son Empire*. Paris: Michel Levy.

Alldridge, T.J. 1910. *A Transformed Colony: Sierra Leone As It Was, and As It Is. Its Progress, Peoples, Native Customs, and Undeveloped Wealth*. London: Seeley and Co.

Allen, Robert C. 1995. Introduction. In R.C. Allen, ed., *To Be Continued. . . . : Soap Operas Around the World*, 1–26. London: Routledge.

Alvares, Manuel. [c. 1615] 1990. *Ethiopia Minor and a Geographical Account of the Province of Sierra Leone*. Ed. and trans. by P.E.H. Hair. Department of History, University of Liverpool, photocopy.

Anderson, Benedict. 1983. *Imagined Communities: Reflections on the Origin and Spread of Nationalism*. London: Verso.

___. 1990. "The Languages of Indonesian Politics." In *Language and Power: Exploring Political Cultures in Indonesia*, 123–51. Ithaca, N.Y.: Cornell University Press.

___. 1991. *Imagined Communities: Reflections on the Origin and Spread of Nationalism* Rev. and ext. ed. London: Verso.

Annan, Noel G. 1955. "The Intellectual Aristocracy." In J.H. Plumb, ed., *Studies in Social History: A Tribute to G.M. Trevelyan*, 243–87. London: Longmans, Green & Co.

Appadurai, Arjun. 1986. "Introduction: Commodities and the Politics of Value." In A. Appadurai, ed., *The Social Life of Things: Commodities in Cultural Perspective*, 3–63. Cambridge, England: Cambridge University Press.

Ardouin, Beaubrun. [1853–65] 1958. *Etudes sur l'histoire d'Haïti*. Port-au-Prince: Dalencourt.

Arya Patrika (Journal). 1886. 2(December 7).

Arya Pratinidhi Sabha. 1889. *The Rules and the Scheme of Studies of the Proposed Gurukula Sanctioned by the Arya Pratinidhi Sabha*. Lahore: Mufid-'i'-am Press.

Asad, Talal. 1973. Introduction, *Anthropology and the Colonial Encounter*, 9–18. New York: Humanities Press.

———. 1993. *Genealogies of Religion*. Baltimore and London: Johns Hopkins University Press.

Ashforth, Adam. 1996. "Of Secrecy and Commonplace: Witchcraft in Soweto." *Social Research* 63(4):1183–234.

Baker, James W. 1996. "White Witches: Historic Fact and Romantic Fantasy." In J.R. Lewis, ed., *Magical Religion and Modern Witchcraft*, 171–192. New York: State University of New York Press.

Banegas, Richard. 1998. *La démocratie 'à pas de caméléon': Transition et consolidation démocratique au Bénin*. Ph.D. thesis. Paris: IEP.

Bann, S., ed. 1994. *Frankenstein: Creation and Monstrosity*. London: Reaktion Books.

Barber, Karin. 1997. "Preliminary Notes on Audiences in Africa." *Africa* 67(3):347–62.

Barrow, Logie. 1986. *Independent Spirits: Spiritualism and English Plebeians, 1850–1910*. London: Routledge and Kegan Paul.

Barton, Tamsyn S. 1994. *Power and Knowledge: Astrology, Physiognomics, and Medicine Under the Roman Empire*. Ann Arbor: University of Michigan Press.

Bastian, T. 1996. *Furchtbare Ärzte: Medizinische Verbrechen im Dritten Reich*. Munich: Verlag C.H. Beck.

Bayart, Jean-François. 1989. *L'Etat en Afrique: La politique du ventre*. Paris: Fayard.

———. 1996. *L'Illusion identitaire*. Paris: Fayard.

Beekman, E.M. 1996. *Troubled Pleasures: Dutch Colonial Literature from the East Indies, 1600–1950*. Oxford: Clarendon Press.

Beets, Jeroen, and Irene Stengs. 1992. "De heksen zijn nog onder ons: Junkies als representanten van het kwaad in onze samenleving." *Etnofoor* 5(1/2):45–60.

Bekeerde. 1916. "Oostersche Mysteriën." *De Reflector* 1(30):714–16.

Benamou, Georges-Marc. 1996. *Le dernier Mitterand*. Paris: Plon.

Benedict, Ruth. 1934. "Magic." In E.R.A. Seligman, ed., *Encyclopaedia of the Social Sciences*. Vol. 9, 39–44. New York: Macmillan.

Benjamin, Walter. 1977. *Illuminationen*. Frankfurt am Main: Suhrkamp Verlag.

———. [1955] 1979. *Baudelaire: Een dichter in het tijdperk van het hoogkapitalisme*. Trans. from German. Amsterdam: Arbeiderspers/Synopsis.

Bennett, Gillian. 1987. *Traditions of Belief: Women and the Supernatural Today*. Harmondsworth, England: Penguin Books.

Benot, Yves. 1989. *La Révolution Française et la fin des colonies*. Paris: Editions de la Découverte.

Bhabha, Homi K. 1994. *The Location of Culture*. London and New York: Routledge.

Binding, Karl, and Alfred Hoche. 1920. *Die Freigabe der Vernichtung lebensunwerten Lebens: Ihr Mass und ihre Form*. Leipzig: no publisher listed.

Binford, M. 1971. "Stalemate: A Study of Cultural Dynamics." Ph.D. Dissertation in Anthropology, Michigan State University.

Blackburn, Robin. 1988. *The Overthrow of Colonial Slavery*. London: Verso.

Blavatsky, Helena Petrovna. 1877. *Isis Unveiled: A Master-Key to the Mysteries of Ancient and Modern Science and Theology*. Wheaton, Ill.: Theosophical Publishing House (reprinted 1972).

___. 1888. *The Secret Doctrine*, 2 vols. Pasadena, Calif.: Theosophical Society Press (reprinted 1997).

___. 1889. *The Key to Theosophy*. London: Theosophical Publishing House (reprinted 1987).

___. 1893–97. *The Secret Doctrine: The Synthesis of Science, Religion, and Philosophy*, 6 vols. Wheaton, Ill.: Theosophical Press (5th ed. 1945).

Bleiler, E.F., ed. 1966. *Three Gothic Novels (The Castle of Otranto, Vathek, and The Vampyre)*. New York: Dover.

Bloch, Maurice. 1989. "Symbols, Song, Dance and Features of Articulation." In *Ritual, History and Power: Selected Papers in Anthropology*. London: Athlone Press.

Bloch, S., and P. Reddaway. 1977. *Russia's Political Hospitals: The Abuse of Psychiatry in the Soviet Union*. London: Gollancz.

Boas, Franz. 1895. *The Social Organization and Secret Societies of the Kwakiutl Indians*. Washington, D.C.: United States National Museum Report.

Boas, Franz, and George Hunt. 1930a. "Religion of the Kwakiutl Indians." In Helen Codere, ed., *Kwakiutl Ethnography*. Chicago: University of Chicago Press (reprinted 1966).

___. 1930b. "Talk about the Great Shaman of the Nakkwaxdax Called Fool." In *Religion of the Kwakiutl Indians*, part 2, *Translations*, 41–45. New York: Columbia University Press.

Boddy, Janice. 1994. "Spirit Possession Revisited: Beyond Instrumentality." *Annual Review of Anthropology* 23:407–34.

Bogoras, Waldemar. 1904–9. *Memoirs of the American Museum of Natural History*. Vol. 11. Ed. by Franz Boas.

Boshier, A. 1974. "African Apprenticeship." In A. Angoff and D. Barth, eds., *Parapsychology and Anthropology*, 273–293. New York: Parapsychology Foundation.

Bowlby, John. 1990. *Charles Darwin: A New Life*. New York: Norton.

Brantlinger, Patrick. 1988. *Rule of Darkness: British Literature and Imperialism, 1830–1914*. Ithaca, N.Y., and London: Cornell University Press.

Braude, Ann. 1989. *Radical Spirits: Spiritualism and Women's Rights in Nineteenth-Century America*. Boston: Beacon Press.

Brewster, A.B. 1937. *The King of the Cannibal Isles*. London: Robert Hale and Company.

Bridges, Lucas. [1949] 1988. *Uttermost Part of the Earth*. New York: Dover.

Bringa, Tone. Forthcoming. "Haunted by the Imaginations of the Past: Robert Kaplan's *Balkan Ghosts*." In Hugh Gusterson and Caroline Besteman, eds., *Why America's Top Pundits Are Wrong About the World*, n.p.

Britten, Emma Hardinge. 1883. *Nineteenth Century Miracles, or, Spirits and Their Work in Every Country of the Earth: A Complete Historical Compendium*. Manchester, England: William Britten.

Brooks, George E. 1993. *Landlords and Strangers: Ecology, Society, and Trade in Western Africa, 1000–1630*. Boulder, Colo.: Westview Press.

Brown, Karen McCarthy. 1989. "Systematic Remembering, Systematic Forgetting: Ogou in Haiti." In Sandra Barnes, ed., *Africa's Ogou: Old World and New*, 65–89. Bloomington: Indiana University Press.

___. 1991. *Mama Lola: A Vodou Priestess in Brooklyn*. Berkeley: University of California Press.

Brunvand, J.H. 1986. *The Choking Doberman and Other "New" Urban Legends*. New York/London: W.W. Norton & Company.

Buck-Morss, Susan. 2000. "Hegel and Haiti," *Critical Inquiry* 26:4:821–65.

Bulwer-Lytton, Edward. [1871, 1859] 1928. *The Coming Race and the Haunted and the Haunters*. London: Humphrey Milford/Oxford University Press.

Burger, P. 1995. *De gebraden baby: Sagen en geruchten uit het moderne leven*. Amsterdam: Prometheus.

Burleigh, M. 1994. *Death and Deliverance. "Euthanasia" in Germany c. 1900–1945*. Cambridge, England: Cambridge University Press.

Burridge, Kenelm. 1969. *New Heaven, New Earth*. Oxford: Blackwell.

Buruma, Ian. 1997. "Royal Tragedy." *New York Review of Books* (October 9):7–9.

Calvert, Rev. James. 1858. *Fiji and the Fijians*. Vol. 2, *Mission History*. Suva: Fiji Museum (reprinted 1983).

Campbell, Bruce F. 1980. *Ancient Wisdom Revived: A History of the Theosophical Movement*. Berkeley: University of California Press.

Campbell, Colin. 1987. *The Romantic Ethic and the Spirit of Modern Consumerism*. Cambridge, Mass.: Blackwell.

Cannadine, David. 1983. "The Context, Performance and Meaning of Ritual: The British Monarchy and the 'Invention of Tradition,' c. 1820–1977." In E. Hobsbawm and T.O. Ranger, eds., *The Invention of Tradition*, 111–164. Cambridge, England: Cambridge University Press.

___. 2001. *Ornamentalism*. Oxford: Oxford University Press.

Carrier, James, ed. 1995. *Occidentalism: Images of the West*. Oxford: Oxford University Press.

Carroll, N. 1990. *The Philosophy of Horror or Paradoxes of the Heart*. New York and London: Routledge.

Carville, James. 1996. *We Are Right and They Are Wrong*. New York: Random House.

Carville, James, with Mary Matalin and Peter Knobler. 1995. *All's Fair: Love, War and Running for President*. New York: Random House.

Castaneda, Carlos. 1968. *The Teachings of Don Juan*. New York: Ballantine Books.

Césaire, Aimé. 1983. *The Collected Poetry*. Trans. by Clayton Eshleman and Annette Smith. Berkeley: University of California Press.

Chambers, Robert. [1844] 1969. *Vestiges of the Natural History of Creation*. Leicester, England: Leicester University Press.

Churchland, Patricia Smith. 1986. *Neurophilosophy: Toward a Unified Science of the Mind/Brain*. Cambridge, Mass.: MIT Press.

Cinnamon, John M. 1996. *The Priest, the Villagers and the Culture of Multi-partyism in Gabon*. Paper for ASA (African Studies Association) conference, San Francisco.

Clammer, John. 1974. "Colonialism and the Perception of Tradition in Fiji." In Talal Asad, ed., *Anthropology and the Colonial Encounter*, 199–220. London: Ithaca Press.

____. 1976. *Literacy in Fiji*. Leiden, Netherlands: Brill.

Clarence-Smith, G. 1989. "The Roots of the Mozambican Counter-Revolution." *Southern African Review of Books* (April–May):7–10.

Cliff, Michelle. 1993. *Free Enterprise*. New York: Plume.

Clifford, James. 1988. *The Predicament of Culture*. Cambridge, Mass.: Harvard University Press.

Cohn, Bernard. 1987. *An Anthropologist Among the Historians and Other Essays*. Delhi: Oxford University Press.

____. 1996. "The Command of Language and the Language of Command." In Bernard S. Cohn, ed., *Colonialism and Its Forms of Knowledge: The British in India*, 16–56. Princeton, N.J.: Princeton University Press.

Comaroff, Jean. 1985. *Body of Power, Spirit of Resistance: The Culture and History of a South Africa People*. Chicago and London: University of Chicago Press.

____. 1997. "Consuming Passions: Child Abuse, Fetishism and The New World Order." *Culture* 17:7–19.

Comaroff, Jean, and John Comaroff, eds. 1993. *Modernity and Its Malcontents: Ritual and Power in Postcolonial Africa*. Chicago: University of Chicago Press.

____. 1999. "Occult Economies and the Violence of Abstraction: Notes from the South African Postcolony." *American Ethnologist* 26(2):279–303.

Comaroff, John, and Simon Roberts. 1981. *Rules and Processes: The Cultural Logic of Dispute in an African Context*. Chicago: University of Chicago Press.

Connor, Linda, Patsy Asch, and Timothy Asch. 1986. *Jero Tapakan: Balinese Healer. An Ethnographic Film Monograph*. Cambridge, England: Cambridge University Press.

Cooter, Roger. 1984. *The Cultural Meaning of Popular Science: Phrenology and the Organization of Consent in Nineteenth-Century Britain*. Cambridge, England: Cambridge University Press.

Copet-Rougier, Elisabeth. 1986. "'Le Mal court': Visible and Invisible Violence in an Acephalous Society—Mkako of Cameroon." In D. Riches, ed., *The Anthropology of Violence*, 50–69. Oxford: Blackwell.

Coronil, Fernando. 1997. *The Magical State: Nature, Money and Modernity in Venezuela*. Chicago: University of Chicago Press.

Corrigan, Philip, and Derek Sayer. 1985. *The Great Arch*. Oxford: Blackwell.

Cosentino, Donald. 1995. "It's All for You, Sen Jak!" In Donald Cosentino, ed., *The Sacred Arts of Haitian Vodou*, 243–64. Los Angeles: UCLA Museum of Cultural History.

Coser, Lewis. 1971. *Masters of Sociological Thought*. New York: Harcourt, Brace, Jovanovich.

Couperus, Louis. [1900] 1985. *The Hidden Force*. Trans. by A.T. de Mattos and E.M. Beekman. Amherst: University of Massachusetts Press.

Crapanzano, Vincent. 1973. "Popular Anthropology." *Partisan Review* 40:471–82.

———. 1995. "The Moment of Prestidigitation: Magic, Illusion and Mana in the Thought of Emile Durkheim and Marcel Mauss." In E. Barkan and R. Bush, eds., *Prehistories of the Future: The Primitivist Project and the Culture of Modernism*, 95–113. Stanford, Calif.: Stanford University Press.

Creusesol. 1916. *Bestaat de Stille Kracht?* Semarang, Indonesia; Surabaja, Indonesia; The Hague, Netherlands: G.C.T. van Dorp.

Crick, Malcolm. 1973. "Two Styles in the Study of Witchcraft." *Journal of the Anthropological Society of Oxford* 4:17–31.

———. 1979. "Anthropologists' Witchcraft: Symbolically Defined or Analytically Undone?" *Journal of the Anthropological Society of Oxford* 10:139–46.

Crowder, Michael. 1968. *West Africa Under Colonial Rule*. London: Hutchinson.

Cullen, M.J. 1975. *The Statistical Movement in Early Victorian England*. New York: Harvester Press.

Cushing, Frank Hamilton. 1979. "My Adventures in Zuni." In Jesse Green, ed., *Zuni: Selected Writings of Frank Hamilton Cushing*. Lincoln: University of Nebraska Press.

Dalmas, Antoine. 1814. *Histoire de la révolution de Saint Domingue . . . : Suivi d'un Mémoire sur le rétablissement de cette colonie*. Paris: Mane frères.

Damsté, Henri T. 1924. "Balische Splinters: 22. Nang Moekanis, de wonderdokter." *Koloniaal Tijdschrift* 13(6):650–55.

Darnton, Robert. 1968. *Mesmerism and the End of the Enlightenment in France*. Cambridge, Mass.: Harvard University Press.

———. 1979. *The Business of Enlightenment: A Publishing History of the Encyclopedie 1775–1800*. Cambridge, Mass.: Harvard University Press.

Dash, J. Michael. 1997. *Haiti and the United States: National Stereotypes and the Literary Imagination*. 2d ed. New York: St. Martin's Press.

Daum, P.A. [1889] 1959. *Goena-Goena*. Amsterdam: Querido.

Davies, Rupert. 1963. *Methodism*. Harmondsworth, England: Penguin Books.

Davis-Floyd, R., and J. Dumit, eds. 1998. *Cyborg Babies: From Techno-sex to Techno-tots*. New York and London: Routledge.

Dayan, Joan. 1988. "The Crisis of the Gods: Haiti After Duvalier." *The Yale Review* 77:299–335.

____. 1994. "Erzulie: A Women's History of Haiti." *Research in African Literatures* 25:2:5–31.

____. 1995. *Haiti, History, and the Gods*. Berkeley: University of California Press.

De Blécourt, Willem. 1993. Review of Willem de Blécourt, Willem Frijhoff, and Marijke Gijswijt-Hofstra, eds., *Grenzen van genezing: Gezondheid, ziekte en genezen in Nederland, zestiende tot begin twintigste eeuw* (Hilversum, Netherlands: Verloren, 1993). *Focaal* 21:218–21.

De Brosses, Charles. [1760] 1988. *Du culte des dieux fétiches*. Paris: Fayard.

De Jager, J. 1991. *Kinderachtige voorstellingen van microbiologische begrippen*. Leiderdorp, Netherlands: Reed Health Care Communications B.V.

Deleuze, Gilles, and Felix Guattari. 1988. *A Thousand Plateaus: Capitalism and Schizophrenia*. London: Athlone Press.

Derby, Lauren. 1994. "Haitians, Magic and Money: *Raza* and Society in the Haitian-Dominican Borderlands, 1900 to 1937." *Comparative Studies in Society and History* 36:488–526.

Deren, Maya. 1953. *Divine Horsemen: The Living Gods of Haiti*. New York: Documentext.

____. [1953] 1970. *Divine Horsemen: The Living Gods of Haiti*. New Paltz, N.Y.: McPherson.

Derrick, R.A. [1946] 1950. *A History of Fiji*. Suva, Fiji: Government Press.

Derrida, Jacques. 1981. *Dissemination*. Translation, annotation, and introduction by Barbara Johnson. Chicago: University of Chicago Press.

____. 1994. *Specters of Marx: The State of the Debt, the Work of Mourning, and the New International*. New York: Routledge.

Desmangles, Leslie. 1992. *The Faces of the Gods: Vodou and Roman Catholicism in Haiti*. Chapel Hill: University of North Carolina Press.

Diawara, Manthia. 1992. *African Cinema: Politics & Culture*. Bloomington and Indianapolis: Indiana University Press.

Dickens, Charles. [1843] 1971. "A Christmas Carol." In Charles Dickens, *The Christmas Books*. Vol. 1, 39–134. Harmondsworth, England: Penguin.

Doel, H.W. van de. 1994. *De Stille Macht: Het Europese binnenlands bestuur op Java en Madoera, 1808–1942*. Amsterdam: Bert Bakker.

Donelha, Andre. [1625] 1977. *Descrição da Serra Leoa e dos rios de Guine do Cabo Verde/An Account of Sierra Leone and the Rivers of Guinea of Cape Verde*. Introduction, notes, and appendices by Avelino Teixera da Mota; notes and English translation by P.E.H. Hair. Lisbon: Centro de Estudos de Cartografia Antiga.

Dorigny, Marcel. 1989. "La Societé des Amis des Noirs et les projets de colonisation en Afrique." In Michel Vovelle, ed., *Révolutions aux Colonies*, 85–94. Paris: Annales Historiques de la Révolution Française.

Dorson, Richard M. 1968. *The British Folklorists: A History*. London: Routledge and Kegan Paul.

Douglas, Mary. 1970. "Introduction: Thirty Years After 'Witchcraft, Oracles and Magic.'" In M. Douglas, ed., *Witchcraft: Confessions and Accusations*. ASA (Association of Social Anthropologists) Monograph no. 9. London: Tavistock.

Dowie, M. 1988. *"We Have a Donor": The Bold New World of Organ Transplanting*. New York: St. Martin's Press.

———. 1989. *De jacht op organen: Transplantatie-industrie in een technologische cultuur*. Amsterdam: Uitgeverij De Balie.

Dubois, Laurent. 1996. "A Spoonful of Blood: Haitians, Racism, and AIDS." *Science as Culture* 26:7–43.

———. 1998a. "A Colony of Citizens: Revolution and Slave Emancipation in the French Caribbean, 1789–1802." Ph.D. Dissertation, University of Michigan.

———. 1998b. *Les Esclaves de la République: L'histoire oubliée de la première Emancipation, 1789–1794*. Paris: Calmann-Lévy.

Duchet, Michèle. 1971. *Anthropologie et histoire aux siècle des lumières*. Paris: François Maspero.

Dumesle, Hurault. 1824. *Voyage dans le nord d'Hayti ou révélations des lieux et des monuments historiques*. Cayes, Haiti: Imprimerie du Gouvernement.

Durkheim, Emile. [1912] 1915. *The Elementary Forms of the Religious Life*. London: George Allen and Unwin (reprinted, New York: Free Press, 1965); originally published in French.

———. 1974. "Replies to Objections." In E. Durkheim, ed., *Sociology and Philosophy*, 63–79. New York: Free Press.

———. [1893] 1984. *The Division of Labor in Society*. New York: Free Press; originally published in French.

———. [1895] 1982. *The Rules of Sociological Method*. New York: Free Press; originally published in French.

———. 1992. *Professional Ethics and Civic Morals*. London and New York: Routledge.

Earthy, D. 1933. *Valenge Women: The Social and Economic Life of Valenge Women of Portuguese East Africa*. London: Oxford University Press.

Ellen, Roy F. 1976. "The Development of Anthropology and Colonial Policy in the Netherlands, 1800–1960." *Journal of the History of the Behavioural Sciences* 12:303–24.

———. 1993. Introduction to C.W. Watson and Roy Ellen, eds., *Understanding Witchcraft and Sorcery in Southeast Asia*, 1–25. Honolulu: University of Hawaii Press.

Ellenberger, H. 1970. *The Discovery of the Unconscious*. New York: Basic Books.

Evans-Pritchard, Edward Evan. 1929. "The Morphology and Function of Magic: A Comparative Study of Trobriand and Zande Ritual and Spells." *American Anthropologist* 31:619–41.

———. 1935. "Witchcraft." *Africa* 8:417–22.

———. 1937. *Witchcraft, Oracles and Magic Among the Azande*. Oxford: Clarendon Press.

———. 1970. "Sorcery and Native Opinion." In M. Marwick, ed., *Witchcraft and Sorcery: Selected Readings*, 21–26. Harmondsworth, England: Penguin.

Fabian, Johannes. 1983. *Time and the Other: How Anthropology Makes Its Object*. New York: Columbia University Press.

Fabricius, Johan. 1948. *Eiland der Demonen: Roman over Bali*. Amsterdam: De Muiderkring.

Fairhead, James, and Melissa Leach. 1998. *Reframing Deforestation. Global Analysis and Local Realities: Studies in West Africa*. London and New York: Routledge.

Farmer, Paul. 1992. *AIDS and Accusation: Haiti and the Geography of Blame*. Berkeley: University of California Press.

Fasseur, Cees. 1993. *De Indologen: Ambtenaren voor de Oost, 1825–1950*. Amsterdam: Bert Bakker.

Favret-Saada, Jeanne. [1977] 1980. *Deadly Words: Witchcraft in the Bocage*. Cambridge, England: Cambridge University Press; originally published in French.

Featherstone, M., and R. Burrows, eds. 1995. *Cyberspace/Cyberbodies/Cyberpunk: Cultures of Technological Embodiment*. London: Sage Publications.

Featherstone, Mike, and Scott Lash. 1995. "Globalization, Modernity and the Spatialization of Social Theory: An Introduction." In M. Featherstone, S. Lash, and R. Robertson, eds., *Global Modernities*, 1–18. London: Thousands Oaks; New Delhi: Sage.

Feliciano, J.F. 1989. *Antropologia Econômica dos Thonga Sul de Mocambique*. Tese de Doutoramentoem Antropologia Econômica, Universidade Técnica de Lisboa.

Ferme, Mariane. 1998. *Secrecy and Its Adornments: Embodying Power in Mende (Sierra Leone)*. Paper, Berkeley, University of California.

———. 1999. "'Staging Politisi': The Dialogics of Publicity and Secrecy in Sierra Leone." In J. Comaroff and J.L. Comaroff, eds., *Civil Society and the Political Imagination in Africa*, 160–91. Chicago: University of Chicago Press.

———. 2001. *The Underneath of Things: Violence, History, and the Everyday in Sierra Leone*. Berkeley: University of California Press.

Fick, Carolyn. 1990. *The Making of Haiti: The San Domingo Revolution from Below*. Knoxville: University of Tennessee Press.

Fields, Karen E. 1982. "Political Contingencies of Witchcraft in Colonial Central Africa: Culture and the State in Marxist Theory." *Canadian Journal of African Studies* 16(3):567–93.

———. 1985. *Revival and Rebellion in Colonial Central Africa*. Princeton, N.J.: Princeton University Press.

Fisiy, Cyprian, and Peter Geschiere. 1990. "Judges and Witches, or How Is the State to Deal with Witchcraft? Examples from Southeastern Cameroon." *Cahiers d'Etudes Africaines* 118:135–56.

———. 1991. "Sorcery, Witchcraft and Accumulation: Regional Variations in South and West Cameroon." *Critique of Anthropology* 11:251–78.

Flaherty, Gloria. 1992. *Shamanism and the Eighteenth Century*. Princeton, N.J.: Princeton University Press.

Fleising, U. 2000. "The Ethology of Mythical Images in Healthcare Biotechnology: A Methodological Approach to Uncovering Ritualized Behavior in the Evolution of Sickness and Healing." *Anthropology & Medicine* 7(2):227–51.

Forgacs, D. 1994. "Fascism, Violence and Modernity." In J. Howlett and R. Mengham, eds., *The Violent Muse: Violence and the Artistic Imagination in Europe, 1910–1939*, 5–22. Manchester, England: Manchester University Press.

Foster, Hal. 1993. "The Art of Fetishism: Notes on Dutch Still Life." In E. Apter and W. Pietz, eds., *Fetishism as Cultural Discourse*, 251–65. Ithaca, N.Y., and London: Cornell University Press.

Foucault, Michel. 1970. *The Order of Things: An Archaeology of the Human Sciences*. New York: Vintage Books.

———. 1979. *Discipline and Punish: The Birth of the Prison*. New York: Vintage Books.

France, Peter. 1969. *The Charter of the Land*. Melbourne: Oxford University Press.

Frank, A.W. 1992. "Twin Nightmares of the Medical Simulacrum: Jean Baudrillard and David Cronenberg." In W. Stearns and W. Chaloupka, eds., *Jean Baudrillard: The Disappearance of Art and Politics*. London: Macmillan.

Frazer, Sir James George. 1911. *The Golden Bough*. 3d ed. London: Macmillan.

———. 1922. *The Golden Bough: A Study in Magic and Religion*. New York: Macmillan.

Freud, Sigmund. [1919] 1938. *Totem and Taboo*. Harmondsworth, England: Penguin Books.

Frey, Sylvia. 1991. *Water from the Rock: Black Resistance in a Revolutionary Age*. Princeton, N.J.: Princeton University Press.

Furnivall, J.S. 1944. *Netherlands India: A Study of Plural Economy*. New York: Macmillan.

Fyfe, Christopher. 1962. *A History of Sierra Leone*. London: Oxford University Press.

Gaillard, Roger. 1983. *La guerilla de Batraville, 1919–1934*. Port-au-Prince: Imprimerie Le Natal.

Garrett, Clarke. 1987. *Spirit Possession and Popular Religion from the Camisards to the Shakers*. Baltimore and London: Johns Hopkins University Press.

Gauthier, Florence. 1995. "Le rôle de la députation de Saint-Domingue dans l'abolition de l'esclavage." In Marcel Dorigny, ed., *Les abolitions de l'esclavage*, 200–211. Paris: Presses Universitaires de Vincennes.

Gay, Peter. 1995. *The Naked Heart: The Bourgeois Experience, Victoria to Freud*. Vol. 4. New York: W.W. Norton.

Geduld, H.M., ed. 1983. *The Definitive Dr. Jekyll and Mr. Hyde Companion*. New York and London: Garland Publishing.

Geertz, Clifford. 1973. "Thick Description: Toward an Interpretive Theory of Culture." In Clifford Geertz, *The Interpretation of Cultures: Selected Essays*. New York: Basic Books.

———. 1983. "Slide Show: Evans-Pritchard's African Transparencies." *Raritan* 3(2):62–80.

Geffray, C. 1990. *La cause des armes au Mozambique: Anthopologie d'une guerre civile.* Paris: Credu-Karthala.

Geffray, C., and M. Pedersen. 1986. "Sobre a Guerra na Provincia de Nampula." *Revista Internacional de Estudos Africanos,* 4–5:303–18.

Geggus, David. 2002. *Haitian Revolutionary Studies.* Bloomington: Indiana University Press.

Germain, Gilbert G. 1994. "The Revenge of the Sacred: Technology and Re-enchantment." In A. Horowitz and T. Maley, eds., *The Barbarism of Reason: Max Weber and the Twilight of Enlightenment,* 248–66. Toronto: University of Toronto Press.

Geschiere, Peter. 1988. "Sorcery and the State: Popular Modes of Action in Southern Cameroon." *Critique of Anthropology* 8(1):35–63.

———. 1996. *Witchcraft, Authoritarianism and Political Liberalization: Occult Violence and Problems of Transition in Cameroonian Politics.* Paper for SSRC (Social Science Research Council) conference on Transitions in Africa: Violence and the Politics of Participation, Niamey, Niger, June 1996.

———. 1997. *The Modernity of Witchcraft: Politics and the Occult in Postcolonial Africa.* Charlottesville and London: University Press of Virginia.

Geschiere, Peter, and Diane Ciekawy, eds. 1998. *The Containment of Witchcraft,* special issue, *African Studies Review* 41(3).

Gibbal, Jean-Marie. [1988] 1994. *Genii of the River Niger.* Chicago: University of Chicago Press (first edition in French).

Gifford, Paul. 1994. "Ghana's Charismatic Churches." *Journal of Religion in Africa* 24(3):241–65.

———. 1998. *African Christianity: Its Public Role.* Bloomington and Indianapolis: Indiana University Press.

Gijswijt-Hofstra, Marijke. 1991. "Geloven in genezen: Beschouwingen over recent onderzoek." *Volkskundig Bulletin* 17(2):118–43.

———. 1997. *Vragen bij een onttoverde wereld* (Inaugural lecture). Amsterdam: University of Amsterdam.

Gillespie, Neal C. 1977. "The Duke of Argyll, Evolutionary Anthropology, and the Art of Scientific Controversy." *Isis* 68:40–54.

Gilroy, Paul. 1993. *The Black Atlantic: Modernity and Double Consciousness.* Cambridge, Mass.: Harvard University Press.

Ginzburg, Carlo. 1983a. *Night Battles.* New York: Penguin.

———. 1983b. "Clues: Morelli, Freud and Sherlock Holmes." In U. Eco and T. Sebeok, eds., *The Sign of Three: Dupin, Holmes, Pierce.* Bloomington: Indiana University Press.

Goldberg, Jeffrey. 1995. "A War Without Purpose in a Country Without Identity." *New York Times Magazine* (January 22):36–39.

———. 2000. "A Continent's Chaos: Why do Americans Find it Intolerable in Europe but Inevitable in Africa?" *New York Times Magazine* (May 21):13–14.

Goldman, Irving. 1975. *The Mouth of Heaven*. New York: John Wiley.

Gouda, Frances. 1995. *Dutch Culture Overseas: Colonial Practice in the Netherlands Indies, 1900–1942*. Amsterdam: Amsterdam University Press.

Gould, Warwick. 1990. "Frazer, Yeats and the Reconsecration of Folklore." In R. Fraser, ed., *Sir James Frazer and the Literary Imagination: Essays in Affinity and Influence*, 121–53. London and Basingstoke, England: Macmillan.

Gouldner, Alvin. 1980. *The Two Marxisms: Contradiction and Anomaly in the Development of Theory*. London and Basingstoke, England: Macmillan.

G.T.B. [1853] 1889. Biographical introduction (by the editor). In A.R. Wallace, *A Narrative of Travels on the Amazon and Rio Negro*, xv–xxi. 2d ed. New York: Dover Publications (reprinted 1972).

Guha, Ranajit. 1988. "The Prose of Counter-insurgency." In R. Guha and G. Spivak, eds., *Selected Subaltern Studies*, 45–86. Oxford: Oxford University Press.

Gunning, Tom. 1989. "An Aesthetic of Astonishment." *Art & Text* 34:31–45.

Gusinde, Martin. 1982. *Los indios del Tierra del Fuego*. Vol. 1, *Los Selk'nam*. Buenos Aires: Centro Argentino de Etnología Americana.

Gustafson, Thomas. 1992. *Representative Words: Politics, Literature, and the American Language 1776–1865*. Cambridge, England: Cambridge University Press.

Guthrie, S. 1993. *Faces in the Clouds: A New Theory of Religion*. New York and Oxford: Oxford University Press.

Habbema, J. 1919. "Bestrijding van het bijgeloof in Indië." *Koloniaal Tijdschrift* 8(1):313–15.

Habermas, Jürgen. 1987. *The Philosophical Discourse of Modernity*. Cambridge, Mass.: MIT Press.

Hacking, Ian. 1975. *Why Does Language Matter to Philosophy?* Cambridge, England: Cambridge University Press.

———. 1988. "Telepathy: Origins of Randomization in Experimental Design." *Isis* 79:427–51.

———. 1990. *The Taming of Chance*. Cambridge, England: Cambridge University Press.

———. 1995. *Rewriting the Soul: Multiple Personality and the Sciences of Memory*. Princeton, N.J.: Princeton University Press.

Halen, Pierre. 1994. "Tintin, paradigme du héros colonial belge? à propos de 'Tintin au Congo.'" *Beloeil* (Bologna) 4:39–56.

Hall, E. 1991. *The Mozambican National Resistance Movement (Renamo) and the Reestablishment of Peace in Mozambique*. Paper delivered at a workshop on Security and Cooperation in Post-Apartheid Southern Africa Maputo, September 1991.

Hanegraaff, Wouter. 1996. *New Age Religion and Western Culture: Esotericism in the Mirror of Secular Thought*. Leiden, Netherlands: Brill.

___. 1998. "The Emergence of the Academic Science of Magic: The Occult Philosophy in Tylor and Frazer." In A.L. Molendijk and P. Pels, eds., *Religion in the Making: The Emergence of the Sciences of Religion*, 253–75. Leiden, Netherlands: Brill.

Hansen, Uffe. 1989. "'Neu-Romantik' or 'Neuro-Mantik'? Psychiatry, Literature, and the Unconscious in the 1880s." In M. Harbsmeier and M.T. Larsen, eds., *The Humanities Between Art and Science: Intellectual Developments 1880–1914*, 143–57. Copenhagen: Akademisk Forlag.

Haraway, D.J. 1997. *Modest-Witness@Second-Millennium. FemaleMan-Meets-OncoMouse. Feminism and Technoscience*. New York: Routledge.

Heelas, Paul. 1996. *The New Age Movement: The Celebration of the Self and the Sacralization of Modernity*. Oxford: Blackwell.

___. n.d. *Diana's Self*. Paper presented at Research Centre Religion and Society, University of Amsterdam.

Heestermans, H. 1989. *Luilebol! Het Nederlands Scheldwoordenboek*. Amsterdam: Thomas Rap.

Hefner, Robert W. 1998. "Multiple Modernities: Christianity, Islam and Hinduism in a Globalizing Age." *Annual Review of Anthropology* 27:83–104.

Hegel, G.W.F. [1807] 1977. *Phenomenology of Spirit*. Trans. by A.V. Miller. Oxford: Clarendon Press; originally published in German.

Hekmeijer, F.C. 1918. *Wetboek van Strafrecht voor Nederlandse Indië*. Batavia, Netherlands Indies: G. Kolff.

Helgesson, A.G. 1971. "The Tswa Response to Christianity: A Study of the Religious and Cultural Impact of Protestant Christianity on the Tswa of Southern Mozambique." M.A. Dissertation, University of Witwatersrand, South Africa.

Helman, Cecil. 1988. "Dr. Frankenstein and the Industrial Body: Reflections on 'Spare Part' Surgery." *Anthropology Today* 4(3):14–17.

___. 1991. *Body Myths*. London: Chatto & Windus.

Hersbach, L. 1997. "Prosthetic Reconstructions: Making the Industry, Re-Making the Body, Modelling the Nation." *History Workshop Journal* 44:23–58.

Hevia, James L. 1998. "The Archive State and the Fear of Pollution: From the Opium Wars to Fu-Manchu." *Cultural Studies* 12(2):234–64.

Himmelman, P.K. 1990. "The Medical Body: An Analysis of Medicinal Cannibalism in Europe, 1300–1700." *Dialectical Anthropology* 22:183–203.

Hirsch, John L. 2001. *Sierra Leone: Diamonds and the Struggle for Democracy*. Boulder, Colo.: Lynne Rienner.

Hirschauer, S. 1991. "The Manufacture of Bodies in Surgery." *Social Studies of Science* 21:279–319.

Hitzka. 1930. "Over de Magie in Indië." *Onze Stem* 11:1073–76, 1097–1100, 1114–17, 1139–42, 1161–64, 1210–13, 1229–32, 1258–62, 1282–85, 1301–4.

Hives, Frank, and Gascoigne Lumley. 1930. *Ju-Ju and Justice in Nigeria*. London: John Lane, the Bodley Head Ltd.

Hobsbawm, Eric, and Terence O. Ranger, eds. 1983. *The Invention of Tradition*. Cambridge, England: Cambridge University Press.

Hodgkin, Thomas, and Richard Cull. 1854. "A Manual of Ethnological Inquiry, prepared for the Ethnological Society of London in 1851." *Journal of the Ethnological Society of London* 3:193–208.

Hoffman, Léon-Francois. 1993. "Un mythe national: La cérémonie du Bois-Caïman." Gérard Barthélemy and Christian Girault, eds., *La République Haïtienne: Etat des Lieux et Perspectives*, 434–48. Paris: Editions Kharthala.

Hollis, Martin, and Steven Lukes. 1982. *Rationality and Relativism*. Oxford: Blackwell.

Holt, Thomas. 1992. *The Problem of Freedom: Race, Labor, and Politics in Jamaica and Britain, 1932–1938*. Baltimore: Johns Hopkins University Press.

Honwana, Alcinda. 1996. "Spiritual Agency and Self-Renewal in Southern Mozambique." Ph.D. Dissertation in Social Anthropology. SOAS (School of Oriental and African Studies), University of London.

———. 1998. "Sealing the Past, Facing the Future: Trauma Healing in Rural Mozambique." In *Accord: International Review of Peace Initiatives*, 3:75–81. London: Conciliation Resources.

———. 1999a. "Negotiating Post-war Identities: Child-Soldiers in Mozambique and Angola." *CODESRIA Bulletin* 1/2:4–13.

———. 1999b. "Healing for Peace: Traditional Healers and Post-war Reconstruction in Southern Mozambique." In J. Hinnels and R. Porter, eds., *Religion, Health, and Suffering*, 237–55. London: Kegan Paul.

Honwana, J. 1995. "The United Nations and Mozambique: A Sustainable Peace?" In *Lumiar Papers* no. 7. Lisbon: Instituto de Estudos Estrategicos e Internacionais.

———. 2000. *No Easy Task: Building Peace in Mozambique*. Manuscript.

Hörisch, Jochen. 1998. *Kopf oder Zahl: Die Poesie des Geldes*. Frankfurt am Main: Suhrkamp.

Horkheimer, Max, and Theodor Adorno. 1969. *Dialectic of Enlightenment*. New York: Continuum.

———. [1944] 1987. *Dialektiek van de Verlichting*. Nijmegen, Netherlands: SUN; originally published in German.

Horton, Robin. 1971. "African Conversion." *Africa* 41:85–108.

Hufford, D.J. 1982. *The Terror That Comes in the Night: An Experience-Centered Study of Supernatural Assault Traditions*. Philadelphia: University of Pennsylvania Press.

Hunt, Lynn. 1984. *Politics, Culture and Class in the French Revolution*. Berkeley: University of California Press.

Hunter, William Wilson. 1885. *The Imperial Gazetteer of India*, 9 vols. London: Trübner and Co.

Hurbon, Laennec. 1988. *Le barbare imaginaire*. Paris: Editions du Cerf.

____. 1995. "American Fantasy and Haitian Vodou." In Donald Cosentino, ed., *The Sacred Arts of Haitian Vodou*. Vol. 2. Los Angeles: UCLA Museum of Cultural History.

Huxley, Leonard. 1900. *The Life and Letters of Thomas Henry Huxley*, 2 vols. London: Macmillan.

Huxley, Thomas Henry. 1881. "On the Method of Zadig: Retrospective Prophecy as a Function of Science." In T.H. Huxley, *Science and Culture and Other Essays*, 128–48. London: Macmillan.

Ijagbemi, E. Ade. 1968. "A History of the Temne in the Nineteenth Century." Ph.D. thesis, Department of History, University of Edinburgh.

____. 1973. *Gbanka of Yoni*. Freetown: Sierra Leone University Press.

Iyer, Pico. 1988. *Video Night in Kathmandu. And Other Reports from the Not-So-Far East*. New York: Random House.

Jackson, John William. 1858. *Mesmerism in Connection with Popular Superstitions*. London: H. Ballière; Edinburgh: MacLachlan & Stewart.

____. 1863. *Ethnology and Phrenology as an Aid to the Historian*. London: no publisher listed.

James, C.L.R. 1963. *The Black Jacobins*. New York: Vintage.

Jasper, J.E. 1901. "'n Critiekje." *Soerabaiaasch Handelsblad* (February 27, 28).

____. 1904. "Godsdienst, bijgeloof en adat." *Weekblad voor Indie* 1(11):129–32.

____. 1932. "Van Doekoens" In *Pharmaceutisch-Tijdschrift voor Nederlandsch-Indië* 9:34–38.

Jay, Martin. 1993. *Downcast Eyes: The Denigration of Vision in Twentieth-Century French Thought*. Berkeley: University of California Press.

Johns, Adrian. 1998. *The Nature of the Book: Print and Knowledge in the Making*. Chicago: University of Chicago Press.

Johnson, Paul C. 1995. "Shamanism from Ecuador to Chicago: A Case Study in New Age Ritual Appropriation." *Religion* 25:163–78.

Jones, Kenneth W. 1976. *Arya Dharm: Hindu Consciousness in 19th Century Punjab*. Berkeley: University of California Press.

____. 1989. *Socio-religious Reform Movements in India: The New Cambridge History of India*. Vol. 3.1. Cambridge, England: Cambridge University Press.

Junod, H.A. 1927. *The Life of a South African Tribe*. Vol. 2, *Mental Life*. 2d ed. London: Macmillan.

Kalff, S. 1925. "Indisch Occultisme." *Vragen van den Dag* 40:444–57.

Kaplan, Fred. 1974. "The 'Mesmeric Mania': The Early Victorians and Animal Magnetism." *Journal of the History of Ideas* 35:691–702.

____. 1975. *Dickens and Mesmerism: The Hidden Springs of Fiction*. Princeton, N.J.: Princeton University Press.

Kaplan, Martha. 1989. "Luveniwai as the British Saw It." *Ethnohistory* 36(4):349–71.

___. 1990. "Christianity, People of the Land, and Chiefs in Fiji." In John Barker, ed., *Christianity in Oceania*. Lanham, Md.: University Press of America.

___. 1995. *Neither Cargo Nor Cult: Ritual Politics and the Colonial Imagination in Fiji*. Durham, N.C.: Duke University Press.

___. 1996. "Blood on the Grass and Dogs Will Speak." In Robert Foster, ed., *Nation Making: Emergent Identities in Postcolonial Melanesia*. Ann Arbor: University of Michigan Press.

Kaplan, Robert D. 1993. *Balkan Ghosts: A Journey Through History*. New York: Vintage Books, Random House.

___. 1994. "The Coming Anarchy: How Scarcity, Crime, Overpopulation, Tribalism, and Disease Are Rapidly Destroying the Social Fabric of Our Planet." *Atlantic Monthly* (February):44–76.

___. 1996. *The Ends of the Earth: A Journey to the Frontier of Anarchy*. New York: Vintage Books, Random House.

___. 2000. *The Coming Anarchy: Shattering the Dreams of the Post Cold War*. New York: Vintage Books, Random House.

Kaplan, Steven. 1995. *Farewell, Revolution: France 1789/1989*. Ithaca, N.Y.: Cornell University Press.

Kelly, John D. 1999a. "Time and the Global: Against the Homogeneous, Empty Communities in Contemporary Social Theory." In Birgit Meyer and Peter Geschiere, eds., *Globalization and Identity: Dialectics of Flow and Closure*, 239–71. Oxford: Blackwell.

___. 1999b. "Fiji's Fifth Veda: Exile, Sanatan Dharm, and Countercolonial Initiatives in Diaspora." In Paula Richman, ed., *Questioning Ramayans*. Berkeley: University of California Press.

Kelly, John D., and Martha Kaplan. 1990. "History, Structure and Ritual." In *Annual Review of Anthropology* 19:119–50.

___. 2001. *Represented Communities: Fiji and World Decolonization*. Chicago: University of Chicago Press.

Kerremans, W. 1923. "Over de psychische mutaties bij Europeanen in de Tropen." *Vragen van den Dag* 38:886–91.

Kiernan, J. 1994. "Variation on a Christian Theme: The Healing Synthesis of Zulu Zionism." In C. Stewart and R. Shaw, eds., *Syncretism/Anti-Syncretism: The Politics of Religious Synthesis*, 69–84. London and New York: Routledge.

Kipp, Rita Smith. 1990. *The Early Years of a Dutch Colonial Mission: The Karo Field*. Ann Arbor: University of Michigan Press.

Klee, E. 1997. *Auschwitz, die NS-Medizin und ihre Opfer*. Frankfurt am Main: S. Fischer.

Koenigsberg, Richard A. 1975. *Hitler's Ideology: A Study in Psychoanalytic Sociology*. New York: Library of Social Science.

___. 1977. *The Psychoanalysis of Racism, Revolution and Nationalism*. New York: Library of Social Science.

____. 1995. "Content Analysis of the Writings and Speeches of Hitler: How Manifest Content Reveals Latent Meaning." *The Psychoanalytic Psychotherapy Review* 6(2–3):78–85.

Koentjaraningrat. 1985. *Javanese Culture*. Singapore: Oxford University Press.

Kohlbrugge, J.M.F. 1907. *Blikken in het zieleleven van den Javaan en zijner overheerschers*. Leiden, Netherlands: E.J. Brill.

Kopf, David. 1969. *British Orientalism and the Bengal Renaissance: The Dynamics of Indian Modernization, 1773–1835*. Berkeley: University of California Press.

Kottler, Malcolm Jay. 1974. "Alfred Russel Wallace, the Origin of Man, and Spiritualism." *Isis* 65:145–91.

Kramer, Fritz W. 1987. *Der rote Fes: Über Besessenheit und Kunst in Afrika*. Frankfurt am Main: Athenäum.

____. 1993. *The Red Fez: Art and Spirit Possession in Africa*. London: Verso.

Krueger, K. 1953. *I Was Hitler's Doctor*. New York: Boar's Head Books.

Lafitau, Joseph-François. [1724] 1983. *Mœurs des sauvages amériquains*, 2 vols. Ed. by E.H. Lemay. Paris: Maspéro.

La Fontaine, Jean. 1992. "Concepts of Evil, Witchcraft and the Sexual Abuse of Children in Modern England." *Etnofoor* 5(1/2):6–20.

Lambek, M. 1996. "The Past Imperfect: Remembering as Moral Practice." In P. Antze and M. Lambek, eds., *Tense Past: Cultural Essays in Trauma and Memory*. New York and London: Routledge.

Lan, D. 1985. *Guns and Rain: Guerrillas and Spirit Mediums in Zimbabwe*. London: James Currey.

Largueche, Abdelhamid. 1995. "L'abolition de l'esclavage en Tunisie (1841–1846)." In Marcel Dorigny, ed., *Les abolitions de l'esclavage*, 200–211. Paris: Presses Universitaires de Vincennes.

Larkin, Brian. 1998–99. "Theatres of the Profane: Cinema and Colonial Urbanism." *Visual Anthropology Review* 14(2):46–62.

Latour, Bruno. 1987. *Science in Action: How to Follow Scientists and Engineers Through Society*. Cambridge, Mass.: Harvard University Press.

____. 1988. *The Pasteurization of France*. Trans. by Alan Sheridan and John Law. Cambridge, Mass.: Harvard University Press.

____. 1993. *We Have Never Been Modern*. Trans. by Catherine Porter. Cambridge, Mass.: Harvard University Press.

____. 1999. "The Slight Surprise of Action: Facts, Fetishes, Factishes." In *Pandora's Hope: Essays on the Reality of Science Studies*, 266–92. Cambridge, Mass. Harvard University Press.

Lauriciano, G. 1990. "Espírito Mungoi: Um poder Alternativo ou mais um Fenómeno da Guerra." *Jornal Domingo* (September 9).

Leach, Edmund. 1957. "The Epistemological Background to Malinowski's Empiricism." In R. Firth, ed., *Man and Culture. An Evaluation of the Work of Bronislaw Malinowski*, 119–37. London: Routledge and Kegan Paul.

Leahey, Thomas H., and Grace E. Leahey. 1983. *Psychology's Occult Doubles: Psychology and the Problem of Pseudo-Science*. Chicago: Nelson-Hall.

Lefebvre, Lucien, and Henri-Jean Martin. [1929] 1997. *The Coming of the Book*. London: Verso.

Leger, Jacques Nicolas. 1891. *Receuil des traités et conventions de la République d'Haïti*. Port-au-Prince: Imprimerie de la Jeune.

Leibovici, S. 1998. "Zuiverheid als utopie: De foute kinderen van Pasteur." In R. van der Laarse et al., eds., *De hang naar zuiverheid: De cultuur van het moderne Europa*, 85–123. Amsterdam: Het Spinhuis.

Lemaire, W.L.G. 1934. *Het wetboek van strafrecht voor Ned.-Indië vergeleken met het Nederlandse wetboek van strafrecht*. Batavia, Netherlands Indies: Noordhoof-Kolff.

Lenga-Kroma, James Samuel. 1978. *A History of the Southern Temne in the Late Nineteenth and Early Twentieth Centuries*, vols. 1 and 2. Ph.D. thesis, Department of History, University of Edinburgh.

Lesquillier, Nicolaas Willem. 1934. *Het adatdelictenrecht in de magische wereldbeschouwing*. Leiden, Netherlands: N.V. Boek–en Steendrukkerij Eduward Ijdo.

Levinas, Emmanuel. 1981. *Otherwise than Being or Beyond Essence*. Trans. by Alphonso Lingis. The Hague, Netherlands: Martinus Nijhoff.

Lévi-Strauss, Claude. 1963. *Totemism*. Boston: Beacon Press.

———. 1966. *The Savage Mind*. Chicago: University of Chicago Press.

———. 1967. "The Sorcerer and His Magic." In *Structural Anthropology*, 161–80. New York: Doubleday.

Lichtblau, Klaus. 1993. "The Protestant Ethics Versus the 'New Ethic.'" In H. Lehmann and G. Roth, eds., *Weber's Protestant Ethic: Origins, Evidence, Contexts*, 179–93. Washington/Cambridge: German Historical Institute/Cambridge University Press.

Loewenberg, Bert J. 1957. *Darwin, Wallace, and the Theory of Natural Selection; Including the Linnean Society Papers*. New Haven, Conn.: G.E. Cinamon.

Lovric, Barbara J.A. 1987. "Rhetoric and Reality: The Hidden Nightmare. Myth and Magic as Representations and Reverberations of Morbid Realities." Ph.D. Dissertation, University of Sydney.

Ludden, David. 1993. "Orientalist Empiricism." In C. Breckenridge and P. v.d. Veer, eds., *Orientalism and the Postcolonial Predicament: Perspectives on South Asia*, 250–78. Philadelphia: University of Pennsylvania Press.

Luhrmann, Tanya. [1989] 1994. *Persuasions of the Witch's Craft: Ritual Magic in Contemporary England*. London: Picador.

Lundin, S., and M. Ideland, eds. 1997. *Gene Technology and the Public: An Interdisciplinary Perspective*. Lund, Sweden: Nordic Academic Press.

Lupton, D. 1994. *Medicine as Culture: Illness, Disease and the Body in Western Societies*. London: Sage Publications.

Machel, Samora. 1981. "Speech to the Second Conference of Frelimo's Department of Education and Culture, September 1970." *President Speeches and Brochures*, page 34. Frelimo.

MacIntyre, Alisdair. 1981. *After Virtue: A Study in Moral Theory*. Notre Dame: University of Notre Dame Press.

Madiou, Thomas. [1847–48] 1989. *Histoire d'Haïti*. Port-au-Prince: Editions Henri Deschamps.

Malinowski, Bronislaw. [1935] 1966. *Coral Gardens and Their Magic*. Vol. 2, *The Language of Magic and Gardening*. London: Allen & Unwin.

———. [1935] 1965. "An Ethnographic Theory of the Magical Word." In *Coral Gardens and their Magic*. Vol. 2, *The Language of Magic and Gardening*, 213–50. Bloomington: Indiana University Press.

Malthus, Thomas R. [1798] 1970. *An Essay on the Principle of Population*. Harmondsworth, England: Penguin.

Martin, E. 1991. *Flexible Bodies: Tracking Immunity in American Culture—From the Days of Polio to the Age of Aids*. Boston: Beacon Press.

Martin, Kingsley. 1937. *The Magic of Monarchy*. London: Thomas Nelson & Sons Ltd.

Marwick, Max. 1952. "The Social Context of Cewa Witch Beliefs." *Africa* 22:120–35, 215–33.

Marx, Karl. [1867] 1974. *Das Kapital: Kritik der politischen Ökonomie*. Vol. 1. Berlin: Dietz Verlag.

Masco, Joseph. 1995. "'It's a Strict Law Which Binds Us Dance': Cosmologies, Colonialism, Death, and Ritual Authority in the Kwakwaka'wakw Potlach, 1849 to 1922." *Comparative Studies in Society and History*, 41–75.

Mauss, Marcel. 1960. *Les techniques du corps*. Paris: PUF.

Mauss, Marcel, and Henri Hubert. [1902] 1972. *A General Theory of Magic*. London and Boston: Routledge and Kegan Paul.

Mazlish, B. 1993. *The Fourth Discontinuity: The Co-evolution of Humans and Machines*. New Haven, Conn., and London: Yale University Press.

Mbembe, Achille. 2001. *On the Postcolony*. Berkeley: University of California Press.

McKinney, H. Lewis. 1972. *Wallace and Natural Selection*. New Haven, Conn.: Yale University Press.

McLuhan, Marshall. [1964] 1995. *Understanding Media: The Extensions of Man*. London: Routledge.

McNaughton, Patrick R. 1982. "The Shirts That Mande Hunters Wear." *African Arts* 15:54.

McQuire, Scott. 1998. *Visions of Modernity: Representation, Memory, Time and Space in the Age of the Camera*. London: Sage.

Meijer, D.G. 1935. "Bijgeloof in Dienst van de Politie en de Misdadigers." *Djawa* 15:107–22.

Mensah, G.B. 1989. "The Film Industry in Ghana: Development, Potentials and Constraints." Thesis, University of Ghana, Legon.

Metraux, Alfred. 1959. *Voodoo in Haiti*. New York: Schocken Books.

Meyer, Birgit. 1992. "'If You Are a Devil You Are a Witch and, If You Are a Witch You Are a Devil': The Integration of 'Pagan' Ideas into the Conceptual Universe of Ewe Christians in Southeastern Ghana." *Journal of Religion in Africa* 22:98–132.

———. 1995. "'Delivered from the Powers of Darkness': Confessions about Satanic Riches in Christian Ghana." *Africa* 65(2):236–55.

———. 1998a. "Commodities and the Power of Prayer: Pentecostalist Attitudes Towards Consumption in Contemporary Ghana." *Development and Change* 29:751–76.

———. 1998b. "'Make a Complete Break with the Past': Memory and Post-colonial Modernity in Ghanaian Pentecostalist Discourse." *Journal of Religion in Africa* 28(3):316–49.

———. 1999a. *Translating the Devil: Religion and Modernity Among the Ewe in Ghana*. Edinburgh: Edinburgh University Press.

———. 1999b. "Popular Ghanaian Cinema and 'African Heritage.'" *Africa Today* 46(2):93–114.

———. 2001a. "Money, Power and Morality: Popular Ghanaian Cinema in the Fourth Republic." *Ghana Studies* 4:65–84.

———. 2001b. "Prières, fusils et meurtre rituel: le cinéma populaire et ses nouvelles figures du pouvoir et du succès au Ghana." *Politique Africaine* 82:45–62.

———. 2002. "Pentecostalism, Prosperity and Popular Cinema in Ghana." *Culture and Religion* 3(1):67–87.

Michelet, Jules. 1967. *History of the French Revolution*. Chicago: University of Chicago Press.

Micklethwait, John, and Adrian Wooldridge. 1996. *The Witch Doctors: What the Management Gurus Are Saying, Why It Matters and How to Make Sense of It*. London: Heinemann.

Middleton, John, and E. Winter, eds. 1963. *Witchcraft and Sorcery in East Africa*. London: Routledge and Kegan Paul.

Middleton-Mends, Kofi. 1995. *Video-Production: Which Direction?* Paper. National Film and Television Institute, Accra, Ghana.

Miller, Daniel. 1994. *Modernity: An Ethnographic Approach. Dualism and Mass Consumption in Trinidad*. Oxford and New York: Berg Publishers.

Ministry of Information, Ghana. n.d. (c. 1995). *Draft of the National Film and Video Policy for Ghana*. Manuscript. Accra.

Mintz, Sidney, and Michel-Rolph Trouillot. 1995. "The Social History of Haitian Vodou." In Donald Cosentino, ed., *The Sacred Arts of Haitian Vodou*, 123–47. Los Angeles: UCLA Fowler Museum of Cultural History.

Mitchell, J. Clyde. 1956. *The Kalela Dance: Aspects of Social Relationships Among Urban Africans in Northern Rhodesia*. Rhodes-Livingstone Paper no. 27. Manchester, England: Manchester University Press.

Mitchell, Timothy. 1991a. "The Limits of the State: Beyond Statist Approaches and their Critics." *American Political Science Review* 85(1):77–96.

___. 1991b. *Colonizing Egypt*. Berkeley: University of California Press.

Mitscherlich, A., and F. Mielke, eds. 1960. *Medizin ohne Menschlichkeit: Dokumente des Nürnberger Ärzteprozesses*. Frankfurt am Main: Fischer Bücherei.

Mitzman, Arthur. 1970. *The Iron Cage: An Historical Interpretation of Max Weber*. New York: Alfred Knopf.

Moerman, D.E. 1979. "Anthropology of Symbolic Healing: With CA Comment." *Current Anthropology* 20(1):59–67.

Moore, Rachel O. 2000. *Savage Theory: Cinema as Modern Magic*. Durham, N.C., and London: Duke University Press.

Morris, Dick. 1997. *Behind the Oval Office: Winning the Presidency in the Nineties*. New York: Random House.

Morton-Williams, P. 1953. *Cinema in Rural Nigeria: A Field Study of the Impact of Fundamental-Education Films on Rural Audiences in Nigeria*. West African Institute of Social and Economic Research, University College, Ibadan, Nigeria.

Mourik, Ruth. 1996. "Mechanical Being: Thoughts of Scientists at Massachusetts Institute of Technology on the Relation Between Technology and Being Human." M.A. Thesis in Cultural Anthropology, University of Amsterdam.

Mritak Shrāddha Khandan (no author noted). 1893. *Mritak Shraddha Khandan*. Lahore: Virajanand Yantralaya.

Muana, Patrick. 1997. "The Kamajoi Militia: Violence, Internal Displacement and the Politics of Counter-Insurgency." *Africa Development* 22:77–100.

Nadel, Siegfried F. 1957. "Malinowski on Magic and Religion." In R. Firth, ed., *Man and Culture: An Evaluation of the Work of Bronislaw Malinowski*, 189–208. London: Routledge and Kegan Paul.

National Media Commission. n.d. *National Media Policy*. Accra, Ghana: Friedrich Ebert Stiftung.

Niehaus, Isaac E., with Eliazaar Mohlala and Kally Shokane. 2001. *Witchcraft, Power and Politics: Exploring the Occult in the South African Lowveld*. London: Pluto Press.

Nietzsche, Friedrich. 1968. "The Birth of Tragedy." In Walter Kaufmann, ed., *Basic Writings of Nietzsche*, 23. New York: Modern Library.

___. [1886] 1974. "Preface for the Second Edition." In *The Gay Science*. New York: Vintage.

___. [1886] 1989. *Beyond Good and Evil*. Trans. by Walter Kauffmann. New York: Vintage.

Nieuwenhuys, Rob. 1978. *Oost-indische spiegel: Wat Nederlandse schrijvers en dichters over Indonesië hebben geschreven, vanaf de eerste jaren der compagnie tot op heden*. Amsterdam: Querido.

Noordman, J. 1989. *Om de kwaliteit van het nageslacht: Eugenetica in Nederland 1900–1950*. Nijmegen: SUN.

Nye, Robert. 1995. "Savage Crowds, Modernism and Modern Politics." In E. Barkan and R. Bush, eds., *Prehistories of the Future: The Primitivist Project and the Culture of Modernism*, 42–55. Stanford, Calif.: Stanford University Press.

Olivier de Sardan, Jean-Pierre. 1992. "Occultism and the Ethnographic 'I': The exoticizing of magic from Durkheim to 'postmodern' anthropology." *Critique of Anthropology* 12:5–25.

Onghokham. 1978. "The Inscrutable and the Paranoid: An Investigation into the Sources of the Brotodiningrat Affair." In Ruth T. McVey, *Southeast Asian Transitions: Approaches Through Social History*, 112–57. New Haven, Conn., and London: Yale University Press.

Opala, Joseph. 1982. "*The Limba* hu-ronko." Seminar-paper presented at the Department of Africa, School of Oriental and African Studies, University of London, March 4.

Owen, Alex. 1989. *The Darkened Room: Women, Power and Spiritualism in Late Victorian England*. London: Virago Press.

Ozouf, Mona. 1988. *Festivals of the French Revolution*. Trans. by Alan Sheridan. Cambridge, Mass.: Harvard University Press.

Pagden, Anthony. 1986. *The Fall of Natural Man: The American Indian and the Origin of Comparative Ethnology*. Cambridge, England: Cambridge University Press.

Pānchāl Panditā. [1900] 1901. *Sakhi* Samvād (Hindi) 4(7, May).

Parham, Althéa de Puech, ed. 1959. *My Odyssey: Experiences of a Young Refugee from Two Revolutions, by a Creole of Saint Domingue*. Baton Rouge: Louisiana State University Press.

Parsons, T. 1951. *The Social System*. Glencoe, Ill.: Free Press.

Pattynama, Pamela. 1998. "Secrets and Danger: Interracial Sexuality in Louis Couperus's *The Hidden Force* and Dutch Colonial Culture." In Julia Clancy-Smith and Frances Gouda, eds., *Domesticating the Empire: Race, Gender and Family Life in French and Dutch Colonialism*, 84–107. Charlottesville: University Press of Virginia.

Peabody, Sue. 1996. *There Are No Slaves in France: The Political Culture of Race and Slavery in the Ancien Régime*. Oxford: Oxford University Press.

Péan, Pierre. 1983. *Affaires africaines*. Paris: Fayard.

Pels, Peter. 1992. "*Mumiani*: The White Vampire. A Neo-diffusionist Analysis of Rumor." *Etnofoor* 5(1/2):165–187.

____. 1995. "Spiritual Facts and Super-Visions: The Conversion of Alfred Russel Wallace." *Etnofoor* 8(2):69–91.

____. 1997. "The Anthropology of Colonialism: Culture, History and the Emergence of Western Governmentality." *Annual Review of Anthropology* 26:163–83.

____. 1998a. "The Spirit of Matter: On Fetish, Rarity, Fact and Fancy." In Patricia Spyer, ed., *Border Fetishisms: Material Objects in Unstable Spaces*, 91–121. London: Routledge.

___. 1998b. "The Magic of Africa: Reflections on a Western Commonplace." *African Studies Review* 41(3):193–209.

___. 1999a. *A Politics of Presence: Contacts Between Missionaries and Waluguru in Late Colonial Tanganyika*. Chur, Switzerland, and Reading, England: Harwood Academic Publishers.

___. 1999b. "The Rise and Fall of the Indian Aborigines: Orientalism, Anglicism, and the Emergence of an Ethnology of India." In Peter Pels and Oscar Salemink, eds., *Colonial Subjects: Essays on the Practical History of Anthropology*, 82–116. Ann Arbor: University of Michigan Press.

___. 1999c. "Professions of Duplexity: A Pre-history of Ethical Codes in Anthropology." *Current Anthropology* 40(2):101–14.

___. 2000. "Occult Truths: Race, Conjecture and Theosophy in Victorian Anthropology." In R. Handler, ed., *History of Anthropology*. Vol. 9, *Excluded Ancestors, Inventible Traditions: Essays Toward a More Inclusive History of Anthropology*, 11–41. Madison: University of Wisconsin Press.

Pels, Peter, and Oscar Salemink. 1994. "Introduction: Five Theses on Ethnography as Colonial Practice." *History and Anthropology* 8:1–34.

Peukert, Detlev J.K. 1989. *Max Weber's Diagnose der Moderne*. Göttingen, Germany: Vandenhoeck u. Ruprecht.

Pietz, William. 1988. "The Problem of the Fetish, IIIa: Bosman's Guinea and the Enlightenment Theory of Fetishism." *Res* 16:105–23.

___. 1993. "Fetishism and Materialism: The Limits of Theory in Marx." In E. Apter and W. Pietz, eds., *Fetishism as Cultural Discourse*, 119–51. Ithaca, N.Y., and London: Cornell University Press.

___. 1999. "The Fetish of Civilization: Sacrificial Blood and Monetary Debt." In P. Pels and O. Salemink, eds., *Colonial Subjects: Essays on the Practical History of Anthropology*, 53–81. Ann Arbor: University of Michigan Press.

Pocock, David. 1972. Foreword. In M. Mauss and H. Hubert, *A General Theory of Magic*. London and Boston: Routledge and Kegan Paul.

Poensen, C. 1879. "Djimat." *Mededeelingen van Wege het Nederlandsche Zendelinggenootschap* 23:229–66.

Polak, F.L. n.d. *De toekomst doorzichtig verpakt: Fantasiebeelden over het dagelijks levenspakket in 2000+*. Deventer, Netherlands: Thomassen & Drijver-Verblifa N.V.

Pott, H. 2000. *Survival in het mensenpark: Over kunst, cyborgs en posthumanisme*. Inaugural lecture. Erasmus Universiteit, Rotterdam, Netherlands.

Powdermaker, Hortense. 1950. *Hollywood: The Dream Factory*. Boston: Universal Library, Little Brown, and Company.

Prakash, Gyan. 1999. *Another Reason: Science and the Imagination of Modern India*. Princeton, N.J.: Princeton University Press.

Prasad, Durga. 1889. *A Triumph of Truth*. Lahore: Virajanand Press.

Pressman, J.D. 1998. *Last Resort Psychosurgery and the Limits of Medicine*. Cambridge, England: Cambridge University Press.

Primary Colors (anonymous author). 1996. *Primary Colors: A Novel of Politics*. New York: Warner Books.

Proctor, R. 1988. *Racial Hygiene: Medicine Under the Nazis*. Cambridge, Mass.: Harvard University Press.

———. 1999. *The Nazi War on Cancer*. Princeton, N.J.: Princeton University Press.

Rainger, Ronald. 1980. "Philanthropy and Science in the 1830s: The British and Foreign Aborigines Protection Society." *Man*, n.s., 15:702–17.

Rankin, F. Harrison. 1836. *The White Man's Grave*. London.

René, Georges, and Marilyn Houlberg. 1995. "My Double Mystic Marriage to Two Goddesses of Love: An Interview." In Donald Cosentino, ed., *The Sacred Arts of Haitian Vodou*, 287–99. Los Angeles: UCLA Fowler Museum of Cultural History.

Rennie, J.K. 1973. "Christianity, Colonialism and the Origins of Nationalism Among the Ndau of Southern Rhodesia, 1890–1935." Ph.D. Thesis in History, Northwestern University, Evanston, Ill.

Reno, William. 1998. *Warlord Politics and African States*. Boulder, Colo.: Lynne Rienner.

Reynolds, P. 1996. *Traditional Healers and Childhood in Zimbabwe*. Athens, Ohio: Ohio University Press.

Richards, Audrey. 1935. "A Modern Movement of Witch-Finders." *Africa* 8:448–61.

———. 1977. "The Colonial Office and the Organization of Social Research." *Anthropological Forum* 4:32–53.

Richards, Paul. 1996. *Fighting for the Rain Forest: War, Youth and Resources in Sierra Leone*. Oxford: James Currey; Portsmouth, N.H.: Heinemann.

———. 1999. "Out of the Wilderness? Escaping Robert Kaplan's Dystopia." *Anthropology Today* 15(6):16–18.

Richards, Thomas. 1993. *The Imperial Archive: Knowledge and the Fantasy of Empire*. London: Verso.

Ricklefs, M.C. 1993. *A History of Modern Indonesia Since c. 1300*. 2d ed. Stanford, Calif.: Stanford University Press.

Rodley, C., ed. 1993. *Cronenberg on Cronenberg*. Rev. paperback ed. London/Boston: Faber and Faber.

Rodney, Walter. 1970. *A History of the Upper Guinea Coast 1545 to 1800*. Oxford: Oxford University Press.

Roesch, O. 1992. "Renamo and the Peasantry in Southern Mozambique: A View from Gaza Province." *Canadian Journal of African Studies* 26(3):462–84.

Romein-Verschoor, Annie. 1971. *Omzien in Verwondering: Herinneringen*. Amsterdam: De Arbeiderspers.

Rose, Nikolas. 1996. "Authority and the Genealogy of Subjectivity." In P. Heelas, S. Lash, and B. Morris, eds., *Detraditionalization*, 295–327. Oxford: Basil Blackwell.

Rosny, Eric de. 1981. *Les yeux de ma chèvre: Sur les pas des maîtres de la nuit en pays douala*. Paris: Plon.

Rouget, Gilbert. 1980. *Music and Trance*. Trans. by B. Biebuyck. Chicago: University of Chicago Press.

Routledge, David. 1985. *Matanitu*. Suva: University of the South Pacific.

Rowlands, Michael, and Jean-Pierre Warnier. 1988. "Sorcery, Power and the Modern State in Cameroon." *Man*, n.s., 23:118–32.

Rubin, Elizabeth. 1997. "An Army of One's Own: In Africa, Nations Hire a Corporation to Wage War." *Harper's Magazine* (February):44–55.

S. (anonymous author) 1921. "Iets over djimat's en misdrijf." *De Nederlandsch-Indische Politiegids* 5(2):33–34.

Sahlins, Marshall. 1985. *Islands of History*. Chicago: University of Chicago Press.

Sakyi, Kwamina. 1996. "The Problems and Achievements of the Ghana Film Industry Corporation and the Growth and Development of the Film Industry in Ghana." Thesis, University of Ghana, Legon.

Sala-Moulins, Louis. 1988. *Le Code Noir, ou le calvaire de Canaan*. Paris: Presses Universitaires de France.

Sanchez, Rafael. n.d. *Plaza Bolivar: The Public Square as Fantasy Screen of the Nation (Venezuela)*. Paper presented at conference Fantasy Spaces, Amsterdam, August 1998.

Sarasvati, Dayanand. [1882] 1963. *Satyārth Prakāsh* (Hindi). Delhi: Dehati Pustak Bhandar.

Śāstrārtha. 1896. *Śāstrārta*. Essay written by two unidentified scholars.

Schenkhuizen, Marguérite. 1993. *Memoirs of an Indo Woman: Twentieth-Century Life in the East Indies and Abroad*. Ed. and trans. by Lizelot Stout van Balgooy. Southeast Asia Series, no. 92. Athens, Ohio: Ohio University Press.

Scheper-Hughes, N. 1993. "Theft of Life: The Globalization of Organ Stealing Rumours." *Anthropology Today* 12(3):3–12.

____. 2000a. "The Global Traffic in Human Organs." *Current Anthropology* 41(2):191–211.

____. 2000b. *Neo-Cannibalism: The Body and Commodity Fetishism*. Paper presented at the Conference on Processes of Inclusion and Exclusion in Western Societies, Amsterdam, October 5–7.

Schlenker, C.F. 1861. *A Collection of Temne Traditions, Fables and Proverbs*. London: Church Missionary Society.

Schluchter, Wolfgang. 1988. *Religion und Lebensführung*. Vol. 1, *Studien zu Max Webers Kultur- und Werttheorie*. Frankfurt am Main: Suhrkamp.

Schmidt, Nelly. 1994. *Victor Schoelcher et l'abolition de l'esclavage*. Paris: Fayard.

Sears, Laurie. 1996. *Shadows of Empire: Colonial Discourse and Javanese Tales*. Durham, N.C.: Duke University Press.

Sewell, William. 1996. "Historical Events as Transformations of Structures: Inventing Revolution at the Bastille." *Theory and Society* 15:841–88.

Shapin, Steven. 1988. "The House of Experiment in Seventeenth-Century England." *Isis* 79:373–404.

____. 1994. *A Social History and Truth: Civility and Science in Seventeenth-Century England*. Chicago: University of Chicago Press.

Shapin, Steven, and Arnold Thackray. 1974. "Prosopography as a Research Tool in History of Science: The British Scientific Community, 1700–1900." *History of Science* 12:1–28.

Sharp, L.A. 2000. "The Commodification of the Body and Its Parts." *Annual Review of Anthropology* 29:287–388.

Shaw, Rosalind. 1997. "The Production of Witchcraft/Witchcraft as Production: Memory, Modernity, and the Slave Trade in Sierra Leone." *American Ethnologist* 24(4):856–76.

———. 2002. *Memories of the Slave Trade: Ritual and the Historical Imagination in Sierra Leone*. Chicago: University of Chicago Press.

Shiraishi, Takashi. 1990. *An Age in Motion: Popular Radicalism in Java, 1912–1926*. Ithaca, N.Y.: Cornell University Press.

Sibley, D. 1995. *Geographies of Exclusion: Society and Difference in the West*. London: Routledge.

Simmel, Georg. 1923. *Soziologie: Untersuchingen über die Formen des Vergesellschaftung*. Vol. 2, 3d ed. Berlin: Duncker & Humblot.

Simpson, Jacqueline. 1994. "Margaret Murray: Who Believed Her, and Why?" *Folklore* 105:89–96.

Slaats, Herman, and Karen Portier. 1993. "Sorcery and the Law in Modern Indonesia." In C.W. Watson and Roy Ellen, eds., *Understanding Witchcraft and Sorcery in Southeast Asia*, 135–48. Honolulu: University of Hawaii Press.

Slezkine, Yuri. 1994. "Naturalists Versus Nations: Eighteenth-century Russian Scholars Confront Ethnic Diversity." *Representations* 47:170–95.

Sloterdijk, P. 1992. *Kritiek van de cynische rede*. Trans. from German by T. Davids. 2d ed. Amsterdam: Uitgeverij De Arbeiderspers.

Soeriokoesoemo, R.M.S. 1919. "Het Djimat in Woelige Tijden." *Wederopbouw* 2:160–63.

Sommers, Marc. 1997. *The Children's War: Toward Peace in Sierra Leone*. New York: Women's Commission for Refugee Women and Children.

Sontag, S. 1979. *Illness as Metaphor*. New York: Vintage Books.

Spencer, Herbert. 1844. "A New View of the Functions of Imitation and Benevolence." *The Zoist: A Journal of Cerebral Physiology & Mesmerism and Their Applications to Human Welfare* 1:369–85.

Stagl, Justin. 1990. "The Methodizing of Travel in the 16th Century: A Tale of Three Cities." *History and Anthropology* 4:303–38.

———. 1995. *A History of Curiosity: The Theory of Travel, 1550–1800*. Chur, Switzerland: Harwood Academic Publishers.

Stallybrass, Peter. 1998. "Marx's Coat." In Patricia Spyer, ed., *Border Fetishisms: Material Objects in Unstable Spaces*, 183–207. London: Routledge.

Starker, Steven. 1989. *Evil Influences: Crusades Against the Mass Media*. New Brunswick and London: Transaction Publishers.

Staub, E. 1989. *The Roots of Evil: The Origins of Genocide and Other Group Violence*. Cambridge, England: Cambridge University Press.

Stein, H.F. 1990. "In What Systems Do Alcohol/Chemical Addictions Make Sense? Clinical Ideologies and Practices as Cultural Metaphors." *Social Science and Medicine* 30(9):987–1000.

Stephanopoulos, George. 1999. *All Too Human: A Political Education.* Boston: Little, Brown and Company.

Stewart C., and R. Shaw, eds. 1994. *Syncretism/Anti-syncretism: The Politics of Religious Synthesis.* London and New York: Routledge.

Stivers, R. 1982. *Evil in Modern Myth and Ritual.* Athens, Ga.: University of Georgia Press.

Stocking, George W. 1971a. "Animism in Theory and Practice: E.B. Tylor's Unpublished 'Notes on Spiritualism.'" *Man*, n.s., 6:88–104.

___. 1971b. "What's in a Name? The Origins of the Royal Anthropological Institute." *Man*, n.s., 6:369–90.

___. [1968] 1982. *Race, Culture and Evolution: Essays in the History of Anthropology.* Chicago: University of Chicago Press.

___. 1991, ed. *Colonial Situations: Essays on the Contextualization of Ethnographic Knowledge.* Madison: University of Wisconsin Press.

Stoler, Ann Laura. 1995. *Race and the Education of Desire: Foucault's History of Sexuality and the Colonial Order of Things.* Durham, N.C.: Duke University Press.

Stoler, Ann Laura, and Frederick Cooper. 1997. Between Metropole and Colony: Rethinking a Research Agenda. In Frederick Cooper and Ann Laura Stoler, eds., *Tensions of Empire: Colonial Cultures in a Bourgeois World*, 1–58. Berkeley: University of California Press.

Stoller, Paul. 1989. *The Taste of Ethnographic Things: The Senses in Anthropology.* Philadelphia: University of Pennsylvania Press.

___. 1995. *Embodying Colonial Memories: Spirit Possession, Power, and the Hauka in West Africa.* New York: Routledge.

Stoller, Paul, and Cheryl Olkes. 1987. *In Sorcery's Shadow: A Memoir of Apprenticeship Among the Songhay of Niger.* Chicago: University of Chicago Press.

Sundkler, B.G.M. 1961. *Bantu Prophets in South Africa.* London: Oxford University Press.

Swarg Men Subject Committee (no author noted). 1895. *Swarg Men Subject Committee.* Danapur, India: Aryavarta Patra.

Tambiah, Stanley Jeyaraja. 1973. "Form and Meaning in Magical Acts: A Point of View." In Robin Horton and Ruth Finnegan, eds., *Modes of Thought*, 199–229. London: Faber and Faber.

___. 1985a. "The Magical Power of Words." In Stanley J. Tambiah, *Culture, Thought and Social Action: An Anthropological Approach*, 17–59. Cambridge, Mass., and London: Harvard University Press.

___. 1985b. "A Performative Approach to Ritual." In Stanley J. Tambiah, *Culture, Thought and Social Action: An Anthropological Approach*, 123–66. Cambridge, Mass., and London: Harvard University Press.

___. 1990. *Magic, Science, Religion and the Scope of Rationality*. Cambridge, England: Cambridge University Press.

Taussig, Michael. 1980. *The Devil and Commodity Fetishism in South America*. Chapel Hill: University of North Carolina Press.

___. 1987. *Shamanism, Colonialism and the Wild Man: A Study in Terror and Healing*. Chicago: University of Chicago Press.

___. 1993a. "Maleficium: State Fetishism." In E. Apter and W. Pietz, eds., *Fetishism as Cultural Discourse*, 217–47. Ithaca, N.Y.: Cornell University Press.

___. 1993b. *Mimesis and Alterity*. New York and London: Routledge.

___. 1997. *The Magic of the State*. New York and London: Routledge.

Teissier, Elizabeth. 1997. *Sous le signe de Miterrand*. Paris: Jacob.

Ten Have, H., and G. Kimsma. 1987. *Geneeskunde tussen droom en drama: Voortplanting, ethiek en vooruitgang*. Kampen, Netherlands: Kok Agora.

Thoden van Velzen, H.U.E. 1995. "Revenants That Can Not Be Shaken: Collective Fantasies in a Maroon Society." *American Anthropologist* 97(4):722–32.

Thomas, Keith. 1971. *Religion and the Decline of Magic*. New York: Scribners.

___. 1973. *Religion and the Decline of Magic: Studies in Popular Beliefs in Sixteenth- and Seventeenth-Century England*. Harmondsworth: Penguin Books.

Thomas, Nicholas. 1990. "Sanitation and Seeing." *Comparative Studies in Society and History* 32:149–70.

Thomashausen, A. 1983. "The National Resistance of Mozambique." *Africa Insight* 13(2):125–26.

Thornton, Robert, and Peter Skalnik. 1993. "Introduction: Malinowski's Reading, Writing, 1904–1914." In R.J. Thornton and P. Skalnik, eds., *The Early Writings of Bronislaw Malinowski*, 1–64. Cambridge, England: Cambridge University Press.

Timmers, Pastoor M. 1918. "Bijgeloof." In *Berichten uit Nederlandsch Oost-Indië voor de Leden van den Sint-Claverbond* 1:190–97.

Tiryakian, Edward A. 1974. *On the Margins of the Visible: Sociology, the Esoteric, and the Occult*. New York: Wiley.

Tohill, C., and P. Tombs. 1994. *Immoral Tales: Sex and Horror Cinema in Europe 1956–1984*. London: Primitive Press.

Toren, Christina. 1988. "Making the Present, Revealing the Past." *Man* 23(4):696–717.

Trouillot, Michel-Rolph. 1991. "From Planter's Journals to Academia: The Haitian Revolution as Unthinkable History." *Journal of Caribbean History* 25(1, 2):81–99.

___. 1995. *Silencing the Past: Power and the Production of History*. Boston: Beacon Press.

___. 2001. "The Anthropology of the State in the Age of Globalization: Close Encounters of the Deceptive Kind." *Current Anthropology* 42(1):125–38.

Tsing, Anna. 1994. *In the Realm of the Diamond Queen*. Princeton, N.J.: Princeton University Press.

Tudor, A. 1989. *Monsters and Mad Scientists: A Cultural History of the Horror Movie*. Oxford: Blackwell.

Turner, Bryan S. 1992. "Preface to the Second Edition." In E. Durkheim, *Professional Ethics and Civic Morals*, xiii–xlii. London and New York: Routledge.

Turner, Frank Miller. 1974. *Between Science and Religion: The Reaction to Scientific Naturalism in Late Victorian England*. New Haven, Conn., and London: Yale University Press.

Tyler, Parker. [1947] 1971. *Magic and Myth of the Movies*. London: Secker & Warburg.

Tylor, Edward Burnett. 1872a. "Ethnology and Spiritualism" (reply to Wallace). *Nature* 5:343.

_____. 1872b. "Quetelet's Contributions to the Science of Man." *Nature* 5:358–63.

_____. 1873. *Primitive Culture*, 2 vols., 2d ed. New York: Brentano's (reprinted 1924).

_____. 1888. "On a Method of Investigating the Development of Institutions, Applied to Laws of Marriage and Descent." *Journal of the Anthropological Institute* 18:245–72.

_____.[1871] 1958. *Primitive Culture*. Vol. 1, *The Origins of Culture*. New York: Harper.

Ukadike, Nwachukwu Frank. 1994. *Black African Cinema*. Berkeley, Los Angeles, and London: University of California Press.

Van Binsbergen, Wim. 1991. "Becoming a Sangoma: Religious Anthropological Field-Work in Francistown, Botswana." *Journal of Religion in Africa* 21:309–44.

Van der Geest, Sjaak. 1990a. "Medicijn, metafoor en metonymia." *Medische Antropologie* 2(1):3–20.

_____. 1990b. "Medicijn, metafoor en metonymia: een repliek." *Medische Antropologie* 2(2):227–32.

_____. 1998. "Yèbisa Wo Fie: Growing Old and Building a House in the Akan Culture of Ghana." *Journal of Cross Cultural Gerontology* 13:333–59.

Van der Veer, Peter. 1998. "The Global History of 'Modernity.'" *Journal for the Economic and Social History of the Orient* 41(3):285–94.

_____. 2001. *Imperial Encounters: Religion and Modernity in India and Britain*. Princeton, N.J.: Princeton University Press.

Van Dijk, Rijk. 1997. "From Camp to Encompassment: Discourses of Transsubjectivity in the Ghanaian Pentecostal Diaspora." *Journal of Religion in Africa* 27(2):135–60.

Van Dijk, Rijk, and Peter Pels. 1996. "Contested Authorities and the Politics of Perception: Deconstructing the Study of Religion in Africa." In T.O. Ranger and R. Werbner, eds., *Postcolonial Identities in Africa*, 245–70. London: Zed Books.

Van Hien, H[endrik] A. 1924. *De Formulieren voor de Stille Kracht*. Weltevreden, Indonesia: N.V. Boekhandel Visser & Co.

_____. 1934. *De Javaansche Geestenwereld en die betrekking die tusschen de geesten en de zinnelijke wereld bestaat*. Batavia, Netherlands Indies: G. Kolff & Co.

Van Rijn–Van Tongeren, G.W. 1997. *Metaphors in Medical Texts*. Amsterdam and Atlanta, Ga.: Editions Rodopi B.V.

Van Soest, R. 1982a. "Psychochirurgie: wondermiddel of blind geweld?" *Intermediair* 18(27):15–22.

___. 1982b. "Psychochirurgie: De uitwassen." *Intermediair* 18(28):27–34.

Van Swieten, J[an]. 1872. Varia. "Een zoek geraakt document over het gebeurde in 1831 te Sumedang." *Tijdschrift voor Nederlands Indië* 1(2):493–96.

Van Vegchel, G. 1991. *Medici contra kwakzalvers: De strijd tegen niet-orthodoxe geneeswijzen in Nederland in de 19e en 20e eeuw.* Amsterdam: Het Spinhuis.

Van Wermeskerken, Henri. 1922. *Roemah Angker: Roman van Stille Kracht en Indisch Bijgeloof.* Haarlem: J.W. Boissevain.

Velander, W.H., H. Lubon, and W.M. Drohan. 1997. "Transgenic Livestock as Drug Factories." *Scientific American* 276(1):54–59.

Vermeulen, Han. 1995. "Origins and Institutionalization of Ethnography and Ethnology in Europe and the USA, 1771–1845." In H. Vermeulen and A.A. Roldán, eds., *Fieldwork and Footnotes: Studies in the History of European Anthropology,* 39–59. London: Routledge

Verrips, Jojada. 1992. "Vampiers en virussen: Over de anthropomorfisering van kwaad." *Etnofoor* 5(1/2):21–43.

___. 1994. "The Thing Didn't 'Do' What I Wanted." In J. Verrips, ed., *Transactions: Essays in Honor of Jeremy F. Boissevain,* 35–53. Amsterdam: Het Spinhuis.

___. 1996. "Anthropology as Myth." *Etnofoor* 9(2):107–23.

___. 1998. "Enige speculaties en reflecties over magie, wetenschap en glas." *Amsterdams Sociologisch Tijdschrift* 25(1):153–55.

___. 2001. "The State and the Empire of Evil." In J. Mitchell and P. Clough, eds., *Powers of Good and Evil.* 185–209. Oxford: Berghahn Books.

Verwey, G. 1998. *Zinverlies, "Kontingenzbewältigung" en herbetovering: Argumenten voor een wijsgerig-antropologische herformulering van de onttoveringsthese.* Paper voor Sociaal-Wetenschappelijke Studiedagen (for Social Science Study), Amsterdam, April 16–17, 1998.

Vidyarthi, Guru Datta. n.d. *Wisdom of the Rishis or Complete Works of Pandita Guru Datta Vidyarthi.* Ed. by Swami Vedananda Tirtha. Lahore: Arya Pustakalyaya.

Vines, Alex. 1991a. *Renamo: Terrorism in Mozambique.* Centre for Southern African Studies, University of York. In Association with James Currey. London and Bloomington: Indiana University Press.

___. 1991b. "Lisbon Diary: Watching Twin Peaks with Renamo." *Southern Africa Review of Books* (July/October):31–32.

Vorderman, A.G. 1893. "Inlandsche Vergiften." *Tijdschrift voor Inlandsche Geneeskundigen* 1(6):81–83.

Vyse, S.A. 1997. *Believing in Magic: The Psychology of Superstition.* New York and Oxford: Oxford University Press.

Waite, Arthur Edward. 1891. *The Occult Sciences: A Compendium of Transcendental Doctrine and Experiment.* Secaucus, N.J.: University Books (reprinted 1974).

Walens, Stanley. 1981. *Feasting with Cannibals: An Essay on Kwakiutl Cosmology.* Princeton, N.J.: Princeton University Press.

Wallace, Alfred Russel. 1864. "The Origin of Human Races and the Antiquity of Man Deduced from the Theory of 'Natural Selection.'" *Journal of the Anthropological Society of London* 2:clvii-clxxxvii.

___. 1869. "Geological Climates and the Origin of Species." *London Quarterly Review* 126:187–205.

___. 1870. *Contributions to the Theory of Natural Selection*. London: Macmillan.

___. 1872a. "Physical Science and Philosophy" (Review of Tylor, "Primitive Culture"). *The Academy* (February 15):69–71.

___. 1872b. "Ethnology and Spiritualism" (Reply to Tylor), *Nature* 5:363–64.

___. [1874] 1896. *Miracles and Modern Spiritualism*. 3d rev. ed. London: George Redway.

___. 1908. *My Life: A Record of Events and Opinions*. 2d rev. and condensed ed. London: Chapman and Hall.

___. [1869] 1962. *The Malay Archipelago: The Land of the Orang-Utan and the Bird of Paradise*. New York: Dover Publications.

___. [1853] 1972. *A Narrative of Travels on the Amazon and Rio Negro*. Reprint of 2d (1889) ed. New York: Dover Publications.

Warner, Michael. 1990. *The Letters of the Republic*. Cambridge, Mass.: Harvard University Press.

Washington, Peter. 1993. *Madame Blavatsky's Baboon: Theosophy and the Emergence of the Western Guru*. London: Secker and Warburg.

Webb, James. 1974. *The Occult Underground*. LaSalle, Canada: Open Court Publishing Company.

Weber, Max. 1930. *The Protestant Ethic and the Spirit of Capitalism*. Trans. by Talcott Parsons. London: Harper Collins (21st impression).

___. 1947. *Gesammelte Aufsätze zur Religionssoziologie I. Teil*. Tübingen, Germany: J.C.B. Mohr.

___. 1948. "Science as a Vocation." In H.H. Gerth and C. Wright Mills, *From Max Weber: Essays in Sociology*, 129–56. London: Routledge and Kegan Paul.

___. 1956. *Wirtschaft und Gesellschaft: Grundriss der verstehenden Soziologie*. Ed. by J. Winckelmann. Tübingen, Germany: J.C.B. Mohr.

___. 1958. *The Protestant Ethic and the Spirit of Capitalism*. New York: Scribner.

Weizenbaum, J., and K. Haefner. 1992. *Sind Computer die besseren Menschen? Ein Streitgespräch*. Ed. by M. Haller. Munich and Zurich: Piper.

Wendl, Tobias. 1999. "The Return of the Snakeman: Horror Films Made in Ghana." *Revue Noire* 32:48–51.

West, M. 1975. *Bishops and Prophets in a Black City*. Cape Town: David Philip.

White, D.G. 1991. *Myths of the Dog-Man*. Chicago and London: University of Chicago Press.

White, Luise. 1993. "Vampire Priests of Central Africa: African Debates About Labor and Religion in Colonial Northern Zambia." *Comparative Studies in Society and History* 35:746–72.

Wideman, John Edgar. 1994. *Fatheralong*. New York: Pantheon.

Wiebel-Fanderl, O. 1997. "Kulturshock Herztransplantation." *Bios Zeitschrift für Biographieforschung und Oral History* 10(1):1–17.

Wiener, Margaret. 1995. *Visible and Invisible Realms: Power, Magic, and Colonial Conquest in Bali*. Chicago: University of Chicago Press.

———. n.d. *Dangerous Liaisons and Other Tales from the Twilight Zone: Sex, Race, and Sorcery in Colonial Java*. Manuscript.

Wilder, Gary. 1999. "Subject-Citizens in Interwar France: Negritude, Colonial Humanism, and the Imperial Nation-State." Ph.D. Dissertation, University of Chicago.

Williams, Raymond. 1977. *Marxism and Literature*. Oxford: Oxford University Press.

William, Rev. Thomas. 1858. *Fiji and the Fijians*. Vol. 1, *The Islands and Their Inhabitants*. Suva: Fiji Museum (republished 1983).

Willis, Roy. 1968. Kamcape: *An Anti-sorcery Movement in South-West Tanzania*. *Africa* 38:1–15.

———. 1985. "Magic." In Adam Kuper and Jessica Kuper, eds., *The Social Science Encyclopedia*, 478–79. London, Boston, and Henley, England: Routledge & Kegan Paul.

Wills, Garry. 1997. "The Real Scandal" (review of Morris 1997). *New York Review of Books* 44(3):411.

Wilson, Bryan R., ed. 1970. *Rationality*. Oxford: Blackwell.

Wilson, K. 1992. "Cults of Violence and Counter-violence in Mozambique." *Journal of Southern Africa Studies* 18(3).

Wolff, Kurt, ed. 1950. *The Sociology of Georg Simmel*. Glencoe, Scotland: Free Press.

Woodham-Smith, Cecil. 1955. *Florence Nightingale*. Harmondsworth, England: Penguin Books.

Worsley, Peter. 1968. *The Trumpet Shall Sound*. New York: Schocken Books.

Yates, Frances. 1972. *The Rosicrucian Enlightenment*. London: Routledge and Kegan Paul.

Young, S. 1978. *What Have They Done with the Rain? Twentieth Century Transformations of Ceremonial Practice and Belief In Southern Mozambique*. Paper delivered at the Annual Meeting of the African Studies Association, November.

Zack-Williams, A.B. 1997. "Kamajors, 'Sobels' and the Militariat: Civil Society and the Return of the Military in Sierra Leone Politics." *Review of African Political Economy* 24.

Zulaika, J. 1988. *Basque Violence: Metaphor and Sacrament*. Reno: University of Nevada Press.

Laurent Dubois is Assistant Professor of History at Michigan State University. He is the author of *Les Esclaves de la République: L'histoire oubliée de la première Emancipation, 1789–1794* (1998) and of the forthcoming *A Colony of Citizens: Revolution and Slave Emancipation in the French Caribbean, 1787–1804*. He has published articles in *Cultural Studies, Transition*, and the *William and Mary Quarterly*.

Peter Geschiere is Professor of the Anthropology of Africa at both Leiden University and the University of Amsterdam. His recent publications include *The Modernity of Witchcraft: Politics and the Occult in Postcolonial Africa* (1997), *Globalization and Identity: Dialectics of Flow and Closure* (edited with Birgit Meyer, 1999), and *The Forging of Nationhood: History, Ethnicity and Nationalism in Latin America, Africa and Asia* (edited with Gyanendra Pandey, 2002). His main research interests are autochthony, citizenship, and belonging in Africa and elsewhere, and the struggle over the Cameroonian rain forest from the German rubber boom to the present-day ecological movement.

Alcinda Honwana is currently a Program Director at the Social Science Research Council (SSRC) in New York. She was previously based in the Anthropology Department of the University of Cape Town, and worked at the United Nations Office of the Special Representative of the Secretary-General for Children and Armed Conflict before joining the SSRC. She holds a Ph.D. in Social Anthropology from the School of Oriental and African Studies of the University of London. She has carried out extensive research in Mozambique on spirit possession, traditional healing, and cultural politics, as well as on the impact of political conflict on children and young people.

Martha Kaplan is Associate Professor of Anthropology at Vassar College, Poughkeepsie, New York. A specialist in ritual, historical anthropology, and the anthropology of decolonization and postcolonialism who conducts fieldwork in Fiji, she is the author of publications including "History, Structure and Ritual" (coauthored with John D. Kelly, 1990), "Panopticon in Poona: An Essay on Foucault and Colonialism" (1995), *Neither Cargo Nor Cult: Ritual Politics and the Colonial Imagination in Fiji*

(1995), and *Represented Communities: Fiji and World Decolonization* (coauthored with John D. Kelly, 2001).

Birgit Meyer is a Senior Lecturer at the Research Centre Religion and Society (Department of Sociology and Anthropology, University of Amsterdam). She has conducted research on missions and local appropriations of Christianity, Pentecostalism, popular culture, and video films in Ghana. Her publications include *Translating the Devil: Religion and Modernity Among the Ewe in Ghana* (1999) and *Globalization and Identity: Dialectics of Flow and Closure* (edited with Peter Geschiere, 1999). In April 2000 she was awarded a PIONIER grant from the Netherlands Foundation for Scientific Research (NWO) for a comparative research program on modern mass media, religion, and the postcolonial state in West Africa, India, Brazil, and the Caribbean. She is currently working on a book on religion, popular cinema, and the postcolonial state in Ghana.

Peter Pels lectures at the Research Centre Religion and Society, University of Amsterdam. His publications include *Constructing Knowledge: Authority and Critique in Social Science* (edited with Lorraine Nencel, 1991), *A Politics of Presence: Contacts Between Missionaries and Waluguru in Late Colonial Tanganyika* (1999) and *Colonial Subjects: Essays on the Practical History of Anthropology* (edited with Oscar Salemink, 1999). He is currently finishing a book provisionally titled *Imagining Elections: Politics, Publicity, and Secrecy in Late Colonial Tanganyika*, along with working on a history of the interconnections between anthropology and occultism in the nineteenth and twentieth centuries. He was an Editor of *Critique of Anthropology* (1987–93) and Advisory Editor of *Current Anthropology* (1999–2001), and he is now editor-in-chief of *Social Anthropology*.

Gyan Prakash is Professor of History at Princeton University and a member of the Subaltern Studies Editorial Group. He is the author of *Bonded Histories: Genealogies of Labor Servitude in Colonial India* (1990) and has edited several volumes of essays on colonial history, including *After Colonialism: Imperial Histories and Postcolonial Displacements* (1995). His recent book is *Another Reason: Science and the Imagination of Modern India* (1999).

Rosalind Shaw is an Associate Professor of Anthropology at Tufts University. She is coeditor of *Syncretism/Anti-Syncretism: The Politics of Religious Synthesis* (1994) and *Dreaming, Religion and Society in Africa* (1992) and author of *Memories of the Slave Trade: Ritual and the Historical Imagination in Sierra Leone* (2002). She is currently conducting research on displaced youth and Pentecostal healing in Sierra Leone.

Michael Taussig teaches Anthropology at Columbia University and previously taught Performance Studies at New York University. His books include *Defacement* (1999), *The Magic of the State* (1997), *Mimesis and Alterity* (1993), *The Nervous System* (1992), and *Shamanism, Colonialism, and the Wild Man: A Study in Terror and Healing* (1987).

Jojada Verrips is Professor of European Anthropology at the University of Amsterdam. He has written and edited a number of books in Dutch and is currently working on a book titled *The Wild (in the) West*.

Margaret J. Wiener is Associate Professor of Anthropology at the University of North Carolina at Chapel Hill. She is the author of *Visible and Invisible Realms: Power, Magic, and Colonial Conquest in Bali* (1995), which won the Victor Turner Prize in Ethnographic Writing (1995). At present, she is working on a book on the production of magic as an object of knowledge and fascination, focusing mainly on the Dutch East Indies and tentatively entitled *Hidden Forces*.